Digital Cities

Digital Cities

THE INTERNET AND THE GEOGRAPHY OF OPPORTUNITY

KAREN MOSSBERGER, CAROLINE J. TOLBERT,

and

WILLIAM W. FRANKO

OXFORD
UNIVERSITY PRESS

Oxford University Press is a department of the University of Oxford.
It furthers the University's objective of excellence in research,
scholarship, and education by publishing worldwide.

Oxford   New York
Auckland   Cape Town   Dar es Salaam   Hong Kong   Karachi
Kuala Lumpur   Madrid   Melbourne   Mexico City   Nairobi
New Delhi   Shanghai   Taipei   Toronto

With offices in
Argentina   Austria   Brazil   Chile   Czech Republic   France   Greece
Guatemala   Hungary   Italy   Japan   Poland   Portugal   Singapore
South Korea   Switzerland   Thailand   Turkey   Ukraine   Vietnam

Oxford is a registered trade mark of Oxford University Press
in the UK and certain other countries.

Published in the United States of America by
Oxford University Press
198 Madison Avenue, New York, NY 10016

Library of Congress Cataloging-in-Publication Data
Mossberger, Karen.
Digital cities : the internet and the geography of opportunity / Karen Mossberger,
Caroline J. Tolbert, and William W. Franko.
p.   cm.
Includes bibliographical references and index.
ISBN 978-0-19-981293-6 (hardcover : alk. paper)—ISBN 978-0-19-981295-0 (pbk. : alk. paper)
1. Internet—Government policy—Illinois—Chicago.   2. Computer networks—Social aspects—
Illinois—Chicago.   3. Digital divide—Illinois—Chicago.   4. Internet—Government policy—
United States.   5. Computer networks—Social aspects—United States.   6. Digital divide—United
States.   I. Tolbert, Caroline J.   II. Franko, William W.   III. Title.
TK5105.875.I57M677   2012
384.30977311—dc23   2012010284

1 3 5 7 9 8 6 4 2

Printed in the United States of America
on acid-free paper

Contents

List of Tables

List of Figures

Acknowledgments

While there are only three authors formally listed on the cover of this book, there are many more people who have made essential contributions along the way. This book is the product of several years of research that began in Chicago. As national surveys appeared again during the Obama administration (through the Bureau of the Census and the FCC), we seized upon these resources to better understand how Internet access and use are patterned by place, and the implications this has for communities. In order to tell this story—through numbers, maps, and interviews—we have drawn upon the help of many individuals and organizations. Of course, we bear full responsibility for any errors or omissions, as well as the conclusions and arguments presented here. We make no assumptions that the people we thank here agree with what we have written, but we have gained from our discussions and work with them nonetheless.

We would like to thank the Chicago partners who first set us on this path, thinking about the potential of technology in cities, as well as the inequalities that hinder that potential. The John D. and Catherine T. MacArthur Foundation and the Illinois Department of Commerce and Economic Opportunity provided funding for a study of technology use that was commissioned by the City of Chicago in 2008. Julia Stasch of the John D. and Catherine T. MacArthur Foundation was instrumental in supporting this research, and in providing leadership on the Mayor's Advisory Council on Closing the Digital Divide and subsequent efforts for the city's digital excellence agenda. We have greatly benefited from working with Alaina Harkness and Craig Howard of the foundation as well. We are currently involved in evaluating the Smart Communities programs and in further studies of technology use in the City of Chicago, through the support of the MacArthur Foundation, Illinois Department of Commerce and Economic Opportunity, the Partnership for a Connected Illinois, and the Institute for Policy and Civic Engagement at the University of Illinois at Chicago. This has given us a chance to observe on the ground the evolution of the federal broadband initiatives (and to have some great policy discussions with Charles Benton, Drew Clark, John Horrigan, Norma Ramos, and Joe Hoereth, among others).

The Chicago programs we describe in chapter 9 were begun under Mayor Daley, and they continue under Mayor Emanuel. Both mayors have had the vision to make technology issues a priority. John Karnuth, Matt Guilford, Danielle DuMerer, Francesca Rodriguez, Kate McAdams, Hardik Bhatt, John Tolva, and Jason DeHaan are dedicated city officials who have worked on these projects over the years. We especially miss Matt's energy and wisdom, but we know he is doing good things at Harvard. Tom Irvine, Concepcion Prado, Kyla Williams and Dan O'Neill have been guiding future planning for technology initiatives at the Chicago Community Trust. We thank Dan also for making sure that no meeting is dull. Susana Vasquez and Dionne Baux of LISC, and all the Smart Communities lead agencies and partners, have been extremely generous and patient with their time, allowing us to watch their efforts unfold in Chicago's neighborhoods. They are doing the hard work required for social change.

We owe a special thanks to Daniel Bowen, now on faculty at the College of New Jersey and a former University of Iowa graduate student in Political Science, for his statistical analysis of the Chicago survey. Originally shared as a report from the City of Chicago, that survey laid the foundation for this study and some analysis found in chapter 6. Dan's careful analysis merging aggregate census-level data with the individual-level survey data allowed us to map the Chicago neighborhoods. We are indebted for his hard work and detailed precision. We also thank former UIC graduate assistant Benedict Jimenez, now on faculty at Rutgers-Newark, for his role in the analysis of the Chicago survey.

The Chicago study we analyze here was based on a random digit-dialed telephone survey of Chicago residents merged with measures of neighborhood attributes; that survey was conducted by David Redlawsk, who was at the University of Iowa at the time, but is now the director of the Eagleton Poll at Rutgers University. As a former city council member in New Jersey, David approached this project with great enthusiasm, and we are lucky to have had the benefit of his expertise.

To generalize beyond Chicago, we interviewed officials in other cities as well—New York, San Francisco, Seattle, Los Angeles, Minneapolis, and Boston. We truly appreciate the time that these officials spared from their busy schedules and also the policy work they are doing to create the digital cities of the future. We would also like to thank those at the NTIA and Census Bureau who graciously provided their assistance when we had questions related to the Current Population Survey data used throughout our study.

Many graduate students and others at our universities have been involved in segments of this research, modeling and remodeling the statistical data, poring over the literature, and assisting with interviews. These include Allison Hamilton at the University of Iowa and Jennifer Benoit-Bryan, Adrian Brown, Mona Noriega, and Meng-Hao Li at the University of Illinois at Chicago (UIC). The Great Cities Urban Data Visualization Laboratory at UIC geocoded the Chicago survey and produced the maps in chapters 5, 6, and 8. A special thank you goes to Nina Savar, Sarah Barr, and Max Dieber for their work and their good humor in meeting our multiple requests. The UIC College of Urban Planning and Public Affairs provided financial assistance for the mapping. The University of Iowa Department of Political Science generously provided funding for a graduate research assistant for this project.

Part of this research has been presented in various venues—at Oxford University, at the Joan Shorenstein Center on the Press, Politics & Public Policy at Harvard's Kennedy School of Government, at Georgetown University, the Brookings Institution, the University of Texas at Austin, the University of Louisville, and the annual conferences of the American Political Science Association, the Midwest Political Science Association, and E-Chicago, among them. The findings were presented as a Public Policy Lecture at Iowa, and for the Departments of Urban Planning and Communications at Iowa. The UIC library also invited a presentation at its symposium. We thank many of those who heard these presentations for their comments, and we received valuable insights on this project from discussions with colleagues, including Eszter Hargittai, Darrell West, Golin Gordan, Bob Boynton, and James King. Chapter 8 in this book borrows heavily from the journal article "Unraveling Differences in Barriers to Technology Use: Urban Residents and Neighborhood Effects" in *Urban Affairs Review.* We thank the editors and publisher of *UAR* for their permission to print the adaptation of the journal article here.

We benefitted considerably from the advice of the anonymous reviewers for Oxford University Press and *UAR.* And finally, we are grateful to Andy Chadwick, the series editor, and Angela Chnapko, of Oxford University Press. Our admiration for Andy's work attracted us to this series, and we are truly fortunate to have worked with Angela and the Oxford staff as well. We are thankful to Oxford for their support and expertise throughout the publication process.

We end with an acknowledgment of the significance of youth, digital creativity, and hope for the future. On the cover of this book, we proudly display the work of You Media student Diego Barragan. Our involvement in evaluating the Smart Communities led us to the impressive work of the Digital Youth Network and the YouMedia program at the Chicago Public Library. Mentor and artist Niq Tognoni generously worked with a number of YouMedia students to produce original artwork for the book cover. We received submissions from Aixa Dones, Charlise Jacox, Daniel Aguado, James Taylor, Jessi Lopez, Oliver Dillard, Tramain Cheney, and Zachary Tidwell, who participate in YouMedia programs at the Harold Washington, Thurgood Marshall, Rudy Lozano, and Richard M. Daley branches of the Chicago Public Library. We could only choose one graphic, but we appreciate the thought and talent invested in all the submissions. For us, this is a chance to highlight the work of young people who are achieving "digital excellence" in meaningful and creative ways.

Digital Cities

1

Cities and a Digital Society

Google created a frenzy by announcing that by the end of 2010 it would select "one or more" cities for a lightning-fast fiber-optic network with speeds of up to one gigabyte—nearly 75 times faster than current average broadband speeds in the United States.[1] Before the late March 2010 deadline for applications, the mayor of Duluth, Minnesota waded through an ice-strewn shoreline and plunged into the frigid waters of Lake Superior to draw attention to his city's bid. Not to be outdone, the mayor of Topeka issued a proclamation changing the city's official name to Google, Kansas—at least for the month of March (Helft 2010). Over 1,000 other cities frantically posted YouTube videos and recruited Facebook fans in an effort to show public support for their projects (Steketee Greiner and Co. 2010; Settles 2011).[2] In March 2011, Google chose Kansas City, Kansas, and Kansas City, Missouri, for its experiment with super-fast broadband (Settles 2011).

The circuslike atmosphere surrounding the Google competition distracted from a serious message underlying the theatrics—new technology matters to cities, but local governments have limited resources to address technology needs on their own. Beyond Google, broadband policy in the United States is at a historical crossroad, with $7.2 billion worth of investments expended in the federal stimulus budget,[3] a comprehensive National Broadband Plan (NBP), and changes to the Universal Service Fund allocating an additional $4 billion annually to broadband.[4]

The emphasis of federal policy, however, has been on the construction of rural broadband infrastructure, largely neglecting cities. Yet, it is cities and metropolitan areas that promise the most substantial payoffs for these broadband investments, which were part of the economic stimulus. Urban areas, with their density of economic activity, offer the largest economic gains from high-speed networks and their varied uses (Forman, Goldfarb, and Greenstein 2005, 2008, 2009). Affordable broadband options in cities could have done far more to address disparities in Internet access and use, which was another goal of federal policy. The nation's population is concentrated in cities and metropolitan areas, including many who are offline or less-connected. By focusing on rural infrastructure (where there is little existing private investment), current federal programs avoid competition and political conflict with the major telecommunications firms, but the programs also fail to address either the opportunities or policy problems associated with broadband use. The consequences for the nation as a whole may be inefficient and ineffective public policies.

Broadband has become the standard for Internet use, and the United States lags behind many other developed countries in terms of speed, affordability, and adoption.

According to the Organization for Economic Cooperation and Development (OECD), the average advertised download speed in the United States in 2010 was only 14 megabits per second (mbps), compared with 85 in Sweden and 37 for the OECD average. Twelve of 24 OECD nations had lower average monthly subscription costs than the United States for the slowest broadband speeds, and the United States did relatively worse in price in higher speed categories. The United States ranked 15th in broadband subscribers per 100 inhabitants in 2010 (OECD 2011).

In a December 2011 *New York Times* editorial, law professor Susan Crawford described the state of broadband policy in the United States, where

> video-on-demand, online medicine and Internet classrooms have redefined the state of the art: they require reliable, truly high-speed connections, the kind available almost exclusively from the nation's small number of very powerful cable companies. Such access means expensive contracts, which many Americans simply cannot afford. While we still talk about "the" Internet, we increasingly have two separate access marketplaces: high-speed wired and second-class wireless. High-speed access is a superhighway for those who can afford it, while racial minorities and poorer and rural Americans must make do with a bike path. (Crawford 2011, 1)

The data lends support to these claims. In 2010, 72% of Americans used the Internet in some setting, and 65% had broadband at home (NTIA 2011). Thus, nearly 4 in 10 Americans (35%) were either offline or less-connected. Latinos were the least likely to have broadband at home (45%), followed by African Americans (50%), and both groups significantly lagged behind white non-Hispanics. One in two African Americans and the majority of Latinos lacked broadband at home.

Nationwide, technology disparities were clearly not driven by a lack of rural infrastructure. Overall, broadband adoption was seven percentage points higher in urbanized areas than in rural communities (see chapter 3). Yet large cities and poor suburbs contain neighborhoods where poverty is heavily concentrated and residents have limited use of information technology. According to the study of Chicago that we examine in chapters 6 and 8, entire neighborhoods with tens of thousands of residents meet the federal definition of "underserved," as less than 40% of the population has broadband connections at home.

The United Nations recently declared that access to the Internet is a human right (Kravets 2011). While the announcement was in response to authoritarian governments blocking Internet access, the UN's position demonstrates the significance of information technology in modern life. Those who are offline because of poverty or lack of education and skills also suffer from a diminished ability to exercise their human rights. Home access and high-speed access are necessary for "digital citizenship," or the regular access and effective use that enable full participation in society online (Mossberger, Tolbert and McNeal 2008). It matters little whether home broadband access is achieved through a mobile air card and laptop or through a wired Internet connection and desktop. The point is that individuals need frequent, convenient, and flexible use of technology, with the full functions of the Internet (rather than limited access through mobile phones). Research has shown that home access is important for education, income, health care, finances, politics, and civic engagement (Hassani 2006; DiMaggio and Bonikowski 2008). These are precisely the applications envisioned in the National Broadband Plan.

While popular rhetoric argues that cell phones will bridge the digital inequalities, we demonstrate in the following pages that mobile phones are insufficient as the primary means of going online. As we show in chapter 4, those who rely primarily on cell phones to use the Internet are disadvantaged in terms of the range of economic and political activities they perform online and the skills they acquire. While Crawford and others have made important arguments to this effect, we provide new empirical ground for this debate. Though smartphones have many benefits, the "second-class access" noted by Crawford constitutes, in effect, second-class digital citizenship. The growth in mobile phone use among African Americans and Latinos has not erased disparities in society online.

Federal policies have the potential to address broadband costs and speeds, bringing the nation closer to universal access and opportunity in an increasingly digital society. Yet new federal initiatives have fallen short in many ways, especially in American cities. Federal policy for expanding Internet access in the United States is focused largely on infrastructure in rural areas and has not sufficiently addressed the disparities or the barriers that exist in urban areas. Affordability as a reason for being offline is even more important in urban than rural areas and for certain segments of the population, such as the poor and minorities. The cost for neglecting both the opportunities and the inequalities in cities may be the failure to reach national goals and to realize either the economic or social benefits of broadband.

What We Can Gain from Cities: Urban Innovation

Today, 84% of the U.S. population lives in urbanized areas, where technology policies are liable to have the greatest impact (Brookings Institution 2010). One reason for paying attention to broadband needs in cities and their surrounding metropolitan areas is this scale. Urban areas, however, produce more than their fair share of innovation, apart from their overwhelming proportion of the population. Economist Edward Glaeser has argued in a recent book that through their density, "Cities enable collaboration, especially the joint production of knowledge that is mankind's most important creation" (2011, 247). A multidisciplinary consensus is forming that "compared with suburban or rural areas, cities do more with less. And the bigger cities get, the more productive and efficient they tend to become" (Bettencourt and West 2011, 52). Simply put, "cities concentrate, accelerate, and diversify social and economic activity" (ibid.). Place matters for the location of broadband investments as well: cities generate a disproportionate share of economic and social gains from technology use. Businesses in urban areas use the Internet in more sophisticated ways and produce higher wage growth from the use of the Internet in firms (Forman, Goldfarb, and Greenstein 2005, 2008, 2009). This is due to the capabilities of urban firms and workers, and the exchange of knowledge in dense urban areas, which allow technology investments to be more fully exploited. Some preliminary research indicates that community institutions such as schools, libraries, and hospitals also employ broadband more intensively in metropolitan areas (Forman, Goldfarb, and Greenstein 2011).

Moreover, local governments are often willing partners for policies aimed at improved broadband deployment and increased adoption; the issues were on local government agendas long before Google's competition or federal stimulus spending. But, history has shown that despite some creative initiatives, local governments lack the resources to affect technology investments or the cost of broadband on a widespread or sustained basis. They are dependent on other actors, especially the private sector. After Philadelphia announced its plans for a municipal wireless network in 2004, many other cities considered forming such partnerships, described in chapter 2. The networks were intended to offer "hot spots" around the cities and to provide low-cost access for residents and businesses. Most of these efforts failed in large cities because of the withdrawal of private-sector partners. Yet, the municipal wireless initiatives demonstrate a history of technology policy as a priority on city agendas, even at a time when the federal government under George Bush had abandoned the issue of digital inclusion.

Many cities examined other options in the wake of the wireless movement. Chicago began to plan for more targeted efforts in several low-income communities, before the election of the Obama administration in 2008 and the resurgence of broadband on the federal agenda. These programs are described in more detail in chapter 9, along with the problems they face in addressing the costs of access for low-income residents.

Why do cities care about broadband, even though they do not control many of the resources needed to affect its deployment and use? The revolution in information and communications technology parallels historic developments such as the printing press. Competition for local economic development and the potential for cutting-edge applications in public safety and municipal services clearly motivated many cities that considered or built municipal networks (Gillett 2005). The Google frenzy in particular suggests economic competition as a cause, as does the literature on urban policy (Peterson 1981).

Local governments in the United States have been captivated by the idea of "smart cities" driven by ubiquitous broadband networks that can power electrical grids, manage public transit systems, protect public safety, conserve energy, and promote sustainability.[5] National governments such as South Korea's or Japan's have promoted ubiquitous networks in cities through a combination of "next generation" wireless and fiber-optic infrastructure, but the United States is a relative laggard in this area (Berkman Center 2010). The complex economic, transportation, and energy systems of major cities could function as important test beds for smart city concepts. To truly test the idea of ubiquity, however, cities need more than the appropriate infrastructure; they need many citizens who can afford wired and wireless broadband access.

As the low-cost access envisioned by municipal wireless proposals suggests, one goal of many local governments is to bring more residents online. Cities have multiple reasons to attend to technology disparities. Local school districts and municipal governments must prepare students for the future, even when those students lack technology access at home. Local libraries are critical venues for public access in poor communities, in an age when an Internet connection is increasingly necessary to search for or apply for a job. Adults who lack technology skills diminish the attractiveness of the local workforce. City governments cannot fully realize the efficiencies and service improvements made possible by e-government if a substantial portion of residents remain offline. Neighborhood organizations can utilize technology for organizing and mobilizing residents to participate in their communities. At the local level, economic development, education, e-government, civic engagement and other community needs have encouraged cities to address digital inclusion, despite the difficulties they face.

Broadband, Cities, and the National Interest

In Barack Obama's speech announcing his presidential candidacy in 2007, he promised to "lay down broadband lines through the heart of inner cities and rural towns all across America."[6] Subsequently, part of the economic stimulus package was devoted to broadband, primarily for infrastructure development but also to map the availability of broadband nationally, to provide some funds for public computer centers, and to encourage broadband adoption. As part of the stimulus bill, Congress directed the Federal Communications Commission (FCC) to devise a long-term national broadband plan. Through public investments in infrastructure, the stimulus program held out the possibility of addressing costs and promoting home broadband access and use.

In that plan, the FCC laid out the goal of universal broadband access and defined the mission of creating "a more productive, creative, efficient America in which affordable broadband is available everywhere and everyone has the means and skills to use valuable broadband applications" (FCC 2010a, 9). The plan spells out important national purposes for broadband policy, including economic opportunity, education, energy and the environment, health care, government performance, civic engagement, and public safety/homeland security. In many ways, the broadband stimulus program represents a significant break from past federal policy, which funded only public access and training. Blair Levin, one of the authors of the National Broadband Plan, has since argued, however, that the plan failed to provide adequate solutions for low-income Americans and that "in terms of priorities, we spend too much on deployment to real estate and not enough on adoption by people" (High 2011, 1). The following chapters will show that costs for home access pose significant difficulties for adoption.

Despite the far-reaching goals articulated in federal plans, implementation of the economic stimulus program indicates that urban communities are being *left behind* in broadband policy.[7] Cities were eligible to apply for infrastructure and other grants to assist "underserved areas" with broadband adoption of 40% or less (Federal Register 2009). Many cities unquestionably had underserved areas, as the neighborhood data from the Chicago study in this book indicates. Yet, not a single city received federal funding for broadband infrastructure in the first round. As we will discuss in chapter 2, cities were disadvantaged from the beginning, because of requirements that were nearly impossible to meet and unequal information advantages for incumbent providers who wished to block city proposals. In the second round, a few urban areas received grants for public safety infrastructure, and only Washington, D.C. was awarded funding for infrastructure deployment to other public and nonprofit institutions. None of these projects provided low-cost broadband to local residents.

Some major cities did receive funding for Public Computer Centers (PCC grants) and Sustainable Broadband Adoption (SBA grants) that supported outreach and training.[8] Training and public access address only part of the policy problem, however, leaving aside the cost barrier that presents such a hurdle for home access in low-income communities. Yet, grantees of the training programs are expected to track outcomes in terms of broadband subscriptions,[9] and many have struggled to find ways to offer affordable solutions for low-income populations.[10]

The Public Sector and Federal Roles

Historically, broadband development in the United States has been left to the private sector, in a thin market that is dominated by a few firms, with little pressure to compete over costs or to develop faster networks (Berkman Center 2010; West 2011, ch. 5). Economists define thin markets (with few providers) as a form of market failure related to monopolies; in thin markets providers set costs too high, resulting in undersupply and market inefficiency or deadweight loss (Munger 2000). Cable dominates the U.S. market, and many regions have a single cable provider (Crawford 2011).[11] In contrast with most other nations, those that build the networks in the United States are not required to lease access to their infrastructure to other providers (Berkman Center 2010; Crawford 2011). Open-access requirements are one policy solution that has been shown to introduce greater competition (Berkman Center 2010). Without addressing the problems of cost and monopoly supply, universal access will remain an elusive goal in cities and in the rest of the country.

Another source of competition could be municipal projects that lease infrastructure to various providers. Federal policy in the stimulus program has avoided creating competition with incumbent private telecommunications providers yet competition is exactly what economists recommend to address supply and demand in thin markets, such as broadband access (Munger 2000). Internet service providers have opposed municipal wireless networks in state legislatures and the courts for years (Feld et al. 2005; McCann 2012) and appear to have influenced current federal policy. This represents a case of government failure (Munger 2000), when federal policy is either captured by the economic interests of incumbent providers or constrained from acting in the public interest by their opposition.

Globally, nations with the fastest networks have also featured long-term public sector investments alongside private provision—for example, in South Korea, Japan, and Sweden (West 2011; Berkman Center 2010). The $7.2 billion allocated to broadband in federal stimulus programs is modest in comparison with the public investments in other countries and hardly enough to deliver affordable broadband everywhere (West 2011, ch. 5). The FCC has estimated that universal availability at 100 megabits per second will cost $350 billion in public and private investments (West 2011; FCC 2010). Federal funding is not likely to fulfill this need, given the private-sector model of provision in the United States, where the nation has relied on private companies for broadband infrastructure. For example, AT&T and Verizon have invested over $40 billion each in recent years in building broadband and wireless networks, and Comcast has spent nearly $15 billion. These are followed by Sprint at $10 billion and T-Mobile with $8.5 billion (West 2011).

But, federal investments could play a catalytic role, supporting municipal and nonprofit use of high-speed infrastructure that could provide better information for public policy through experiments with lower levels of pricing as well as new applications. The higher speeds and lower costs made possible by public infrastructure investment in cities could benefit community institutions such as schools, hospitals, libraries, and government agencies and assist with other national goals such as health care and education reform. Only a few infrastructure grants went to urban public institutions, in contrast with rural networks for institutions, businesses, and residents.

Additionally, the public sector has an important role to play in supporting access for low-income populations. The concluding chapter in this book discusses the development of some low-income assistance programs in the United States, such as the Internet Essentials program that Comcast offered in return for regulatory permission for a merger, and the changes to the Low-Income Program of the Universal Service Fund administered by the FCC. These are important and welcome initiatives and are discussed in more detail in the conclusion. Only a portion of those in need, however, are likely to be covered by these programs. In contrast, broadband access is a legal right in Finland (West 2011).

While the absence of broadband infrastructure in rural areas is clearly a case of market failure, so are the under provision of cutting-edge technologies in cities and the under consumption of broadband in urban areas. Cost poses a dilemma for urban broadband that requires federal assistance, whether that is through legislation that encourages greater competition in the market, public investments and incentives, or subsidies for low-income individuals. The National Broadband Plan defines broadband as a public good, and we argue that federal policy is needed for urban and metropolitan areas, as well as local government programs. The market alone will not produce anything close to universal access and adoption.

How Place Matters: Uncovering Multiple Layers of the Policy Context

Cities are strategic venues for national broadband policy, for addressing both innovation and inequality. In the next chapters, however, we make the argument that "place matters" for broadband policy on many levels. This is true for a number of reasons. First, the United States has a decentralized federal system, where local governments are responsible for a variety of policies, and where programs are more dependent on local own-source revenues than in many other political systems (Wolman 2012). Second, in the United States, social inequality is often spatially patterned, across jurisdictions within metropolitan areas and across neighborhoods within cities. Taking differences across place into account allows for a more accurate definition of the scope and nature of digital disparities and needs, as well as potential policy solutions.

Peeling through the multiple layers of this policy context, we see in chapter 3 that urban, suburban, and rural differences are visible. But these are inadequate for fully depicting policy needs and the influence of place. A more nuanced understanding would allow us to compare variation across cities and metropolitan areas, and across neighborhoods within cities. These variations affect economic and social opportunities for residents. Metropolitan areas form the labor markets and regional economies that provide jobs and income for technology use and access. How poverty and tax wealth are distributed across municipal boundaries within these metropolitan areas affects resources for institutions such as schools and libraries, which provide not only public access but also education for the information age. Central cities (along with poor suburbs) may offer fewer resources for residents. Differences within cities are worthy of investigation as well. Urban scholars have argued that the "neighborhood effects" of living in high-poverty areas constrain individual opportunities for education, employment, health, and more (Wilson 1987; Jargowsky 1997; Sampson, Morenoff, and Gannon-Rowley 2002; Newburger, Birch, and Wachter 2011).

Xavier de Souza Briggs (2005) has described these spatially patterned inequalities as the geography of opportunity in the United States. Here we explore how geography matters across multiple levels for opportunity in terms of both broadband innovation and inequality. Broadband is far from an arcane, technical issue, but rather a matter of access to information and communication, cutting across policy areas, and fulfilling social and individual needs.

Focusing on the nation's cities—and especially the neighborhoods within them—illuminates the diversity of experiences and challenges that must be taken into consideration for increasing broadband adoption and realizing federal objectives. To do this, we analyze three sources of survey data from the period when recent federal programs were launched: two national surveys fielded in 2009, and a 2008 survey of Chicago (conducted by the authors). The October 2009 Current Population Survey (CPS) sponsored by the U.S. Bureau of the Census contains 134,000 respondents, permitting us to analyze subsamples for central city, suburban, and rural residents (NTIA 2010a). In addition to the CPS data, a national survey of 5,000 respondents was conducted by the Federal Communications Commission in November 2009 (Horrigan 2010). This survey replicates the CPS and includes additional questions about activities online, mobile use, knowledge, and skills. Statistics based on the 2010 CPS are cited in the text and generally track the 2009 figures. The Chicago survey has a sample of more than 3,000 respondents, including data on technology use across the city's 77 neighborhoods and over 300 census tracts. Thus, we are able to compare unique neighborhood-level data with national trends in a similar time period, during the development of recent federal policies.

While a variety of methods are used to analyze the data, and are explained in more detail below, in several chapters we employ multilevel statistical models. These allow us to simultaneously test the significance of neighborhood-level and individual-level factors, for example. Multilevel models also allow us to create estimates of technology use in cities and neighborhoods, mapping the geography of broadband use. While federal programs have mapped broadband availability based on service-provider data, we are able to portray actual use based on estimates of the percentage of the population with high-speed Internet at home, for example, and barriers to technology use.

Within these chapters, we also present the voices of policy participants, supplementing the trends revealed by the data. To better understand city goals and activities for broadband, interviews were conducted with local officials in seven major cities that have active technology initiatives: New York, Boston, Chicago, Minneapolis, Seattle, San Francisco, and Los Angeles. The survey data on Chicago is complemented by a rich description of the Smart Communities program in the five Chicago neighborhoods that received $7 million in federal funding through the Sustainable Broadband Adoption (SBA) program.

A Few Words on Methods

Readers without a background in quantitative research methods will be able to track our findings through maps, graphs, and results that are as easy to interpret as simple percentages. But, we want to emphasize the methods that are used in the study and why they matter. Many studies of Internet use have relied on descriptive statistics or other methods of analysis that lack multivariate controls to untangle overlapping influences. Descriptive statistics, such as the *percentage* of mobile phone users who are Latino, are useful for tracking trends, as many of the following chapters show. But understanding, for example, the effect of home broadband versus mobile access on online political activities, requires the use of methods that can better isolate cause and effect. The limitation of descriptive studies is that individuals who use mobile access may be different in a number of ways beyond their race or ethnicity; they may also be younger, less affluent, less educated, or live in poorer neighborhoods. Multivariate methods allow us to examine which factors are statistically significant for predicting outcomes, holding other factors constant.

For most of the analysis in this book, we use a number of sophisticated multivariate methods that allow us to explore the causes of trends, including the relative role of overlapping influences such as individual-level income and education, and place-based or geographic factors. Multilevel statistical models are used to break new ground in several chapters: to rank Internet use and access in the 50 largest cities and in suburban areas in chapter 5 (something not done before), and also to create estimates of technology use across Chicago's neighborhoods in chapters 6 and 8. For these purposes, we use a method of hierarchical linear modeling with post-stratification weights to create the city and suburban-level estimates of Internet use at home and in any location, as well as by neighborhoods, within cities. These neighborhood-level estimates are mapped. To do so, we build on work by Lax and Phillips (2009a, 2009b) and others to create geographic estimates from the multilevel models drawn from both individual- and aggregate-level variables (Steenbergen and Jones 2002; Raudenbush and Bryk 2002).

For those familiar with multivariate regression analysis, the methods we use also include logistic regression (for binary outcome variables) and ordinal logistic regression (for ordinal outcome variables). Depending on the coding of the dependent variables, these methods are used in models in various chapters. In our analysis of the large-sample CPS data, we use "subsample" analyses, predicting technology access or frequency of Internet use for subsamples of the population, such as African Americans or Latinos. These fine-grained analyses allow us to more accurately isolate the factors that encourage technology use by disadvantaged groups than standard statistical methods, taking into account context or place factors.

Despite the advanced methods underlying the findings, we present the results in a format accessible to readers without a background in statistics. We will use tables that list statistically significant factors and figures based on probability simulations (or predicted values) that are as easy to understand as simple percentages, but that are based on the multivariate regression coefficients and illustrate the relative size of the impact on outcomes. Stated another way, the multivariate regression models (including the more specific type of multilevel modeling we use here) are interpreted by generating predicted values using simulations holding other variables in the models constant at mean values (King, Tomz, and Wittenberg 2000). The predicted values for the regression models can be read and interpreted the same as simple percentages—but they provide a more accurate picture of technology opportunity and inequality.

Through maps and graphs, we allow the data to tell the story about place and public policy. The predicted values (or point estimates) discussed earlier are used to generate maps based on geographic patterns or graphs based on demographic factors.

All multivariate regression tables are included in appendix A for those who wish to examine our data and results in greater detail.

Plan of the Book

Chapter 2 frames the policy issues for broadband, discussing current federal policy and examining the central role of cities and metropolitan areas for achieving national goals. We review research on the benefits of broadband use in urban areas and explore the relationship between cities and the policies prioritized by the National Broadband Plan. We offer a brief history of municipal broadband efforts, including descriptions of those funded through the federal stimulus and others launched through independent city initiatives. The chapter includes interviews with government officials in seven major cities regarding their goals for broadband policy, and their views on the role of the public sector at the local level.

In chapter 3, we begin to explore the different levels of the policy context. Chapter 3 examines patterns of technology use anywhere, home access, and home broadband adoption—nationally, and in subsamples for urban, suburban, and rural respondents from the Current Population Survey. This allows for a detailed view of patterns of technology use, for example, differentiating between urban and rural Latinos, and between low-income and more affluent urban or rural residents. We analyze the data using multivariate models, and unlike the federal reports, which document metropolitan versus nonmetropolitan results, we separate central cities from their suburbs. The very large sample size of the CPS (over 100,000 respondents) allows us to provide accurate estimates of technology use and access nationwide—the closest to "truth" we can obtain. The national FCC survey, which has a smaller sample but some additional questions, offers similar results. The picture that emerges on this first level portrays the impact of social inequalities as well as some similarities and differences between urban and rural communities.

Chapter 4 extends this analysis and compares broadband users with mobile-phone-only Internet users and others that are "less-connected" across urban, suburban, and rural areas. Mobile phone use is rising among low-income African Americans and Latinos, provoking debates about whether new technologies are erasing disparities. Drawing on both the CPS and FCC national surveys, we contrast broadband users to those who rely on cell phones, public access, or slow dial-up connections. We describe these less-connected populations across geographic areas but also examine measures of skill and online activities for different types of less-connected Internet users. Neither smart-phones nor other modes of access offer anything rivaling the capacities enabled by home broadband.

Chapter 5 offers an unprecedented snapshot of variation across cities and suburban areas, digging into the metropolitan and city-level contexts. Comparative data have only been available at the state level in the past, so this chapter offers new information for policymakers. The CPS has sufficiently large samples in each of the 50 largest metropolitan areas that allow us to create estimates of overall home broadband access and barriers to access, for these central cities and their suburban regions, using multilevel models. We rank the 50 largest cities and suburban metropolitan areas in terms of the percentage of the population with home broadband and Internet use anywhere for 2007 and 2009, as these questions were repeated in these years. In addition to tracking change over this period, the chapter also separately ranks outcomes for use anywhere and home broadband for African Americans and Latinos across cities and suburban regions. The rankings show substantial differences between cities, as well as notable inequalities within metropolitan areas. Context clearly matters for technology opportunities.

Examining technology use and access at the metropolitan or city level still obscures the experiences of low-income communities within cities, including distinctive differences across high-poverty neighborhoods. The data on Chicago neighborhoods fills this gap and is introduced in chapter 6. This study provides a truly unique view of technology use in low-income communities. Using a citywide survey of 3,453 respondents conducted by the authors, we examine patterns of technology use across census tracts and the city's 77 community areas. This study, which was commissioned by the City of Chicago and funded by the MacArthur Foundation and the State of Illinois, breaks new ground by using multilevel models that produce estimates of technology access and use at the neighborhood level.

Chicago functions as a critical case. By studying this diverse city, in chapter 6 we are able to examine the relationship between technology use and place factors, such as concentrated poverty and segregation. Low- and high-broadband-use neighborhoods can be contrasted in terms of the activities that residents engage in online—job searches, political participation, employment, health, and e-government. This offers a concrete view of the impact of technology inequality in poor neighborhoods.

After describing these disparities, we turn to the reasons why people are offline or less-connected. Chapter 7 discusses national data on barriers to technology use from the Current Population Survey. As in chapters 3 and 4, multivariate analysis is used for subsamples of urban, suburban, and rural residents. While there are some urban and rural differences, nationally, affordability is the most common barrier for home broadband adoption.

Returning to the Chicago survey in chapter 8, we examine barriers to home access at the neighborhood level, where we find significant differences across demographic groups and neighborhoods. Living in segregated and poor neighborhoods magnifies barriers to technology use, as we show with multilevel models and interactions.

Chicago is also a city with active neighborhood groups and a history of technology initiatives, and we describe the efforts of the Smart Communities partners in the conclusion (chapter 9). The material on the Chicago Smart Communities program is based on interviews with key participants from community groups, nonprofit organizations, city departments, foundations, and other organizations, as well as documents and websites. We conclude by considering policy solutions at various levels of government, again considering the layers of geography and policy context. By focusing on place, we offer information to policymakers for fine-tuning policy regarding the nature and extent of policy problems, and the need for place-based targeting, or for national solutions. Broadband policy should embrace grassroots initiatives, local experimentation, and broader state and federal programs.

Across these multiple layers of geography, telling the stories of neighborhoods, cities, and the nation—both in data and in participants' experiences—brings to life the significance of broadband, wireless, and other forms of Internet access as the means to accomplish important social ends and to produce widespread public benefits. Some scholars have described urban inequalities in terms of the geography of opportunity (Briggs 2005). Digital cities are central for addressing both inequality and innovation, and for creating the opportunities of the future.

2

The Need for Urban Broadband Policy

Like railroads and highways, broadband accelerates the velocity of commerce, reducing the costs of distance. Like electricity, it creates a platform for America's creativity to lead in developing better ways to solve old problems. Like telephony and broadcasting, it expands our ability to communicate, inform and entertain. Broadband is the great infrastructure challenge of the early 21st century. But as with electricity and telephony, ubiquitous connections are means, not ends. It is what those connections enable that matters.

Federal Communications Commission
—National Broadband Plan 2010

Broadband policy landed on the federal agenda with the Obama election and the stimulus act's designs to spur the economy forward. Along with infrastructure projects, such as roads and highways, the stimulus funding passed in early 2009 included $7.2 billion for broadband projects in infrastructure, mapping, public access, and training. To place these investments within a longer term perspective, Congress required the FCC to develop a national broadband plan to guide future federal policy. As the epigraph shows, the FCC recognized that broadband is both an infrastructure investment and a platform for a variety of activities. It is the applications for high-speed Internet across policy areas, the abilities of users, and the information flowing through those networks that create value for society. At the heart of broadband policy is the use of information, and cities have the dense and diverse networks needed to utilize information in the most efficient and effective ways. Federal policy is needed to fill gaps in private-sector investment and to promote affordability of broadband access.

The $7.2 billion expended on broadband in the stimulus funding was a down payment on the anticipated $350 billion that the national plan estimates will be needed to achieve the long-term goal of at least 100 million homes with affordable access to actual download speeds of 100 megabits per second (mbps) and actual upload speeds of 50 mbps by 2020 (FCC 2010a, 10). This raises questions about how future funding should be allocated beyond current programs.

Cities are important for national broadband policy because urban areas are uniquely positioned for producing broadband's social and economic benefits. The density of population and institutions enhances the impact of broadband use in economic development, multiple policy domains, and the community. Density creates critical needs for information technology in areas such as public safety, energy, education, health care, and mass transit. But, it also offers the conditions for solutions like ubiquitous broadband and the bottom-up development of new applications in many of these policy areas (Bettencourt and West 2011, 52). Overall, the many uses and specialized activities in urban areas allow for more complex applications and greater innovation for national economic growth and policy. Research shows that the economic benefits of broadband are highest in urban areas (Forman, Goldfarb, and Greenstein 2005, 2008, 2009). For many reasons, the nation's cities are most likely to produce the broadband applications of the future.

The vast majority of the national population is urban: nearly 85% of Americans reside in metropolitan areas. Large central cities (and some suburbs) confront problems of poverty and reflect an increasingly diverse society, and thus are opportune places to devise solutions that fit the needs of different populations. Programs that address barriers to broadband use in urban areas can affect a large number of those who are technologically disadvantaged, which can therefore have a significant impact on fostering more widespread and equitable access to the information and communication opportunities online.

These benefits have the potential to ripple throughout the larger society and are not just confined to urban areas.

Yet, in the broadband stimulus program, less than 8% of the funding went to projects in metropolitan areas.[1] National broadband policy so far is a rural infrastructure policy and is referenced as such in speeches by President Obama (Kang 2011). Urban grants were primarily limited to public access, training, and outreach rather than the infrastructure that could support higher speeds for innovation and affordable solutions for low-income residents. The issue is not whether cities have been slighted in the distribution of federal funding, but whether the United States will realize the potential offered by technology. "Place" matters for effective public policy.

In this chapter, we examine the role of cities and metropolitan areas for achieving national goals. We review research on the benefits of urban broadband and explore the relationship between cities and the policy areas prioritized by the National Broadband Plan. We conclude with a discussion of local broadband programs, both those funded through the federal stimulus programs and a few undertaken by cities themselves. Based on interviews with local officials, we discuss the goals and needs of cities, and their role in national broadband policy.

Cities and National Purposes

Following years of neglect, the promotion of information technology use is on the federal agenda again.[2] With the deep economic recession as the backdrop, the Obama administration promoted broadband policy as a solution that would have future implications for the economy and society, as well as a short-term impact on hiring (Reuters 2010). In this vein, congressional legislation authorizing the broadband spending required that the FCC produce a national broadband plan with a detailed strategy for

> *achieving affordability and maximizing use of broadband* to advance 'consumer welfare, civic participation, public safety and homeland security, community

development, health care delivery, energy independence and efficiency, education, employee training, private sector investment, entrepreneurial activity, job creation and economic growth, and other national purposes.[3]

The National Broadband Plan (NBP) was announced in March 2010, more than a year after the passage of the stimulus legislation, and following months of public hearings, testimony from experts, and the gathering of research and other evidence.[4] The discussion of national purposes in the broadband plan focuses on both the social benefits of broadband use and the costs of inequality in these areas—including economic development, health, education, public safety, government services, civic engagement, energy, and the environment. We review the relationship between cities and the national broadband goals in the next section.

Urban areas have two characteristics that are important for national broadband policy. One is their density, which fosters innovation and supports institutions and activities with national significance. The other distinguishing feature of urban areas is their diversity, with populations that face different challenges, needs, and resources for technology use. The concentration of activity and diversity within cities adds to their significance for national policy, beyond sheer numbers.

Cities and their metropolitan areas are the engines of prosperity and innovation for the nation (Brookings Institution 2007, 6; Glaeser 2011), because of agglomeration economies in the dense networks of interrelated activity, with clusters of firms, suppliers, research and development, skilled workers, and more (Brookings Institution 2007; see also Kantor and Turok 2012). According to economists, urban areas are more innovative due to this density: "Ideas flow readily from person to person...Urban density creates a constant flow of new information that comes from observing other's successes and failures" (Glaeser 2011, 247). Technology has in many ways enhanced the advantages of cities, increasing the influence of global cities beyond national borders (Glaeser 2011, 248; Sassen 2001).

The advantages of urban density, however, are not limited to business and trade. Some preliminary research on "community anchor institutions" indicates that urban organizations are more likely to adopt high-bandwidth broadband, and that they enjoy the same agglomeration economies that affect firms—the knowledge spillovers and skills in urban labor markets (Forman, Goldfarb and Greenstein 2011). Density supports cultural institutions such as museums, research libraries, and medical centers. Sixty-seven percent of the nation's research universities are located in the largest 100 metropolitan areas (Brookings Institution 2007, 32).

Broadband is a cross-cutting technology, necessary for greater use of geographic information systems, telemedicine, virtual reality, supercomputing (including cloud computing), video conferencing, distance education, and wireless networks that bring urban spaces and streets to life (West 2011). It is in densely populated cities and regions where technology can have the greatest impact in areas such as transportation, environment, energy, health, education, public safety, and homeland security. Technology firms IBM, Cisco, and Siemens have supported experiments with "smart city" initiatives to use "networks, sensors, and analytics to make cities more efficient, productive, and habitable" (Swabey 2012), by managing energy grids, traffic, public safety, and other city services. Fast broadband and wireless connections enable the deployment of sensors in city vehicles and public transit shelters, for example. But human connections also promote the potential for the information flows in smart cities, as residents make service requests or report problems, "crowd-sourcing" information that can be used to respond to crime, traffic jams, severe weather, and other developments (Swabey 2012; Ratti and Townsend 2011). Cities are thinking about new ways to analyze these information flows, to improve services, or to develop indicators to evaluate the socioeconomic health of neighborhoods (Tolva 2012). Through open data portals, some of the nation's largest cities are in turn making more of the information they collect available online to citizens. The aim is to improve transparency and governance as well as services (Mossberger and Wu 2012). Cities are important test beds for social innovation as well as economic growth. Yet, the employment of many smart city solutions depends on speeds and coverage that are not always available. Moreover, the cost of broadband limits the participation of some businesses, organizations, and residents.

Cities are also economically and demographically diverse, including higher proportions of populations that are technologically disadvantaged. Targeting resources in poor urban neighborhoods can effectively reach many who are offline or less-connected. Urban areas represent the multiracial and multicultural mosaic of the nation, where non-Hispanic whites will soon be a minority of the population (Brookings Institution 2010; Baldassare 2000; Hero 1992, 1998, 2003; Hero and Tolbert 1996; Barreto et al. 2010). Combined, African Americans, Latinos, and Asian Americans represent over a third of the population nationally, but a majority in large cities (Frey 2011). Projections by the U.S. Census Bureau indicate that by 2050, white non-Hispanics will account for only 50% of America's population, with Latinos comprising 30%. Hero (1998) writes of the unstoppable demographic forces of race and ethnicity reshaping America. Diversity is a theme that will grow in importance in the coming decades (Tolbert 2010), and major cities are at the forefront of these trends.

The racial and ethnic diversity of cities can foster approaches to technology use that fit the needs of different populations. Analyses in later chapters show that patterns of technology use and barriers differ for African Americans and Latinos, and for Spanish-speaking and English-speaking Latinos. If effective and responsive policy solutions are developed for varied populations in cities, they will have broader resonance as well for an increasingly multiracial and multiethnic nation. We further explore these issues of density and diversity, of innovation and inequality, following the purposes set out in the National Broadband Plan.

ECONOMIC DEVELOPMENT AND ECONOMIC OPPORTUNITY

Information technology firms and those that use research and development extensively tend to be located in metropolitan areas (Hackler 2006), because of the knowledge spillovers and specialized skills discussed earlier. Knowledge-intensive industries that rely upon technology use are concentrated in major cities and cluster together in downtowns to take advantage of face-to-face interactions (Kasarda 1990). These industries include sectors such as finance, publishing, insurance, real estate, government, and administrative and business services. Information technology has complemented these advantages of proximity and face-to-face interaction rather than erasing them. Just as online social networking such as Facebook can augment face-to-face interactions among individuals, technology supplements rather than eliminates the need for traditional interpersonal communication.

Cities and metropolitan areas, however, host a variety of industries beyond these information-intensive sectors, and the benefits of technology are not restricted to high-tech jobs. Productivity growth throughout the economy since the 1990s has been linked to information technology use (Stiroh 2004), including its applications in the "old economy" sectors (Litan and Rivlin 2002). Technology applications will be the primary source of innovation and productivity growth in the coming decades (Byrnjolfsson and Saunders 2010). Research has revealed positive outcomes for communities with broadband (Gillett et al. 2006), across a range of economic sectors—including manufacturing, health care, finance, insurance, real estate, and education (Crandall, Lehr, and Litan 2007)—and in most industries (Kolko 2010).

The benefits for technology use are highest in cities and metropolitan areas (Crandall, Lehr, and Litan 2007; Kolko 2010). While the clustering of technology in places like Silicon Valley, California, and Seattle, Washington, is well-known (Saxenian 1996), cities more generally are able to create agglomeration economies for the use of technology. Forman, Goldfarb and Greenstein have demonstrated the significance of what they call "urban leadership" for technology use and innovation among businesses (2005, 2008, 2009). This means that firms in metropolitan areas with large populations are more likely to adopt advanced technologies because of "thicker" labor markets with more skilled workers and knowledge spillovers between firms. In cities, the cost of innovation is lower because firms are less dependent on internal resources, or the need to develop knowledge and talent from within (Forman et al. 2008). Urban businesses employ more complex uses of technology that generate greater productivity and economic growth in the national economy. In contrast, rural firms tend to use the Internet for basic purposes such as email and web browsing. Rural firms do not have the same skilled labor markets that allow them to enhance production processes with technology (Forman et al. 2005, 2009). Benefits, such as wage growth associated with Internet use, are also concentrated disproportionately in large, urbanized counties (Forman, Goldfarb, and Greenstein 2009).

However, urban areas also contain many workers who are less skilled or unemployed, and small businesses that struggle with few resources. One of the most effective strategies for economic development, according to Bartik (2003), is to connect workers with jobs that pay relatively better for the level of skill that workers possess. Internet use in general is associated with higher wages, controlling for other factors. This is true for Internet use at home as well as Internet use on the job (DiMaggio and Bonikowski 2008). Internet use at work is important for economic opportunity for less-educated employees as well as more highly educated workers. One analysis of national data indicated that the wage premium for Internet use on the job was nearly as much for those with only a high school education as for all workers—about $100 per week, controlling for other factors (Mossberger, Tolbert, and McNeal 2008).

Technology skills are also increasingly necessary for job searches. According to the American Library Association, "classified job ads have gone the way of the mimeograph—nearly obsolete. Nearly three-quarters of job seekers now use the Internet to seek employment, in part because this is the only way to apply for many job opportunities" (ALA Office for Research and Statistics 2010, 1). Inequalities in access to the Internet and online employment information further disadvantage poor urban residents in the job market.

Small businesses in inner-city neighborhoods lag behind in technology use, lacking connections to metropolitan markets and to suppliers with competitive prices. According to the 2010 FCC Survey of Small Businesses, only 24% of small businesses use e-commerce to sell online (FCC 2010a, 266). The key problem for such small businesses is understanding and utilizing applications rather than the availability of broadband connections. Small businesses comprise 99% of establishments and 80% of total employment in "inner cities and economically challenged areas" (FCC 2010a, 269).

HEALTH AND EDUCATION

High-speed networks support advances in medical research, including the exchange of information across the globe. Moreover, broadband networks can improve the quality of care in cities by linking medical centers to other local institutions with fewer resources, such as community clinics in low-income neighborhoods. Telehealth is not just a rural phenomenon. Home broadband access facilitates remote patient monitoring for chronic conditions such as high blood pressure, providing more regular attention to patient health. Trends toward home health care are increasing, and information technology use is vital for coordination and communication (National Academy of Sciences 2011; West 2011). Additionally, doctors and other health care professionals can better engage patients in decision making with access to test results and health education online if patients are connected and know how to use technology. Such steps can improve the quality of care and lower costs through prevention, providing health benefits to the community and savings for tax-supported health care programs such as Medicare and Medicaid (FCC 2010a). Access to these publicly funded health insurance programs also increasingly relies on information online, and those most in need of these services, including the elderly and the poor, are using government websites for these services (Schmeida and McNeal 2007).

High-speed connections are important for remaining on the cutting edge of research, and U.S. universities have a critical need for high bandwidth for supercomputing, visualization, and other research needs. Thirty universities recently launched Gig.U: The University Community Next Generation Project, which seeks to promote ultra-high-speed broadband on campuses and their surrounding communities to further both research and economic development. Many of these projects will affect urban areas.[5]

Broadband-enabled technology in classrooms has produced new ways of teaching, using digital media, mobile devices, online collaboration for group projects, and social media among others. Schools are turning to iPads and netbooks for interactive e-textbooks and are replacing traditional textbooks (Schwarz 2011). The Department of Education has supported such initiatives, and companies like Google and Apple are fostering the development of educational content for tablets (Nicolai 2012; also see http://www.google.com/edu/). Urban schools have many low-income and low-achieving students (Jacob and Ludwig 2011), and high school graduation rates for central cities are considerably lower than national averages, or even rural areas (Orfield 2004). Achievement gaps are growing nationally between low-income and high-income students

(Reardon 2011), and this clearly has an impact in urban school districts. Some education scholars argue that new media have special relevance for reaching urban minority students (Nolan 2011; Barseghian 2011). For example, school districts are using iPads to address needs for remedial reading (Misur 2012). Educational software programs can assist English-language learners (Stansbury 2012). More generally, technology in the K–12 classroom allows for individualized, differentiated learning, including remedial education, individual practice and research, and access to online courses for districts unable to provide specialized and advanced courses. A White House education initiative, called the Digital Promise Center, was recently formed through a number of foundations and the National Science Foundation to evaluate the impact of technology in education (Quillien 2011). Innovations enabled by broadband that improve urban educational outcomes may generate substantial benefits for society.

Broadband connections are needed at home as well as in school. The web has become an indispensible source of information for research, and moves toward the adoption of online textbooks and other digital applications raise problems for continued learning at home. While libraries and other public access sites are now available in many urban neighborhoods, students without regular access at home have limited time to do homework because of waiting times and limited hours of availability, and this problem is greatest in urban areas, according to a recent nationwide library study (Hoffman et al. 2011).

Improvements in library resources could increase the assistance available in urban communities but would not replace the need for home broadband access. Students do homework primarily in the evenings, when many libraries and other public access sites are closed. School districts post information for students and parents using platforms such as "Power Schools." Parents without home Internet connections have less access to school schedules, their child's grades, class syllabi, and other resources that facilitate parental involvement in education. Recognizing this need, the Broadband Technology Opportunities Programs (BTOP) in New York and Boston, discussed later in this chapter, have provided technology training for students and parents, along with computers and discounted home broadband. The rationale is to support student success and new opportunities for families.

ENERGY, ENVIRONMENT, AND SAFETY IN DENSELY POPULATED AREAS

Because so much of the national population resides in urban areas, they are essential for achieving national purposes such as energy efficiency, environmental conservation, and homeland security. Density has its drawbacks as well, creating problems such as traffic congestion, high energy-use during peak periods, greater vulnerability to crime and terror, and a need for crowd control during public events. High-speed networks are necessary for managing smart grids and improving mass transit, as well as for safety and security.

One of the few infrastructure grants awarded to cities under BTOP was for a public safety network in Los Angeles, and public safety has been highlighted as a national goal for high-speed networks (FCC 2010a).[6] Technology innovation in public safety seeks to increase the performance and efficiency of the police, whether for neighborhood patrols, disaster management, or homeland security. There is also a need for interoperability and coordination of public safety and emergency preparedness nationally and across the many different governments within metropolitan areas, which can number in the hundreds (U.S. Department of Homeland Security 2007).[7] Cutting-edge communication systems are critically needed in major cities.

Citizen broadband connections are important as well. Cities such as Chicago offer searchable data on crime as part of their community policing programs. Online weather provides up to the minute information on hurricanes, tornados, flash floods, blizzards, fires, earthquakes, and other natural disasters. Sophisticated maps allow citizens and public safety officials to track the path of natural disasters, improving life-saving evacuations, for example. Internet connections have aided recovery from disasters in major cities, including Hurricane Katrina in New Orleans (Bertot et al. 2006) and more recently, through social media after the Japanese tsunami (Blackburn 2011).

Overloading the electrical grid can be a problem in densely populated cities, and the payoff for more efficient management of energy resources is also greatest in population centers. Broadband enables "smart grids" that manage these networks and also permit consumers to control their own energy use through home Internet connections. The City of Boston has an innovative program using broadband to coordinate electric delivery during peak loads (FCC 2010a, 254). With real-time information, consumers are able to make energy-efficient choices or to take advantage of lower cost electricity during off-peak hours. As smart grids become more common, they offer new ways to conserve energy and to lower electricity costs, and their implementation in large cities can increase their early impact.

There are other uses for the smart city concept of utilizing networks, sensors, and data to solve policy problems. Working with the Massachusetts Institute of Technology, the City of Seattle tracked more than 2,000 items of trash with electronic tags and cellular networks. The city was able to monitor where the trash ended up, including illegal disposal sites and some far-flung destinations across the country. This information can facilitate the design of more efficient waste management policies, including recycling programs (Ratti and Townsend 2011).

Intelligent transportation systems have the potential to manage traffic flows, improving driver safety and reducing the need to build additional highways (Ezell 2010). Already, San Francisco and other cities have used real-time data to facilitate the search for parking spaces (Ezell 2010). Use of Google maps to avoid traffic congestion has become common among mobile wireless drivers, and Google has recently unveiled biking, mass transit, and walking maps.

Mass transit systems conserve energy and provide other social benefits, for example, relief of traffic congestion and pollution. Internet connectivity makes possible mass transit improvements such as the delivery of real-time transportation information to customers. In Chicago, "bustracker" and "traintracker" systems allow riders to find arrival times on computers or cell phones (based on the current location of the vehicle). Enhancements in the quality of public transportation can encourage greater use among those who have alternative transportation and better mobility for those who do not. High-speed networks can improve information flows with sensors and data analysis for the estimation of demand, management of fleets, and scheduling, increasing cost-savings as well as quality, and coordinating across systems within metropolitan areas.

GOVERNMENT SERVICES, CIVIC ENGAGEMENT, AND COMMUNITY ORGANIZING

E-government presents a number of possible benefits for government and society; these benefits are maximized with a larger number of citizens who are online. Online delivery of services and information has been pursued by governments as a way to save on costs (West 2000; Tolbert and Mossberger 2006). Government websites also serve as venues for communicating with citizens through email, social media, online surveys, and complaint forms. E-government improves access to government services and information for citizens and businesses in many ways: eliminating the need to travel to offices or play phone tag; increasing convenient access through portals, links, and search engines; and extending availability around the clock. Online information has the potential to produce greater government transparency and accountability. Large cities in the United States tend to outperform other local governments in the sophistication and features on their government websites (Ho 2002; Moon 2002; Mossberger, Wu, and Jimenez 2010). City size is associated with better information and more participatory opportunities online. (Mossberger, Wu, and Jimenez 2010). Major cities have been early adopters in the "open data" movement, offering an eclectic mix of government data online, from vacant properties and crime statistics to city budgets. New York, San Francisco, Portland, and Chicago are among the cities providing such online open data. Many of these cities have also held contests to develop applications for using the data on these portals (Mossberger and Wu 2012). Major cities have used their websites to promote transparency in other ways. Minneapolis displays citywide goals formulated during neighborhood planning processes and to report on performance measures tracking those goals. Seattle has long hosted discussions of policy issues using online forums and, more recently, social media (Mossberger and Jimenez 2009; Mossberger and Wu 2012).

Technology inequality in cities limits the ability of local governments to realize potential cost savings, service improvements, and online communication with citizens. Low-income individuals are more reliant on government services, and technology disparities exclude them from equal access to government services and civic information. Such disparities have an impact on the public sphere and citizenship more generally. For example, e-government use at the local level is uniquely related to higher trust and confidence in government (Tolbert and Mossberger 2006). Overall, citizens who have access to political information online are more likely to participate in politics, whether online or offline. Previous research has shown that Internet use for news is positively related to civic engagement, volunteering, and many forms of political participation (Mossberger, Tolbert, and McNeal 2008; Tolbert and McNeal 2003; Shah et al. 2005; Bimber 2003; see Boulianne 2009 for a review). Social media users are also more likely to be civically engaged, controlling for other factors (Hampton et al. 2011). One study of the 2008 election campaign using panel surveys where respondents were repeatedly interviewed over nine months found that individuals who became active politically online were more likely to engage in politics in traditional ways not involving the Internet. The effects were the most pronounced for older citizens, who had not been politically active online before (Hamilton and Tolbert 2011). To the extent that low-income urban residents are excluded from political information and participation online, both cities and society suffer from a democratic deficit. The benefits of technology to low-income urban residents, like the elderly just cited, may be disproportionate.

Urban neighborhoods are important venues for community organizing and political participation (Berry, Portney, and Thomson 1993). Community revitalization, school reform, immigrant rights, and community policing are just a few examples of neighborhood civic participation in recent years (Grogan and Proscio 2000; Stone et al. 2001; Pallares and Flores-Gonzalez 2011; Fung and Wright 2003; Briggs 2008). Technology offers new methods and new skill sets for participation (Krueger 2006), using social media, videos, neighborhood listservs, and community portals for local engagement. Case studies suggest that technology use can foster civic engagement in low-income communities (Hampton 2010), and this is an explicit goal of neighborhood-focused outreach and training programs in some cities. Seattle's community technology program is intended to strengthen technology use for participation. Chicago's Smart Communities program, discussed in chapter 9, includes "Civic 2.0" training in technology resources for block clubs, school groups, and other neighborhood organizations.

Cities and National Policy

In this section, we discuss cities and the broadband stimulus program, and offer a view of broadband policy from the local level. Following a brief history of municipal wireless efforts, we describe current programs in several major cities, drawing on interviews, city websites, grant summaries, and reports. These programs illustrate some of the activities cities engage in, although they are by no means exhaustive.

The interviews were conducted in June and July of 2011, by phone and in person, with a purposive sample of seven cities that have been active in broadband policy. The seven cities are Chicago, Minneapolis, San Francisco, Seattle, Los Angeles, Boston, and New York.[8] These include cities where governments have received stimulus grants, as well as cities that have independent local initiatives such as citywide wireless or community technology programs.

The interviews allowed us to ask about goals for technology, how officials view the role of local governments, and the challenges they face. Interview participants included chief information officers, policy analysts, deputy commissioners, and managers for the BTOP or other programs in information technology departments. Some cities included more than one respondent, with both the BTOP manager and chief information officer involved, for example, to cover different aspects of city policy.[9] Respondents were knowledgeable about broadband policy across issues, as we asked questions about both digital-inclusion initiatives and broadband deployment. Before turning to the interviews, however, we review the broadband stimulus program and its role in broadband policy.

BTOP: BROADBAND FUNDING IN THE STIMULUS PROGRAM

Despite the strategic significance of urban areas for achieving many national goals, federal investment so far has prioritized rural broadband infrastructure development over other needs. Of the $7.2 billion allocated for broadband stimulus funding, we estimate from the data on BTOP awards that less than $500 million (or less than 7%) was spent in metropolitan areas.[10] Disentangling the investments in urbanized or metropolitan areas is difficult, because there are many statewide grants and multilocational grants.[11] Assuming that one-third of these benefit urban areas, then less than 7% of the spending has affected metropolitan regions. Even a more generous assumption, that half of these broader grants benefit urbanized areas, would mean that metropolitan grantees received only 8% of the funding from the federal government. The reason for the disproportionate spending is that there were only a few infrastructure grants awarded within urban regions, while the majority of the program's funding supported rural infrastructure initiatives. Metropolitan grants were predominantly for Public Computer Centers (PCC) or Sustainable Broadband Adoption (SBA) programs that offer technology awareness and training. This helped to expand inclusion efforts by local governments and nonprofits. But, urban infrastructure grants could have generated other important public benefits by supporting experiments in affordable broadband in some low-income neighborhoods and higher speeds and creative applications for community anchor institutions, businesses, and residents. Previous policies have encouraged public access and training alone. The BTOP grants missed the opportunity to address other issues that have been neglected in the past, such as the cost of home access and the speeds and agility of urban networks.

Legislation set aside part of the American Recovery and Reinvestment Act (ARRA) funds for rural infrastructure but also allowed different types of communities to apply for some of the funding.[12] The National Telecommunications and Information Administration (NTIA) distributed $4.7 billion on a competitive basis through the Broadband Technology Opportunities Program (BTOP).[13] BTOP allowed both unserved areas (lacking broadband networks) and underserved areas with low adoption rates to compete for infrastructure funding as well as for public access and training programs. Underserved areas, defined by federal requirements as having less than 40% broadband subscribership, appeared to qualify many urban neighborhoods for the infrastructure grants.[14] But, the hurdles for eligibility were onerous. Program rules required underserved areas to present evidence that subscribership was below 40% for infrastructure proposals. The catch is that subscribership data is proprietary and not released by Internet providers. The six-week window for preparing applications for the first round made data collection through surveys impossible.[15] Moreover, the same incumbent providers who were not required to release data on subscribership were allowed to use that information to challenge urban infrastructure applications during the award process without publicly releasing that data, according to interviews.

One possible explanation for these restrictions is that private companies feared competition from citywide broadband networks and successfully lobbied for rules to prevent their development. Telecommunications firms have used political lobbying in the past to ward off competition from municipal networks or public-private partnerships (Tapia, Stone, and Maitland 2005; Munger 2000). The impossible data requirements clearly tipped the scales against proposals by the cities.

As a result, not a single major city received an infrastructure grant during the first round of funding. Our interviews indicate that some cities did not even apply for infrastructure grants because of the requirements. San Francisco dropped its plans to submit an infrastructure proposal that included major medical centers and health clinics, despite initial work invested in the project. Based on survey data collected a few months before, Chicago submitted an infrastructure proposal to serve community anchor institutions and residents in two low-income neighborhoods. The application was denied, despite having extensive evidence for the project area that less than 40% of the population had broadband at home.

According to interviews, cities such as San Francisco, Chicago, and Seattle had planned to coordinate infrastructure investments with proposals to upgrade public computer centers and to provide outreach and training. This would allow a holistic approach to facilitating broadband adoption, providing affordable service along with the support to build skills and to promote a variety of uses among residents and businesses in low-income neighborhoods.

There was some prioritization of broadband infrastructure for community anchor institutions in the second round, especially a provision for public safety use.[16] As a result, Washington, D.C. received an infrastructure grant to serve community anchor institutions in low-income wards. Public safety infrastructure grants were awarded to a special district in the greater Los Angeles region and to Motorola for a project in the San Francisco Bay area.[17]

Because cities and other urban organizations did receive some funding for important technology programs, the stimulus grants provided a welcome source of support and some exciting opportunities, according to our interviews with city officials. Yet, neither technology inclusion nor the potential for technology innovation in urban areas were sufficiently addressed by federal policy.

CITIES AS POLICY CATALYSTS

Local governments can contribute ideas, grassroots involvement, and policy experimentation in this arena, although they do not have the resources to address broadband policy alone. Digital-inclusion efforts have a long history at the local level, especially through schools, libraries, and job-training programs. Before the emergence of the Internet, Santa Monica, California, hosted the Public Electronic Network (PEN) to share information and discuss community issues (Van Tassel 1994). Economic development has also been an important motivation for local government initiatives to attract technology investments (Hackler 2003). Several years ago, the municipal broadband movement caught the imaginations of a number of city leaders. While not all the efforts evolved as planned, they raised the visibility of technology issues at a time when they were dormant on the federal agenda, and they laid the groundwork for many of the current city programs.

In 2004, Mayor John Street declared that Philadelphia would become the nation's first "wireless city" with coverage across all 135 square miles within city boundaries (Aaron 2008). Until Philadelphia's announcement, municipal broadband networks had been constructed primarily in rural towns where private providers had not invested (*Economist* 2007). Soon a number of other major cities followed suit, with San Francisco, Chicago, and Minneapolis among those who announced intentions to provide wireless access everywhere.

The Philadelphia plan was to achieve universal access by offering low-cost broadband along with training and hardware distributed through nonprofit organizations (Jain, Mandviwalla, and Banker 2007). Originally, the city envisioned a municipally owned or nonprofit network. After objections about unfair competition from an existing provider, Comcast, the city instead awarded an exclusive franchise to Earthlink in return for establishing a wireless network using city utility and light poles. The public-private partnership soon faltered, however, as the quality of coverage was poor and subscribership levels were too low to ensure profitability. In 2008, Earthlink sold the network to a group of local investors who provided service citywide for free. Usage soared, but the financial model was not sustainable. In 2010, the City of Philadelphia purchased the network with the provision that it would be used primarily for government business (see Forlano et al. 2011 and the *Economist* 2007). The failure of Philadelphia's network cast a long shadow on other cities and the national municipal broadband movement.

As events unfolded in Philadelphia, plans for municipal wireless networks derailed in most other large cities. For example, San Francisco's deal for free citywide wireless with Earthlink and Google fell apart, and Chicago failed to receive acceptable bids on their request for proposals. Earthlink withdrew from other agreements to provide wireless networks. Some small- and medium-sized cities continue to offer municipal broadband through wired and wireless networks, but often these are municipally owned, much like public water utilities (Forlano et al. 2011; Aaron 2008). The municipally owned networks tend to flourish in areas where there is little competition from private incumbent providers or where service is restricted to government use. In 2010, estimates identified 110 cities with citywide municipal wireless networks that were open to public use (either free or for a fee), 56 municipalities with citywide or nearly citywide networks that were reserved for government use only, and 84 cities with hot spots in downtowns or public areas (Vos 2010).

After Philadelphia's program initially inspired other cities to examine the possibilities for wireless networks, Internet companies lobbied hard in Washington and in state capitals to prevent cities from providing broadband (Tapia, Stone, and Maitland 2005). This opposition is still visible in state legislatures in recent years, for example in Georgia (McCann 2012). The impact of this opposition is evident in the restrictive eligibility requirements for BTOP as well, including the right of incumbent providers to challenge city data on broadband adoption without disclosing their own subscription data.

What was the impact of the municipal wireless initiatives, given that most cities did not build such networks? One chief information officer described the municipal wireless movement as responsible for elevating technology issues on city agendas around the country. To date, however, cities have had limited success in addressing the issues that motivated the municipal broadband movement, such as access to innovative speeds and affordable prices.

CONTEMPORARY PROJECTS: FROM INCLUSION TO INFRASTRUCTURE

Most major cities address broadband in a variety of programs, especially libraries and schools. Several of the cities interviewed have conducted studies to document needs for technology use and developed plans to target resources for e-government, economic development, and inclusion. New York recently issued a "road map" for technology; Chicago has a Digital Excellence Agenda; and planning efforts were mentioned by San Francisco, Los Angeles, and Boston. Minneapolis and Seattle offer interesting examples of local projects that preceded the federal BTOP grants.

In contrast to other large cities, Minneapolis built a citywide wireless network through a public-private partnership that offers a number of benefits for the community. The network was completed in 2009 by U.S. Internet Wireless (USIW), which is a local Internet provider. The agreement requires the company to build, finance, and operate the network, in exchange for nonexclusive rights to use city-owned poles and buildings and a commitment that the city will purchase all of its wireless and wired Internet services from USIW. The city serves as the anchor tenant, purchasing broadband for city departments, schools, and libraries (Forlano et al. 2011). The most affordable level of residential broadband service costs $14.95 per month, and vouchers are available for free service during a one-month trial period. This sum is more than $30 less than national averages for broadband (Horrigan 2009). Wireless hot spots in some public spaces throughout the city provide free access.

Minneapolis has also leveraged the partnership to fund training and public access. The partnership arrangements support a Digital Inclusion Fund, which requires USIW to make an initial contribution of $500,000 and to invest 5% of its profits each year. The city estimates that this will produce $11 million for the fund over the 10-year lease. So far, the fund has assisted nonprofit technology projects for homeless youth, seniors, organizations in low-income Latino neighborhoods, and a YMCA afterschool success center, among others.

Other aspects of the Minneapolis wireless program address resources for inclusion and for civic participation. There is an online Technology Literacy Collaborative that centralizes training materials and other resources for community technology centers. Free Internet access is available to community technology centers, and the city provides neighborhood portals at no cost. A "Civic Garden" portal aggregates government and community content by area of the city.

Minneapolis is one of the few large cities that has successfully sustained a public-private partnership for broadband. One reason may be the participation of a locally based provider, according to interviews, and such partners may not be available in other cities. With comparatively low rates for basic broadband and funding for inclusion programs, Minneapolis illustrates the difference that city policy can make. Yet, officials acknowledge that there are still many residents who cannot afford broadband access at home and that more remains to be accomplished.

Seattle has supported the efforts of community technology centers since 1996, with a Community Technology division in its Department of Information Technology. Its website lists over 200 places for public access, posts training materials and other resources, and features reports, articles, blogs, and other materials on information technology for health, small businesses, and neighborhoods. The department advises other city agencies on inclusion and IT as part of the city's Racial and Social Justice Initiative. As in Minneapolis, there is an emphasis on supporting neighborhood efforts—evident in the "Communities Online" pages filled with neighborhood information, links to neighborhood data in the city's open data website, and advice for neighborhoods developing online tools. "Neighborhoods on the Net" aggregates websites, blogs, wikis, and social media related to specific communities. The Bill Wright Technology Matching Fund is supported by cable franchise fees and awards grants of up to $20,000 to community technology organizations to "increase residents' use of technology for community problem solving, civic engagement, and community building" (www.seattle.gov/tech/tmf).

Seattle has also been concerned with the quality and affordability of broadband across the city and has tried to encourage more competition and high-speed service. Currently, the city is leasing conduit to Comcast in the Pioneer Square neighborhood to increase bandwidth for development in that area. The mayor has directed Seattle Public Utilities to create a business plan for a fiber-to-the-premises network for the entire city.

While both Minneapolis and Seattle have established funds for digital inclusion, other cities have institutionalized these programs as well to support public access and training. Federal law allows cities to collect up to 5% of cable revenues for rights of way. New York has set aside these revenues for public access and inclusion, and has leveraged in-kind benefits from private providers as well, such as the wiring of parks and other public places. Having a dedicated pool of funds allows cities to sustain training programs, technical support, and public access. Using a somewhat different approach, Chicago has established a partnership with the MacArthur Foundation and the Chicago Community Trust called the Smart Chicago Collaborative. The fund intends to make grants for innovative uses of technology in low-income neighborhoods. Local programs have primarily supported public access or programs for digital literacy, rather than infrastructure serving homes or businesses.

FEDERAL BTOP GRANTS

As mentioned, the urban BTOP grants were awarded for public access and technology training. In some of these initiatives, cities have attempted to reduce the cost of home access for BTOP participants by negotiating agreements with Internet providers. The special rates are important benefits that cities have obtained through their inclusion programs, yet they are usually for a limited time. In summer 2011, midway through the BTOP initiative, Comcast announced a program called Internet Essentials, which offered basic broadband at $9.95 per month to households with children enrolled in the school free-lunch program. This kind of initiative has the potential to affect many families nationwide and is an important program that will be discussed further in the concluding chapter. Yet, there is no comprehensive policy that offers assistance to all low-income individuals, including disadvantaged groups such as the elderly and people with disabilities. What do some of the major urban BTOPs look like, and how are they addressing barriers to inclusion?

The BTOP Public Computer Center (PCC) grants have enabled cities to expand existing public access programs and to reach many different constituencies. In Los Angeles, the $7.5 million grant supports public access at 188 locations, including libraries, parks, recreation centers, and workforce development sites. The funds are used to upgrade 72 of these facilities, and to purchase 2,741 desktop computers and 132 laptops. The project grant description emphasizes non-English speaking and low-income communities, and city officials describe their priority as reaching youth and preparing future generations. Connected Communities, the New York City PCC grant of $14 million adds over 1,000 workstations to public access sites, upgrades community centers, dispatches mobile vans, and increases training options. Broadband speeds and hours are being increased at public libraries, and new connections serve parks and housing authority residents. Low-income neighborhoods, seniors, and limited-English speakers are targeted. The Chicago PCC grant of $9 million improves facilities and provides equipment for public housing, libraries, senior centers, city colleges, parks, after-school programs, and workforce centers. Additionally, free digital literacy training is provided in the 150 locations participating in the program. The Boston PCC grant of nearly $2 million provides for 600 computers and free workshops and classes at 50 facilities owned by Boston Family and Youth Services, the Boston Housing Authority, and the Boston Public Library. The range of organizations affected by the grant in all these cities suggests the kind of impact that city programs can have, despite limited funding, across many different institutions and neighborhoods.

The Sustainable Broadband Adoption (SBA) programs employ strategies for digital inclusion and often feature partnerships with nonprofits or businesses. Funding supports outreach and training. San Francisco's $8 million SBA program has a three-part focus: seniors and adults with disabilities, community media, and youth. The city has created small sites for public access and training within senior centers and adult residential treatment facilities. Community media projects in San Francisco focus on training for content creation and a digital-media delivery system for the neighborhoods. Programs for youth target participants who are low-income or who speak English as a second language. In addition to projects in schools funded by the grant, a program run by the nonprofit Street Side Stories operates mobile labs to conduct training and teach youth to tell their stories digitally. The SBA grant helped to leverage other funding for a program called Neighborhood Network News, which trains young people in digital media and journalism at a Boys and Girls Club.

Both the $6 million New York and $4.3 million Boston SBA grants address the needs of school-age children and their families, and these cities have sought partnerships to provide low-cost access for a limited time. The New York Connected Learning program provides training, computers, and reduced-cost home broadband for two years, for 18,000 sixth graders and their families. Teacher training and tech support are also included in the program. Students receive training at school, but they attend Saturday workshops with parents before taking home their desktop computers loaded with educational software. The program has been popular with families, with 86% attendance at the Saturday workshops. A related program called Connected Foundations targets schools with 16 to 21 year-old students at risk of dropping out and provides digital-literacy training and a laptop. In Boston, a partnership between several public agencies and the nonprofit Timothy Smith Network has supported a program called Tech Goes Home for 11 years. The SBA grant enabled Boston to increase the number of participants by 5,800. Eligible students and their guardians receive training and a subsidized netbook, costing $50. The SBA grant also provides for technology-training programs run by Connected Living in three senior Boston Housing Authority communities. A third program, Online Learning Readiness, focuses on workforce skills and serves 800 unemployed adults, who also receive netbooks. Before the announcement of the Internet Essentials program, the city was able to negotiate special pricing for all SBA program participants through Comcast, offering $10.95 a month for the first year and $15.95 a month for the second year of the subscription.

The City of Chicago's Smart Communities program is supported through a $7 million SBA grant and is targeted to five low-income neighborhoods, operated by community organizations with the support of many partners. The project is described in more detail in chapter 9 of this book. It includes a variety of activities intended to create a "culture" of technology use in these communities, through FamilyNet Centers, Business Resource Networks, YouMedia programs in libraries, Digital Youth Network afterschool programs and summer jobs, Civic 2.0 training for community groups, and neighborhood portals.

As shown by these descriptions, the various BTOPs have employed a range of approaches for different populations. A commonality, however, is that the lack of infrastructure grants has limited options for combining training and public access with affordable home broadband. The SBA grants require recipient cities to track home broadband subscriptions, but the underlying assumption is that outreach and training will increase home adoption without addressing affordability. As indicated by the arrangements in some of the SBA programs described, cities have attempted to address the barrier of cost, often by negotiating for special deals with providers. The available alternatives, however, often apply to only one segment of the population in need, or provide temporary discounts. As one official remarked in an interview, cities have more resources to address issues such as training and public access but affecting the cost barrier is more difficult.

INFRASTRUCTURE NEEDS: UBIQUITOUS, FAST, AFFORDABLE

City technology programs have multiple goals, for the development of the economy and public services, as well as for digital inclusion. There is widespread sentiment for obtaining what one respondent called "ubiquitous, ultra-high speed at affordable prices" for public institutions, businesses and residents. But, most respondents perceived that cities had a limited ability to achieve these goals on their own. Many have adopted incremental strategies for improving various aspects of broadband infrastructure. For example, Los Angeles encourages hot spots and infrastructure improvements through the private sector and some public facilities, incrementally "lighting up the city" with higher speeds. The City of Chicago is experimenting with wireless in a few small neighborhood business districts. San Francisco offers free broadband in its public housing units, single-room occupancy housing, and some nonprofit low-income housing. All the cities have wireless access in some public places, but all want to do more to address ubiquitous access, speeds, and costs. Hospitals and telehealth programs are priorities in San Francisco and Seattle and were part of the BTOP infrastructure proposals not submitted or funded. In cases where cities recognized a need for better infrastructure, they felt constrained from making such investments by tight budgets and the current recession.

Local governments view themselves as solving problems of market failure, but they must do so mostly through the market, with government leadership to facilitate public benefits. Respondents described themselves as looking for ways to "incent" the private sector, bringing companies to the table to work with community groups, and making a case for various partnerships. One city official said, "We have to play a role because we don't believe the current commercial offering allows residents to take advantage of information and services." Other cities were more positive about cooperation with the private sector, but still saw city governments as important participants in broadband policy.

City officials also recognized how their position was different from the private sector and critical for realizing the public goods characteristics of broadband. One official told us, "The private sector is not looking to ubiquitous solutions. Every company aligns services or products to segments of the world. The city is not looking at broadband as a product to sell, but trying to level the playing field to allow access to the digital society. The goal is to reach every business and residence."

Conclusion: Pursuing Benefits and Capabilities

Cities are important for achieving national purposes for broadband, and current federal government policy fails to recognize the opportunities in urban broadband. Investments in cities, whether for infrastructure or inclusion, have the potential to affect many. The density and diversity of cities create powerful resources for economic growth and spillover benefits that span policy areas identified in the National Broadband Plan. There are many reasons to believe, based on prior research and economic theory, that the economic and social benefits for closing the gaps and supporting innovation in urban areas will greatly exceed the costs involved.

The federally funded public access and training efforts aimed at urban areas, while important, are incomplete because they do not address the core problem of affordability. Federal policy has shied away from clashing with incumbent providers and the private sector, even when this might introduce more competition and provide lower cost alternatives. More generally, there is a lack of competition in many markets, and this may be particularly true in low-income communities in urban areas (Dunbar 2011). Rural areas will also face the same barriers of cost if rural infrastructure programs merely follow existing patterns of provision. While policies such as subsidies for low-income individuals are another option, these have been available only for telephone services and not for broadband.

Cities have been at the forefront as advocates for both high-speed deployment and digital inclusion, despite having few resources to affect many of the barriers to ubiquitous technology use. Why do cities view deployment and technology use as public policy issues? The expected benefits of technology cited by officials were often related to human capital and economic development—jobs, education, skills, business development, investment in strategic areas such as biotechnology, and the creation of a globally competitive city. In other cases, respondents discussed technology's role in facilitating relationships between government and citizens—civic participation, responsive services, and support for different needs across neighborhoods. This goes to the heart of cities as democratic institutions.

For city governments, information technology policy is related to equality of opportunity for individuals as well. Respondents often used terms such as social justice, equity, or the city's responsibility to all residents to describe the motivation for addressing digital inclusion. As one official explained, "We are interested in serving all of our communities, not just some—that everybody has access, that everybody participates." Young people, or "future generations" were another theme. Others simply described it as an issue for "quality of life" in their communities.

Scholars have written about the "just city" as one that enhances the capabilities needed by all residents to participate fully in society (Campbell and Fainstein 2012; see also Sen 1993). Comparing technology use to education, one respondent commented on the role of cities in broadband policy:

> Society has moved away from agreeing that we would ensure that all have a staple of basic capabilities. I think we need to go back to that. Unless government forces the issues, we will always have a divide... Those with access have a tremendous advantage over those who do not. Feeling comfortable with technology is a necessary requirement... Participating fully in digital society is also a necessary requirement.

3

Place and Inequality:
Urban, Suburban, and Rural America

From its inception, the concept of the "digital divide" encompassed a number of different factors associated with lower rates of Internet access and use: age, education, income, race, ethnicity, and urban and rural disadvantage (NTIA 1995). The first report on the digital divide released by the National Telecommunications and Information Administration (NTIA) was in fact entitled *Falling Through the Net: A Survey of the "Have-Nots" in Rural and Urban America* (NTIA 1995). Identifying urban and rural residents as less likely to use computers or the Internet than their suburban counterparts, this report defined geography as an important aspect of disparities. Many years later, are urban and rural communities still disadvantaged? Are policy problems similar in both geographic areas?

While the 1995 report defined digital haves and have nots as a dichotomy, the ensuing diffusion of Internet connectivity in schools, libraries, and other public places such as cafes and hot spots calls for a more nuanced view of different levels of access and how that affects the ability of individuals to use technology. The advent of mobile technologies, including Internet-enabled smartphones, affords access in new and different ways. Prior research suggests that broadband access at home may still offer distinctive opportunities, and we examine this issue further in the next chapter on mobile use and the "less-connected." Our purpose in this chapter is to define levels of use across places, including those who are offline completely, those who are less-connected, and those who have full access to the rich information and interactivity of the Internet. While previous research has identified variation in technology access, we go beyond prior studies by mapping the individual-level factors predicting technology access and use for urban, suburban, and rural residents separately. We make the geography of opportunity a central part of the analysis.

In this chapter, we analyze survey data from the Current Population Survey (CPS) and the FCC to understand differences in types of Internet adoption and access using subsamples for urban, suburban, and rural residents. We further explore the effects of individual-level factors such as poverty, race, and ethnicity within these varied contexts. In other words, we investigate the differences in outcomes for African Americans in urban and suburban communities, for example, or for the urban and rural poor. What this analysis reveals is that there is indeed still variation by place, with both urban and rural disadvantage. The lack of infrastructure clearly accounts for some of the rural disparities that persist. But of much more consequence are the social inequalities that drive technology disparities across geographic areas. While these play out somewhat differently across places (and it is important to understand these differences for policy), the story told by the numbers throughout is an echo of other inequities in society, and this speaks louder than rural infrastructure needs. Chapter 7 on barriers to broadband adoption will examine this further, supplementing the patterns of access that we document here with survey responses on the reasons people give for not having broadband at home.

We begin by defining the policy problem as a matter of the capacity to use technology, with a brief review of access as a policy issue, including both technology availability and determinants of adoption. Next, we describe the two data sets we use in the analysis of national trends in this book and track different levels of access with simple percentages (or descriptive data). We further examine these patterns using multivariate regression models that yield a more accurate account of the factors that account for apparent differences. The graphs and probabilities (that are based on these more rigorous models but read like percentages) make the findings accessible for those who do not have a background in such statistical methods.

Access and Digital Citizenship

A clear-cut division between those who are online and those who are not is, of course, a simplification of the challenges for both individuals and society. As noted by a city official quoted in the last chapter, the public policy issue is the extent to which individuals have acquired the capacity to use technology—what has elsewhere been called "digital citizenship" (Mossberger, Tolbert, and McNeal 2008, 1). The Internet revolution in communications technology parallels that of the printing press in nineteenth-century America, which saw the rise of the penny press, widespread literacy, and advances in public education. In both cases, it was the change in the capacity of individuals and institutions to use information that ultimately mattered, but this was enabled by new technologies. The term "digital citizenship" emphasizes the public interest characteristics of technology use; it is the "ability to participate in society online" (Mossberger, Tolbert, and McNeal 2008, 1). In much the same way that education and literacy have promoted democracy and economic growth, the Internet has the potential to benefit society as a whole and to facilitate political participation of individuals within society. Like education, the capacity to use the Internet provides skills and information needed for democratic engagement and economic opportunity (Krueger 2006; Mossberger, Tolbert, and McNeal 2008). It facilitates social inclusion through greater access to resources for individual well-being such as government services and health care information (DiMaggio et al. 2001).

Digital citizenship requires regular and effective access and use. This suggests multiple needs—for access to the Internet, access to hardware and software, the technical skills to use technology, and critical-thinking skills needed to evaluate and utilize information online. The latter has been called "information literacy" (see Mossberger, Tolbert, and Stansbury 2003 for a review), but basic literacy and educational competencies also greatly enrich the capacity to use the Internet. Both access and skills vary in quality, defying a simple dichotomy or divide (Mossberger, Tolbert, and Stansbury 2003; Hargittai 2002; Warschauer 2003; Van Dijk 2008).

Previous research suggests that the combination of broadband and home use supports the development of digital citizenship. High-speed connections and home access are both predictors of more frequent Internet use, especially daily use, which we have used as an indicator of digital citizenship in the past (Mossberger, Tolbert, and McNeal 2008). Those who have limited experience online are less likely to possess the skills they need to find information and to use the technology. They are less likely to use the Internet for a broad range of activities (Howard, Rainie, and Jones 2001), including information-seeking activities that can enhance individual opportunity—for jobs, health, education, and political participation among them (Hargittai 2002; Mossberger, Tolbert, and Stansbury 2003). Home access is strongly associated with these human-capital-enhancing activities, controlling for other factors (Hassani 2006). It affords more flexibility and convenience than public access or the workplace, allowing individuals to explore a greater range of uses and to gain experience (DiMaggio et al. 2004; Hargittai and Hinnant 2008). While use in multiple venues is even more strongly related to human capital activities online, home access is particularly important as a resource for digital citizenship.

The higher speeds and capabilities of broadband convey even more advantages for frequency of use, broader use, and skill. Higher speeds facilitate navigation, video streaming, downloading and uploading, content creation, and the full multimedia experience of the Internet. The Internet is simply built for broadband today. Dial-up users are more likely to go online less often and for fewer tasks (Horrigan 2004; NTIA 2004; Mossberger, Tolbert, and McNeal 2008).

A common argument by industry officials, policymakers, and the mass media is that mobile phones with Internet capabilities (also called "smartphones") will close gaps in access, and thus markets and new technology will naturally solve the problem of inequality in Internet access. Some of the fastest-growing segments of the smartphone market include minorities (Latinos and African Americans), the poor and the young, who increasingly do not have landlines and instead only use mobile phones (Lenhart 2010). In the next chapter, we examine the characteristics and activities of those who rely on mobile phones as their primary means of Internet access. Because handheld devices such as smartphones have limited functions in comparison with laptops (or even their less powerful cousins, netbooks), we include smartphone-only Internet users, public-access-only users, and dial-up users as among the less-connected.

Wireless networks do offer some advantages, including ubiquity and mobility of access. Yet, the CEO of Motorola Corporation predicts that wired broadband service offered by the cable industry to individual homes will continue to be the central mechanism for accessing the Internet. The Motorola CEO, Sanjay Jha, said, "the wireless spectrum in the U.S. remains 'very limited'" (Worden 2011, 1). Thus our focus on the importance of home broadband compared with mobile wireless remains important.

Public Access: Demand Exceeds Supply

In measuring different levels of access, we measure Internet use anywhere, including outside the home. Libraries, community centers, and other places offering public access provide a technology lifeline for many, with and without home Internet connections. Such public access sites offer training and support, and help finding information online. A large-scale national study on public libraries aptly describes them as a "key element of America's digital infrastructure" (Becker et al. 2010, iv). Technology users at libraries include people from all walks of life and all ages, but 44% of households below the poverty level report using computers or the Internet at a public library. Youth and minorities are among those who are most frequent public access users (Becker et al 2010; see also Gant et al. 2010).

Those who depend on public access as their primary means of going online do not have the regular, around-the-clock access to the Internet afforded by home Internet connections. Yet, it is abundantly clear from activities and help offered by libraries that the Internet is essential for access to basic services and fundamental opportunities in today's society. Most frequently, patrons use technology at the library for education (42%), employment (40%), health (37%), or government and legal services (34%) (Becker et al. 2010, 5). As a result, librarians have been challenged to play a variety of roles: helping with resumes, job applications, income taxes, and applications for unemployment, social security, and Medicare (Becker et al. 2010; Hoffman et al. 2011). The majority of libraries report that they cannot fill the demand for their services, leading to long waits and time limits. Funding has not kept pace with the need, and this has been especially true during the recession (Becker et al. 2010). In 2010–2011, 76% of public libraries reported that they do not have enough computers to meet demand, and 56% believed they did not have enough staff to assist with job seeking (ALA 2011). Additionally, many local governments are cutting back library services at the very time when more people are depending on them for an Internet connection and for help applying for jobs and services (Hoffman et al. 2011; Dailey et al. 2010). Strains on existing resources and budget cuts are most severe in urban public libraries, according to national surveys. Because "six percent of U.S. public libraries serve almost 60% of the population and make up nearly 60% of total library expenditures," these urban library cuts are exacting a heavy toll (Hoffman et al. 2011, 12). Public access is an important mainstay for the multiple venues of use that support digital citizens and digital communities, but those who depend on public access alone face many challenges.

If home adoption and high-speed access are necessary for full participation in society online, only 65% of Americans in 2010 had the required access to qualify as digital citizens. Thus, more than one-third of the U.S. population is still offline or has limited technology access (NTIA 2011).

Place, Infrastructure, and People

The market has provided uneven access to broadband in both cities and rural areas, but for different reasons. Access to high-speed Internet service involves two components: (1) availability of infrastructure and service, and (2) individual adoption of the technology. Availability of broadband varies by place, but the socioeconomic and demographic characteristics of communities also affect patterns of adoption once the technology is available.

According to the FCC, broadband service meeting the minimal performance speeds of 4 mbps for downloads and 1 mbps for uploads is available in 95% of the nation. Only 1% of the population in urban areas or urban clusters qualifies as unserved, using this definition of broadband (FCC 2010b).[1] The challenges for connecting these areas through high-speed networks are considerable. Scattered housing units in remote areas make wired and even wireless broadband expensive for the number of individuals or households served. The FCC estimates that with current technologies, it will cost $23.5 billion to provide Internet service meeting the Commission's standards across 100% of the nation (FCC 2010b), and this could translate into expenditures of up to $4,800 of infrastructure subsidy for each broadband subscriber (Rosston and Wallsten 2011).

There are indeed some infrastructure challenges within cities, according to our interviews with city officials, including poor quality of service, lack of choice, high costs, slow speeds, and limited capacity, as well as pockets that are unserved. For the most part, however, availability is less of a problem than adoption in many urban areas. For example, a recent report by New York City estimated that some type of broadband is available in 98% of its jurisdiction (City of New York 2011), and the Chicago survey discussed in chapters 6 and 8 indicated little problem with availability from some provider.

From the first NTIA reports to the most recent research, studies have demonstrated that a number of individual-level factors influence adoption—education, income, race, ethnicity, age, parental status, and occupation among them (Horrigan 2010; Hargittai and Hinnant 2008; Fairlie 2007; Gant et al. 2010; NTIA 2011; Norris 2001; Bimber 2003; Mossberger, Tolbert, and Stansbury 2003). While women continue to differ from men in Internet use, Internet adoption gaps based on gender have largely disappeared over time (Tolbert, Mossberger, King, and Miller 2007). Age disparities have narrowed. As baby boomers age into the over-65 group, a higher percentage of these individuals are technology adopters (Horrigan 2010). The presence of children in the household increases the probability of home access (Mossberger, Tolbert, and McNeal 2008, 184; Horrigan 2010). Occupations are also related to home adoption. Those who work in professional, managerial, sales, secretarial, or repair jobs are more likely to have Internet access at home (Mossberger, Tolbert, and McNeal 2008, 185–86).

Inequalities associated with poverty, education, race, and ethnicity are embedded in different social structures in urban, suburban, and rural areas. Education and income are strongly related to access, across racial and ethnic groups (NTIA 2011; Fairlie 2007). Race and ethnicity are significant predictors of Internet use, controlling for other factors (NTIA 2011; Fairlie 2007). Adoption rates are growing for African Americans and Latinos, but it is minorities earning $50,000 or more who have achieved parity with non-Hispanic whites (Gant et al. 2010). Latinos lag furthest behind in technology adoption and use, according to recent research (Livingston 2010; Fairlie 2007; Ono and Zavodny 2008). This is especially true for those who speak Spanish primarily (Fairlie 2007; Livingston 2010). Some debate exists about whether it is language or immigrant status that drives these disparities for (and among) Latinos (Ono and Zavodny 2008; Fairlie 2007). Spanish dominance may indicate recent immigration and a lack of exposure to the Internet, as well as the effect of language per se.

The subsamples we analyze here allow us to follow these trends (and variation in trends) across urban, suburban, and rural areas. While there are consistent patterns of urban and rural disparity, these are more pronounced for African Americans, Latinos, and the poor, especially when we use statistical controls to disentangle the effects of overlapping factors.

Survey Data for the U.S. Population

Our study of Internet use and accessibility relies mainly on two data sources. The first is the Current Population Survey (CPS) Internet Use Supplement, which was conducted by the Census Bureau in October of 2007 and 2009 (and updated in October of 2010).[2] Later chapters explore the city of Chicago and its community areas in detail, drawing on a large and representative sample of over 3,000 Chicago residents conducted in summer 2008. To make parallel inferences between the city and national-level data, we focus primarily on the 2009 CPS survey data and provide data from 2010 and 2007 to show trends over time. While broadband use has been slowly increasing over this period, the patterns of use and inequality remain constant, and that is what our analyses show.

The CPS Internet Use Supplement interviewed approximately 157,000 U.S. residents in 2009, asking a variety of questions about Internet use along with more general population characteristics, making it one of the best (and largest) samples to explore technology use in the American population. Only respondents 18 years of age and older were included in our analysis, bringing the total number of respondents down to 101,000. The CPS is the source of the official government statistics on employment and unemployment and has been conducted monthly for over fifty years. The CPS interviews about 57,000 households monthly, randomly selecting respondents on the basis of area of residence to represent the nation as a whole, individual states, and metropolitan and nonmetropolitan areas.[3] The very large sample size obtained by the CPS is particularly useful for this research since an emphasis is placed on the differences in Internet use and accessibility in U.S. cities. Having large samples from metropolitan areas gives us a high degree of confidence in the resulting statistical inferences made throughout this study and in ranking the 50 largest cities and suburbs in terms of the population online. The CPS is also unique in providing detailed and current information on occupation and industry, which are included as controls in the statistical analysis.[4]

Official government reports from the U.S. Census Bureau and NTIA (*Digital Nation*) show trends for metropolitan and nonmetropolitan areas only, with central cities and suburbs (or balance areas) collapsed into metropolitan areas. A unique aspect of this study is separate mapping of trends for (1) central cities, (2) suburbs, and (3) rural areas. We define "urban" as the central city within each metropolitan area rather than the "primary cities" often cited in Census reports. These primary cities include larger suburbs, and our purpose is to differentiate more precisely central city and suburban patterns of access. While our focus is Internet use in cities, throughout the book we draw parallels to suburban and rural residents. All the statistical analyses provided in this chapter report results for urban, suburban, and rural areas. We find quite different patterns in access, use, and inequality in these three geographic areas.

The second data source is a survey of 5,005 U.S. residents conducted by the FCC in October and November of 2009, making it comparable to the large-sample CPS survey.

While the FCC survey includes information about Internet use and access similar to the CPS data, the FCC survey asks more detailed questions about the role of the Internet in the lives of the American public. The FCC study includes information about how people connect to the Internet (including mobile devices); the types of economic and political activities individuals use the Internet for; barriers to Internet use; and views about technology in general, including measures of technology skill or familiarity with the technology. The FCC study is a random digit-dialed telephone survey. Because the FCC survey has a smaller sample size, we include binary variables measuring residence in central cities, suburbs, or rural areas, rather than separate subsamples of respondents living in cities, suburbs, or rural areas. Both resources are used to evaluate Internet access and use from geographic and national perspectives.

Two questions are used to measure Internet use, providing two levels of Internet access for both the CPS and FCC surveys. The first and most important question asks whether the respondent uses a high-speed Internet connection at home (*Uses High-Speed at Home*). Since broadband or high-speed Internet at home provides the most flexibility for a variety of political and economic tasks, this is the gold standard for access. The second question is whether the individual uses the Internet at any location, which can include work, school, a public library, cafe, etc. (*Uses Internet Anywhere*). Responses to these questions are dichotomized into binary variables that are analyzed in this and the following chapters.

Individual responses to questions about Internet use in the CPS and FCC surveys are used to estimate the likelihood of different levels of Internet access when controlling for a number of individual and geographic factors. In contrast, the U.S. Census reports data on broadband use for households, rather than for individuals. Individual-level analyses offer more fine-grained analysis with less error. We cluster respondents by household to control for errors that may be introduced by multiple responses per household.

Internet Use and Place

Since an important aspect of this study is the influence of geography on Internet use, each of the three dependent variables are modeled using the entire sample (nationally), and then separately by geographic subsamples, where only respondents from central cities are included, or from suburbs or from rural areas. The geographic area types were identified by using the U.S. Census Bureau metropolitan statistical areas (MSA): the central city within an MSA, areas within an MSA but not located in the central city (also called balance cities), and nonmetropolitan areas. These geographic areas are referred to as urban, suburban, and rural areas, respectively, and are defined similarly for the FCC sample.[5] Focusing on central cities is a unique aspect of our study. To draw comparisons, results from both samples are reported unweighted below, but weighted data for the cross-tab results are in the following tables.

Table 3.1 states that in 2009 61% of Americans had high-speed Internet access at home via DSL or a cable modem (this number increased to 65% in the 2010 CPS). Thus, a little over 6 in 10 Americans are "digital citizens" with 24-hour daily access to the Internet that is both fast and convenient (at home) (Mossberger, Tolbert, and

Table 3.1 **Percent of Americans with Internet Use by Residence in Central Cities, Suburbs, and Rural Areas (2009 CPS)**

	National (All)	Central Cities	Suburbs	Rural
Broadband Internet Access at Home (High speed)	61 (62,313)	59 (12,422)	65.5 (38,845)	52 (11,046)
Connect to Internet from Home (Slow speed)	66 (66,782)	63 (13,128)	70 (41,309)	58 (12,345)
Use Internet at Any Location	71 (71,966)	68.5 (14,348)	74 (43,945)	64 (13,673)

Note: N = 101,529 (unweighted); sample sizes in parentheses.

McNeal 2008). National rates of broadband access at home in 2009 are slightly lower in central cities (59%) and modestly higher (65.5%) in the suburbs. Consistent with previous research, the lowest rate of home broadband access is for those living in rural areas, with just 52% of Americans. This very large sample of Americans (over 100,000 respondents) gives us the highest level of confidence in the patterns we report here. The percent of Americans that indicate they can connect to the Internet from home via broadband or slow dial-up is higher, including 70% of individuals living in suburbs and 58% in rural areas. Nationally, 71% of Americans say they use the Internet in any location (including public access, school, work, or cell phone); the same is true for 68.5% of central city residents, almost three in four suburban residents, and 64% of rural residents. Clearly Internet access in any location is much higher than high-speed access at home, and 10% of Americans are "less-connected" Internet users who lack broadband at home.

Table 3.2 draws on the 5,000-person 2009 FCC telephone survey. Broadband access at home nationally is comparable but somewhat lower (54%) than in the CPS for the same year. The FCC oversampled for nonadopters, so the unweighted sample is slightly different. Again, suburban residents report the highest rates of broadband access at home (almost 60%) with the lowest rates of access in rural areas (40%). Residents of central cities fare much like the national average, with 56% reporting broadband access at home. Again, we see higher rates of Internet use when measuring use in any place, including outside the home. In general, the comparable patterns reported in Tables 3.1 and 3.2 provide a robustness check showing that the FCC sample, while smaller, provides similar patterns of technology use for the nation as a whole and our three geographic areas of focus.

INTERNET USE BY DEMOGRAPHIC FACTORS AND GEOGRAPHY

Tables 3.3–3.7 provide detailed descriptive statistics on our two key variables of interest—home broadband and Internet use at any location—nationally and by geographic subsamples (urban, suburban, and rural residents). Survey weights are used. The numbers show that Internet use varies by race/ethnicity, language spoken at home, income, education, and age. The most important variations in high-speed use at home are by racial and ethnic groups, language, income, and age.

Racial and ethnic minorities continue to lag behind white non-Hispanics in this primary form of communication in the 21st century as Table 3.3 demonstrates. Nationally, as of 2009, 64% of white non-Hispanics had broadband access at home compared with 46% of African Americans and 42% of Latinos, an 18-point difference based on race and more than a 20-point difference based on ethnicity. Minorities live disproportionately in urban and rural areas, and access rates in these areas are lower than the national averages. Only 38% of Latinos living in central cities have broadband at home and only 45% of African Americans. Statistically, less than one in two urban minorities are digital citizens, according to our definition. For respondents reporting that Spanish is spoken exclusively at home, only a little over one in five (or 23.5%) has high-speed Internet at home, compared with 62% who speak English at home (see Table 3.4). In central cities,

Table 3.2   **Percent of Americans with Internet Use by Residence in Central Cities, Suburbs, and Rural Areas (2009 FCC Survey)**

	National (All)	Central Cities	Suburbs	Rural
Broadband Internet Access at Home (High speed)	54 (2,654)	56 (756)	59 (1,389)	40 (417)
Broadband Internet Access	54	56	59	40
Connect to Internet from Home (Slow speed)	62.5 (3,077)	62 (837)	67 (1,582)	53 (557)
Use Internet at Any Location	71 (3,477)	70 (948)	74 (1,735)	64 (673)

Note: N = 5000 (unweighted); sample sizes in parentheses.

Table 3.3 **Internet Use by Race and Ethnicity (2009 CPS)**

| | Race | | | Ethnicity | |
	White	*Black*	*Asian*	*Hispanic*	*Non-Hispanic*
National (All):					
Use Internet at Any Location	75.27 (55,684)	60.19 (5,612)	73.33 (3,255)	50.76 (5,747)	73.41 (66,219)
Access Internet at Home Using High-Speed	66.05 (48,863)	46.40 (4,326)	67.85 (3,012)	41.67 (4,718)	63.85 (57,595)
Central City:					
Use Internet at Any Location	78.99 (8,574)	59.75 (2,386)	70.46 (1,171)	47.6 (1,886)	73.45 (12,462)
Access Internet at Home Using High-Speed	71.14 (7,722)	45.30 (1,809)	66.00 (1,097)	38.14 (1,511)	64.31 (10,911)
Suburbs:					
Use Internet at Any Location	77.72 (34,858)	65.60 (2,784)	76.03 (1,929)	53.69 (3,466)	76.59 (40,479)
Access Internet at Home Using High-Speed	69.40 (31,126)	53.02 (2,250)	70.08 (1,778)	44.96 (2,902)	68.00 (35,943)

	Race				Ethnicity	
	White	Black	Asian		Hispanic	Non-Hispanic
Rural:						
Use Internet at Any Location	67.07 (12,252)	40.66 (442)	64.58 (155)		43.65 (395)	65.13 (13,278)
Access Internet at Home Using High-Speed	54.82 (10,015)	24.56 (267)	57.08 (137)		33.70 (305)	52.69 (10,741)

Note: Entries are weighted percentages with sample sizes in parentheses.

Table 3.4   **Internet Use by Language (2009 CPS)**

	Spanish-Only Spoken	
	No	*Yes*
All:		
Use Internet at Any Location	71.70	29.96
	(71,370)	(596)
Access Internet at Home Using High-Speed	62.13 (61,845)	23.53 (468)
Central City:		
Use Internet at Any Location	70.14	25.94
	(14,154)	(194)
Access Internet at Home Using High-Speed	60.81 (12,272)	20.05 (150)
Suburbs:		
Use Internet at Any Location	74.89	33.10
	(43,570)	(375)
Access Internet at Home Using High-Speed	66.27 (38,553)	25.77 (292)
Rural:		
Use Internet at Any Location	64.42	25.00
	(13,646)	(27)
Access Internet at Home Using High-Speed	52.02 (11,020)	24.07 (26)

Note: Entries are weighted percentages with sample sizes in parentheses.

only 20% of individuals whose primary language is Spanish have high-speed Internet at home, compared with 26% of Spanish speakers living in the suburbs and 24% in rural areas. Thus, Latinos living in urban areas who speak primarily Spanish have some of the lowest access rates of any ethnic group in the United States.

Wide disparities in technology use are also found based on income, as shown in Table 3.5. Nationally, of individuals earning $20,000 or less per year, only 32% have home broadband, compared with almost 90% of those with incomes of $100,000 or more; a 60% difference from the poorest to the most affluent. These figures are roughly the same for residents of central cities. In contrast, only 27% of very poor rural residents (with an annual income of $20,000 or less) have broadband compared with 83% of the rural wealthy (with $100,000 or more in income). The highest-income rural residents lag behind urban and national averages for that category by only six percentage points. This suggests that poverty has a much greater influence on rural broadband adoption than infrastructure availability.

Table 3.5 **Internet Use by Income (2009 CPS)**

				Income		
	Less than 20,000	*20,000 to 39,999*	*40,000 to 59,999*	*60,000 to 99,999*	*100,000 or more*
National (All):						
Use Internet at Any Location	44.93 (6,090)	59.62 (11,233)	76.72 (11,273)	86.44 (16,520)	93.24 (14,302)
Access Internet at Home Using High-Speed	32.32 (4,381)	46.86 (8,828)	65.49 (9,623)	78.69 (15,039)	89.58 (13,740)
Central City:						
Use Internet at Any Location	46.87 (1,642)	59.93 (2,387)	76.02 (2,108)	84.92 (2,957)	93.1 (2,766)
Access Internet at Home Using High-Speed	33.69 (1,180)	47.83 (1,905)	66.10 (1,833)	78.46 (2,732)	89.63 (2,663)
Suburbs:						
Use Internet at Any Location	46.83 (2,973)	61.23 (6,266)	77.73 (6,681)	87.33 (10,460)	93.64 (9,939)
Access Internet at Home Using High-Speed	34.51 (2,191)	49.15 (5,030)	67.46 (5,798)	79.95 (9,576)	90.67 (9,624)

(continued)

Table 3.5 **(continued)**

	Income				
	Less than 20,000	*20,000 to 39,999*	*40,000 to 59,999*	*60,000 to 99,999*	*100,000 or more*
Rural:					
Use Internet at Any Location	39.83 (1,475)	55.81 (2,580)	74.68 (2,484)	84.99 (3,103)	91.05 (1,597)
Access Internet at Home Using High-Speed	27.28 (1,010)	40.95 (1,893)	59.89 (1,992)	74.80 (2,731)	82.84 (1,453)

Note: Entries are weighted percentages with sample sizes in parentheses.

Table 3.6 **Internet Use by Education (2009 CPS)**

	Education				
	Less than High School	High School Graduate	Some College, Associate's	Bachelor's or Higher
National (All):				
Use Internet at Any Location	30.48 (3,826)	59.38 (18,825)	81.72 (23,580)	90.56 (25,735)
Access Internet at Home Using High-Speed	23.25 (2,918)	48.53 (15,384)	70.57 (20,363)	83.21 (23,648)
Central City:				
Use Internet at Any Location	28.41 (899)	54.88 (3,066)	79.51 (4,385)	90.02 (5,998)
Access Internet at Home Using High-Speed	20.76 (657)	44.41 (2,481)	67.94 (3,747)	83.10 (5,537)
Suburbs:				
Use Internet at Any Location	33.49 (2,152)	62.63 (11,290)	83.56 (14,404)	91.36 (16,099)
Access Internet at Home Using High-Speed	26.23 (1,685)	52.54 (9,470)	73.64 (12,694)	85.10 (14,996)

(continued)

Table 3.6 (continued)

	Education			
	Less than High School	High School Graduate	Some College, Associate's	Bachelor's or Higher
Rural:				
Use Internet at Any Location	26.16 (775)	55.25 (4,469)	78.49 (4,791)	87.98 (3,638)
Access Internet at Home Using High-Speed	19.44 (576)	42.44 (3,433)	64.25 (3,922)	75.33 (3,115)

Note: Entries are weighted percentages with sample sizes in parentheses.

Table 3.7 **Internet Use by Age (2009 CPS)**

	Age			
	18–29	30–49	50–64	65 +
National (All):				
Use Internet at Any Location	81.59 (16,431)	79.47 (29,014)	71.75 (19,103)	40.63 (7,418)
Access Internet at Home Using High-Speed	69.45 (13,986)	69.97 (25,544)	62.48 (16,635)	33.68 (6,148)
Central City:				
Use Internet at Any Location	79.98 (3,980)	75.36 (5,842)	65.93 (3,266)	38.81 (1,260)
Access Internet at Home Using High-Speed	68.27 (3,397)	65.83 (5,103)	58.11 (2,879)	32.12 (1,043)
Suburbs:				
Use Internet at Any Location	83.70 (9,613)	82.50 (17,981)	75.25 (11,764)	44.12 (4,587)
Access Internet at Home Using High-Speed	72.95 (8,378)	74.29 (16,190)	66.47 (10,392)	37.37 (3,885)

(continued)

Table 3.7 **(continued)**

	Age			
	18–29	30–49	50–64	65 +
Rural:				
Use Internet at Any Location	77.18 (2,838)	74.55 (5,191)	67.46 (4,073)	34.06 (1,571)
Access Internet at Home Using High-Speed	60.13 (2,211)	61.05 (4,251)	55.71 (3,364)	26.45 (1,220)

Note: Entries are weighted percentages with sample sizes in parentheses.

As reported in earlier research, skills and literacy are necessary to use the Internet, and gaps in use of broadband at home based on education remain important. Nationally, only 23% of Americans with less than a high school degree have high-speed access at home, compared with 83% who hold a bachelor's degree or higher, a 60% gap based on educational attainment, as shown in Table 3.6. Again, the less educated in central cities and rural areas are the worst off. Only 20% of those with less than a high school degree residing in urban or rural areas have home broadband. Disparities in high-speed access based on generations remain but are abating somewhat, according to Table 3.7. Seventy percent of 18–29 year-olds have broadband at home, compared with 34% of those 65 years and older nationwide. These patterns are fairly consistent for central cities, with slightly higher access rates in the suburbs and lower rates in rural areas.

PREDICTING INTERNET USE ACROSS GEOGRAPHY

We are not only interested in patterns of Internet use by geography, but how demographic factors shape technology use across geographic areas, especially in cities. As discussed in chapter 1, many variables overlap in predicting Internet use, including race, ethnicity, age, income, and education (Mossberger, Tolbert, and Stansbury 2003). We need to use multivariate regression to isolate the independent effects of different factors on the probability of access; for example, the effects of Latino ethnicity, holding income and education levels constant, since Latinos on average are poorer and have less formal education than white non-Hispanics. If we do not control for overlapping influences, we could overestimate or underestimate the true effect of Latino ethnicity on the probability of home broadband access. The figures reported in this chapter are from multivariate statistical models, but the results are presented as predicted probabilities—in graphs—that are as easy to read and compare as simple percentages. No training in statistical methodology is necessary to read the findings of this book, but for readers trained in these methods, the full models are available in appendix A.

Our multivariate analyses model high-speed Internet at home or Internet use in any location as outcome variables and how this varies by place of residence. We model Internet use as a function of several demographic and economic variables. These variables include race (black, Asian); ethnicity (Latino); Spanish language; total yearly income from all sources (on a 1–16 scale from less than $5,000 a year to over $150,000); education (on a 1–5 scale from less than a high school graduate to a post-graduate education); age measured in years; gender (binary variable for males with females as the reference category); marital status; parental status, an interaction term to capture a single parent with children; and business ownership, assuming owning a business increases the need for information online. The CPS includes detailed occupation questions that measure employment in economic sectors, including categories such as professional, service, sales, and construction, among others. A series of binary variables is used to measure each occupational category with production as the reference category. Please see appendix B for details on the survey question wording, response options, and variable coding. For the national sample, binary variables measure whether the individual resides in an urban or rural area, with suburban respondents as the reference category.

Explanatory variables were selected and coded to be as similar as possible for the CPS and FCC surveys, allowing a robustness test across the two surveys conducted in the same year (2009). Some differences do exist. In general, the CPS data has more detailed demographic information about the respondents than the FCC data. Two main advantages of the CPS data are that we can isolate how Internet use is influenced by being Spanish-dominant and how use is influenced by relatively specific occupational categories.

Results

Appendix Table A3.1.1 presents a multivariate logistic regression model predicting broadband access at home (coded 1 and 0 for no access) using the CPS survey and Appendix Table A3.1.2 presents a similar model using the FCC survey. In column one of both tables the sample is the entire nation (all respondents), column 2 only includes respondents residing in central cities, column 3 shows respondents residing in suburbs, and column 4 refers to rural residents. Appendix Tables A3.2.1 and A3.2.2 model the probability of using the Internet anywhere for CPS and FCC surveys, respectively. Because the dependent variables measuring Internet use are binary, logistic regression coefficients are reported. For the CPS models standard errors are clustered by household using VCE (variance-covariance estimator).

The results are consistent with the previous literature on Internet adoption, showing variation in high-speed Internet access based on race/ethnicity, Spanish language, income, education, age, occupation, and more (Norris 2001; Bimber 2003; Mossberger, Tolbert, and Stansbury 2003). The national sample of all respondents in column 1 indicates that both rural and urban residents are less likely to have broadband at home than those living in the suburbs, all else being equal. Because these are logistic regression estimates, it is difficult to understand the substantive effects by the size of coefficients. Instead, we convert the logistic regression coefficients from the appendix tables (based on the CPS survey) into predicted probabilities, with all other variables in the model held constant at mean/modal values. These probabilities can be interpreted like simple percentages, but they are based on the multivariate regression models and thus allow us to hold constant the overlapping factors that are related to Internet access and use.

RACE/ETHNICITY AND INTERNET USE BY GEOGRAPHY

Figure 3.1 (based on Appendix Table A3.1.1) shows one of the most important patterns reported in this book. Racial and ethnic minorities significantly lag behind white non-Hispanics in Internet use, as measured by the estimated probability of having broadband access at home, and these patterns are found across geographic areas. We find that socioeconomic inequalities trump place in defining access and use of the Internet. Overall, Latinos have the lowest rates of broadband access. Only 47% of Latinos who reside in central cities or in rural areas have broadband at home, while 55% of suburban Latinos have high-speed Internet at home, holding other factors constant. This compares to 70% of white non-Hispanics with broadband home access in central cities, 73% in suburbs and 64% in rural areas. On average, white non-Hispanics have access rates

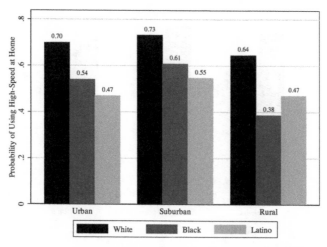

Figure 3.1 Predicted Probability of High-Speed Home Access by Race/Ethnicity (from Appendix Table A3.1.1). Note: All other explanatory variables held constant at mean values.

30% greater than Latinos. African Americans also lag behind white non-Hispanics but have slightly higher access rates than Latinos. Fifty-four percent of urban blacks have broadband at home, compared with 61% of black suburban residents and only 39% of blacks who reside in rural areas. By these estimates—which hold constant the respondents' income, education, age, gender, occupation, et al.—**one in two American minorities is offline or less-connected as defined by broadband Internet access at home**.

Figure 3.2 (based on Appendix Table 3.2.1) graphs the probability, holding other demographic factors constant, of using the Internet anywhere by race/ethnicity and geography. The higher estimates for blacks and Latinos reflect the widespread use of technology outside of home and in public places. Seventy percent of African Americans residing in central cities use the Internet anywhere, compared with the 54% who use broadband at home, a 16% difference, and 76% of African-Americans who live in the suburbs use the Internet at any location. This suggests that a lack of interest in the Internet is not the reason fewer African Americans are online at home. Latinos are also more likely to use the Internet outside the home, with almost 59% of Latinos living in central cities and 63% in rural areas having used the Internet somewhere, compared with 47% home broadband access for urban Latinos. These graphs help us understand the contours of these access disparities and the effects of place.

While gaps in Internet access based on race/ethnicity have received a fair amount of attention, less is known about access rates based on language acquisition, especially across different geographic areas. Figure 3.3 shows the probability of a broadband connection at home among Latinos who speak Spanish only, compared with Latinos who speak English (or English and Spanish). Among urban Latinos who speak only Spanish, 29% have high-speed access at home, compared with almost 50% of Latinos who speak

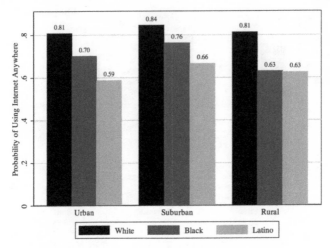

Figure 3.2 Predicted Probability of Internet Use Anywhere by Race/Ethnicity
(from Appendix Table A3.2.1). Note: All other explanatory variables held constant at mean
values.

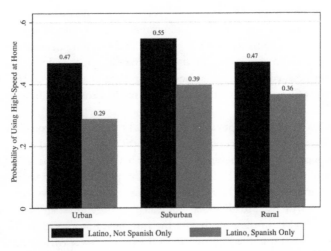

Figure 3.3 Predicted Probability of High-Speed Home Access by Language (from
Appendix Table A3.1.1). Note: All other explanatory variables held constant at mean values.

English or are bilingual, an 18-point difference. Similar differences are found for
Spanish-speaking Latinos residing in the suburbs and rural areas. Most notable is that
the lowest use of broadband at home is among Latinos in central cities. While the probability of using the Internet at any location rises to 36% for urban Latinos who speak
Spanish, this is still very low compared with national averages (see Figure 3.4). Spanish-
speaking Latinos who live in suburban or rural areas have slightly higher rates of using
the Internet in any location.

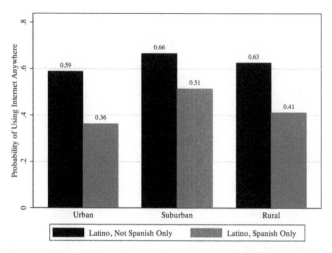

Figure 3.4 Predicted Probability of Internet Use Anywhere by Language (from Appendix Table A3.2.1). Note: All other explanatory variables held constant at mean values.

INCOME/EDUCATION/AGE AND INTERNET USE BY GEOGRAPHIC REGION

Figure 3.5 (based on Appendix Table 3.1.1) graphs the probability of high-speed access at home by income for suburban residents (solid line), rural residents (dashed line), and urban residents (dotted line). The steadily upward sloping three lines show that the probability of access rises significantly with increased income, from a low of 35% for the poorest Americans (incomes of $5,000 per year) who live in rural areas to a high of almost 85% for the wealthiest citizens (incomes over $150,000) who live in the suburbs. Here we see clearly that socioeconomic disparities outweigh variation based on geography. While there are some differences among the geographic regions, with home broadband the lowest in rural areas and highest in the suburbs, the results for the poor in all three areas track each other closely, showing that home broadband access, regardless of region, is still driven by income. Broadband adoption rates at home are roughly the same in central cities and suburbs for the least affluent. Figure 3.6 demonstrates that increased income is associated with a higher probability of being online regardless of whether the respondent resides in an urban area, the suburbs, or a rural community. In fact, the lines for urban and rural residents cross. Internet use anywhere is higher for wealthier rural residents than affluent urban residents. This may indicate more use of public access or mobile devices for high-income rural residents.

The literature on digital inequality has shown education to be an important predictor of being online (Norris 2001; Mossberger, Tolbert, and Stansbury 2003). Figure 3.7 (based on Appendix Table 3.1.1) indicates that for a rural resident with less than a high school degree, the probability of having broadband at home is only 45%. This rises to over 70% for college graduates, holding other demographic and

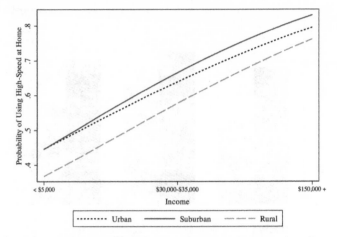

Figure 3.5 Predicted Probability of High-Speed Home Access by Income (from Appendix Table A3.1.1). Note: All other explanatory variables held constant at mean values.

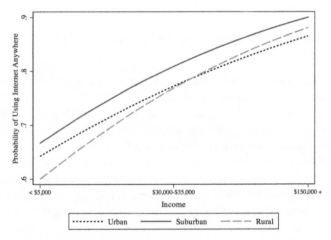

Figure 3.6 Predicted Probability of Internet Use Anywhere by Income (from Appendix Table A3.2.1). Note: All other explanatory variables held constant at mean values.

occupational factors constant. Those with less formal education (less than a high school degree) living in urban areas have a 50% chance of home broadband access, rising to nearly 80% for college graduates. Less-educated suburbanites (with less than a high school degree) have a 65% chance of having high-speed Internet at home; 15% higher than their urban counterparts, again rising to above 80% among those with a college degree. Figure 3.8 (based on Appendix Table 3.2.1) plots similar estimates for the probability of using the Internet at any location. Central city and rural residents have virtually identical probabilities of Internet use anywhere, increasing

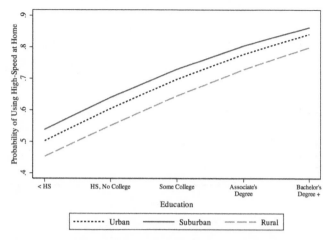

Figure 3.7 Predicted Probability of High-Speed Home Access by Education (from Appendix Table A3.1.1). Note: All other explanatory variables held constant at mean values.

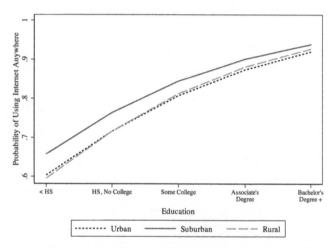

Figure 3.8 Predicted Probability of Internet Use Anywhere by Education (from Appendix Table A3.2.1). Note: All other explanatory variables held constant at mean values.

as education rises from a high school graduate to post-graduate degree, while suburban residents have access rates by about five percentage points higher across educational categories.

Figures 3.9 and 3.10 (based on Appendix Tables 3.1.1 & 3.2.1) plot the probability of having a high-speed connection at home or using the Internet anywhere by age, measured in years. Regardless of geographic location, young Americans (age 20) have a .80 to .90 probability of having broadband Internet at home, decreasing to between 50–55% for those 60 years of age. Unlike the income and education graphs, which show a steadily sloping upward probability curve, these graphs indicate a downward

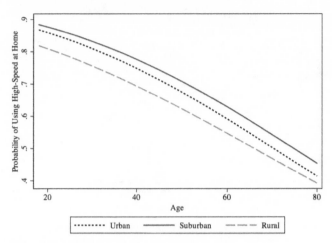

Figure 3.9 Predicted Probability of High-Speed Home Access by Age (from Appendix Table A3.1.1). Note: All other explanatory variables held constant at mean values.

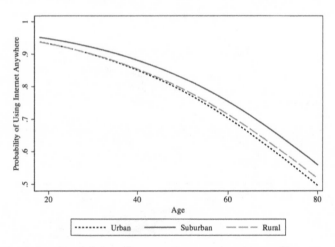

Figure 3.10 Predicted Probability of Internet Use Anywhere by Age (from Appendix Table A3.2.1). Note: All other explanatory variables held constant at mean values.

trend, with the oldest age group the least likely to have Internet access. Differences between rural, suburban, and urban residents are relatively small compared with the gaps based on generations. For young people, Internet use is a necessity regardless of location. For Internet use at any location (Figure 3.10), the young (age 20) have a .95 probability of use, and there is almost no difference by geographic region. The slope reduces as age increases, but remains relatively constant up until 40 years of age, and then drops off sharply. Age continues to define large gaps in access, more than a decade and a half after the first federal reports of a digital divide between "haves" and "have nots."

Conclusion: Disaggregating Disparities

While there are differences by geographic location for all levels of adoption, the gaps are visible, but relatively modest, when we simply compare the percentages of urban, suburban, and rural residents. Suburban residents have higher rates of access overall, with urban residents somewhat ahead of or sometimes on par with rural respondents.

Controlling for overlapping influences, however, reveals more pronounced inequalities in access for both urban and rural residents based on race, ethnicity, and poverty. This allows us to compare the differences based on poverty alone, or race alone, across places; it suggests more about possible causes for disparities. Poverty decreases the probability of home broadband access at an almost identical rate in all geographic areas. There are some interesting patterns by race and ethnicity. African Americans do relatively worse in rural areas (although city residents trail suburban African Americans). On the other hand, urban Latinos have the lowest rates of use anywhere, controlling for other factors.

In all types of communities there is increased diversity, with a U.S. population that will soon have a non-white majority. Most of the 50 largest cities have already reached this threshold. Latinos are the fastest-growing group nationally (Frey 2011), and yet they are the most technologically disadvantaged. A better understanding of the challenges they face is needed for the future.

Less-educated individuals have a noticeably higher likelihood of use anywhere in the suburbs, compared with similarly situated urban and rural residents. A possible reason for this may be the availability of public access and help in suburban locations where there is less competition for resources outside the home. Location matters little for age-related disparities until age 40. In fact, the youngest respondents have nearly universal experience with having used the Internet in some location, at 95%, holding other factors constant. The federal E-Rate program, which has funded an almost uniform presence of Internet connections in libraries and schools (Becker et al. 2010; National Center for Education Statistics 2011), likely explains this finding. For those who have any interest in using the Internet, nearly all can access it at least occasionally.

Statistical controls allow us to disentangle factors that affect Internet access. Yet, there is clearly variation within categories that is not entirely captured by these results. Some rural places are poorer than others, and there are affluent neighborhoods as well as areas of concentrated poverty within urban areas. Later chapters disaggregate these results further, at lower levels of urban geography, including the neighborhood. Places may magnify social inequalities because of the concentration of poverty, segregation, or fiscal inequities affecting public resources.

What is clear even from this first layer of geographic analysis, however, is that social inequalities are related to unequal access in any environment. Universal broadband access will require more than infrastructure, especially focused only in rural areas. Fostering universal access and digital citizenship will require attention to the effects of poverty, education, discrimination, and immigrant needs. Rural communities will still lag behind, as well as poor urban neighborhoods, without greater policy attention to barriers other than availability. Universal access, as Blair Levin argues, depends on adoption as well as infrastructure.

While we examined a continuum of technology access—from use anywhere to home broadband adoption—these patterns of access alone do not explain the extent to which individuals can exercise digital citizenship. How are varied types of access related to activities online and to measures of skill? Because there is almost universal experience with Internet use in some settings among younger people, does that mean that there are few place-based differences in those experiences? The next chapter on the "less-connected" offers a better view of how technology is used and the inequalities that remain for those who have more limited access.

4

Mobile Access and the Less-Connected

The proliferation of mobile devices is unquestionably changing the way in which many people go online, and cell phone adoption is high among minorities and the young. As of 2012, nearly half the American population has mobile Internet access on smartphones (Zickhur and Smith 2012). How are these trends likely to affect the prospects for digital citizenship or full participation in society online?

The mass media have frequently portrayed mobile wireless, particularly Internet-enabled smartphones, as the solution to disparities in Internet access. Using the language of human rights and equity, legal scholar Susan Crawford (2011) has countered that dependence on mobile phones (as well as dial-up) are second-class forms of access to the Internet. There has been little prior research using appropriate statistical methods examining whether mobile access facilitates a range of activities online, especially regarding health, economic opportunity, and democratic participation. The National Broadband Plan depicts universal broadband access as essential because of what it enables, yet there is limited evidence on how different forms of access matter. Can those who rely on smartphones participate in society online in a meaningful way? How do cell-phone-only Internet users compare with those who have broadband at home? Do they differ from other Internet users who are "less-connected," such as those who depend on public access or dial-up connections?

In this chapter we investigate the skills and activities of mobile-phone-only Internet users and others who are less-connected. The results show that quality of access matters considerably for individual capabilities and potential public benefits. Interestingly enough, smartphone users are more likely than other less-connected individuals to perform a few select activities online; overall, however, all are strikingly less engaged online than individuals with home broadband. The findings underscore quite clearly the need for home broadband access and use as an anchor for more robust participation in society online.

Mobile Access: Is it a Game Changer?

As mobile devices, especially cell phones, have evolved in their online capabilities, questions have arisen about the extent to which they can substitute for home broadband access.

Moreover, high rates of mobile phone adoption by African Americans and Latinos seem to pose prospects for closing the gaps in connectivity that were evident in chapter 3. In 2012, adoption of Internet-enabled smartphones was slightly higher nationally for

African Americans and Latinos (at 49%) than for non-Hispanic whites (at 45%), just as cell phone adoption in general is slightly higher among these groups (Zickuhr and Smith 2012; Smith 2010). This contrasts with home broadband adoption, where African Americans and Latinos lag behind (NTIA 2011; Horrigan 2012). Most mobile phone Internet users, however, also have home broadband (Horrigan 2012) and are generally younger, higher income, and more educated than those without smartphones (Zickuhr and Smith 2012).

But smartphones as an alternative to home broadband access can offer some cost advantages. Mobile phones can replace landlines, and as devices for connecting to the Internet they require less of an upfront investment than laptops or desktop computers (Kang 2010). Families with children who compete for a single computer may opt instead to provide individualized Internet access through phones (Gallaga 2010).

Smartphones are in fact used by low-income youth at higher rates. A national study of teenagers showed that on average 25% used the Internet on their phones, especially for social networking sites. For teens in households with incomes less than $30,000, that figure jumps to 41%. Similarly, 44% of African American youth and 35% of Latino teens use the Internet on their phones. Low-income teenagers frequently pay for their own mobile Internet bills, and pay higher costs because they are not on less expensive family plans. They are also more likely to lack Internet access at home (Brown, Campbell, and Ling 2011).

Could affordable smartphone use remedy disparities in access, given the enthusiasm for the devices among many demographic groups that are offline or less-connected? This is an argument often reflected in popular headlines: "Mobile Use Shrinks the Digital Divide" in the *New York Times* (Wortham 2009); "A Digital Revolution in the Palm of Your Hand," on National Public Radio (Peterson 2010). Such speculation certainly corresponds to the increased capabilities of phones. These include mobile banking and contactless payments through applications like Google Wallet. News and other print media now use formats that make it easier to read copy on smartphones. The portability of mobile phones affords continuous access to the Internet, especially for locational information or real-time updates (for example, for mass transit).

Despite the development of many new applications, reliance on cell phones as the primary way to go online offers a more functionally limited Internet. Mobile phones may be useful for social networking, texting, and gaming, but with their smaller screens and more challenging keyboards they are not likely to replace high-speed access on laptop or desktop computers for activities such as applying for jobs or researching health issues (Washington 2011; Wortham 2009). Slow speeds on wireless networks often make it difficult to download or upload information, and data-usage caps (common in most wireless plans) may discourage online exploration (Goldman, 2012; Wortham, 2011).

Measuring Activities Online as Digital Citizenship

The activities that individuals engage in online provide a good measure for comparing modes of access against their potential for individual inclusion and spillover benefits for society. As Crawford (2007) has argued, the Internet's value is grounded not in the nature of the connections themselves, but in the human relations the connections facilitate. Eszter Hargittai has called variation in activities online the second-order digital divide emerging in a society where some experience with the Internet is becoming more widespread (Hargittai 2002).

To what extent do forms of access matter for participating in society online? The growth of online information and communication suggests that those who are excluded from this medium are indeed outside the social mainstream. A 2012 Pew survey found that 8 in 10 Internet users check the weather online, 75% read the news online (up from 61% in 2011), and over 6 in 10 look up political information online. They also seek out government information; 67% visited a local, state, or federal government website (up from 56% in 2011). Economic activity online is widespread; 60% do banking, and 56% look for information about a job. Online information even affects where you live; 4 in 10 Internet users search online for housing (Zickuhr and Smith 2012).[1]

We argue that digital citizenship can be measured in terms of economic and political activities online. As we noted, liberal ideas of citizenship and equality of opportunity are grounded in the belief that individuals should have fair access to the tools necessary to compete economically (Smith 1993; Hartz 1955; Mossberger, Tolbert, and McNeal 2008). Civic republicanism, which also forms a part of the American political heritage, emphasizes the need for citizen participation (Skocpol 1992; Smith 1993). Thomas Jefferson, for example, argued for the establishment of public education to foster democratic citizenship, and the Internet today provides additional resources for civic engagement (Mossberger, Tolbert, and McNeal 2008).

Building on these traditions of citizenship, we examine in this chapter how different forms of access are related to economic and political participation, and other activities related to health, education, and government services that have been called human-capital-enhancing activities (DiMaggio and Celeste 2004; Hargittai 2002; Hassani 2006). Together these types of activities promise to create spillover benefits for society as well as resources and opportunities for individuals.

We hypothesize that home broadband is a significant predictor of digital citizenship and that mobile access as a primary means of going online is not. Previous research suggests that home access is strongly associated with human-capital-enhancing activities and digital citizenship, controlling for other factors (Hassani 2006; DiMaggio and Bonikowski 2008). It affords greater flexibility and convenience than public access or the workplace. Additionally, home access allows Internet users more time to explore a range of uses and to gain experience more than work or public access sites such as libraries (DiMaggio et al. 2004; Hargittai and Hinnant 2008). Perhaps for these reasons, longitudinal research indicates that the acquisition of home access is a significant predictor of increased wages (DiMaggio and Bonikowski 2008). The higher speeds and capabilities of broadband convey additional advantages for frequency of use, broader use, and skill. Broadband users perform more activities online, and this is so even when other influences, such as education, are held constant (Horrigan 2004; Mossberger, Tolbert, and McNeal 2008). We explore how mobile-only Internet users and others who are less-connected participate in varied types of activities using the Internet.

Who Are Mobile Phone Users Without Home Access?

This is a small but growing segment of the American population that is the topic of much debate regarding the future of digital inequality. Fortunately, the FCC telephone survey used in chapter 3 included a question asking respondents whether they "use their cell phone for email and or Internet use" (questions #30a and 30e); thus, we are able to analyze a large-sample national survey to better describe this population and to measure their activities online. In contrast with other reports on cell phone use, we use multivariate regression to assess the role of race, for example, holding constant other influences such as income, age, gender, and education. In keeping with our focus on geographic differences, we explore variation across urban, suburban, and rural areas.

Of the respondents in the survey using their mobile phones to access the Internet, the vast majority (86%) also have high-speed Internet access at home. Three and a half percent connect to the Internet at home via slow speed, and 6% do not have Internet access at home but use the Internet. Surprisingly, another 5% of individuals who use their cell phones for email or the Internet say they are not Internet users; this may be because they connect to the Internet without a standard computer. We thus use the full sample of 5,000 respondents in the following analysis, rather than only Internet users, as we did for the previous less-connected analysis. The patterns of use and inequality for mobile phone Internet users lacking a home broadband connection parallel the general findings for the less-connected in important ways.

Overall, in our sample, about 4% of Americans use mobile phones for access but do not have high-speed Internet at home as of 2009. This is an important variable in this chapter for comparison with individuals with home broadband. Of respondents in the survey who self-identify as Latino, almost 11% use a cell phone to connect to the Internet but do not have home broadband, and 7% of African Americans do the same. This is compared with only 2% of white non-Hispanics who use mobile Internet without broadband at home. Of the poor, defined as individuals earning less than $20,000 a year, 8% use smartphones without high-speed access at home, compared with 1% of respondents who earn over $75,000 a year. We see the same pattern for education. Of individuals with less than a high school degree, 8% use mobile phone Internet without home access, compared with 1% of college graduates. The young are also much more likely to have only smartphones (8% of those age 18–24), but mobile-phone-only Internet users account for less than 1% of those 65 and older.

Geography is an important variable in our study, but descriptive data suggests there are not major differences here. Among individuals living in rural areas, 5% are mobile phone Internet users with no home broadband, compared with 3% of those living in the suburbs and almost 4.5% of urban residents. Reliance on cell phones to access the Internet appears less about a lack of infrastructure and more about cost and convenience.

Following the format of the multivariate logistic regression models presented in chapter 3, Appendix Table A4.1 uses the 5,000 person 2009 FCC survey to model the factors predicting mobile phone Internet use without high-speed home access, controlling for other demographic and economic influences. Column 1 includes the full sample of respondents, modeling wireless Internet users nationally, while columns 2, 3, and 4 provide subsamples for urban, suburban, and rural residents, respectively. The same set of predictor variables and coding used in chapter 3 is included in these models. Controlling for income, education, age, geographic residence, and other factors, we find that Latinos and African Americans are much more likely to connect through mobile phones than white non-Hispanics, consistent with mass media reports. Asian Americans are no different than whites in their dependence on smartphones to go online.

Race and ethnicity predict mobile phone reliance differently across geography. Among urban residents, African Americans are more likely to have only mobile Internet, but not Latinos. Of individuals living in the suburbs, Latinos are more likely to connect to the Internet on mobile devices than whites, but African Americans are no different (statistically) than whites. Among rural residents, African Americans are more likely to use mobile phone Internet than whites, but Latinos and whites are not different. Figure 4.1 shows the predicted probability of being a mobile-phone-only Internet user lacking home high-speed access by race/ethnicity for urban, suburban, and rural residents, holding other demographic and economic factors constant at mean values. The dark-gray bars represent African Americans, the light-gray bars Latinos, and the black bars non-Hispanic whites. Urban African Americans have a 5% chance of relying exclusively on their mobile phone to connect to the Internet in 2009, compared with 1% of whites and 2% of Latinos. Similarly, suburban Latinos have an 8% probability of being a mobile-only Internet user compared with 4% of African Americans and 3% of non-Hispanic whites. Reliance on cell phones in the suburbs is highest among Latinos, and among African-Americans in cities. This may reflect the geography of poverty within these groups, apart from individual income. Low-income African Americans have traditionally experienced more residential segregation, focused on central cities, whereas low-income Latinos within metropolitan areas often live in poor neighborhoods in suburban communities as well as central city neighborhoods (Logan 2011).

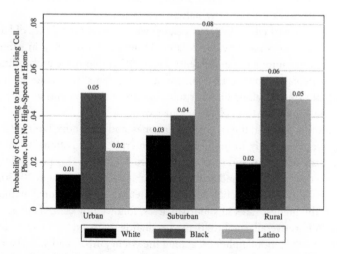

Figure 4.1 Predicted Probability of Mobile Access (Cell Phone), but No High-Speed at Home by Race/Ethnicity (from Appendix Table A4.1). Note: All other explanatory variables held constant at mean values.

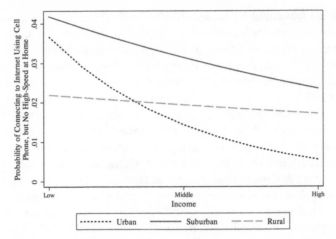

Figure 4.2 Predicted Probability of Mobile Access (Cell Phone), but No High-Speed at Home by Income (from Appendix Table A4.1). Note: All other explanatory variables held constant at mean values.

Appendix Table A4.1 shows that nationwide, less affluent individuals are statistically more likely to rely on mobile phone Internet access (lacking home access) in urban areas, but this is not the case for suburban or rural residents. Rural residents may use mobile phone Internet because broadband is not available. Figure 4.2 graphs the probability of connecting to the Internet via mobile phones for those without broadband at home by income level. Low-income individuals living in urban areas (dotted black line) have a high probability of being exclusively mobile users, and this probability drops steeply as income rises. In contrast, rural and suburban residents have a roughly equal probability of connecting to the Internet via cell phones without home access regardless of income level. This shows that this form of limited connectivity is driven primarily by income in urban areas and minority status across place.

Similarly, increased education is associated with a lower probability of having only mobile Internet access nationwide (column 1) among those living in suburban and rural areas, but not among urban residents. Figure 4.3 graphs these probabilities as education levels increase, showing a flat line for urban residents (no change with increased education), but steeply falling lines for suburban and rural residents as education rises to a high school graduate to a college graduate or more.

Age is another factor in the rise of smartphones, and Appendix Table A4.2 indicates the young are more likely to be mobile-only Internet users nationally, among those living in urban, suburban, and rural areas. Figure 4.4 graphs this probability, holding constant other demographic and economic variables. The young, ages 20–30, have the highest probability of connecting to the Internet via mobile phones without home access, with the highest rates in suburban areas, followed by central cities, and lastly, rural areas. While, overall, rural residents are slightly more likely to rely exclusively on wireless Internet via mobile phones, among the young, urban and suburban residents have the highest probability of connectivity in this form. Access rates via only mobile phones drop significantly as age increases across urban, suburban, and rural areas. This graph suggests that future trends point to an increasingly mobile Internet.

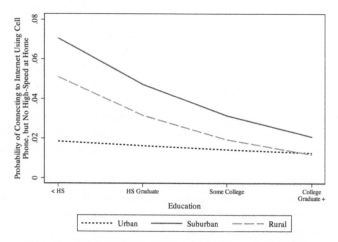

Figure 4.3 Predicted Probability of Mobile Access (Cell Phone), but No High-Speed at Home by Education (from Appendix Table A4.1). Note: All other explanatory variables held constant at mean values.

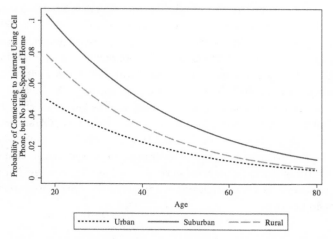

Figure 4.4 Predicted Probability of Mobile Access (Cell Phone), but No High-Speed at Home by Age (from Appendix Table A4.1). Note: All other explanatory variables held constant at mean values.

Who Are the Less-Connected, Overall?

Among the 39% of Americans who lack broadband access at home, many have some experience with Internet use and try to maintain connectivity in some way. The predominance of traditionally disadvantaged groups among cell-phone-only Internet users suggests that such individuals are motivated to gain access to the Internet but may not have the same quality of access that is afforded through home broadband. It is useful, therefore, to compare mobile-only Internet users with other individuals who are less-connected. As chapter 3 (Table 3.1) showed, nationally at least 10% of Americans are Internet users who do not have regular or full access to the Internet. They rely upon public access or other connections outside the home, such as wireless hot spots, coffee houses, or the homes of friends and relatives. They have slow dial-up connections at home and cannot access the full content of the Web. Or, they use the Internet on their phones but do not have regular broadband access otherwise.

To what extent do mobile-only users resemble the overall population of Internet users without home broadband? How do the less-connected vary by place and demography?

We examine the less-connected as a group using the 2009 Current Population Survey (CPS), discussed in chapter 3. While the CPS did not include questions on mobile phone use specifically, its size allows us to examine subsamples for the more general category of less-connected Internet users.

Simple frequencies are useful as an initial step for understanding the composition of the less-connected. They are much more likely to be minority than white. Of Latinos online, 24% have no high-speed Internet at home. This compares with 19% of African Americans who are less-connected and only 14% of white non-Hispanics. Of female Internet users, 18% are less-connected compared with 13% of males, a 5% difference. The less-connected are poorer. Of individuals earning less than $20,000 a year, 31% are less-connected, compared with 25.5% of income earners in the $20,000–$30,000 range, and only 5% of individuals earning $75,000 or more. Nationwide, the less-connected have lower educational attainment. Of those online, but with less than a high school degree, 34% are less connected, compared with 22% of those with a high school degree or GRE, 14% of individuals with some college and only 8% of college graduates. There is also a geographic component to the profile of the less-connected, in part due to a lack of infrastructure for wired broadband in many rural areas. Of individuals living in rural areas that use the Internet, 28% are less-connected, compared with 15% of those residing in urban areas and 12% of those living in the suburbs. As chapter 3 indicated, about half of the less-connected in rural areas have home access but with slow dial-up connections. In contrast, nearly two-thirds of the urban less-connected lack any type of home access.

Subsamples by Race/Ethnicity and the Less-Connected

African Americans and Latinos comprise an important segment of the less-connected, according to the descriptive statistics mentioned (and the literature on public access and reliance on mobile access). However, are there certain groups within the minority population that are most at risk for being less-connected? How do we understand the relative impact of poverty versus education or language?

We again draw on the large-sample 2009 CPS and multivariate regression analysis, but this time home in on only African Americans or Latinos in the survey. Appendix Table A4.2 presents two models predicting Internet use, drawing on a subsample of African American respondents (columns 1 and 3) and a subsample of Latino respondents (columns 2 and 4). Models predicting high-speed Internet at home are in columns 1 and 2 and Internet use anywhere in columns 3 and 4.

A striking finding is that Spanish-dominant Latinos have a considerably lower probability of Internet use (high-speed or in any location) than English-speaking Latinos. They are more likely to be offline completely rather than among the less-connected. Figure 4.5 graphs the probability of having high-speed Internet at home for Latinos based on the model in column 2 of Appendix Table A4.2, holding all other variables constant at mean values. Latinos who speak only Spanish have a .35 probability of home broadband adoption compared with English-speaking Latinos, who have a .50 probability of access, controlling for other factors. Figure 4.6 shows that the probability Latinos will use the Internet at any location is only 44% if they only speak Spanish, compared with 62% for English-speaking Latinos, an 18-point difference. Thus, an important dimension of technology use for Latinos in the United States is language acquisition and skill, which may also indicate other constraints, such as immigrant status and a lack of exposure to the Internet.

Appendix Table A4.2 also shows subsamples of African American respondents modeled to predict Internet use. In all four models in the table, income is positive and statistically significant. More affluent and educated minorities are significantly more likely to have broadband at home and to use the Internet at any location. This is consistent with descriptive statistics in other studies (Gant et al. 2010), but these relationships remain significant using appropriate statistical controls.

Figure 4.7 graphs the probability of having high-speed Internet at home based on income for the African American and Latino subsamples, with all other demographic and economic variables held constant at average values. The lines for blacks and Latinos are very similar, and both show a steeply sloping upward curve. Increased wealth is significantly related to a higher probability of minorities having home access. Both blacks and Latinos with high incomes ($150,000 +) have almost a 70% chance of having

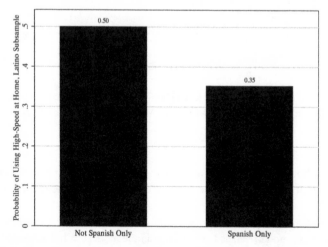

Figure 4.5 Predicted Probability of Home High-Speed Access by Language Spoken/ Latino Subsample (from Appendix Table A4.2). Note: All other explanatory variables held constant at mean values.

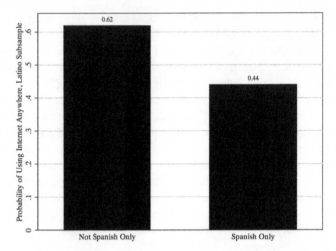

Figure 4.6 Predicted Probability of Internet Use Anywhere by Language Spoken/Latino Subsample (from Appendix Table A4.2). Note: All other explanatory variables held constant at mean values.

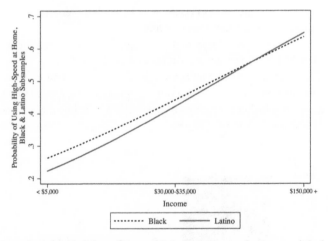

Figure 4.7 Predicted Probability of Home High-Speed Access by Income/Black vs. Latino Subsample (from Appendix Table A4.2). Note: All other explanatory variables held constant at mean values.

broadband at home, but the poor have a very low probability. Thus, poverty and minority status overlap in important ways in shaping digital inequality, especially for African Americans.

Figure 4.8 graphs the probability of using the Internet at any location for African Americans (subsample model) versus Latinos (subsample model). While increased wealth is associated with Latinos and African Americans using the Internet at any location, across income categories blacks are roughly 5 percentage points more likely to be online than Latinos, the most technologically disadvantaged ethnic group in America.

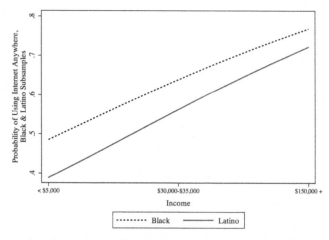

Figure 4.8 Predicted Probability of Internet Use Anywhere by Income/Black vs. Latino Subsample (from Appendix Table A4.2). Note: All other explanatory variables held constant at mean values.

Comparing Mobile-Only Access and the Less-Connected Overall

So far we have described those who connect to the Internet via mobile phones but lack high-speed access at home. Next, we examined patterns among those who lack high-speed Internet at home but connect to the Internet via slow dial-up access at home or use the Internet outside the home. Some differences are apparent in the composition of these groups.

Surprisingly, 5% of mobile phone Internet users claim they do not use the Internet in any location, suggesting some cognitive difference between access on a cell phone and through a computer. The mobile-only users also differ from the less-connected as a whole because mobile phone users tend to be younger and located in roughly similar proportions in urban, suburban, and rural areas. But these two populations also share many common features in that racial and ethnic minorities are overrepresented, as are the poor, and those with less formal education. Urban residents who are less-connected, including mobile phone users, tend to have no Internet access at home, and Latinos are least likely to be online through any mode of access. In the next section, we investigate activities online for cell-phone-only Internet users comparing them with those with broadband at home.

Why Broadband Matters: Economic and Political Activities

Previous research has found that home broadband promotes digital citizenship, with spillover benefits that provide economic and political advantages not only to the

Table 4.1   **Economic and Political Activities Online for the Less-Connected versus Home High-Speed Access (Percent)**

Economic and Political Activities	Less-Connected	Home Broadband	Difference Less-Connected
Use Internet to get local or community news	55	80	−25
Use Internet to visit local, state, or federal government website	57	79	−22
Use Internet to get national or international news	52	77	−25
Use Internet to get information or apply for job	45	60	−15
Use Internet to get information from a government agency on health/safety	35	54	−10
Use Internet to take a class for credit toward a degree	12	24	−12
Use Internet for online banking	35	70	−35

Note: Reported frequencies are weighted. Sample based on the 3,477 respondents who use the Internet. 2009 Federal Communications Commission (FCC) Survey of 5,000 respondents nationwide. Less connected = dial-up Internet or no Internet at home, including individuals with mobile access only.

individuals using the technology but also to society as a whole (Mossberger, Tolbert, and McNeal 2008). The FCC survey introduced in chapter 3 includes questions about a number of activities online, allowing us to compare the types of activities performed on the Internet by mobile-only Internet users, other less-connected individuals, and those with home broadband. We analyze economic, political, educational, and health-related activities associated with digital citizenship, as well as the public policy objectives of the broadband plan. Table 4.1 (2009 FCC survey) compares activities online for the less-connected (Internet users without home broadband) and home broadband adopters. Frequencies are weighted and the sample is based on the 3,477 respondents who use the Internet.

Disparities in use of the Internet for broadband adopters and less-connected users are dramatic. Only 55% of Americans with slow or no home access use the Internet to get local or community news, compared with 80% of those with broadband at home, a 25% difference. Reading national and international news online reveals the same gap, with 52% of the less-connected doing so, compared with 77% of those with high-speed access at home. Of the less-connected, only 57% used e-government (state, local, or federal government websites) compared with 79% with broadband at home, a 22% difference. Thirty-five percent of Americans with slow access or no access at home used the Internet to get information from a government agency about health or safety, compared with 54% of Americans with broadband at home. While less common in general, 24% of those with broadband used the Internet to take a class for credit toward a degree, while only 12% of the less-connected did so—half the rate.

Reported economic activities online reveal an equally wide gap for the less-connected compared with those who have broadband at home. Sixty percent of home broadband adopters used the Internet to get information or apply for job, compared with only 45% of the less-connected group, a 15% difference. Seventy percent of Americans with broadband at home used online banking compared with only 35% of those with slow or no access at home, a dramatic 35% gap. This may be partly due to limited privacy or the difficulty in using encrypted logins required for financial information with public access. Online banking makes it possible for individuals to manage their finances in real time and can be a boon to consumers across different levels of income. These simple descriptive statistics show that broadband access at home matters and encourages the migration of daily economic, political, health, and educational activities online. The disparities shown in Table 4.2 illustrate the more limited capacity of the less-connected.

Table 4.2   **Technology Skills for the Less-Connected versus Home High-Speed Access (Percent)**

Skills	Less-Connected	Home Broadband	Difference Less-Connected
Very comfortable...using a computer.	45	70	−35
Very well...understand what spyware/malware are.	20	41	−21
Very well.....understand what an operating system is.	21	44	−23
Very well....understand what refresh or reload are.	37	62	−25
Very well....understand what a widget is.	5	17	−12
Very well....understand what a JPEG file is.	18	42	−14

Note: Reported frequencies are weighted. Sample based on the 3,477 respondents who use the Internet. 2009 Federal Communications Commission (FCC) Survey of 5,000 respondents nationwide. Less connected = dial-up Internet or no Internet at home, including individuals with mobile access only.

Individuals lacking broadband access at home report fewer skills to use the Internet effectively, a critical component of digital citizenship as discussed in the literature (Mossberger, Tolbert, and Stansbury 2003). The FCC survey included a self-reported measure of comfort with technology, as well as questions about Internet terms that have been correlated with demonstrated skill in previous research (Hargittai and Hsieh 2011).[2]

Table 4.2 indicates the less-connected are 35% less likely to say they are "very comfortable" using a computer and 23% less likely to say they understand "very well" what an operating system is. They are 25% less likely to understand how to refresh or reload a webpage, and they are less likely to know what a widget or JPEG file is, or to understand the dangers of computer viruses.

Conventional Wisdom: Mobile Access or Smartphones Will Close the Gap

The conventional wisdom in the mass media, and among some industry officials and policymakers is that the mobile phone Internet can remedy technology disparities, providing new forms of access to disadvantaged segments of the population. To some extent, this is occurring, especially with the proliferation of mobile applications. Wireless Internet via cell phones is increasingly common among Latinos, African Americans, and the young (Lenhart 2010; Smith 2010). But, a critical question is whether mobile access via smartphones can provide a substitute for a lack of home broadband Internet access. Absent from this debate are the data and statistical analyses needed to compare and contrast the online activities and capacity of individuals with home broadband versus access limited to mobile devices.

Appendix Table A4.3 draws on the 2009 FCC survey of 3,500 respondents that report using the Internet, to estimate seven logistic regression models (columns 1–7). The outcome variables are seven political and economic activities reported in Table A4.1.[3] If the respondents use the Internet for local news, for example, they are coded 1, and coded 0 for those that do not. The same coding is used for each of the activities. The primary explanatory variables are whether the individual has high-speed access at home (coded 1 for yes, and 0 for no) and whether the individuals connect to the Internet via a mobile phone with no access at home (coded 1 for yes, and 0 for no). We thus have two variables: one measuring mobile access (cell phones) only, and one measuring the highest level of connectivity. The statistical models control for the respondents' race/ethnicity, income, education, age, gender, marital status, parental status, employment, and geographic location, following the variables examined in the previous chapters.

The results show broadband access at home is statistically associated with an increased probability of engaging in each of the seven activities, including using the Internet for local and community news (column 1), using e-government websites (column 2), national and international news (column 3), getting information or applying for a job (column 4), getting government information about health care (column 5), using online banking (column 6), or taking a class online for credit (column 7), even after controlling for other demographic factors associated with being online.

Individuals with mobile access (cell phones) only are more likely to use the Internet than those with slow dial-up access to get local or community news; to search local, state, or federal government websites (e-government); and to obtain national or international news. These findings may reflect the impact of news formats (applications) for mobile phones, although the e-government results are interesting as well. To the extent that mobile-phone-only users are lower income, this may be tied to greater use of public services, including mass transit. But, those who rely on mobile phone access are not more likely to use the Internet to search for information about employment or to apply for a job, which are more data- and time-intensive activities. They are not more likely to use online banking, to use the Internet for government information on health care, or to take a class online. With a few exceptions, more demanding online activities are not fostered by Internet access via portable mobile phones.

Figure 4.10, for example, shows that individuals with broadband at home have a .70 probability of using online banking, holding all other demographic and economic factors constant, compared with mobile phone users with no high speed, who have a .46 probability of doing so. While more rare among the general population, Figure 4.11 indicates that individuals with home broadband have a .17 probability of taking a class online, compared with mobile phone Internet users, who have only a .08 probability of engaging in this activity. Individuals with broadband at home have a .78 probability of reading local news online, compared with those with mobile-phone-only Internet, who have a .69 probability of doing so (see Figure 4.9). Similar disparities and patterns are found for using government websites or reading national or international news online.

Despite the conventional wisdom that smartphones will erase technology disparities, we provide statistical evidence that the online capacity of smartphone users who do not have home high-speed access is limited.

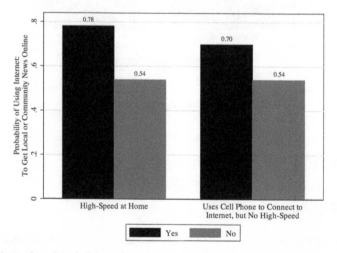

Figure 4.9 Predicted Probability of Reading Online News by Type of Access (from Appendix Table A4.3). Note: All other explanatory variables held constant at mean values.

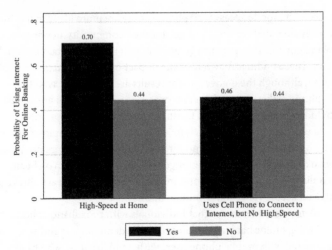

Figure 4.10 Predicted Probability of Using Online Banking by Type of Access (from Appendix Table A4.3). Note: All other explanatory variables held constant at mean values.

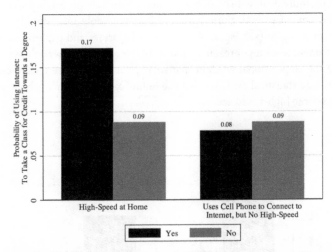

Figure 4.11 Predicted Probability of Taking an Online Course by Type of Access (from Appendix Table A4.3). Note: All other explanatory variables held constant at mean values.

The Capacity of Smartphone Users versus Home Broadband for Disadvantaged Subsamples

We conclude the empirical analysis for this chapter with what we consider the most important empirical evidence that Internet use via smartphones cannot close technology gaps, even for racial and ethnic minorities, or the poor who lack access is any other way. Table 4.3 displays the results for a subsample of African Americans in the 2009 FCC survey that answered the questions on use of the Internet for the seven political and economic activities (see Table 4.1). It compares the probability of engaging in each activity online for African Americans with home broadband (column 1) compared with blacks lacking home broadband (column 2). Column 3 reports the difference and a chi-square test of statistical significance using independent sample t-tests. The asterisks in the table indicate differences between the two groups (broadband at home versus without home broadband) that are statistically significant. That is, they could not occur just by chance. In comparison with those who lack such connections, African Americans with home broadband are more likely to engage in each of the seven human-capital-enhancing activities, such as reading online news or applying for a job online, and the differences are statistically significant. For example, African Americans with broadband at home are 19% more likely to search for information online about employment or to apply for a job than those without broadband, and they are 27% more likely to take a class for credit than African Americans without broadband. Education and employment are important for economic welfare. Thus home Internet access is statistically related to an increased probability of being an African American digital citizen.

Table 4.3 also compares the probability of engaging in these seven valuable online activities for those with mobile phone Internet only (column 4) compared with other African American Internet users who do not rely exclusively on mobile phone Internet (column 5) and the difference (column 6). The difference in the frequency of engaging in each activity is much smaller and none of the differences are statistically significant. Because we are only analyzing African American respondents, we have some empirical evidence that smartphones do not provide African Americans the same benefits for political and economic opportunity as home broadband.

Table 4.4 repeats this analysis, but for Latinos in the survey using the same format as the previous table for African Americans. Latinos with broadband at home are more likely to visit a local, state, or federal government website than Latinos without high-speed access at home. Latinos with broadband are 26% more likely to get information from a government agency, including heath care, and almost 30% more likely to use online banking than Latinos without high-speed access at home. These differences are statistically significant, as shown by the chi-square test.

However, Latinos with mobile phone Internet only are not more likely to engage in any of the seven economic and political activities than Latino Internet users without smartphones, similar to African Americans. Despite what appear to be differences in some activities online for mobile Internet users and other Internet users, the number of cases is small, and we cannot be confident that these gaps did not just occur by chance. For Latinos, the most disadvantaged of ethnic groups, broadband enables digital citizenship, but mobile wireless does not.

Finally, Table 4.5 presents these data for a subsample of survey respondents who earn incomes of $30,000 a year or less, what we define as the "poor." In every case, the poor with home broadband are more likely to read local, national, and international news online; to use government websites; apply for a job online; or take a class online than the poor without high-speed Internet at home. In each case the differences are statistically significant and range between 15 and 25 percentage points. However, columns

Table 4.3 **Online Activities for African Americans**

Uses the Internet:	High-Speed at Home			Internet Access on Cell Phone but No Home Broadband		
	Yes	No	Diff.	Yes	No	Diff.
To Get Local or Community News Online	84.54 (82)	64.44 (29)	20.1*	86.36 (19)	76.67 (92)	9.69
To Visit Local, State or Federal Government Website	77.32 (75)	60.00 (27)	17.32*	81.82 (18)	70.00 (84)	11.82
To Get National or International News	74.76 (77)	51.35 (19)	23.41*	66.67 (4)	68.66 (92)	–1.99
To Get Information or Apply for a Job	75.73 (78)	56.76 (21)	18.97*	100.00 (6)	69.40 (93)	30.6
To Get Information from a Government Agency	57.84 (59)	32.43 (12)	25.41*	66.67 (4)	50.38 (67)	16.29
For Online Banking	59.22 (61)	24.32 (9)	34.9*	33.33 (2)	50.75 (68)	–17.42
To Take a Class for Credit Toward a Degree	34.95 (36)	8.11 (3)	26.84*	0.00 (0)	29.10 (39)	–29.1

Note:* indicates the difference is significant at the .05 level. Numbers in parentheses indicate sample size.

Table 4.4 Online Activities for Latinos

Uses the Internet:	High-Speed at Home			Internet Access on Cell Phone, but No Home Broadband		
	Yes	No	Diff.	Yes	No	Diff.
To Get Local or Community News Online	80.68 (71)	64.71 (22)	15.97	71.43 (10)	76.85 (83)	–5.42
To Visit Local, State, or Federal Government Website	73.56 (64)	44.12 (15)	29.44*	64.29 (9)	65.42 (70)	–1.13
To Get National or International News	76.00 (57)	58.33 (21)	17.67	80.00 (8)	69.31 (70)	10.69
To Get Information or Apply for a Job	64.47 (49)	50.00 (18)	14.47	70.00 (7)	58.82 (60)	11.18
To Get Information from a Government Agency	53.95 (41)	28.57 (10)	25.38*	30.00 (3)	47.52 (48)	–17.52
For Online Banking	65.79 (50)	36.11 (13)	29.68*	50.00 (5)	56.86 (58)	–6.86
To Take a Class for Credit Toward a Degree	26.32 (20)	16.67 (6)	9.65	20.00 (2)	23.53 (24)	–3.53

Note: * indicates the difference is significant at the .05 level. Numbers in parentheses indicate sample size.

Table 4.5　Online Activities for Low-Income Households (Less than $30,000)

	High-Speed at Home			Internet Access on Cell Phone, but No Home Broadband		
Uses the Internet:	Yes	No	Diff.	Yes	No	Diff.
To Get Local or Community News Online	75.82 (207)	51.35 (95)	24.47*	71.79 (28)	65.23 (272)	6.56
To Visit Local, State or Federal Government Website	72.69 (197)	55.19 (101)	17.5*	76.32 (29)	64.73 (268)	11.59
To Get National or International News	70.15 (188)	45.90 (84)	24.25*	59.26 (16)	60.38 (256)	−1.12
To Get Information or Apply for a Job	56.88 (153)	40.98 (75)	15.9*	66.67 (18)	49.41 (210)	17.26
To Get Information from a Government Agency	42.38 (114)	30.22 (55)	12.16*	25.93 (7)	38.21 (162)	−12.28
For Online Banking	51.88 (138)	29.51 (54)	22.37*	33.33 (9)	43.36 (183)	−10.03
To Take a Class for Credit Towards a Degree	23.51 (63)	12.02 (22)	11.49*	11.11 (3)	19.34 (82)	−8.23

Note:　* indicates the difference is significant at the .05 level. Numbers in parentheses indicate sample size.

4–6 show that low-income Americans with Internet access only via smartphones are not more likely to engage in any of the seven activities than the poor without smartphones. None of the differences between the group that relies exclusively on smartphones for access and other Internet users are statistically significant. Thus any differences or gaps seen between the two groups may have occurred by chance.

The pattern across Tables 4.3–4.5 is unmistakable. In every case, broadband use by these subgroups—African Americans, Latinos, or the poor, respectively—leads to a higher probability of using the Internet for activities related to employment, jobs, and political engagement. But smartphone use by these same disadvantaged groups has no measurable effects. While we do not have experimental data, with treatment and control conditions, the survey data strongly suggests the benefits of broadband at home and questions the conventional wisdom that mobile or wireless Internet on cell phones can compensate for lack of home broadband access.

Conclusion: Mobile Access and Digital Inequality

The analysis in this chapter demonstrates a strong link between different levels of access and capabilities for digital citizenship, including skills and activities online. Despite popular conceptions about mobile access as a solution for the disadvantaged, there is little evidence to support these claims. For most, smartphones are a convenient supplement to other forms of Internet access. Their mobility and the evolution of new applications give them advantages for certain uses over other modes of Internet access, but they have not replaced PCs or laptops, as demonstrated by the data here. It is the combination of modes of access—what has elsewhere been called ubiquitous access—that has the most promise for the future. The mobile Internet, public access and support, and high-speed connections at home are together most likely to foster digital citizenship and the public benefits of information technology.

Those who are mobile-only users are, like other less-connected Internet users, more likely to be low-income, less-educated, African American, or Latino. Both mobile-only and other less-connected Internet users perform fewer activities online and they have less knowledge about the Internet. The final part of the analysis, examining subsamples of mobile-only Internet users by race, ethnicity, and income underscores the benefits of broadband at home for digital citizenship. Even among disadvantaged groups, mobile-only access does not confer equal access to the Internet, or enable the same activities online.

For mobile-only Internet users and other individuals who are less-connected, there may be some optimistic signs. All these forms of more limited access provide a gateway or a first step online. Mobile use is especially interesting in this regard. Some patterns of use—for news and e-government—are similar for smartphone-only and home broadband users. We do not know from the survey responses exactly how smartphone users are navigating government websites, and surely what they can do is more limited than on a laptop or desktop. But, smartphone users have somewhat slightly more diverse activities online than the rest of the less-connected. Will gaps narrow further, with improvements in smartphone applications? Mobile-only Internet users are also younger than other less-connected individuals (such as dial-up users), raising the possibility that smartphone users will gain fuller access in the future.

In the meantime, however, the less-connected continue to experience significant marginalization from society online. A recent report by the Social Science Research Council concluded that employment, education, and government services as the "strongest drivers by far" for broadband adoption, and the needs of many in low-income communities are "urgent" (Dailey et al. 2010, 15, 16), as "educational systems, employers, and government agencies at all levels have shifted services online—and are pushing rapidly to do more" (4). In the next chapter, we examine patterns of broadband connectivity and Internet use at the community level in cities and metropolitan areas. What does the geography of opportunity look like in the nation's major urban areas?

5

Ranking Digital Cities and Suburbs

While federal stimulus funds are supporting the mapping of broadband availability across the United States, little information *on broadband adoption or use* exists for geographies below the state level. A few cities have collected data on their own through surveys.[1] But, the reports issued by the NTIA contain only national or state-level data. Policymakers in many cities and regions have little information about technology use in their area. Moreover, there is often no way to draw firm comparisons across the cities that do have some data, because of variation in methods and questions in the surveys conducted by individual cities. Rankings by magazines have used proxies for Internet use, rather than direct measures of the percentage of the population online (Bushwick 2011).

This chapter presents estimates of broadband adoption and Internet use for each of the 50 largest metropolitan cities and their suburban areas in 2007 and 2009, comparing places by ranking the results. We know of no comparable data ranking Internet use for cities and suburban areas across the United States. We also examine technology use by race and ethnicity in each of the cities and their balance (suburban) areas and find that while gaps between these groups persist across places, minorities do substantially better in some cities and suburbs than others.

Chapter 3 demonstrated that, overall, a noticeable gap in technology use exists comparing cities and suburbs. Peeling off another layer of the geography of Internet use reveals variation across cities and metropolitan areas. By further disaggregating the data and ranking cities, we can provide important information for public policy. We can locate the cities and suburban regions that have the highest levels of technology adoption and use, as well as those that lag behind. We can also compare inequalities within regions, identifying where central city and suburban contrasts are greatest, and we rank outcomes for subsamples of African Americans and Latinos across cities and suburbs. There are several reasons to make such assessments.

Estimating Internet use at the metropolitan level is a measure of technology skills in the area labor market. Within cities and suburbs, technology use is an indicator of community capacity for many policy areas. Estimates of Internet use suggest the potential for local governments to modernize services and to improve transparency through digital government, or to pursue technologically advanced strategies in education, health care, transportation, or other domains. Disparities in technology use within and between regions follow more generally the landscape of inequality and increase challenges for fostering greater equity across policy areas.

Through rankings, we can encourage action. In an innovative book, Heather Gerken (2009) diagnoses failures in the election system and proposes a simple solution: a democracy index that would rate the performance of state and local election systems. A rough equivalent to the *U.S. News and World Report* ranking of colleges and universities or the Environmental Performance Index (EPI) of nations, the index would focus on problems that matter. The index works for the simple reason that no government wants to be at the bottom of the ranking. The index encourages change by quantifying performance, replacing anecdotes and rhetoric with hard data and verifiable outcomes. Rather than mandating policy change via regulation, ranking states, cities, or localities uses competition to stimulate policy change.

This competition is evident in popular technology indices, like the rankings for the 10 most tech-friendly cities or the top 10 for best Internet access, compiled by *Wired* and *Forbes* magazines, respectively. Noting that "not all of the above lists were created using conventional statistical or scientific methods, therefore their validity could be suspect," *Scientific American* blended these lists to rank overall technology performance (Bushwick 2011, 2). This places Seattle at the top, followed by Orlando, Florida, Washington, D.C., San Francisco, Atlanta, Boston, Los Angeles, New York City, and Minneapolis (Bushwick 2011). The rankings combine a number of criteria, including presence of information sector firms, Wi-Fi hot spots, and some murkier measures such as high-tech gadgetry and geek culture. We employ somewhat different measures, with more reliable data and rigorous methods, and find both similarities and differences from these popular lists.

We hope that these rankings contribute to public policy discourse and response. We highlight the cities with higher levels of technology access and those that lag behind. We are, of course, not rating performance per se—Internet use in cities and suburbs reflects complex social and economic dynamics, including the structure of the local economy, educational attainment, and poverty. But, policy actions matter too, and places with inequality may or may not prioritize change. Counting is a form of policy argument, according to Deborah Stone (2002). It provokes policy attention, defines issues, and mobilizes effort. Ranking cities and suburban areas allows local policymakers and residents to identify strengths to build on and problems to address. Additionally, it provides information for other levels of government about the relative distribution of need and how that affects the ability of local actors to devise solutions.

Preceding our presentation of the rankings, we discuss how place might matter for technology use within the metropolitan context and influences that may drive differences across cities and suburbs.

The Policy Ecology of Cities and Suburbs

Metropolitan areas include central cities and their balance areas, or suburbs. Scholars and policymakers alike increasingly refer to urban issues as being metropolitan in scope and call for city and suburban regional cooperation on public policy (Brookings Institution 2007; Pastor et al. 2000; Dreier, Mollenkopf, and Swanstrom 2004; Orfield 1997). There are two divergent tendencies affecting broadband policy on the metropolitan level—the regional scope for economic innovation and growth that unite the region on the one hand, and the political boundaries within metropolitan areas that divide them on the other, reinforcing social and economic inequalities. Metropolitan areas with the greatest gaps between cities and suburbs are least likely to flourish as a region, and so these inequalities affect the area as a whole (Pastor et al. 2000; Ledebur and Barnes 1998). In metropolitan regions as in broadband policy more generally, both innovation and inequality deserve policy attention.

Local economies and labor markets are metropolitan in scale, and so to understand the economic impacts of broadband, the regional lens is useful. Metropolitan areas, in fact, are defined by the U.S. Bureau of the Census based on commuting patterns for (Brookings Institution 2007, 30). Because of this interconnectedness, the Brookings Institution has defined metropolitan regions as "more than the sum of their parts" (ibid., 8) and the drivers of national prosperity. In a similar vein, others have argued that the U.S. economy resembles a "common market" composed of many regional economies that compete with each other and across the globe (Ledebur and Barnes 1998, cf. Pastor et al. 2000, 4). Innovation, infrastructure, and human capital are key determinants of metropolitan economic outcomes, according to the Brookings Institution (2007, 6). City and suburban levels of technology use, discussed in this chapter, affect the talent available within the regional workforce and metropolitan resources for economic development. Other policies are also regional in scope because they have spillover effects across jurisdictional boundaries or are implemented through special districts or intermunicipal cooperation. Technology use within regions has the potential to influence service delivery and outcomes in areas such as health, social services, emergency preparedness, environmental policy, and regional mass transit.

At the same time, these urban regions are fragmented into many different jurisdictions, often numbering into the hundreds within a single metropolitan area (Hendrick 2012). There is no metropolitan government that sets policy for most regions, and so policymaking depends on the separate and collective actions of municipalities and other local governments, such as counties and special districts.[2] Central cities are the largest municipalities within their regions, and they matter for outcomes in the region as a whole (Ledebur and Barnes 1998; Pastor et al. 2000). For these reasons, the metropolitan lens alone is inadequate to describe the policymaking environment. We rank the 50 largest central cities in terms of technology use, as well as their suburban areas, rather than metropolitan areas. Technology use may be affected by factors such as local labor markets that account for differences between metropolitan regions. Within metropolitan areas, differences in technology use may be influenced by the spatial distribution of needs and resources across local governments in the region, and the neighborhood effects of concentrated poverty and segregation within municipalities.

LABOR MARKETS AND TECHNOLOGY USE

The first level of variation we examine is across cities and suburbs, and technology use may be affected by regional economies. Metropolitan areas differ in the structure of their local economies, having diverse industries and occupations. The jobs available to residents provide both motivation for acquiring technology skills and resources for Internet use (such as on-the-job learning, as well as income sufficient for home broadband adoption). In places where many jobs require information technology use, even at basic levels, there should be higher incentives to acquire the needed skills. The presence of the information technology industry in a locale may attract or develop a tech-savvy population. Technology use spans a number of occupations and sectors of the economy, beyond the information industry. Employment in some service sectors, especially finance, education, and healthcare, is positively related to broadband deployment across states, which could be defined as a rough proxy measure of demand for use within these industries (Crandall, Lehr, and Litan 2007). Metropolitan areas with larger populations and more educated residents are likely to be places where technology is used more intensively (Forman et al. 2005, 2008).

INEQUALITIES WITHIN METROPOLITAN REGIONS: NEED AND FISCAL CAPACITY

The *distribution* of need within regions has important implications for the resources available to their populations for technology use. The fragmented institutional context of metropolitan areas means that local governments are a major source of funding for many of the programs that can promote technology use, such as K–12 schools, community colleges, senior programs, public housing, and libraries. Local governments in the United States are also highly dependent on their tax bases and local revenues (Wolman 2012). As a result, there are significant disparities in local fiscal capacity to support public institutions that address digital inclusion. Municipalities with high poverty rates and greater need for public access and training usually have the least ability to raise revenues because of lower property values and insufficient sources of revenue, such as income and sales taxes. To the extent that the poor cluster within central cities (and other municipalities such as poor suburbs), there is a dichotomy between local needs and resources (Hendrick 2012, ch. 1; Dreier, Mollenkopf, and Swanstrom 2004). In recent years, higher income individuals have also become more geographically segregated from the poor within metropolitan areas, affecting tax support for services for poor residents (Reardon and Bischoff 2011); income segregation coupled with metropolitan fragmentation widens the gap between needs and resources. Thus, poor cities get poorer and wealthier cities get richer. The extent of metropolitan fragmentation varies across states and regions, with the older metropolitan areas of the Northeast and Midwest tending toward more fragmentation (Rusk 1995) and greater levels of income inequality (Swanstrom et al. 2004).

Despite the greater suburbanization of poverty in recent years (Kneebone 2011; Allard and Roth 2010), central city poverty rates are still nearly double those in suburban communities. In 2009, the poverty rate was 19.5% for central cities, compared with 10.4% for the suburbs (Kneebone 2011). In general, minority households continue to be overrepresented in the low-income population (Brookings Institution 2007, p. 134). Among the 50 largest metro areas (which we examine here), only a little over one-third (or 18) had central cities with majority white populations in 2010 (Frey 2011).

SEGREGATION AND CONCENTRATED POVERTY IN TECHNOLOGY USE

Within metropolitan areas, segregation and concentrated poverty create environments that limit opportunity, including technology use. Decades after the Fair Housing Act, progress in racial integration has been steady but also slow, especially for African Americans (Logan and Stults 2011). Latinos experience less segregation than African Americans, but the growth of Latino immigration has led to higher levels of segregation in places with larger Latino populations in recent years (Logan and Stults 2011; Lewis and Hamilton 2011). According to recent research, residential segregation in metropolitan areas affects technology access, with detrimental effects for Latinos (Fong and Cao 2008).

"Neighborhood effects" in areas with many poor residents (Wilson 1987 and 1996; Jargowsky 1997) may magnify the challenges that individuals face in acquiring regular Internet access and skills. Environments of concentrated poverty are characterized by higher levels of crime, drug use, single-parent families, and school dropout rates (Wilson 1987; Jargowsky 1997). But, why would they matter for technology use? Possible place-based influences include lack of knowledge about technology in localized social networks, lack of exposure to Internet use on the job because of neighborhood effects on employment, unequal educational opportunities in schools, and the higher costs of goods and services in such neighborhoods. We will examine these possible explanations in chapter 8, when we explore the influence of neighborhood characteristics on barriers to Internet use. Previous research indicates the need to examine neighborhood differences within cities, and the chapters on Chicago (chapters 6, 8, and 9) offer a unique view of place effects and the potential for community-based solutions.

Racial segregation and concentrated poverty are highly correlated (Jargowsky 1997; Massey and Denton 1993). Segregation of minorities (whether African American, Latino, or Asian American) is higher when these groups represent a larger share of the population. It is more prevalent in larger cities and metropolitan areas. Older cities in the Northeast and Midwest are among those that are most segregated and have the most concentrated poverty, although there has been some growth in both trends in the West (Lewis and Hamilton 2011; Jargowsky 1997, 46–48; Jargowsky 2003). Some metropolitan areas and/or cities have developed immigrant gateway neighborhoods that are also very poor (Federal Reserve and Brookings Institution 2008). Given the previous findings on Spanish-speaking Latinos, areas with a large percentage of Latino immigrants may be particularly disadvantaged in Internet use. Concentrations of poverty are emerging in some suburban communities (Federal Reserve and Brookings Institution 2008; Allard and Roth 2010), and where clusters of poverty involve a greater proportion of the suburban population, this may introduce some variation in technology use across metropolitan areas.

Data and Methods

In this chapter we build on the multivariate models of high-speed Internet use at home and Internet use at any location using the 2009 CPS Internet Use Supplement presented in chapter 3. The digital cities ranking is replicated using the 2007 CPS to show how much change in use (if any) is experienced in the cities over a two-year period (2007 to 2009). Estimates are produced for both central cities and their suburbs (MSA balance areas), which allow us to rank Internet use and broadband access by both of these geographic designations.

The first step in creating the digital cities ranking is to identify the cities to be analyzed. We focus on the 50 largest U.S. metropolitan areas, highlighting variation in Internet use (1) across large central cities, (2) between central cities and suburbs, and (3) between the suburban areas of these particular metropolitan regions. In addition to the overall estimates and rankings for cities and suburbs, we replicate these by race and ethnicity across places. All rankings compare rates of home broadband adoption, as emphasized by federal policy, and Internet use anywhere, to include the less-connected. Population data for the 50 largest MSAs were obtained from the U.S. Census to select the sample and to create the city and suburban rankings by merging census data with the CPS. Even with the large sample size provided by the CPS data it would be difficult to conduct rigorous statistical analyses for places smaller than the 50 most populous regions given small sample sizes for these places in the CPS. Similarly, small subsample sizes also prevent an analysis of the rural residents outside the metropolitan areas we examine.

We rank the U.S. cities by first estimating broadband use at home and Internet use anywhere for only those individuals residing in central cities and again for only respondents in suburban areas. This is similar to the subsample models discussed in chapter 3, in that these models only include respondents from the 50 largest MSAs from the CPS sample, omitting rural residents. In contrast to chapter 3, here we use multilevel statistical models that include both individual-level survey data from the CPS and aggregate-level variables to control for demographic and economic factors unique to each region. The central-city-level aggregate data was obtained from the American Community Survey (three-year estimates 2007–2009), and the *State and Metropolitan Area Data Book* for the suburban area model estimates.[3] Aggregate-level variables in the statistical models include population size, per capita income, and the percent of the MSA or central city that is African American, Latino, educated with a high school diploma, over 65 years of age, and employed in the information sector (see appendix B for the variable coding).[4]

To create the digital cities ranking, a multilevel logistic regression with random intercepts is used (see Appendix Tables A5.1–A5.3). This approach to modeling the data allows us to predict separate probability estimates of Internet use for each central city and its suburbs. We specifically model Internet use for individual respondents using logistic regression but also "nest" individuals within their respective MSA or central city. The constant term for each MSA or central city is allowed to vary, which provides an estimate of how different Internet use is, on average, for each city or suburban area. Since a variety of aggregate-level factors are being controlled for (see above), any variance in Internet use that is found is due to characteristics specific to that area (urban or suburban). City rankings are produced by estimating the probability of using the Internet for the average resident of each central city and its suburbs, with all individual-level covariates held constant at average values. Additionally, the likelihood of Internet use for each city and its suburbs is calculated separately for whites (non-Hispanics), African Americans, and Latinos.

Appendix Table A5.1 shows the multilevel regression models predicting the probability of using the Internet anywhere (column 1); having Internet connectivity at home, slow or high-speed Internet (column 2); and having high-speed Internet at home (column 3) for residents of America's 50 largest central cities in 2009. The models in columns 1 and 3 are the most important and are used to rank the cities.

Results: Digital Cities Ranking of Central Cities

BROADBAND AT HOME

Table 5.1 ranks the 50 largest central cities in terms of the estimated percent of the city population with high-speed Internet at home, and Table 5.2 ranks the cities based on the estimated percent of the population that uses the Internet at any location, including public access. The first column, entitled "Average Use," is based on a simple frequency of respondents in the 2009 CPS aggregated to the city level and should be used for a comparison only. This figure includes no statistical controls for either individual attributes or city-level economic and social characteristics. The second column entitled "Probability of Use" is the estimated percent of the population online based on the multilevel statistical models reported in Appendix Table A5.1. The ranking of the top 50 central cities is in parentheses. The third, fourth, and fifth columns report the estimated probability of high-speed access for white non-Hispanics, African Americans, and Latinos, respectively, showing disparities in access based on race and ethnicity within cities and across cities. The final column reports the sample size for each city. The same format is used for every ranking table presented in this chapter. Notably, with a few exceptions, most cities have a sample of at least 100 respondents. Many large cities have samples well over 500, including Chicago with 800 respondents and Los Angeles with 1,204 respondents. Where possible, estimates of Internet use are based on the largest city within a principal city area, but in a few cases the largest city within each area could not be identified and the principal city area is used instead.

Seattle is ranked the highest in the nation in terms of the overall percent of its population with broadband Internet at home (83%). Seattle is followed by the Portland, OR area, San Francisco, and San Jose, which all tied for second place with 80% of the population having broadband at home. The top 10 digital cities are rounded out by Virginia Beach ranked fifth, Boston and San Diego tied for sixth, and the Austin area, Phoenix, and Jacksonville, FL tied for tenth. In some ways these rankings are not surprising, given the extensive information technology employment sector in many of these cities, including Microsoft Corporation in Seattle and Silicon Valley in Northern California. But our interviews in chapter 2 indicate that the rankings also reflect policy innovation on the part of some cities to take a leadership role in technology use and inclusion.

Table 5.1 also notes the cities lagging behind, some of which have high minority populations. They include a few surprises, including technology-savvy Denver, ranked 39th, just shy of the bottom 10. Tied for 40th are Houston, Las Vegas, Louisville MSA, and Philadelphia. This is despite the fact that Philadelphia has been an innovator in being one of the only cities to attempt to create a free, citywide Wi-Fi network, as discussed in chapter 2. Los Angeles ranks 44th, followed by Miami and the Cleveland area at 46th and 47th. Tied for 48th, second to last, are Rochester, NY and San Antonio. Ranked last is Buffalo. The estimated percent of the population with broadband at home in these cities ranges from a high of 53% for those ranked 40, to a low of 39% in Buffalo. This latter score is literally half that of first-ranked Seattle. Thus, the range in the probability of broadband at home across America's 50 largest cities is very large.

Table 5.1 Central City Rankings, Uses High-Speed Internet At Home (2009 CPS)

City	Average Use Percent (Rank)	*Predicted Probability of Use Prob. (Rank)	Probability of Use by Race White	Black	Latino	N
Seattle, WA	76% (2)	0.83 (1)	0.85	0.74	0.68	309
Portland-Vancouver-Beaverton, OR-WA	75% (4)	0.80 (2)	0.82	0.70	0.63	380
San Francisco, CA	73% (6)	0.80 (2)	0.85	0.74	0.68	335
San Jose, CA	76% (2)	0.80 (2)	0.86	0.75	0.69	251
Virginia Beach, VA	78% (1)	0.79 (5)	0.83	0.71	0.64	123
Boston, MA	75% (4)	0.78 (6)	0.83	0.70	0.64	350
San Diego, CA	73% (6)	0.78 (6)	0.83	0.71	0.65	367
Austin-Round Rock, TX	68% (10)	0.76 (8)	0.82	0.70	0.63	239
Phoenix, AZ	70% (8)	0.74 (9)	0.80	0.66	0.59	368
Jacksonville, FL	69% (9)	0.73 (10)	0.78	0.63	0.56	192
Raleigh-Cary, NC	66% (12)	0.73 (10)	0.79	0.65	0.58	155
Washington-Arlington-Alexandria, DC-VA-MD-WV	64% (17)	0.73 (10)	0.80	0.66	0.60	1933
Salt Lake City, UT	66% (12)	0.72 (13)	0.74	0.59	0.51	98
Atlanta, GA	66% (12)	0.71 (14)	0.78	0.64	0.57	201

City	Average Use		*Predicted Probability of Use		Probability of Use by Race			N
	Percent (Rank)		Prob. (Rank)		White	Black	Latino	
Minneapolis, MN	65%	(15)	0.71	(14)	0.74	0.59	0.52	492
Nashville-Davidson-Murfreesboro, TN	64%	(17)	0.70	(16)	0.76	0.61	0.54	182
Orlando-Kissimee, FL	68%	(10)	0.70	(16)	0.78	0.64	0.57	72
Pittsburgh, PA	63%	(19)	0.70	(16)	0.73	0.57	0.50	97
Sacramento, CA	65%	(15)	0.69	(19)	0.78	0.63	0.56	203
Tampa-St. Petersburg-Clearwater, FL	63%	(19)	0.67	(20)	0.73	0.57	0.50	196
Columbus, OH	60%	(24)	0.65	(21)	0.70	0.54	0.47	189
Milwaukee, WI	61%	(22)	0.65	(21)	0.72	0.57	0.49	293
Providence, RI	61%	(22)	0.64	(23)	0.70	0.53	0.46	676
Riverside, CA	60%	(24)	0.63	(24)	0.73	0.58	0.50	176
St. Louis, MO-IL	62%	(21)	0.62	(25)	0.70	0.54	0.47	128
Indianapolis-Carmel, IN	57%	(26)	0.61	(26)	0.67	0.50	0.43	218
Charlotte, NC	56%	(29)	0.60	(27)	0.68	0.52	0.45	238

(continued)

Table 5.1   (continued)

City	Average Use		*Predicted Probability of Use		Probability of Use by Race			N
	Percent (Rank)		Prob. (Rank)		White	Black	Latino	
Hartford, CT	57%	(26)	0.60	(27)	0.68	0.52	0.44	190
Kansas City, MO-KS	56%	(29)	0.59	(29)	0.67	0.50	0.43	224
Birmingham-Hoover, AL	57%	(26)	0.58	(30)	0.70	0.53	0.46	81
Dallas, TX	56%	(29)	0.58	(30)	0.70	0.54	0.46	349
Richmond, VA	47%	(46)	0.58	(30)	0.67	0.50	0.43	76
Memphis, TN-MS-AR	55%	(32)	0.57	(33)	0.68	0.51	0.44	185
Oklahoma City, OK	53%	(36)	0.57	(33)	0.63	0.46	0.39	206
Chicago, IL	53%	(36)	0.56	(35)	0.66	0.49	0.42	841
Cincinnati-Middletown, OH-KY-IN	51%	(38)	0.56	(35)	0.65	0.48	0.40	93
New York, NY	54%	(33)	0.56	(35)	0.67	0.51	0.43	2291
Baltimore-Towson, MD	54%	(33)	0.55	(38)	0.66	0.49	0.42	321
Denver, CO	50%	(41)	0.54	(39)	0.64	0.47	0.40	472
Houston, TX	50%	(41)	0.53	(40)	0.66	0.49	0.42	584

City	Average Use Percent (Rank)	*Predicted Probability of Use Prob. (Rank)	Probability of Use by Race White	Black	Latino	N
Las Vegas, NV	50% (41)	0.53 (40)	0.62	0.44	0.37	359
Louisville-Jefferson County, KY-IN	51% (38)	0.53 (40)	0.58	0.41	0.34	97
Philadelphia-Camden-Wilmington, PA-NJ-DE-MD	54% (33)	0.53 (40)	0.63	0.46	0.39	387
Los Angeles, CA	49% (44)	0.49 (44)	0.63	0.46	0.39	1204
Miami, FL	51% (38)	0.48 (45)	0.63	0.46	0.38	202
Detroit, MI	48% (45)	0.47 (46)	0.60	0.43	0.36	339
Cleveland-Elyria-Mentor, OH	46% (47)	0.44 (47)	0.54	0.37	0.30	126
Rochester, NY	39% (49)	0.43 (48)	0.53	0.36	0.30	58
San Antonio, TX	44% (48)	0.43 (48)	0.59	0.42	0.35	324
Buffalo, NY	38% (50)	0.39 (50)	0.44	0.28	0.23	131

Note: For each of the 50 metropolitan areas, the probability of using the Internet is based on responses from only those living in the largest city within a metropolitan area when identification of the largest city is possible. For some areas, the CPS does not provide information that identifies each city within a designated principal city area. In these cases, the principal city area, which may include multiple cities, was used to estimate the probability of Internet use. The ranking entries with multiple cities listed are those that did not have identifying information for each individual city.

*Probabilities estimated from random intercept model reported in Appendix Table A5.1, column 3.

Comparing these Internet use rankings with the *Scientific American* list shows that digital inclusion does not necessarily occur in cities with high-tech gadgets and geek culture. Seattle and San Francisco top both rankings, but other cities that placed high in the magazine list, such as Los Angeles, are low in terms of Internet use by the population. Los Angeles and other low-ranking Internet use cities have substantial minority populations, and we explore this issue further, with interesting results.

OUTCOMES BY RACE AND ETHNICITY ACROSS CITIES

We create rankings for the probability of having broadband at home for each city in terms of the African American population (column 4) and Latino population (column 5), compared with the white non-Hispanic population (column 3). African Americans have the highest probability of having high-speed Internet at home in San Jose (75%), followed by Seattle and San Francisco (74%). In general, cities with more of the population online tend to produce better outcomes for racial and ethnic minorities. In all the cities ranked in the top 10 for overall broadband access, African Americans do fairly well, with broadband access rates ranging from 66–75%. However, they lag behind whites by roughly 10 percentage points. Likewise, Latinos have the highest probability of home broadband in San Jose (69%), with average access rates when residing in the top 10 cities ranging from 60–69%, noticeably lower than their African American counterparts. Cities with a general climate of technology use encourage higher rates of minority adoption as well.

The range in terms of access rates for minorities is large. In Denver, we estimate only 40% of Latinos and 47% of African Americans have high speed Internet at home, compared with 64% of whites. Latinos in San Antonio have just a one in three chance of having broadband at home, with four in ten African Americans having home broadband in the city. The former manufacturing centers of the Midwest fare poorly, with an estimated 37% of blacks and a dismal 30% of Latinos with home broadband in the Cleveland area. Estimates are comparable for Detroit. In Los Angeles, home to one of the numerically largest minority populations in the United States, 39% of Latinos and 46% of African Americans have home broadband, compared with 63% of white non-Hispanics.[5] Across central cities, Latinos and African Americans lag considerably behind white non-Hispanics in broadband access. But what about usage rates at any location, including public access?

INTERNET USE AT ANY LOCATION

Table 5.2 ranks the 50 largest cities by the percent of the population that reports using the Internet at any location. Again, "average use" (column 1) is merely the percent of the citywide sample saying yes to this question and should be used as a baseline comparison only. Column 2 provides the probability of using the Internet in any location based on the multilevel statistical model found in Appendix Table A5.2, with rankings again noted in parentheses. For Internet use at any location, San Francisco ranks number one in the nation, with an estimated 87% of its population using the Internet, followed by Seattle (ranked second), and the Portland, OR area ranked third, San Jose ranked fourth, and Boston ranked fifth. Jacksonville, FL and San Diego are tied for seventh (with 80%

of their populations online), and the Austin, TX area, Raleigh, NC, and the Washington, D.C. area are tied for ninth place. With just two exceptions, the top 10 cities in terms of Internet use at any location are the same for home broadband access. These are America's leading digital cities.

The lowest-ranked central cities for Internet use at any location also overlap with the broadband ranking. Tied for 40th are Denver, Houston, and the Philadelphia area with only 57% of their population online. Ranked 43rd is Los Angeles with 56% of residents online. The Louisville area is ranked 45th, followed by Detroit (46), the Cleveland area (47), Rochester (48), and San Antonio (49). Again, Buffalo ranks last with an estimated 41% of its population using the Internet at any location.

Table 5.2 also ranks the cities by Internet use at any location for white non-Hispanics, African Americans, and Latinos. Internet use rates range from a high of 78% for Latinos and 83% for African Americans in San Francisco to lows of 24% for Latinos and 31% for African Americans in Buffalo, a 50-plus point difference between cities ranked at the top and bottom. Results range across the continuum from these high and low estimates with 68% of African Americans using the Internet in Atlanta, to 58% in Chicago. Latino Internet use rates range from 44% in Miami to 36% in San Antonio to 46% in Los Angeles, well behind African Americans. We argue it is important to not only consider overall or average rankings in terms of Internet use but also disparities in access for disadvantaged groups across cities.

Results: Digital Cities Ranking of Suburbs

BROADBAND AT HOME

Table 5.3 ranks the nation's 50 largest suburban regions (or MSA balance areas) based on the probability of high-speed Internet use at home, and Table 5.4 does the same for these suburbs based on Internet use at any location. Estimates in both tables are calculated from the multilevel logistic regression models found in Appendix Table A5.2. The format is identical to the previous tables ranking the central cities. For the top 10 ranked suburbs, broadband access rates are comparable to the central cities. Five suburban areas are ranked number one, with an estimated 80% of their population having high-speed Internet at home: Boston, Denver, Milwaukee, Seattle, and the Washington, D.C. area. Five additional suburban areas are tied for sixth place in terms of broadband use, including, the suburbs of Austin, Kansas City, MO, Minneapolis, Rochester, NY, and Salt Lake City. With the inter-city collaboration around Google Fiber in both Kansas Citys, broadband use may increase in both cities and suburbs in the future—but it is already relatively high in the suburbs. Finally, four suburban areas are tied for 11th place, including New York City, Philadelphia, Phoenix, and San Francisco.

Several places have strikingly divergent findings for their cities and suburbs. The official government census reports only distinguish between metropolitan and nonmetropolitan areas, but we separate central cities and their suburbs to provide a clearer picture of the geography of technology access and use. Denver and Milwaukee ranked relatively low in terms of access rates for the central city, and Rochester was ranked at the very bottom; yet these cities have highly connected suburbs ranked in the top 10. Possible

Table 5.2 Central City Rankings, Uses Internet Anywhere (2009 CPS)

City	Average Use Percent (Rank)		*Predicted Probability of Use Prob. (Rank)		Probability of Use by Race				
					White	Black	Latino	N	
San Francisco, CA	83%	(5)	0.87	(1)	0.91	0.83	0.78	335
Seattle, WA	86%	(2)	0.86	(2)	0.88	0.79	0.73	309
Portland-Vancouver-Beaverton, OR-WA	84%	(4)	0.85	(3)	0.87	0.77	0.71	380
San Jose, CA	81%	(6)	0.83	(4)	0.89	0.80	0.74	251
Boston, MA	80%	(7)	0.82	(5)	0.86	0.76	0.69	350
Virginia Beach, VA	79%	(8)	0.81	(6)	0.85	0.74	0.67	123
Jacksonville, FL	88%	(1)	0.80	(7)	0.83	0.72	0.65	192
San Diego, CA	78%	(10)	0.80	(7)	0.86	0.75	0.68	367
Austin-Round Rock, TX	71%	(22)	0.79	(9)	0.85	0.74	0.67	239
Raleigh-Cary, NC	78%	(10)	0.79	(9)	0.84	0.73	0.66	155
Washington-Arlington-Alexandria, DC-VA-MD-WV	73%	(18)	0.79	(9)	0.85	0.74	0.67	1933
Nashville-Davidson-Murfreesboro, TN	78%	(10)	0.76	(12)	0.81	0.69	0.61	182

City	Average Use		*Predicted Probability of Use		Probability of Use by Race			N
	Percent (Rank)		Prob. (Rank)		White	Black	Latino	
Phoenix, AZ	75%	(14)	0.76	(12)	0.82	0.70	0.62	368
Minneapolis, MN	79%	(8)	0.75	(14)	0.78	0.65	0.57	492
Pittsburgh, PA	73%	(18)	0.75	(14)	0.78	0.64	0.56	97
Sacramento, CA	75%	(14)	0.75	(14)	0.83	0.72	0.64	203
Atlanta, GA	71%	(22)	0.74	(17)	0.80	0.68	0.60	201
Salt Lake City, UT	76%	(13)	0.74	(17)	0.76	0.62	0.53	98
Birmingham-Hoover, AL	85%	(3)	0.73	(19)	0.82	0.70	0.62	81
Orlando-Kissimee, FL	74%	(17)	0.73	(19)	0.81	0.69	0.61	72
Tampa-St. Petersburg-Clearwater, FL	72%	(20)	0.71	(21)	0.76	0.62	0.54	196
Milwaukee, WI	75%	(14)	0.70	(22)	0.77	0.63	0.55	293
Columbus, OH	72%	(20)	0.68	(23)	0.73	0.58	0.49	189
Charlotte, NC	70%	(26)	0.66	(24)	0.73	0.59	0.50	238
Providence, RI	66%	(31)	0.66	(24)	0.72	0.57	0.48	676
St. Louis, MO-IL	71%	(22)	0.66	(24)	0.73	0.58	0.50	128

(continued)

Table 5.2 (continued)

City	Average Use		*Predicted Probability of Use		Probability of Use by Race			
	Percent (Rank)		Prob. (Rank)		White	Black	Latino	N
Chicago, IL	68%	(28)	0.64	(27)	0.73	0.58	0.49	841
Hartford, CT	64%	(35)	0.64	(27)	0.73	0.58	0.49	190
Indianapolis-Carmel, IN	71%	(22)	0.64	(27)	0.70	0.54	0.46	218
Riverside, CA	65%	(33)	0.64	(27)	0.75	0.61	0.52	176
Oklahoma City, OK	70%	(26)	0.63	(31)	0.68	0.52	0.44	206
Kansas City, MO-KS	67%	(30)	0.62	(32)	0.70	0.54	0.46	224
New York, NY	60%	(43)	0.62	(32)	0.73	0.58	0.50	2291
Memphis, TN-MS-AR	65%	(33)	0.61	(34)	0.71	0.56	0.47	185
Richmond, VA	58%	(47)	0.61	(34)	0.70	0.55	0.46	76
Baltimore-Towson, MD	64%	(35)	0.59	(36)	0.70	0.54	0.45	321
Cincinnati-Middletown, OH-KY-IN	68%	(28)	0.59	(36)	0.67	0.51	0.43	93
Dallas, TX	63%	(37)	0.59	(36)	0.71	0.56	0.47	349
Las Vegas, NV	60%	(43)	0.59	(36)	0.67	0.51	0.43	359

City	Average Use		*Predicted Probability of Use		Probability of Use by Race			N
	Percent (Rank)		Prob. (Rank)		White	Black	Latino	
Denver, CO	61%	(39)	0.57	(40)	0.67	0.51	0.42	472
Houston, TX	59%	(46)	0.57	(40)	0.70	0.55	0.46	584
Philadelphia-Camden-Wilmington, PA-NJ-DE-MD	61%	(39)	0.57	(40)	0.67	0.51	0.42	387
Los Angeles, CA	60%	(43)	0.56	(43)	0.70	0.54	0.46	1204
Louisville-Jefferson County, KY-IN	61%	(39)	0.55	(44)	0.60	0.44	0.36	97
Miami, FL	55%	(48)	0.54	(45)	0.68	0.52	0.44	202
Detroit, MI	61%	(39)	0.51	(46)	0.63	0.47	0.38	339
Cleveland-Elyria-Mentor, OH	63%	(37)	0.48	(47)	0.59	0.42	0.34	126
Rochester, NY	66%	(31)	0.47	(48)	0.57	0.41	0.33	58
San Antonio, TX	49%	(50)	0.44	(49)	0.61	0.45	0.36	324
Buffalo, NY	51%	(49)	0.41	(50)	0.47	0.31	0.24	131

Note: For each of the 50 metropolitan areas, the probability of using the Internet is based on responses from only those living in the largest city within a metropolitan area when identification of the largest city is possible. For some areas, the CPS does not provide information that identifies each city within a designated principal city area. In these cases, the principal city area, which may include multiple cities, was used to estimate the probability of Internet use. The ranking entries with multiple cities listed are those that did not have identifying information for each individual city.

* *Probabilities estimated from random intercept model reported in Appendix Table AS.1, column 1.*

explanations for these differences may be greater inequalities in income or metropolitan segregation. In fact, the Milwaukee metropolitan area has the highest level of black-white segregation in the country, according to recent data covering 2005–2009 (Frey 2010).

Suburban areas with the lowest percentage of the population with broadband Internet at home include Los Angeles, Miami, and Oklahoma City (tied for 39th), Houston (42nd), Memphis, and Nashville, tied for 43rd, Louisville (45th), Virginia Beach, (46th), Richmond and Riverside (tied for 47th), San Antonio (again 49th), and Birmingham ranked last (50th). The probability of adoption of broadband at home ranges from 66% to a low of 46%. Notably, all suburbs ranked near the bottom are in the traditional South, with two exceptions in the Southwest. This may reflect cost and affordability concerns, as average incomes tend to be lower in the South. Also, some of these low-ranking suburban areas have large percentages of Latinos, especially foreign-born individuals (Frey 2010).

Visualization permits us to recognize patterns in additional ways. We present maps that categorize cities and suburban regions in terms of broadband use at home. Home broadband adoption represents the highest level of technology access in our measures and is also the target of current policy. The city map in Figure 5.1 and suburban map in Figure 5.2 illustrate this discussion, with some differences in the rankings for cities and suburbs. The maps also indicate some regional patterns, with lower rates of Internet use especially in the Midwest and South.

RACE AND ETHNICITY ACROSS SUBURBS

Minorities living in America's suburbs have considerably higher rates of high-speed Internet at home than minorities living in cities, but African Americans still lag behind whites by roughly 10 percentage points and Latinos by 20 percentage points. African Americans living in the suburbs generally do worse for connectivity in Southern cities and tend to do relatively better when living in other regions of the country. The probability of African Americans using broadband at home ranges from a high of 76% in the Washington, D.C. area to a low of 35% in the Birmingham area; a 40% difference based on geographic location, and almost double the difference for the population as a whole from the most to least connected suburbs. While federal government policy has focused on technology disparities in rural areas, there are vast inequalities in technology use in cities and suburban areas.

SUBURBAN INTERNET USE AT ANY LOCATION

Table 5.4 ranks the 50 largest suburban areas by the probability of Internet use at any location (column 2). Salt Lake City ranks first in the nation with 91% of the population online and Denver and Minneapolis tied for second place at 90% (again, notable since Denver central city ranks so low on this same measure of technology use). Three suburban areas are tied for third place with 89% online: San Francisco, Seattle, and Washington, D.C. Four suburban areas are tied for seventh—Milwaukee, Portland, Rochester, and San Jose. These suburban areas tend to be in the West or Midwest. Tied for 11th

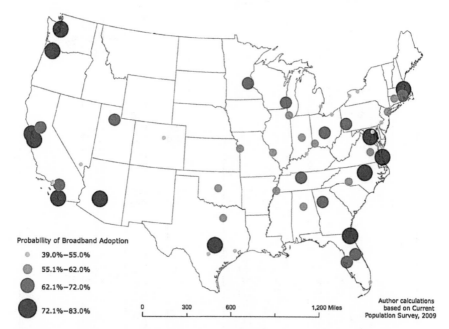

Figure 5.1 Probability of Broadband Adoption for Central Cities in the United States, 2009. Note: Probabilities estimated from random intercept model reported in Appendix Table A5.1, column 3.

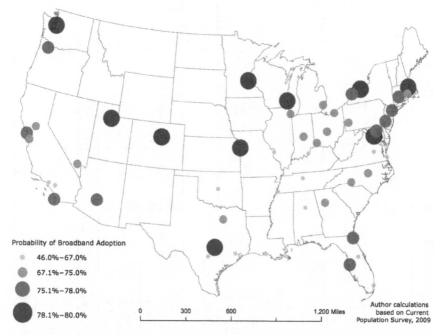

Figure 5.2 Probability of Broadband Adoption for Suburban Areas in the United States, 2009. Note: Probabilities estimated from random intercept model reported in Appendix Table A5.2, column 3.

Table 5.3 **Suburban Rankings, Uses High-Speed Internet At Home (2009 CPS)**

City	Average Use Percent (Rank)		*Predicted Probability of Use Prob. (Rank)		Probability of Use by Race White	Black	Latino	N
Boston, MA	72%	(13)	0.80	(1)	0.82	0.71	0.64	1537
Denver, CO	75%	(1)	0.80	(1)	0.82	0.73	0.66	736
Milwaukee, WI	74%	(3)	0.80	(1)	0.80	0.69	0.62	298
Seattle, WA	74%	(3)	0.80	(1)	0.82	0.72	0.65	738
Washington-Arlington-Alexandria, DC-VA-MD-WV	74%	(3)	0.80	(1)	0.85	0.76	0.69	1702
Austin-Round Rock, TX	74%	(3)	0.79	(6)	0.83	0.73	0.66	192
Kansas City, MO-KS	73%	(8)	0.79	(6)	0.80	0.69	0.62	597
Minneapolis, MN	74%	(3)	0.79	(6)	0.80	0.70	0.62	1102
Rochester, NY	73%	(8)	0.79	(6)	0.80	0.69	0.61	259
Salt Lake City, UT	73%	(8)	0.79	(6)	0.80	0.69	0.62	403
New York, NY	72%	(13)	0.78	(11)	0.81	0.71	0.64	2738
Philadelphia-Camden-Wilmington, PA-NJ-DE-MD	73%	(8)	0.78	(11)	0.80	0.70	0.62	2090

City	Average Use		*Predicted Probability of Use		Probability of Use by Race			N
	Percent (Rank)		Prob. (Rank)		White	Black	Latino	
Phoenix, AZ	72%	(13)	0.78	(11)	0.81	0.71	0.63	608
San Francisco, CA	72%	(13)	0.78	(11)	0.83	0.74	0.67	851
Baltimore-Towson, MD	71%	(20)	0.77	(15)	0.80	0.69	0.62	1026
Hartford, CT	71%	(20)	0.77	(15)	0.78	0.67	0.59	694
Jacksonville, FL	75%	(1)	0.77	(15)	0.78	0.67	0.59	153
Portland-Vancouver-Beaverton, OR-WA	72%	(13)	0.77	(15)	0.79	0.68	0.60	461
San Diego, CA	73%	(8)	0.77	(15)	0.82	0.73	0.65	410
Buffalo, NY	72%	(13)	0.76	(20)	0.76	0.65	0.57	172
Tampa-St. Petersburg-Clearwater, FL	71%	(20)	0.76	(20)	0.79	0.68	0.60	556
Atlanta, GA	70%	(24)	0.75	(22)	0.79	0.68	0.61	1100
Chicago, IL	69%	(26)	0.75	(22)	0.78	0.67	0.59	1588
Cleveland-Elyria-Mentor, OH	70%	(24)	0.75	(22)	0.77	0.65	0.57	454
Columbus, OH	71%	(20)	0.75	(22)	0.76	0.64	0.56	269

(continued)

Table 5.3 (continued)

City	Average Use		*Predicted Probability of Use		Probability of Use by Race			N
	Percent (Rank)		Prob. (Rank)		White	Black	Latino	
Indianapolis-Carmel, IN	68%	(29)	0.75	(22)	0.76	0.64	0.56	257
Providence, RI	72%	(13)	0.75	(22)	0.76	0.64	0.56	1475
Detroit, MI	69%	(26)	0.74	(28)	0.75	0.64	0.55	900
Sacramento, CA	69%	(26)	0.74	(28)	0.78	0.67	0.59	375
Charlotte, NC	67%	(31)	0.72	(30)	0.74	0.62	0.53	222
Cincinnati-Middletown, OH-KY-IN	68%	(29)	0.72	(30)	0.73	0.60	0.52	519
San Jose, CA	65%	(32)	0.72	(30)	0.78	0.67	0.59	288
Las Vegas, NV	65%	(32)	0.70	(33)	0.75	0.63	0.55	958
Raleigh-Cary, NC	62%	(38)	0.70	(33)	0.73	0.61	0.52	136
Dallas, TX	64%	(34)	0.69	(35)	0.74	0.62	0.54	1182
Pittsburgh, PA	63%	(35)	0.68	(36)	0.69	0.56	0.47	630
Orlando-Kissimee, FL	63%	(35)	0.67	(37)	0.74	0.62	0.53	477
St. Louis, MO-IL	63%	(35)	0.67	(37)	0.69	0.56	0.48	791

City	Average Use		*Predicted Probability of Use		Probability of Use by Race			
	Percent (Rank)		Prob. (Rank)		White	Black	Latino	N
Los Angeles, CA	61%	(40)	0.66	(39)	0.75	0.63	0.55	2184
Miami, FL	62%	(38)	0.66	(39)	0.76	0.65	0.57	1278
Oklahoma City, OK	60%	(43)	0.66	(39)	0.68	0.54	0.46	337
Houston, TX	61%	(40)	0.65	(42)	0.72	0.60	0.51	762
Memphis, TN-MS-AR	61%	(40)	0.62	(43)	0.66	0.52	0.44	168
Nashville-Davidson-Murfreesboro, TN	57%	(44)	0.62	(43)	0.63	0.49	0.41	206
Louisville-Jefferson County, KY-IN	55%	(47)	0.61	(45)	0.64	0.50	0.42	317
Virginia Beach, VA	56%	(46)	0.60	(46)	0.65	0.51	0.43	367
Richmond, VA	55%	(47)	0.58	(47)	0.62	0.48	0.40	387
Riverside, CA	57%	(44)	0.58	(47)	0.68	0.55	0.46	845
San Antonio, TX	49%	(49)	0.55	(49)	0.62	0.48	0.40	194
Birmingham-Hoover, AL	43%	(50)	0.46	(50)	0.48	0.35	0.28	302

* Probabilities estimated from random intercept model reported in Appendix Table A5.2, Column 3.

Table 5.4 **Suburban Rankings, Uses Internet Anywhere (2009 CPS)**

MSA	Average Use Percent (Rank)		*Predicted Probability of Use Prob. (Rank)		Probability of Use by Race White	Black	Latino	N
Salt Lake City, UT	84%	(1)	0.91	(1)	0.92	0.87	0.79	403
Denver, CO	84%	(1)	0.90	(2)	0.92	0.87	0.80	736
Minneapolis, MN	83%	(3)	0.90	(2)	0.91	0.86	0.77	1102
San Francisco, CA	83%	(3)	0.89	(4)	0.93	0.89	0.82	851
Seattle, WA	82%	(6)	0.89	(4)	0.91	0.86	0.77	738
Washington-Arlington-Alexandria, DC-VA-MD-WV	80%	(11)	0.89	(4)	0.92	0.87	0.79	1702
Milwaukee, WI	80%	(11)	0.88	(7)	0.88	0.82	0.72	298
Portland-Vancouver-Beaverton, OR-WA	83%	(3)	0.88	(7)	0.90	0.84	0.75	461
Rochester, NY	81%	(8)	0.88	(7)	0.89	0.83	0.73	259
San Jose, CA	80%	(11)	0.88	(7)	0.92	0.87	0.79	288
Austin-Round Rock, TX	78%	(18)	0.87	(11)	0.90	0.84	0.75	192
Baltimore-Towson, MD	79%	(15)	0.87	(11)	0.89	0.83	0.73	1026
Boston, MA	78%	(18)	0.87	(11)	0.89	0.83	0.73	1537

MSA	Average Use		*Predicted Probability of Use		Probability of Use by Race			N
	Percent (Rank)		Prob. (Rank)		White	Black	Latino	
Hartford, CT	79%	(15)	0.87	(11)	0.88	0.81	0.71	694
Kansas City, MO-KS	80%	(11)	0.87	(11)	0.88	0.82	0.72	597
Philadelphia-Camden-Wilmington, PA-NJ-DE-MD	81%	(8)	0.87	(11)	0.89	0.83	0.73	2090
Columbus, OH	81%	(8)	0.86	(17)	0.87	0.80	0.69	269
Phoenix, AZ	78%	(18)	0.86	(17)	0.89	0.83	0.73	608
Buffalo, NY	79%	(15)	0.85	(19)	0.86	0.78	0.67	172
Indianapolis-Carmel, IN	75%	(31)	0.85	(19)	0.86	0.78	0.67	257
Jacksonville, FL	82%	(6)	0.85	(19)	0.86	0.78	0.67	153
Raleigh-Cary, NC	73%	(35)	0.85	(19)	0.87	0.80	0.69	136
Sacramento, CA	78%	(18)	0.85	(19)	0.88	0.82	0.72	375
San Diego, CA	78%	(18)	0.85	(19)	0.89	0.83	0.74	410
Atlanta, GA	77%	(24)	0.84	(25)	0.87	0.80	0.70	1100
Chicago, IL	76%	(28)	0.84	(25)	0.87	0.80	0.70	1588

(continued)

Table 5.4 (continued)

MSA	Average Use		*Predicted Probability of Use		Probability of Use by Race			N
	Percent (Rank)		Prob. (Rank)		White	Black	Latino	
Cleveland-Elyria-Mentor, OH	76%	(28)	0.84	(25)	0.85	0.77	0.66	454
Detroit, MI	77%	(24)	0.84	(25)	0.85	0.78	0.66	900
New York, NY	76%	(28)	0.84	(25)	0.88	0.81	0.71	2738
St. Louis, MO-IL	77%	(24)	0.84	(25)	0.86	0.78	0.67	791
Tampa-St. Petersburg-Clearwater, FL	78%	(18)	0.84	(25)	0.87	0.80	0.69	556
Charlotte, NC	77%	(24)	0.83	(32)	0.85	0.77	0.65	222
Oklahoma City, OK	75%	(31)	0.83	(32)	0.84	0.76	0.64	337
Cincinnati-Middletown, OH-KY-IN	75%	(31)	0.82	(34)	0.83	0.74	0.62	519
Orlando-Kissimmee, FL	73%	(35)	0.81	(35)	0.86	0.79	0.68	477
Providence, RI	75%	(31)	0.81	(35)	0.82	0.74	0.62	1475
Dallas, TX	71%	(38)	0.80	(37)	0.85	0.77	0.65	1182
Las Vegas, NV	72%	(37)	0.80	(37)	0.84	0.76	0.64	958
Pittsburgh, PA	69%	(41)	0.80	(37)	0.80	0.71	0.58	630

MSA	Average Use		*Predicted Probability of Use		Probability of Use by Race			N
	Percent	(Rank)	Prob.	(Rank)	White	Black	Latino	
Houston, TX	71%	(38)	0.79	(40)	0.85	0.77	0.66	762
Richmond, VA	70%	(40)	0.79	(40)	0.81	0.72	0.59	387
Nashville-Davidson-Murfreesboro, TN	67%	(46)	0.78	(42)	0.79	0.69	0.56	206
Los Angeles, CA	69%	(41)	0.77	(43)	0.85	0.78	0.66	2184
Virginia Beach, VA	69%	(41)	0.77	(43)	0.80	0.71	0.58	367
Miami, FL	69%	(41)	0.76	(45)	0.85	0.77	0.66	1278
Memphis, TN-MS-AR	69%	(41)	0.75	(46)	0.78	0.67	0.54	168
San Antonio, TX	62%	(47)	0.74	(47)	0.80	0.70	0.57	194
Louisville-Jefferson County, KY-IN	61%	(49)	0.73	(48)	0.75	0.65	0.51	317
Birmingham-Hoover, AL	58%	(50)	0.68	(49)	0.70	0.58	0.44	302
Riverside, CA	62%	(47)	0.67	(50)	0.77	0.67	0.53	845

* Probabilities estimated from random intercept model reported in Appendix Table AS.2, column 1.

place are the suburban areas of Austin, Baltimore (its first showing in the top rankings), Boston, Hartford, CT (another first showing), Kansas City, MO, and Philadelphia with 87% of the population using the Internet at any location.

Nearly the same group of suburbs ranks last for broadband home access as for Internet use in any location, but in general, Internet use in the suburbs is considerably higher than in central cities. Houston and Richmond are ranked 40th, Nashville (42nd), Los Angeles, and Virginia Beach (43rd), Miami (45th), Memphis (46th), San Antonio (47th), Louisville (48th), Birmingham (49th), and Riverside ranks last at 50. However, the range is smaller from the most connected to the least connected suburbs, ranging from 91% with broadband to 67% with broadband, only a 24% difference from the top to the bottom ranking. Thus, disparities in Internet use are smaller in America's suburbs than in central cities.

Change in Internet Use in Central Cities Over Time

While point estimates or measures taken at one time period are informative, it is also useful to track change over time. We are able to replicate the rankings for the central cities using the 2007 CPS to assess change over a two-year period. The multilevel logistic regression models are reported in Appendix Table A5.3 and yield the estimates found in Table 5.5 (broadband at home) and Table 5.6 (Internet use anywhere).

Which cities have experienced the greatest gains in broadband use at home over the last few years? The last column of Table 5.5 shows the change in the estimated probability of high-speed Internet at home from 2007 to 2009 across the 50 largest central cities. Phoenix increased rates by 32% from 2007 to 2009, and Seattle and Jacksonville increased by 23%. Atlanta and the Birmingham area saw a 25% gain in the percent of the population with broadband at home over this two-year period. In contrast, Charlotte, NC, had only a 5% gain over this period and San Antonio and Rochester a 3% change. Gauging change in the digital cities ranking may be as important (or more important) than the absolute numbers.

In general, those cities ranked in the top 10 stayed near the top over this period, and those cities ranked near the bottom remained. Exceptions are Phoenix, which moved up from 32nd in home broadband use in 2007 to ninth in 2009; Jacksonville, which moved up from 19th to 10th by 2009; and Atlanta, which rose from 24th in 2007 to 14th in 2009. Other cities saw equally large drops in their ranking, including the Tampa area, falling from fifth in 2007 to 20th by 2009, and Charlotte, moving from 15th to 27th over the two-year period.

Table 5.6 presents similar estimates for Internet use at any location. In general these differences (last column) are much smaller; as a larger fraction of the population has used the Internet in any location, there are smaller gains to be made. There are a few exceptions. The Birmingham area ranked near the bottom for cities overall in previous tables but saw a 29% increase in the percent of the city population using the Internet at any location. In contrast, San Antonio saw only a 1% change.

Table 5.5 **Central City Rankings 2007–2009 Comparison, Uses High-Speed Internet at Home (CPS)**

MSA	Average Use				*Predicted Probability of Use*				Difference (2009–2007)
	2007		2009		2007		2009		Prob.
	% (Rank)		% (Rank)		Pr. (Rank)		Pr. (Rank)		
Seattle, WA	56%	(12)	76%	(2)	0.60	(9)	0.83	(1)	+0.23
San Francisco, CA	67%	(1)	73%	(6)	0.70	(1)	0.80	(2)	+0.10
Portland-Vancouver-Beaverton, OR-WA	67%	(1)	75%	(4)	0.69	(2)	0.80	(2)	+0.11
San Jose, CA	61%	(6)	76%	(2)	0.61	(7)	0.80	(2)	+0.19
Virginia Beach, VA	60%	(9)	78%	(1)	0.63	(5)	0.79	(5)	+0.16
Boston, MA	61%	(6)	75%	(4)	0.61	(7)	0.78	(6)	+0.17
San Diego, CA	59%	(10)	73%	(6)	0.57	(11)	0.78	(6)	+0.21
Austin-Round Rock, TX	65%	(4)	68%	(10)	0.65	(3)	0.76	(8)	+0.11
Phoenix, AZ	44%	(35)	70%	(8)	0.42	(32)	0.74	(9)	+0.32
Washington-Arlington-Alexandria, DC-VA-MD-WV	56%	(12)	64%	(17)	0.56	(12)	0.73	(10)	+0.17

(continued)

Table 5.5 (continued)

| MSA | Average Use | | | | *Predicted Probability of Use | | | | Difference (2009–2007) |
| | 2007 | | 2009 | | 2007 | | 2009 | | Prob. |
	% (Rank)		% (Rank)		Pr. (Rank)		Pr. (Rank)		
Jacksonville, FL	51%	(18)	69%	(9)	0.50	(19)	0.73	(10)	+ 0.23
Raleigh-Cary, NC	61%	(6)	66%	(12)	0.65	(3)	0.73	(10)	+ 0.08
Salt Lake City, UT	56%	(12)	66%	(12)	0.60	(9)	0.72	(13)	+ 0.12
Atlanta, GA	47%	(30)	66%	(12)	0.46	(26)	0.71	(14)	+ 0.25
Minneapolis, MN	52%	(17)	65%	(15)	0.54	(16)	0.71	(14)	+ 0.17
Pittsburgh, PA	51%	(18)	63%	(19)	0.56	(12)	0.70	(16)	+ 0.14
Orlando-Kissimee, FL	66%	(3)	68%	(10)	0.54	(16)	0.70	(16)	+ 0.16
Nashville-Davidson-Murfreesboro, TN	49%	(25)	64%	(17)	0.51	(18)	0.70	(16)	+ 0.19
Sacramento, CA	57%	(11)	65%	(15)	0.56	(12)	0.69	(19)	+ 0.13
Tampa-St. Petersburg-Clearwater, FL	63%	(5)	63%	(19)	0.63	(5)	0.67	(20)	+ 0.04
Columbus, OH	47%	(30)	60%	(24)	0.46	(26)	0.65	(21)	+ 0.19

| MSA | Average Use | | | | *Predicted Probability of Use | | | | Difference (2009–2007) |
| | 2007 | | 2009 | | 2007 | | 2009 | | Prob. |
	% (Rank)		% (Rank)		Pr. (Rank)		Pr. (Rank)		
Milwaukee, WI	51%	(18)	61%	(22)	0.49	(22)	0.65	(21)	+0.16
Providence, RI	51%	(18)	61%	(22)	0.49	(22)	0.64	(23)	+0.15
Riverside, CA	42%	(40)	60%	(24)	0.42	(32)	0.63	(24)	+0.21
St. Louis, MO-IL	48%	(27)	62%	(21)	0.44	(30)	0.62	(25)	+0.18
Indianapolis-Carmel, IN	48%	(27)	57%	(26)	0.47	(25)	0.61	(26)	+0.14
Charlotte, NC	56%	(12)	56%	(29)	0.55	(15)	0.60	(27)	+0.05
Hartford, CT	45%	(33)	57%	(26)	0.43	(31)	0.60	(27)	+0.17
Kansas City, MO-KS	44%	(35)	56%	(29)	0.42	(32)	0.59	(29)	+0.17
Dallas, TX	44%	(35)	56%	(29)	0.42	(32)	0.58	(30)	+0.16
Richmond, VA	49%	(25)	47%	(46)	0.38	(40)	0.58	(30)	+0.20
Birmingham-Hoover, AL	36%	(49)	57%	(26)	0.33	(48)	0.58	(30)	+0.25

(continued)

Table 5.5 (continued)

MSA	Average Use				*Predicted Probability of Use				Difference (2009–2007)
	2007		2009		2007		2009		
	% (Rank)		% (Rank)		Pr. (Rank)		Pr. (Rank)		Prob.
Memphis, TN-MS-AR	41%	(42)	55%	(32)	0.38	(40)	0.57	(33)	+ 0.19
Oklahoma City, OK	50%	(23)	53%	(36)	0.49	(22)	0.57	(33)	+ 0.08
New York, NY	42%	(40)	54%	(33)	0.38	(40)	0.56	(35)	+ 0.18
Chicago, IL	44%	(35)	53%	(36)	0.40	(36)	0.56	(35)	+ 0.16
Cincinnati-Middletown, OH-KY-IN	46%	(32)	51%	(38)	0.39	(39)	0.56	(35)	+ 0.17
Baltimore-Towson, MD	37%	(47)	54%	(33)	0.35	(45)	0.55	(38)	+ 0.20
Denver, CO	39%	(44)	50%	(41)	0.37	(43)	0.54	(39)	+ 0.17
Philadelphia-Camden-Wilmington, PA-NJ-DE-MD	38%	(45)	54%	(33)	0.35	(45)	0.53	(40)	+ 0.18
Houston, TX	35%	(50)	50%	(41)	0.32	(49)	0.53	(40)	+ 0.21

| MSA | Average Use | | *Predicted Probability of Use | | Difference |
| | 2007 | 2009 | 2007 | 2009 | (2009–2007) |
	% (Rank)	% (Rank)	Pr. (Rank)	Pr. (Rank)	Prob.
Las Vegas, NV	50% (23)	50% (41)	0.50 (19)	0.53 (40)	+ 0.03
Louisville-Jefferson County, KY-IN	53% (16)	51% (38)	0.50 (19)	0.53 (40)	+ 0.03
Los Angeles, CA	48% (27)	49% (44)	0.46 (26)	0.49 (44)	+ 0.03
Miami, FL	45% (33)	51% (38)	0.36 (44)	0.48 (45)	+ 0.12
Detroit, MI	38% (45)	48% (45)	0.34 (47)	0.47 (46)	+ 0.13
Cleveland-Elyria-Mentor, OH	37% (47)	46% (47)	0.32 (49)	0.44 (47)	+ 0.12
San Antonio, TX	44% (35)	44% (48)	0.40 (36)	0.43 (48)	+ 0.03
Rochester, NY	51% (18)	39% (49)	0.46 (26)	0.43 (48)	– 0.03
Buffalo, NY	40% (43)	38% (50)	0.40 (36)	0.39 (50)	– 0.01

Note: For each of the 50 metropolitan areas, the probability of using the Internet is based on responses from only those living in the largest city within a metropolitan area when identification of the largest city is possible. For some areas, the CPS does not provide information that identifies each city within a designated principal city area. In these cases, the principal city area, which may include multiple cities, was used to estimate the probability of Internet use. The ranking entries with multiple cities listed are those that did not have identifying information for each individual city.

* Probabilities estimated from random intercept model reported in Appendix Table A5.3, column 3 for 2007 and Appendix Table A5.1, column 3 for 2009.

Table 5.6   Central City Rankings 2007–2009 Comparison, Uses Internet Anywhere (CPS)

| MSA | Average Use | | *Predicted Probability of Use | | Difference (2009–2007) |
	2007 % (Rank)	2009 % (Rank)	2007 Pr. (Rank)	2009 Pr. (Rank)	Prob.
Seattle, WA	74% (6)	86% (2)	0.85 (2)	0.93 (1)	+ 0.08
San Francisco, CA	78% (2)	83% (5)	0.85 (2)	0.92 (2)	+ 0.07
Portland-Vancouver-Beaverton, OR-WA	82% (1)	84% (4)	0.88 (1)	0.91 (3)	+ 0.03
Jacksonville, FL	65% (21)	88% (1)	0.72 (19)	0.90 (4)	+ 0.18
Boston, MA	71% (11)	80% (7)	0.77 (11)	0.89 (5)	+ 0.12
Minneapolis, MN	74% (6)	79% (8)	0.83 (6)	0.88 (6)	+ 0.05
Washington-Arlington-Alexandria, DC-VA-MD-WV	71% (11)	73% (18)	0.79 (9)	0.87 (7)	+ 0.08
San Diego, CA	71% (11)	78% (10)	0.75 (15)	0.87 (7)	+ 0.12
San Jose, CA	72% (8)	81% (6)	0.76 (13)	0.87 (7)	+ 0.11

| MSA | Average Use | | *Predicted Probability of Use | | Difference (2009–2007) |
| | 2007 | 2009 | 2007 | 2009 | |
	% (Rank)	% (Rank)	Pr. (Rank)	Pr. (Rank)	Prob.
Virginia Beach, VA	78% (2)	79% (8)	0.84 (4)	0.87 (7)	+ 0.03
Raleigh-Cary, NC	75% (5)	78% (10)	0.84 (4)	0.87 (7)	+ 0.03
Pittsburgh, PA	72% (8)	73% (18)	0.82 (8)	0.86 (12)	+ 0.04
Nashville-Davidson-Murfreesboro, TN	65% (21)	78% (10)	0.73 (17)	0.86 (12)	+ 0.13
Salt Lake City, UT	78% (2)	76% (13)	0.83 (6)	0.86 (12)	+ 0.03
Birmingham-Hoover, AL	51% (45)	85% (3)	0.55 (42)	0.84 (15)	+ 0.29
Milwaukee, WI	66% (19)	75% (14)	0.70 (22)	0.83 (16)	+ 0.13
Austin-Round Rock, TX	71% (11)	71% (22)	0.79 (9)	0.83 (16)	+ 0.04
Atlanta, GA	60% (28)	71% (22)	0.68 (26)	0.82 (18)	+ 0.14
Phoenix, AZ	55% (35)	75% (14)	0.60 (36)	0.82 (18)	+ 0.22

(continued)

Table 5.6 (continued)

| MSA | Average Use | | | | *Predicted Probability of Use | | | | Difference (2009–2007) |
| | 2007 | | 2009 | | 2007 | | 2009 | | |
	% (Rank)		% (Rank)		Pr. (Rank)		Pr. (Rank)		Prob.
Sacramento, CA	69%	(16)	75%	(14)	0.72	(19)	0.82	(18)	+ 0.10
Orlando-Kissimee, FL	72%	(8)	74%	(17)	0.69	(24)	0.82	(18)	+ 0.13
Columbus, OH	68%	(18)	72%	(20)	0.74	(16)	0.82	(18)	+ 0.08
Tampa-St. Petersburg-Clearwater, FL	69%	(16)	72%	(20)	0.77	(11)	0.80	(23)	+ 0.03
Indianapolis-Carmel, IN	66%	(19)	71%	(22)	0.73	(17)	0.80	(23)	+ 0.07
St. Louis, MO-IL	65%	(21)	71%	(22)	0.66	(27)	0.79	(25)	+ 0.13
Cincinnati-Middletown, OH-KY-IN	57%	(32)	68%	(28)	0.61	(34)	0.78	(26)	+ 0.17
Charlotte, NC	70%	(15)	70%	(26)	0.76	(13)	0.78	(26)	+ 0.02
Oklahoma City, OK	65%	(21)	70%	(26)	0.69	(24)	0.78	(26)	+ 0.09
Chicago, IL	58%	(30)	68%	(28)	0.62	(32)	0.77	(29)	+ 0.15

| MSA | Average Use | | *Predicted Probability of Use | | Difference |
| | 2007 | 2009 | 2007 | 2009 | (2009–2007) |
	% (Rank)	% (Rank)	Pr. (Rank)	Pr. (Rank)	Prob.
Richmond, VA	55% (35)	58% (47)	0.55 (42)	0.77 (29)	+ 0.22
Kansas City, MO-KS	61% (27)	67% (30)	0.64 (30)	0.76 (31)	+ 0.12
Providence, RI	60% (28)	66% (31)	0.65 (28)	0.74 (32)	+ 0.09
Memphis, TN-MS-AR	53% (40)	65% (33)	0.57 (40)	0.74 (32)	+ 0.17
Riverside, CA	52% (43)	65% (33)	0.57 (40)	0.71 (34)	+ 0.14
Baltimore-Towson, MD	52% (43)	64% (35)	0.59 (37)	0.71 (34)	+ 0.12
Hartford, CT	55% (35)	64% (35)	0.59 (37)	0.71 (34)	+ 0.12
Denver, CO	55% (35)	61% (39)	0.62 (32)	0.70 (37)	+ 0.08
Louisville-Jefferson County, KY-IN	62% (26)	61% (39)	0.72 (19)	0.70 (37)	− 0.02
Dallas, TX	56% (34)	63% (37)	0.59 (37)	0.69 (39)	+ 0.10
Rochester, NY	58% (30)	66% (31)	0.65 (28)	0.68 (40)	+ 0.03
New York, NY	50% (47)	60% (43)	0.51 (46)	0.67 (41)	+ 0.16

(continued)

Table 5.6 (continued)

| MSA | Average Use | | | | *Predicted Probability of Use | | | | Difference |
| | 2007 | | 2009 | | 2007 | | 2009 | | (2009–2007) |
	% (Rank)		% (Rank)		Pr. (Rank)		Pr. (Rank)		Prob.
Los Angeles, CA	57%	(32)	60%	(43)	0.61	(34)	0.67	(41)	+ 0.06
Houston, TX	48%	(50)	59%	(46)	0.51	(46)	0.67	(41)	+ 0.16
Las Vegas, NV	64%	(25)	60%	(43)	0.70	(22)	0.67	(41)	– 0.03
Philadelphia-Camden-Wilmington, PA-NJ-DE-MD	49%	(49)	61%	(39)	0.52	(45)	0.66	(45)	+ 0.14
Detroit, MI	54%	(39)	61%	(39)	0.54	(44)	0.66	(45)	+ 0.12
Cleveland-Elyria-Mentor, OH	50%	(47)	63%	(37)	0.51	(46)	0.65	(47)	+ 0.14
Miami, FL	53%	(40)	55%	(48)	0.46	(50)	0.58	(48)	+ 0.12
Buffalo, NY	53%	(40)	51%	(49)	0.63	(31)	0.58	(48)	– 0.05
San Antonio, TX	51%	(45)	49%	(50)	0.51	(46)	0.50	(50)	– 0.01

Note: For each of the 50 metropolitan areas, the probability of using the Internet is based on responses from only those living in the largest city within a metropolitan area when identification of the largest city is possible. For some areas, the CPS does not provide information that identifies each city within a designated principal city area. In these cases, the principal city area, which may include multiple cities, was used to estimate the probability of Internet use. The ranking entries with multiple cities listed are those that did not have identifying information for each individual city.

Probabilities estimated from random intercept model reported in Appendix Table A5.3, column 1 for 2007 and Appendix Table A5.1, column 1 for 2009.

Conclusion: Counting, Ranking, and Public Policy

By comparing cities and metropolitan areas, we can see that technology use is not equivalent across places; Seattle has rates of technology use nearly double those in Buffalo. High-ranking cities include those with significant technology industries, educated populations, and policy attention to promotion of technology use (as in Seattle and San Francisco). But other cities with technology initiatives profiled in chapter 2 have lower rates of technology use. Los Angeles ranks low for Internet use in both the city and suburbs, despite its high placement on some technology lists.

Technology disparities largely reflect other inequalities. Many of the low-ranking cities and suburban areas have been burdened by decades of decline and disinvestment. Cities like Buffalo, Detroit, and Cleveland have abysmal poverty rates and unemployment; and in the case of Detroit and Cleveland, high levels of black-white metropolitan segregation (Logan and Stults 2011). Lower ranking suburban areas tend to be in the South and Southwest, suggesting that high Latino populations and lower incomes may play a role. While rates of broadband adoption and Internet use are consistently lower for central cities than suburbs, regional fortunes often rise and fall together. There are some exceptions, though, where a few suburban areas rank much higher than their central cities, including Rochester, Denver, and Milwaukee. One possibility is that high levels of metropolitan segregation or income inequality may contribute to these outcomes.

The concentration of poverty is more prevalent in central cities, which have higher poverty rates overall. Results for many of the low-ranking cities suggest that the concentration of poverty may play a role, given that this is most common in cities of the Northeast and Midwest. But, neighborhoods are varied within cities, and to understand the possible effects of concentrated poverty, it is necessary to examine technology use at the neighborhood level. We will explore these possible place effects in the Chicago chapters, as well as strategies for community building through technology in Chicago.

While gaps between minorities and whites are persistent everywhere, it is also true that African Americans and Latinos have higher rates of use in cities or suburbs where everyone is more likely to be online. This may be a case where "a rising tide lifts all boats" with better access to jobs involving technology, more emphasis on technology use in public institutions and on the political agenda, or a general atmosphere of technology use that leads to more widespread awareness of its possible benefits.

Metropolitan fragmentation suggests that many local governments eager to create a more digitally equitable community lack the resources to do so on their own. Key strategies depend on local institutions, but fiscal capacity may be a barrier. Regional collaboration has been a traditionally weak instrument for addressing segregation or inequality (Lefevre and Weir 2012), and so there is reason to doubt the feasibility of proposing metropolitan solutions for technology disparities. Yet, the regional character of labor markets and some other policy areas affected by broadband suggest that Internet use is a metropolitan concern in many ways, not solely defined by city boundaries. Regional planning organizations and county governments may be well advised to take up technology use as an issue for economic and metropolitan workforce development.

Other levels of government must also make room for cities and poor suburbs on their technology policy agendas, as we argued in earlier chapters. The data available here does not allow us to examine individual suburbs, but there are undoubtedly some that would benefit from political alliances with central cities to make the case for a larger share of state and federal assistance. With shifts in the geography of poverty and the growing diversity of suburbs, political coalition building and cooperative policy solutions may be more feasible than in the past, as Myron Orfield has suggested (1997).

While the rankings reflect socioeconomic structure and labor markets, local and regional policy initiatives addressing inequalities can make a difference as well (Dreier, Mollenkopf, and Swanstrom 2004). Counting and ranking can call attention to policy issues and place them at the top of political agendas, whether local or national. Transparency and competition may initiate solutions from the ground up at the local and regional level, because few communities will want to linger at the bottom. For all these policy conversations, counting and ranking may provide a way to better define problems and solutions.

6

Mapping Opportunity in Chicago Neighborhoods

Not having access to broadband applications limits an individual's ability to participate in 21st century American life.
—National Broadband Plan, FCC 2010a

This chapter focuses on neighborhoods as environments that may affect opportunities to go online and as places that are in turn shaped by the activities of their residents. Does the neighborhood context influence broadband adoption or Internet use? Are there different patterns in low-income African American communities compared with poor Latino neighborhoods? How do technology disparities across neighborhoods impact prospects for improving employment, health, access to government services, and political participation?

To address these questions, this chapter presents neighborhood-level data, drawing on a large-sample survey of nearly 3,500 Chicago residents that was conducted in June and July 2008. Describing urban places or urban residents in the aggregate misses substantial diversity within city boundaries and the levels of need that exist within low-income communities. Chapter 5 provided estimates of broadband adoption and Internet use for Chicago as a whole and for racial and ethnic groups in the city. In this chapter, we use multilevel models to control for the neighborhood context and to generate estimates of technology use and activities online for Chicago's 77 community areas. The Chicago survey was completed just a few months before the 2008 election and the passage of the broadband stimulus program. So it offers a snapshot of conditions close to the enactment of federal broadband policies. It also provides a close match to the 2009 national survey data used in previous chapters, albeit with an in-depth view of neighborhood variation within a large American city.

Chicago as a Case

Historically called the most American of cities (Koval 2006, 3, 6), Chicago embodies many of the contradictions evident in the urban landscape, both the promise of technology innovation and the challenge of connecting more residents to share in that promise. Chicago is a global city with a postindustrial economy, yet it retains traces of an industrial heritage. Chicago is also ideal for comparing trends in African American and Latino neighborhoods, because each group comprises approximately a third of the city's population. In many ways, Chicago reflects both the nation's urban past and the unfolding urban future (Bennett 2010).

Chicago is literally a hub in the physical network of the Internet; it has one of the world's highest capacity Network Access Points (Moskow et al. 2007). More critically, however, its global economy is positioned to benefit from technology use. Information technology supports international connectivity and has changed the scale on which cities compete (Castells 1991; Sassen 2001). Some cities, and some residents, have benefited more than others from these shifts. In 2008, the Chicago metropolitan area ranked eighth in a worldwide global cities index, moving to sixth in 2010 (Foreign Policy 2008, 2010), and earlier rankings consistently placed Chicago within the top 10 cities in the international economy (Wolman and Horak 2010; Moskow et al. 2007). Within the space of a few decades, Chicago has transitioned from a Midwestern manufacturing center to a knowledge economy. Manufacturing dropped from 31.9% of the city's employment in 1970 to 14.2% in 2000.[1] In its place are corporate and legal services, finance, insurance, pharmaceuticals, and a variety of other knowledge-intensive industries (Moskow et al. 2007; Brookings Institution 2007). Although the metropolitan area has information-industry firms such as Motorola, and the locally based Groupon has attracted national attention, it is the broader knowledge economy that has accounted for high levels of technology use in Chicago (Chapple et al. 2004).

Central to the ability to innovate through technology are research and education. Chicago has research-extensive universities such as the University of Chicago, Northwestern University, and the University of Illinois at Chicago, and many other institutions of higher education. Within the metropolitan area are other renowned venues for research, including Fermilab, Argonne National Laboratories, and some of the world's leading centers of medical research. In the 2008 Global Cities Index, which featured subcategories not available in 2010, Chicago ranked second in education and human-capital measures, behind London (Foreign Policy 2008).

Chicago exists, however, with residents at opposite poles of the technology spectrum. Global trade, knowledge-intensive firms, and research and development offer resources for generating substantial benefits from Internet use. Yet, the transition to the new economy has left some without the skills to participate; old jobs disappeared and many positions that do not require a college degree often entail some technology competency.

CHICAGO'S RACIAL AND ETHNIC DIVERSITY

Chicago is one of the most diverse cities in the United States, whether measured in socioeconomic, racial, or ethnic terms. The third-largest city in the United States, Chicago had a 2010 population of just under 2.7 million living within the city limits. The 2010 census showed no racial or ethnic majority in the city, with a population that was 45% white, 33% black, 5.5% Asian, and 29% Hispanic (of all races). The city is a "gateway" for immigration from many countries, but especially Latin America. In 2010, 21% of Chicago residents were foreign born, compared with a little under 13% for the United States as a whole. The poverty rate was also approximately 21%, or about 50%

higher than the national average of less than 14%. This diversity allows us to examine variation within demographic groups and neighborhoods across the city, but it also reveals deep social inequalities within this context.[2]

The Chicago region is one of the most segregated metropolitan areas in the United States (Logan and Stults 2011). Larger metropolitan areas located in the Northeast and Midwest, and also places with a higher share of minorities tend to be more segregated (Frey 2010; Lewis and Hamilton 2011). Immigration, gentrification, and the demolition of high-rise public housing are changing some neighborhoods in the city, and measures of metropolitan segregation dropped slightly since 2000 (Logan and Stults 2011; Bennett 2010; Pattillo 2007). But segregation and the spatial concentration of poverty remain significant factors in many of Chicago's low-income neighborhoods.

There are also stark racial and ethnic disparities in income among Chicago residents. The median household income for African Americans was just a little over $29,000 in 2010, compared with approximately $40,000 for Latinos and nearly $66,000 for non-Hispanic whites.[3] Thus, the median income for African Americans was less than half the median for non-Hispanic whites. Although Latinos fare a little better at the household level than African Americans, they still constitute a predominantly low-income population, with less than two-thirds the income of non-Hispanic white households.

Chicago has many thriving and vibrant neighborhoods as well as areas of disinvestment and poverty. By examining Chicago's neighborhoods, we can explore the variation in technology use among different populations and within different contexts, suggesting urban experiences in the United States more generally.

Neighborhood Context and Technology Use

Whether rich or poor, neighborhoods influence the quality of life for individuals (Dreier, Mollenkopf, and Swanstrom 2004; Newburger, Birch, and Wattner 2011, xi; Reardon and Bischoff 2011). Of particular concern to social scientists has been the neighborhood effects engendered by the spatial concentration of poverty.[4] Because of differences in patterns of racial and ethnic segregation, African Americans are most likely to live in areas of concentrated poverty, followed by Latinos, and less commonly, non-Hispanic whites (Jargowsky 1997; Massey and Denton 1993). During the 1990s, the strong economy was responsible for some reversal of the trends toward growing concentration of poverty, but poverty is increasing and its geographic concentration is now rising as well (Federal Reserve and Brookings Institution 2008). Additionally, what was primarily an inner-city phenomenon has developed elsewhere in metropolitan areas; there has been growth in the concentration of poverty in some inner-ring suburbs as well as central cities (Drier, Mollenkopf and Swanstrom 2004; Berube and Kneebone 2006; Allard and Roth 2010). We focus here on neighborhoods in the city of Chicago, but the findings should have relevance for understanding the geography of opportunity in other urban and even some suburban communities.

How would concentrated poverty affect broadband use, beyond the effects of individual poverty? The concentration of poverty obviously produces weaker markets for many goods and services, including broadband. While most urban neighborhoods have some availability of high-speed Internet, disadvantaged communities may be left out, or have slower and less reliable access, less competition among providers, and higher prices. Although there is little systematic evidence on these issues, one recent study of the Washington, D.C. region found that broadband prices were relatively higher in low-income areas for the speeds delivered (Dunbar 2011), and some case study research suggests limited high-speed service in low-income neighborhoods despite advertised availability (Dailey et al. 2010).

In areas where poor individuals cannot afford home access, they must rely on public institutions, commercial access such as cafes, and the homes of friends and relatives. Demand for public access may far exceed supply where many rely upon it. In Chicago, over 60% of public libraries in 2009 reported wait times of three hours or longer for public access computers.[5]

As one Social Science Research Council study described the situation across the United States, "Communities with a large percentage of non-adopters face multiple, overlapping challenges to broadband use, from skill and language barriers, to problems with providers, to overburdened community intermediaries and overstretched public Internet access points" (Dailey et al. 2010, 6).

High-poverty communities may also offer fewer opportunities for learning and assistance with technology. Although gaps have narrowed in terms of student-to-computer ratios, there are significant differences between schools in how computers are used in the classroom. In schools with lower income students, technology use often focuses on basic skills rather than research, report writing, or multimedia presentations (Warschauer 2010). Subsequently, students become less proficient in technology and are less able to exploit the information online or to create content. Adults often learn about technology on the job, but in places with high unemployment and residents who are in low-skill jobs, there are fewer opportunities to gain new skills in this way. To the extent that friends and neighbors also know little about technology, there are fewer chances for individuals to learn informally. Social networks are important for encouraging technology use and fostering informal learning (Warschauer 2003). Examining technology adoption at the neighborhood level in this chapter allows us to explore whether neighborhood characteristics are related to technology use. Chapter 8 returns to these issues, discussing barriers to technology use in Chicago's neighborhoods.

Information Technology as a Neighborhood Resource

Given the significance of the Internet for so many social and economic activities, patterns of technology use across neighborhoods may ameliorate or exacerbate spatial disadvantage. Among the effects attributed to the concentration of poverty are disparities in health (Currie 2011), education (Jacob and Ludwig 2011; Jargowsky and El Komi 2011), labor markets (Wilson 1987; Granovetter 1973; Bayer, Ross, and Topa 2008), collective efficacy (Sampson, Raudenbush, and Earls 1997), and political participation (Alex-Assensoh 1997). While there are multiple individual-level and community-level factors that affect these outcomes, access to the information and communication opportunities online represent potential resources for addressing needs in many of these policy areas.

Low-income communities often have high rates of chronic disease (Currie 2011). Limited options for safe exercise, poverty-induced stress, and "food deserts" lacking in fresh produce contribute to health disparities. Improved access to health information online may offer strategies for coping with these environmental constraints as well as better knowledge about how to prevent or control illness. Some community organizations and health care institutions have used the Internet to raise awareness around health issues in the neighborhood—for example, the Humboldt Park Smart Communities portal in Chicago features information about diabetes.

High-poverty neighborhoods struggle with many educational disadvantages, including high drop-out rates and low achievement (Orfield and Lee 2005; Orfield et al. 2004; Jacob and Ludwig 2011; Stone et al. 2001). Disparities in Internet access affect the more general educational environment, beyond the burdens they create for individual students. In communities where many families lack Internet access, educators may feel constrained in assigning homework or research outside the classroom. Compared with schools in higher income neighborhoods, where online tools are readily used, teachers can less easily communicate with and involve parents by posting grades, assignments, and announcements.

Residents of poor neighborhoods are often isolated from better paying jobs because they lack sufficient information about opportunities in their informal information networks (Granovetter 1973). Such networks are highly local, with many sources located within a one-mile radius of job seekers (Ioannides and Topa 2009, 14; Wellman 1996; Guest and Lee 1983; Lee and Campbell 1999). To a greater extent than most, residents of high-poverty neighborhoods rely upon strong ties for job referrals; they are less likely to have the weak ties outside their closest circle of friends and relatives to provide links to better jobs (Elliott 1999; Kleit 2001). The Internet can possibly supplement the personal networks of individuals in poor neighborhoods, overcoming some of the constraints of the immediate environment.

Collective efficacy in a neighborhood is based on social cohesion and community enforcement of social norms; such norms can help control crime as well as support mutual assistance (Hampton 2010). Policy experiments have indicated that communication through the Internet on neighborhood listservs may have positive effects for organizing low-income communities for collective efficacy (ibid.). Similarly, residence in an area of concentrated poverty is associated with low rates of political participation (Alex-Assensoh 1997). The Internet can connect residents with online news, e-government, websites, blogs, and social media, supplementing the information available in neighborhood networks. There are already substantial disparities in political participation based on education and income (Schlozman, Verba, and Brady 2010). To the extent that more information, discussion, and communication are moving online, residents of high-poverty neighborhoods will be further excluded from democratic engagement.

A Chicago Survey and Neighborhood Aggregate Data

The data presented in this chapter are drawn from a random-sample telephone survey of 3,453 Chicago residents covering the 77 Chicago community areas. Designed by the authors, the survey was conducted by the University of Iowa Hawkeye Poll in June and July 2008, in Spanish and English. Survey interviewers talked to 12,947 people and obtained a cooperation rate of 26.7%, which is typical for telephone surveys.[6] The survey included five call-backs for nonresponses unless a hard refusal was given. Chicago's zip codes were used to create the overall geographic area from which the random sample was drawn. The survey instrument took 12 minutes to complete (see appendix C for the survey questionnaire).[7] The results obtained in the 2008 study were comparable to national surveys at the time, including the 2009 Current Population Survey.

The survey's sample of residents 18 years and older was fairly representative of Chicago's population. Of survey respondents, 45% were white non-Hispanic, 31% were African American, 3% Asian American, 19% Latino, and 3% other or mixed race. According to the American Community Survey estimates, in 2008, 42% of Chicago residents were white, 35% were black, 28% were Hispanic (of all races), and 5% were Asian.[8]

The survey was merged with census tract level data measuring neighborhood racial and ethnic context, educational attainment, and relative affluence or poverty. The results are briefly presented here, first analyzing the individual-level factors alone and then using multilevel statistical models (individual and aggregate level factors). These multilevel models are used to create probability estimates of technology use at the neighborhood level for Chicago's 77 community areas, similar to the methodology used to create the ranking of central cities and suburbs in chapter 5. These estimates are presented in tables for select neighborhoods and as maps to illustrate the importance of neighborhood geography.

Despite the discussion of neighborhood effects above, the concept of "neighborhood" is inexact in social science, for neighborhoods generally do not have fixed political boundaries in the same way that municipalities or counties do. Rather, the neighborhood context is often measured at the census tract level (Ellen and O'Regan 2011; Currie 2011; Jargowsky and El Komi 2011). The multilevel analysis presented here was modeled in two ways—by census tract and by the larger Chicago community area (CCA), and estimates of technology use were created for each. The probabilities of Internet use (or geographic estimates) are mapped in this chapter utilizing the 77 officially designated community areas. Created by the sociologists who pioneered the "Chicago school" of urban studies at the University of Chicago in the 1920's, community areas are still used by the city and other agencies (Park, Burgess, and Mackenzie 1984). Many decades have passed, and perceived neighborhood boundaries have often changed. But, community areas are more identifiable as distinct neighborhoods than individual census tracts, and policy decisions are often made with some reference to these community areas.

The Connected and Less-Connected in Chicago

In 2008, 61% of Chicago residents had broadband at home, meaning that nearly 40% of Chicagoans were either less-connected or offline entirely. Overall, 25% of Chicago residents did not use the Internet at all, another 6% used the Internet at times but lacked home access, and 8% had more limited and slow dial-up connections rather than high-speed broadband. Thus, 4 in 10 faced technology barriers of varying degrees. These figures are comparable to those reported in chapter 5 based on 2009 survey data in which 56% of Chicago's population was estimated to have broadband at home.

The proportion of Chicago residents who were online daily in 2008 was similar to the percentage who had full access—that is broadband at home. Only 60% of Chicago residents used the Internet on a daily basis. There are clear links between frequency of use and the quality of access. Among those who had Internet connections at home, 83% were online daily in contrast with 7% of those who did not have home access. Similarly, 88% of those who had broadband at home were online every day, compared with 54% of those who had dial-up Internet access. There is a dramatic difference in frequency of use, comparing those who do and do not have home access. This has consequences for the ability to gain experience and skills, and to engage in a variety of activities online (Hassani 2006; Mossberger, Tolbert, and McNeal 2008). As with national statistics, however, citywide averages mask substantial differences within the population.

Difference in Access Based on Individual Characteristics

While the same factors predict Internet access in Chicago as in the rest of the nation, a closer look at the Chicago data reveals important patterns among the less-connected by race, ethnicity, and neighborhood factors. Following the same patterns for digital inequality discussed in Chapter 3, Chicagoans who did not use the Internet at any location were more likely to be older, Latino, African American, lower income, and less educated. The largest gaps in access in Chicago were between Spanish-speaking and English-speaking residents, as only 39% of those who responded to the survey in Spanish used the Internet, compared with 79% of those who answered in English, a 40% difference based on language use. Latinos stood out as among the least connected residents. Age was the most important predictor of Internet use anywhere, accounting for a 26% difference, moving from one standard deviation below to one standard deviation above the mean. Income was the most important factor, however, associated with home Internet access. Income accounted for a 29% gap in the probability of Internet access at home, comparing low ($10,000–20,000) and high income ($75,000–100,000) households.

Patterns based on race and ethnicity revealed differences between African Americans and Latinos, controlling for other factors. African Americans had an 84% probability of using the Internet at any location controlling for other factors, compared with a 90% probability for whites. Yet, African Americans lagged further behind in home access (by about 10 percentage points), with only a 72% probability of having any type of home access (high-speed or a slow dial-up connection). In Chicago, there was a gap of about 12% between Internet use and home access for African Americans. Still, African Americans were much more likely than Latinos to have some online experience. Comparing Latinos to non-Hispanic whites, the gap in Internet use anywhere was substantially larger, at 18% (versus a 6% difference between African Americans and whites).

Examining use of the Chicago public libraries for Internet access demonstrates differences by race and ethnicity as well. A third of Chicago residents reported using the Internet at libraries, and these included both more-connected and less-connected residents. Younger and better educated Chicagoans had a higher likelihood of using the Internet at the public library, but so did low-income residents. African Americans were 14% more likely, and Latinos 8% more likely to use the Internet at a library than white non-Hispanic Chicago residents, holding other factors constant. (See Appendix Tables A6.1–A6.4 for the statistical models for the results reported here.)

Differences in Access Based on Individual and Neighborhood Characteristics

Using multilevel models, we include statistical controls for neighborhood-level factors (percent black, percent Latino, percent Asian-American, percent below the poverty line and percent of high school graduates) (see models in Appendix Tables A6.5–A6.6). Controlling for neighborhood characteristics, the differences between African Americans and whites in Internet use anywhere disappear. Residence in neighborhoods with either a high percentage of African Americans or Latinos is associated with a lower likelihood of being an Internet user. Chicago residents of neighborhoods with a high percentage of Latinos are also less likely to have home access, but those who live in neighborhoods with more Asian Americans have a greater likelihood of home use.

This means that neighborhood-level factors influence technology access, over and above the effects of an individual's income, race, or other characteristics (see Mossberger, Tolbert, and Gilbert 2006). Holding environmental factors constant, there are no longer any differences in Internet use at any location, comparing African Americans and non-Hispanic whites. In other words, it is African Americans who live in relatively segregated (and generally high-poverty) neighborhoods who are offline—not all African Americans. Differences between Latinos and non-Hispanic whites remain significant when we control for neighborhood influences, with Latinos less likely to be online. Living in neighborhoods with a large proportion of Latinos magnifies this effect. Disparities for predominantly African American and Latino neighborhoods are apparent throughout the findings in the Chicago study, although Latino neighborhoods lag furthest behind.

Mapping Chicago's community areas by quartiles (see Figures 6.3 and 6.4) shows the geography of poverty and broadband access. Community areas with higher concentrations of African Americans, Latinos, and the poor on the South and West Sides of the city (Figures 6.1–6.3) tend to be those where home broadband adoption is lowest, as depicted in Figure 6.4. Patterns of broadband adoption mapped in Figure 6.4 indicate there is some variation, especially for African American neighborhoods (see Figure 6.1), which include both very low and average broadband adoption. As shown in the discussion later in the chapter, the neighborhoods that are particularly disadvantaged for technology use and adoption are almost entirely African American or Latino, with high poverty rates.

The results of the Chicago survey are consistent with the findings in a study based on a 2001 national survey that showed the effects of poverty and place for all racial and

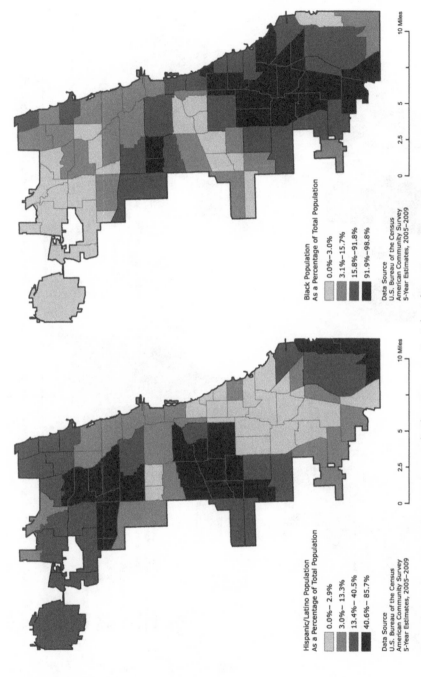

Figures 6.1–6.2 Percent Hispanic/Latino (left) and Percent Black (right) by Chicago Community Area

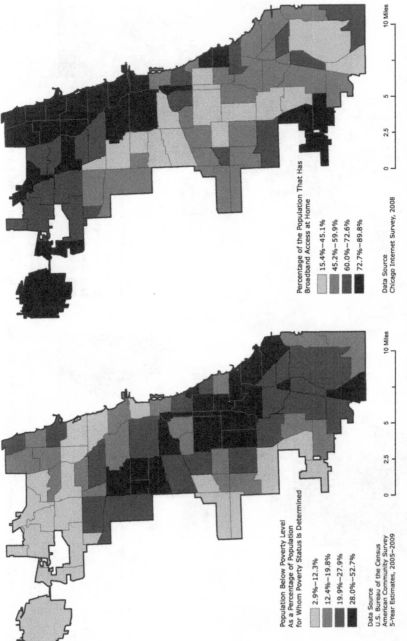

Population Below Poverty Level
As a Percentage of Population
for Whom Poverty Status Is Determined

2.9%–12.3%

12.4%–19.8%

19.9%–27.9%

28.0%–52.7%

Data Source
U.S. Bureau of the Census
American Community Survey
5-Year Estimates, 2005–2009

0   2.5   5   10 Miles

Percentage of the Population That Has
Broadband Access at Home

15.4%–45.1%

45.2%–59.9%

60.0%–72.6%

72.7%–89.8%

Data Source
Chicago Internet Survey, 2008

0   2.5   5   10 Miles

Figures 6.3–6.4 Population Below the Poverty Level (left) and Predicted Probability of High-Speed Home Access (right) by Chicago Community Area (from Appendix Table A6.6) ethnic groups. For African Americans, those who were disadvantaged lived in lower income areas, and disparities with whites were no longer significant controlling for neighborhood characteristics; for Latinos, place mattered but did not entirely account for gaps in technology use (Mossberger, Tolbert, and Gilbert 2006). The Chicago study reveals similar patterns seven years later, in the context of a city with a broad diversity of neighborhoods.

Opportunity and Online Activities in Chicago

The activities people engage in online signal the potential for Internet use to support public goals such as civic engagement, employment, and access to government services and health care. To what extent are low-income communities isolated from this information online? Alternatively, some patterns may suggest activities that low-income communities value on the Internet, even though residents in these areas are less-connected. The Chicago study featured a number of questions about online activities, similar to many in the national FCC survey in chapter 4. Using this data, we first show citywide averages and summarize factors that account for variation across types of residents and neighborhoods using multilevel models. Finally, we use geographic estimates from these models to show differences between activities online for the most and least connected neighborhoods and to map patterns of online activities across the city.

City-wide, residents perform many tasks online, as seen in Table 6.1. Most commonly, they read news online and look up health information. Almost two in three Chicago residents who are online use the Internet to find government information, and more than half use the Internet for information about politics or mass transit. Approximately half the city's residents search for job information online, use the city website, or do work on the Internet as part of the job. Online education is less common; only 31% of Chicago residents have used the Internet for this reason.

Table 6.1 **Activities Online, Chicago Sample**

Have ever used the Internet to...	City Population	Internet Users
Read online news	67%	91%
Find health information	64%	86%
Find information on government	57%	76%
Get information about public transport	56%	74%
Get information on politics	53%	71%
Look for job information	50%	67%
Use City of Chicago website	49%	65%
Do work for your job	48%	64%
Take a class or training	31%	41%

Table 6.2   **Frequency of Internet Use for Job by Education (employed Chicago residents only)**

Educational Attainment	% of Employed Who Use the Internet for Work Daily or a Few Times Per Week
0–8 Years	9%
9–11 Years	13%
High School Graduate	33%
Vocational/Technical Education	35%
Some College	54%
4-Year College Degree	74%
Post-Graduate Study	88%
Total Employed	63%

Internet use at work is a concern for local economic development, but to what extent do less-educated workers use the Internet for their jobs, anyway? While about 48% of all Chicago residents reported using the Internet at work, if we restrict the sample to those who are employed, we find that 63% of Chicago residents who were working used the Internet for their jobs at least a few times per week. As shown in Table 6.2, Chicago residents who used the Internet at work were most prevalent in high-skill occupations held by workers with a baccalaureate or post-graduate degree. Still, Internet use at work was not uncommon for those without a college degree. At least a third of high school graduates and those with some vocational education used the Internet for work, and over half with some college did so.

These figures demonstrate that Internet use was fairly common even in lower skilled occupations that did not require college degrees. Internet use throughout a variety of industries is predicted to grow nationally over a number of years (Litan and Rivlin 2002) and digital skills will be increasingly important for the economic prospects of even less-educated workers and for the city's ability to attract or cultivate a variety of firms seeking technology-skilled employees.

Activities Online: Comparing Highly Connected and Less-Connected Neighborhoods

How do these patterns of Internet use unfold across neighborhoods in Chicago? By looking at Internet use at the neighborhood level, we can add to research on the geography of opportunity. What activities are commonplace in fully connected neighborhoods, and how are some neighborhoods currently excluded from information online? What potential impact does this have for economic development, public services, political representation, health, and quality of life across neighborhoods? Are there activities online that appeal to residents of some poor and less-connected neighborhoods, despite low rates of home adoption?

As mentioned, the Chicago survey was merged with aggregate-level variables to create probability estimates of broadband adoption, Internet use, and a variety of activities online for each of Chicago's 77 community areas. In this section, we map the prevalence of several Internet activities across the city, providing visual evidence of both potential and disparities. Federal agencies have defined "underserved" communities as those with 40% or less broadband subscribership at the census block level. We use that threshold to identify Chicago community areas that average the same rate across a much larger population, with thousands of residents.[9] Based on multilevel models, we estimate that nine community areas have less than 40% of the population with broadband at home (see Table 6.4). We first examine Internet activities in the nine community areas with the highest rates of broadband adoption in Chicago (see Table 6.3) and contrast them with patterns in the underserved community areas.

Many of the highly connected community areas are well-known as affluent neighborhoods in Chicago, including the Lincoln Park and the Gold Coast areas (near North Side). Condominium development in the Loop during recent years has made this a mecca for high-end residential addresses as well. While some of these community areas are predominantly white, others are more integrated, especially Hyde Park near the University of Chicago and Beverly, an attractive middle-class area on the South Side. Latinos are one-fifth to over one-fourth of the population in two of the highly ranked community areas, but they are not a majority in any of the most-connected neighborhoods. Ranked ninth is Armour Square, which is two-thirds Asian American and contains part of Chicago's "Chinatown" neighborhood. This community area is much poorer than the others with high broadband adoption and Internet use, with a 31% poverty rate.

High-speed Internet adoption at home ranged from 82% to 90% in these nine highest-ranked community areas in 2008, with Internet use anywhere from 92–98%. Each of these areas also considerably exceeded city averages for the percentage of the population engaged in most activities online: health information, politics, and use of the city website. Online job search differed, with some of these higher income neighborhoods using the Internet for job search at rates that were slightly below city averages (by a few percentage points). Personal networks are likely richer sources of job contacts in these communities, in comparison with poor neighborhoods (Granovetter 1973). Internet use on the job was generally higher in all these neighborhoods, with the exception of Armour Square. Internet use on the job is particularly low in this poorer and heavily Asian community area, with only 24% of employed residents estimated to use the Internet for work. This compares with a citywide average of 63% and with a range of 70 to 84% for the other high-broadband community areas. The Asian community in Armour Square looks quite different from other high-adopting neighborhoods, but this is consistent with national research that shows high rates of information technology use among Asian Americans (Mossberger, Tolbert, and Stansbury 2003; Fairlie 2007).

Table 6.4 shows the predicted broadband use for Chicago neighborhoods with the lowest access. All nine of the community areas listed in the table are estimated to have

Table 6.3   Internet Activities in Chicago Community Areas with Highest Broadband Adoption, 2008

CCA	Demographic Characteristics (%)								Internet Use (%)			
	Black	Latino	Asian	Poor	High School Grad	Home Broadband	Internet Anywhere	Use for Job*	Job Search	Health Info	Politics	City Web Site
Lincoln Park	5	5	6	11	96	90	98	80	60	91	82	63
Loop	12	4	13	10	97	87	97	84	44	89	82	59
Lakeview	4	8	6	10	97	86	97	78	53	88	79	57
Near North Side	13	5	8	14	96	86	96	78	46	87	77	56
North Center	2	13	4	7	93	85	96	72	58	86	74	57
Hyde Park	34	5	11	20	95	84	96	80	54	86	80	57
Beverly	32	3	1	5	95	83	95	79	47	84	72	58
Lincoln Square	5	19	13	14	86	82	96	70	57	85	72	60
Armour Square	9	4	68	28	65	82	92	24	62	88	62	63
City Avg.	34	27	5	20	79	61	75	63	50	64	53	49

of employed population only.

Sources: U.S. Bureau of the Census, American Community Survey 5 Year Estimates, 2005–2009 for Demographic Characteristics; 2008 Chicago Internet Survey for Internet Use.

Table 6.4 **Internet Activities in Chicago Community Areas with Lowest Broadband Adoption, 2008**

CCA	Demographic Characteristics (%)						Internet Use (%)					
	Black	Latino	Asian	Poor	High School Grad	Home Broad-band	Internet Any-where	Use for Job*	Job Search	Health Info	Politics	City Web Site
Fuller Park	97	0	0	36	69	15	28	19	17	22	15	20
South Lawndale	14	82	0	26	44	25	44	19	37	30	17	31
Grand Boulevard	94	1	0	34	79	35	59	26	39	45	26	33
West Englewood	97	2	0	40	69	35	59	24	44	42	25	34
Hermosa	2	85	3	18	62	36	60	32	40	40	27	34
Gage Park	6	86	0	19	51	38	59	26	40	40	24	36
Auburn Gresham	99	1	0	27	78	38	60	32	40	42	30	33
Lower West Side/Pilsen	3	82	1	30	56	39	61	40	34	43	31	37
New City	32	53	1	34	58	40	65	25	43	47	24	40
City Avg.	34	27	5	20	79	61	75	63	50	64	53	49

* *of employed population only*

Sources: U.S. Bureau of the Census, American Community Survey 5 Year Estimates, 2005–2009 for Demographic Characteristics; 2008 Chicago Internet Survey for Internet Use.

less than 40% of the population with home high-speed Internet access.[10] Just as chapter 4 showed that less-connected individuals engage in fewer activities online, our data indicates that less-connected communities experience unequal access to the information and communication opportunities on the Internet.

These underserved community areas are either predominantly African American or Latino. African American neighborhoods that are underserved are between 96 and 98% African American. Heavily Latino areas range from 80 to 94% Latino. One neighborhood, New City, has a mixture of African Americans and Latinos, but is still over 85% minority. The African American community areas have higher poverty rates, while the Latino community areas have lower high school graduation rates. This suggests some differences in barriers—with income likely to be a higher barrier in these African American neighborhoods, and education a higher hurdle in the Latino communities. Both Internet use anywhere and home broadband adoption are especially low in African American Fuller Park and Latino South Lawndale (also known as "Little Village"). Fuller Park on Chicago's South Side, like other heavily African American neighborhoods, has especially high poverty rates. South Lawndale, on the far West Side, is a significant gateway for recent immigrants in Chicago and is almost entirely Latino.

Outside of Fuller Park and South Lawndale, however, the likelihood of broadband adoption is between 35–40%, and Internet use anywhere is between 59–65% in underserved areas. These are considerably lower than the citywide averages of 61% for broadband and 75% for Internet use anywhere. The gaps are somewhat larger for home broadband adoption, however, than for Internet use in general. Outside of Fuller Park and South Lawndale, approximately 20–25% of the population in these community areas is estimated to have some experience with Internet use. This fits with the findings on Chicago public library Internet use, which show that both African Americans and Latinos are more likely to use public access technology. It is also consistent with research in northeast Ohio, which revealed high rates of Internet use outside the home in very poor, predominantly African American communities (Mossberger, Kaplan, and Gilbert 2008). In Chicago, where there is a larger Latino population, a similar pattern is evident in some Latino neighborhoods.

Unsurprisingly, Internet use for all activities was lower in these underserved neighborhoods. The most glaring differences were for Internet use for politics, which ranged from 15 to 31% (in comparison with 53% citywide) and for use on the job, which ranged between 19 and 40% of employed residents, compared with the citywide average of 63%. Of course, this reflects resident occupation and education in these neighborhoods as well as Internet skills. The lack of Internet use on the job suggests the possibility of a skills mismatch affecting the ability of residents to become employed or secure better paying jobs in the new economy. Low Internet use for politics indicates disadvantages for political information and mobilization in these neighborhoods and possibly for political representation.

Looking up health information online is most common in these communities, as in the city overall, although only 22–47% of underserved area residents are estimated to have done this in comparison with 64% citywide. The next most common activities are job searches and use of the city website. The probability of use of the Internet for a job search was between 17 and 43% in these less-connected communities, although in most it hovered close to 40%. The citywide average for online job searches in this case was only slightly more, at 50%. Gaps between underserved neighborhoods and the rest of the city were also more modest for use of the city website, which ranged from 20–40% in comparison with 49% citywide. Poor communities depend more heavily on public services, and so access to government information online is especially important (Dailey et al. 2010).

Underserved communities were disadvantaged in all respects, especially for online politics and Internet use at work. But, there are some indications that residents in these neighborhoods are more likely to use the Internet for some activities than for others. Those who were online commonly used information on health, jobs, and government services. These are the types of activities online that libraries report among patrons in low-income communities (Becker et al. 2010; Dailey et al. 2010). How do these patterns compare when we look across the city, at all of the neighborhoods? Mapping community areas by quartiles helps to visualize the geography of Internet use and opportunity in Chicago.

Mapping Economic Opportunity: Internet Use at Work and Job Searches

Comparing neighborhoods, we can see in Figure 6.5 that low-income African American and Latino community areas clustered on the South and West sides, like the underserved areas mentioned, have generally low rates of employment involving Internet use at work. Internet use at work is especially concentrated in the community areas on the North Side of the city along Lake Michigan. Some of these North Side areas are wealthy, and others are economically and ethnically diverse, but they stand in contrast to the city's poorest communities. This suggests technology disparities that exacerbate other inequalities in the labor market and may contribute to more limited employment options for residents of the poorest and most segregated neighborhoods.

As in the comparison of low- and high-broadband community areas in Tables 6.1 and 6.2, maps show that the Chicago neighborhood profile differs for job searches, compared with Internet use at work. Figure 6.6 indicates that areas with high Internet job searches include low-income, predominantly African American communities on the West Side like Austin and Garfield Park, as well as Greater Grand Crossing on the south.

The models used to produce these maps (see Appendix Tables A6.7–A6.8) show that Chicago residents who are more likely to search for jobs online are African American, as well as younger, higher income and more educated residents, holding other factors constant. National research indicates that despite having lower rates of Internet use, African Americans are more likely than other groups to search for jobs online.[11] This is true in Chicago as well. Some national studies have shown that English-speaking Latinos are also among those who are most likely to look for job information online (Boyce 2002). However, that is not the case for Latinos in Chicago, when both Spanish- and English-speaking Latinos are included.

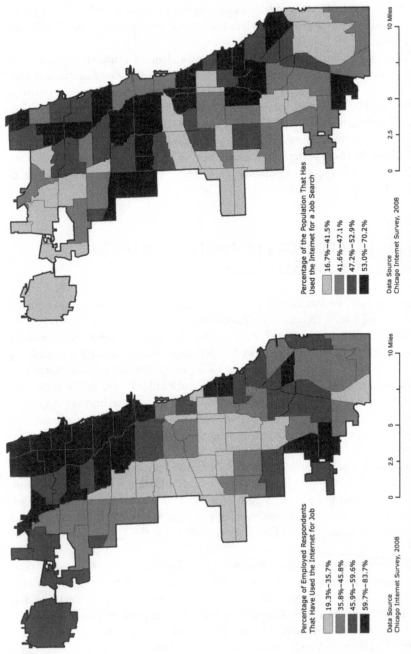

Percentage of Employed Respondents
That Have Used the Internet for Job

19.3%–35.7%
35.8%–45.8%
45.9%–59.6%
59.7%–83.7%

Data Source
Chicago Internet Survey, 2008

Percentage of the Population That Has
Used the Internet for a Job Search

16.7%–41.5%
41.6%–47.1%
47.2%–52.9%
53.0%–70.2%

Data Source
Chicago Internet Survey, 2008

10 Miles

0   2.5   5   10 Miles

Figures 6.5–6.6 Predicted Probability of Using the Internet at Work (left) and for Online Job Search (right) by Chicago
Community Area (from Appendix Tables A6.7 and A6.8)

Mapping Access to Services and Participation: E-government and Politics Online

The maps in Figures 6.7 and 6.8 compare Internet use for e-government and politics online. In Figure 6.8, more affluent neighborhoods with higher Internet use are also those with more residents engaging in politics online, as the most-connected neighborhoods showed. While similar patterns are visible for e-government, there is somewhat more diversity in use for the city's website than for politics. Low-income communities may not have equal access online to local government services and information, but the differences between communities are not as sharp for e-government as for politics. Local government websites offer residents information on services and online transactions, as well as new forms of participation. Neighborhood information is common on local government websites (Mossberger, Wu, and Jimenez 2010), and Chicago is no exception.

Use of the City of Chicago website is most likely for residents who are higher income, better educated, younger, women, and parents. Holding other factors constant, however, there are no racial or ethnic differences at the individual level (see models in Appendix Tables A6.9–A6.10), and this is reflected in the somewhat more diverse use of e-government apparent in the Chicago maps.[12] Local government websites may be particularly relevant for the daily routines of residents, attracting parents and a broader range of users.

The multivariate models in Appendix Table A6.10, demonstrate why the maps show greater disparities for political participation. Chicago residents most likely to be interested in politics online are younger, white non-Hispanic, higher income, better educated, and male. This is consistent with published research.[13] Parents are also less likely than those without children to look for political information on the Internet. This may suggest time constraints for either politics or Internet use.

Mapping Use of Health Information Online

Among the online activities included in the survey, looking for health information is one of the most common, with 64% of the population who have done this at some time. The multilevel models show that in Chicago there are some notable disparities for online health at the individual level and at the neighborhood level (see Appendix Table A6.11). Younger, more affluent, more educated residents, women, and parents are most likely to use the Internet for health. This fits with previous research demonstrating that women and caretakers are among the most frequent users of health information on the Web.[14] Those who are least likely to use health information online include Latinos and residents of neighborhoods with high populations of African Americans and Latinos. At the individual level, however, African Americans are no different from whites in online health information use.

These differences are apparent in the neighborhood map for online health information (see Figure 6.9). Some predominantly African American neighborhoods, such as Austin

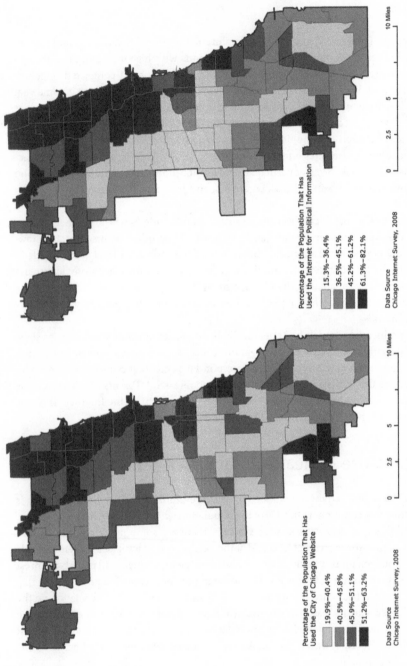

Percentage of the Population That Has
Used the City of Chicago Website

☐ 19.9%–40.4%
☐ 40.5%–45.8%
☐ 45.9%–51.1%
☐ 51.2%–63.2%

Data Source
Chicago Internet Survey, 2008

Percentage of the Population That Has
Used the Internet for Political Information

☐ 15.3%–36.4%
☐ 36.5%–45.1%
☐ 45.2%–61.2%
☐ 61.3%–82.1%

Data Source
Chicago Internet Survey, 2008

Figures 6.7–6.8 Predicted Probability of Using the City of Chicago Website (left) and for Online Political Information (right) by Chicago Community Area (from Appendix Tables A6.9 and A6.10)

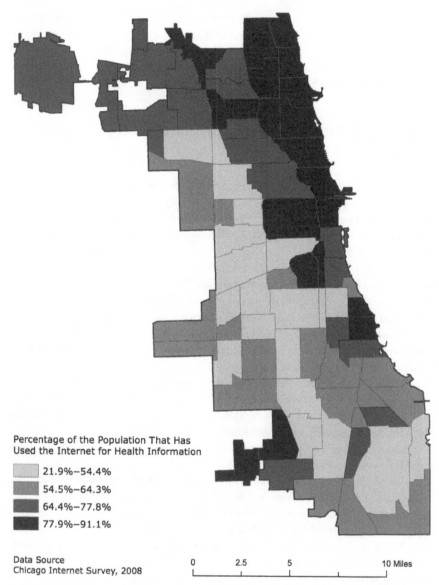

Figure 6.9 Predicted Probability of Using Online Health Information by Chicago Community Area (from Appendix Tables A6.11)

and West Garfield Park are in the second-highest quartile for health information use. While our models show that heavily African American neighborhoods tend to experience greater disparities in health information online, there is some variation among African American neighborhoods. For Latinos, both individual-level and neighborhood demographics predict low use of health information.

There are many challenges for effective use of online health information. Education and information literacy are important for evaluating the validity of different sources of health information. However, even as doctors, nurses, and other health care professionals refer more patients to online health information, residents of some Chicago neighborhoods have had less access to this resource. Given the greater health problems in poor communities, increased patient information and online support could help individuals in such neighborhoods to improve their health.

Conclusion: The Geography of Opportunity in Chicago

Through the neighborhoods of Chicago, a better view of technology inequality and opportunity emerges. Residents who were online daily were most likely to have home connections and have broadband, which encourages frequent use and a wider range of activities online. Yet, approximately 40% of Chicago residents were either offline or less-connected in 2008.

Chicagoans who were statistically more likely to be offline *or* less-connected were older, Latino, African American, low-income, and less educated. Residents of neighborhoods with a high percentage of African Americans and Latinos were particularly disadvantaged in terms of Internet use. The gap between African Americans and whites for Internet use anywhere was relatively small and was concentrated in segregated (and high-poverty) neighborhoods. African Americans were among the most frequent users of public access, although, like Latinos, they were less likely than whites to have home access. Thus, many low-income African Americans numbered among the less-connected, who have some experience with the Internet, and who make the effort to go online without easy access. This replicates findings in other high-poverty African American communities (Mossberger, Kaplan, and Gilbert 2008).

In Chicago, the growing Latino population stood out as the least connected, especially those who are Spanish dominant. Latinos were less likely to use the Internet anywhere than African Americans or non-Hispanic whites, although they also used Internet connections at public libraries more than non-Hispanic whites.

At the same time that the neighborhood context was a significant predictor for technology access, these disparities affected opportunities within neighborhoods as well. The Internet has become a critical resource for work, job information, civic engagement, access to government services, and health. Neighborhoods in Chicago with high rates of broadband access translate this resource into human capital, with high Internet usage at work. Such neighborhoods can convert their broadband access into information capital as well, using nearly every type of information we measured at higher rates than average. This was especially true for political information and may have consequences for democratic representation of neighborhoods. As more information and services move online, the costs increase for residents who are excluded from this medium. Within low-income neighborhoods, technology disparities have the potential to exacerbate existing place-based inequalities in health, the labor market, the democratic sphere, and in access to public goods.

Some activities clearly provide motivation to go online among the less-connected. In neighborhoods with the lowest rates of Internet use, activities such as looking up health information, job searches, and use of the city website were among the most common pursuits, much in the same way that national library studies report use for jobs and e-government (Becker et al. 2010). Earlier research has shown that African Americans, in particular, are likely to have positive attitudes about the connection between Internet use and economic opportunity—for getting a job, starting a business, or moving to a better job (Mossberger, Tolbert, and Stansbury 2003). The Chicago survey findings are consistent with one study of low-income urban and rural communities that concluded, "Broadband access is a prerequisite of social and economic inclusion, and low-income communities know it" (Dailey et al. 2010, 14).

How, then, can that knowledge produce social change? Divergent patterns of Internet use evident here suggest a possible need for different strategies in African American and Latino neighborhoods. Some approaches, such as subsidies, are especially important to assist those who are less-connected. Outreach, as well as multiple types of assistance, may be needed to reach those who are totally removed from Internet use. While the less-connected are relatively disadvantaged, as chapter 4 indicated, the data also suggests the motivation to take a first step forward. The policy problem is to understand how to facilitate the next step. In the next two chapters, we explore the barriers to broadband adoption—at the national level in chapter 7 and in Chicago neighborhoods in chapter 8. As in this chapter, the neighborhood-level perspective offers a more nuanced view of the challenges that the disconnected and less-connected face.

7

The Geography of Barriers to Broadband Adoption

The success of national policy depends on more than laying fiber or constructing wireless networks; it also relies on whether it affects barriers to broadband adoption or information technology use more generally. How can policy address the reasons that people are offline or only tenuously connected? To what extent do these barriers vary across place, or are they similar everywhere?

National survey data on the reasons individuals do not have broadband at home is available in the 2009 Current Population Survey. In this chapter, we analyze the 2009 CPS data by individual-level factors and by geographic subsamples, similar to chapter 3 on access and chapter 4 on the activities of mobile users and the less-connected. In the next chapter, we will compare the results here to similar data from the 2008 Chicago study, exploring the effects of neighborhood-level influences and variation across populations within the city. Together, these two chapters provide a comprehensive view of individual and place-based needs for addressing obstacles to widespread digital citizenship.

Theories of Technology Adoption and Possible Barriers

A number of barriers for Internet use or broadband adoption have been explored through research in the past, and we review some of the findings here within the context of the theory of planned behavior (Ajzen 1991). There are a number of relevant theoretical frameworks for understanding technology adoption (Davis 1989; Rogers 1995). While we make reference to some of these other frameworks, the theory of planned behavior has been widely used across disciplines (Morris and Venkatesh 2000) and has some advantages for exploring social and neighborhood-level variables as well as the individual attitudes or resources that underpin most of these models.

According to this theory, technology adoption is driven by several factors. **Beliefs and attitudes** include perceived usefulness of the technology and perception of fit between the technology and the individual's needs. **Perceived behavior control** involves an individual's perceptions about whether he or she has adequate resources to adopt the technology. Additionally, the social context matters, according to Ajzen (1991). **Subjective norms** that influence adoption refer to peer pressures, opinions within social networks, and community norms. How does this framework relate to prior research on Internet adoption and use? Common barriers cited in past research include a lack of interest, which can be influenced by individual beliefs and attitudes or social norms. Perceived behavioral control (resources for adoption) depends on an individual's assessments of affordability, skill demands, time, and availability of the technology, among other factors. We discuss these issues in relation to prior research. As in previous chapters, our focus is on home broadband adoption, which is a goal of national policy and a resource for digital citizenship.

Individual Attitudes and Subjective Norms—Interest. Choices are made by individuals based on their perceptions of the relevance or usefulness of technology (Ajzen 1991; Davis 1989).[1] People who do not have broadband at home may simply be uninterested in going online anywhere or in making the investment to have home access. Causes for this lack of interest could be varied: a lack of awareness of the uses and potential benefits of the technology, perceived lack of relevance or fit, or rejection of the technology.

Selwyn and colleagues (2005) describe nonusers in Britain as most often choosing not to adopt technology because of a lack of fit with their lives. Many who do not use the Internet simply do not see a reason to change their current routines or do not perceive any relative advantage to going online (Rogers 1995). One policy challenge for attracting those who are not currently online is to engage individuals in ways that respond to their particular needs (Warschauer 2003, 199; Katz and Rice 2002, 94–96). This may involve content that is culturally relevant or particularly useful for different populations. For example, a national nonprofit organization called One Economy addresses a variety of needs for low-income communities on the Beehive website that it hosts for subsidized housing programs, and the Chicago Smart Communities have separate portals for each neighborhood.[2]

Lack of interest may have a number of sources. Individuals who are less educated may be less knowledgeable about or interested in the benefits of technology, while those who have social networks with fewer adopters may not as readily learn about its potential uses (Warschauer 2003; DiMaggio et al. 2004; Hargittai 2003). Ono and Zavodny (2007) indicate that Latino immigrants may be among those with little experience with technology in their social networks. Additionally, nonadopters may avoid technology because of fears about unintended consequences, such as privacy and security threats. Survey data demonstrates that such fears are higher among those who have little or no experience with the technology (Horrigan 2010). All this suggests that outreach about the potential uses of technology and information about how to go online safely may change attitudes toward Internet use.

Selwyn (2003) cautions, however, that lack of interest cannot always be equated with knowledge deficits. Some individuals make a conscious choice not to go online in the same way that others choose to avoid television. This ideological refusal (Selwyn 2003) may be a form of opposition to mainstream culture. Haddon (2000) identified the elderly as more likely to be resistant to innovations and to the values of consumerism.

Given that race and ethnicity are still significant predictors of disparities in broadband access, what role might race, ethnicity (and possibly cultural differences) play in attitudes toward technology? Surveys by the Joint Center for Political and Economic Studies indicate that among individuals who do not use the Internet anywhere, lack of interest is most likely to be cited among all races, and that African Americans are slightly more likely than whites to mention a lack of interest (Gant et al. 2010). These descriptive statistics, however, don't include any controls for other possible explanations affecting lack of interest, such as age or education, nor are they disaggregated by geography. The authors also examine only those who do not use the Internet anywhere and not less-connected Internet users. In contrast, descriptive data on barriers to home Internet adoption or broadband adoption have consistently shown that cost concerns predominate for African Americans and Latinos nationally, in contrast with whites (Mossberger, Tolbert, and McNeal, 2008; Horrigan 2009).

One national survey found that African Americans were more likely than similarly situated whites to express positive attitudes toward Internet use, associating technology use with economic opportunity. Controlling for other factors, Latinos were significantly more likely than non-Hispanic whites to believe that you need the Internet to keep up with the times (Mossberger, Tolbert, and Stansbury 2003). African Americans and Latinos are also frequent users of public access and are somewhat more likely to use cell phones to go online (Gant et al. 2010; Zickuhr and Smith, 2; Livingston et al. 2009). While lack of interest likely influences some individuals across racial and ethnic groups, there is reason to believe that it is less prevalent among those who are socioeconomically disadvantaged, who may instead lack the resources for broadband access and digital citizenship.

Resources—Cost. Income has been found to be a consistent predictor of home access, and the cost of hardware, software, and broadband connections could be expected to pose a barrier for low-income populations (Fairlie 2004; Mossberger, Tolbert, and McNeal 2008; Katz and Rice 2002). Information technology can require a substantial up-front investment, despite falling prices for computers in recent years. Repairs and maintenance may add to costs, and outdated computers may not perform the functions that individuals need (Selwyn 2003). The CPS data examined here lists lack of a computer as a separate category, but we demonstrate in this chapter that conceptually this reason for lacking broadband is a matter of cost.

Internet services, however, require a monthly payment, and this may be a greater hardship for low-income consumers than the initial costs, forcing monthly decisions about competing priorities. Historically, disparities have been greater in telephone use than in radio and pre-cable television, which required one-time purchases (Schement and Forbes 2000). The price of broadband has not decreased as much as hardware (Van Dijk 2008; Greenstein and McDevitt 2010), and prices are higher in the United States than in many other countries.

Lack of consumer information may also magnify the problem of costs for low-income individuals. According to case studies in low-income communities, individual respondents often mentioned losing their Internet access because of extra costs for installation or because of practices such as bundling, which raised monthly bills beyond their ability to pay (Dailey et al. 2010). Costs are a matter of perception as well as dollars, of course, because individuals make choices about what to prioritize. Interviews with low-income respondents indicate, however, that Internet access outranks other expenses such as cable television in such households (Dailey et al. 2010). According to descriptive data, cost is important for African Americans and Latinos (Mossberger, Tolbert, and McNeal 2008, 99). Immigrants cite cost barriers at twice the rates of native born individuals (Ono and Zavodny 2008). Without further analysis, however, it is difficult to tell whether this is because of lower incomes or a difference in how technology is valued.

Resources—Skill. Frustration or anxiety about using technology is expected to discourage broadband adoption. Self-reports of difficulty using the Internet may be a matter of educational competencies, self-confidence, experience, or physical disabilities. Technology use requires a variety of skills or literacies (Warschauer 2003; Van Dijk 2005, 2008). Some measure of technical competence is needed, as well as online information literacy. The latter involves the ability to find, evaluate, and use information in a Web-based environment, and educational disparities are expected to inhibit such skills (Mossberger, Tolbert, and Stansbury 2003). Lack of confidence or anxiety may be a barrier for some individuals. Self-efficacy, self-image, and locus of control influence attitudes toward computer and technology use (Katz 1994; Ellen, Bearden, and Sharma 1991; Todman and Monaghan 1994). Physical disabilities, especially those that affect eyesight or fine motor skills, can make it difficult to use screens or keyboards, discouraging Internet use. Adaptive technologies can compensate for many disabilities, but not everyone is aware of their availability or can afford them. Many individuals with disabilities also have low incomes (Dobransky and Hargittai 2006).

Difficulty using technology is associated with older and less-educated individuals (Van Dijk 2008), although income, race, and ethnicity have also been found to be significant predictors for technical competence and information literacy (Mossberger, Tolbert, and Stansbury 2003). In studies that observed actual performance, women tended to report lower levels of technology skill, yet observations revealed no differences in actual skill based on gender, controlling for other factors (Hargittai and Shafer 2006; Van Deursen and Van Dijk 2009 a and b).

Language may be another skill barrier, and national surveys show large gaps in technology use between English-speaking and Spanish-speaking Latinos in the United States (Fox 2009; Ono and Zavodny 2008; Fairlie 2004). In fact, surveys that include only English-speaking Latinos often find few disparities with non-Hispanic whites.[3] There are different possible explanations for these results. Although the Internet has content available in many languages, English still dominates the Web (Ono and Zavodny 2008). One survey asked respondents how well they read English or Spanish and found that it was English ability rather than reading ability per se that affected Internet use (Livingston, Parker, and Fox 2009). Alternatively, predominantly Spanish-speaking Latinos may be more recent immigrants who had less exposure to the Internet in their countries of origin, especially if they migrated from rural areas (Kim et al. 2007). It is difficult to distinguish the exact reasons, but clearly English proficiency is associated with Internet use and adoption, at least within the United States.

Resources—Availability. Because broadband has unevenly diffused across the country, availability is a barrier to high-speed Internet adoption, especially in rural areas. Availability may be a problem for some metropolitan residents as well. Our interviews with municipal officials and recent case studies (Dailey et al. 2010) indicate that there are pockets without availability in some urban areas, and these may be most likely to affect low-income individuals.

There are other barriers to technology use discussed in the literature, including a lack of time as a resource. In this chapter, we focus on modeling the main reasons that were most common in the 2009 Current Population Survey.

Barriers to Internet Use: Nationally and by Geographic Regions

We are interested in understanding barriers to Internet adoption at home at both the individual level and by geographic region. The data in this chapter reports the main barrier for broadband use cited by respondents, across urban, suburban, and rural residents. This allows individuals to choose whether availability is the main reason they don't have broadband at home, for example, or whether the cost would be prohibitive even if it were available.

Given the descriptive statistics and prior research, at the individual level we expect those who are less interested in technology will be older and white. Those who cite costs are more likely to be African American, Latino, and low income. Those who report difficulty with technology are more likely to be older, less educated, and Latino. While African Americans are among the less-connected, they have a higher probability of Internet use in some settings, so will be less likely to say that they have difficulty using the technology at the level that it presents a barrier to home adoption.

In terms of geography, we expect a lack of availability of broadband to be a more common response among rural residents, and affordability or cost to be a more common barrier for urban residents. We anticipate that the reasons people are not online will vary by individual-level demographic factors but also by place. While scholars have traditionally focused on individual factors in defining disparities in access and use, we explore how these two dimensions overlap in raising obstacles to home broadband adoption.

BARRIERS TO BROADBAND ADOPTION AND GEOGRAPHY

The 2009 October Current Population Survey of 129,000 respondents documents the main reasons that individuals do not have high-speed (broadband) Internet connections at home. Questions on reasons for no home broadband access were asked of people with no Internet access of any kind as well as those with home dial-up. The most common reasons for not having broadband at home are lack of interest, cost, and lack of a home computer (or adequate computer). It is difficult to interpret the "no computer" response, because this begs the question of why the household does not have a home computer. Is this because of cost, skill, or lack of interest? In the following analysis we examine affordability separately but also create a category for individuals who cite either cost or lack a computer, effectively creating a meaningful measure. Responses to these two questions track together, suggesting the lack of a computer is driven by cost more than interest.

Unlike federal government reports drawing on the same census data that show trends for metropolitan and nonmetropolitan areas (NTIA 2010a and 2011), our focus in this chapter is on more detailed geographies and on community areas within cities in chapter 8. Following the format of chapter 3, in this chapter we show trends in barriers to broadband access nationally, and for central cities, suburbs, and rural areas separately. We find different barriers to broadband access matter in these three geographic areas.

We also analyze data for individuals rather than households, in contrast to the U.S. Census and NTIA reports. Following the multivariate models in the previous chapters of this volume, we cluster respondents by household to control for any error that may be introduced by multiple responses per household.

Since an important theme of this book is the influence of place, each of the five outcome variables are analyzed using the entire national sample and then separately by geographic subsamples. Table 7.1 lists the reasons for not having high-speed access nationally (column 1), for central cities (column 2), suburbs (column 3), and for residents of rural areas (column 4). The responses show the main reason that individuals gave for not having high-speed access at home. In Table 7.1 and the following tables, the cell numbers are weighted percentages, with the number of respondents in parentheses. In a few tables, cell sizes may be too small to make valid inferences.

The most commonly mentioned barrier among individuals lacking home broadband in Table 7.1 is the category in which we combined responses for "the cost is too high" and "don't have a computer." This applies to 45% of respondents. The second most frequently cited response is "I don't need it/not interested" at 36%. Taken alone, the response "too expensive" is given by 27% of respondents. Additionally 4.5% say "not available in area," and 2% say they lack confidence or skill to use computers and the Internet. Based on these simple percentages, the most important barriers to Internet use are cost and a lack of interest, not availability in terms of infrastructure, despite the focus of federal government policy on rural broadband.

There are also important variations by geographic region. Residents of central cities are 3% more likely to cite expense as the reason for no access and are almost 6% more likely to mention cost or lack of a computer than the national averages. Thus, cost as a barrier to Internet access is somewhat more prevalent among central city residents than in other parts of the country. Urban residents are somewhat less likely to indicate a lack

Table 7.1   **Reason for No High-Speed Home Access by Central Cities, Suburbs, and Rural Areas (2009 CPS)**

	National (All)	*Central Cities*	*Suburbs*	*Rural*
Don't Need It, Not Interested	36.18 (11,658)	33.26 (2,318)	36.49 (5,979)	37.92 (3,361)
Too Expensive	27.38 (8,821)	30.18 (2,103)	28.19 (4,619)	23.68 (2,099)
Too Expensive or No Computer	45.33 (14,605)	50.68 (3,532)	45.29 (7,422)	41.19 (3,651)
Not Available in Area	4.58 (1,477)	1.03 (72)	4.11 (674)	8.25 (731)
Lack of Confidence or Skill	2.61 (841)	3.07 (214)	2.54 (416)	2.38 (211)

Note: Entries are weighted percentages with sample sizes in parentheses.

of interest than national averages, while suburban and rural residents give this reason at almost the same frequency as national averages. Rural residents are much more likely to say that broadband is not available (8%) than individuals living in central cities (1%), as expected, and they are significantly less likely to say the main barrier is affordability or affordability/no computer. Suburban residents closely match national averages in terms of the main reasons for why they are not online. Very few respondents across geographic areas indicate a lack of confidence or skill as a reason for not having high-speed Internet at home.

BARRIERS TO INTERNET USE: RACE/ETHNICITY AND GEOGRAPHIC REGIONS

Table 7.2 presents descriptive data broken down by geography and by the race/ethnicity of the respondent, paralleling the frequency tables on access from chapter 3. Nationally, African Americans are almost 10% more likely than whites to say the main reason for a lack of high-speed access at home is because it is too expensive; 33% to 23%, respectively. Latinos are 14% more likely to cite affordability than white non-Hispanics. When we combine responses for too expensive or no computer/inadequate computer,

Table 7.2 **Reason for No High-Speed Home Access by Race and Ethnicity (2009 CPS)**

	Race			Ethnicity	
	White	*Black*	*Asian*	*Hispanic*	*Non-Hispanic*
National (All):					
Don't Need It, Not Interested	39.90 (8,233)	31.48 (1,382)	40.60 (350)	26.60 (1,438)	38.12 (10,220)
Too Expensive	23.61 (4,873)	33.01 (1,449)	21.35 (184)	36.92 (1,996)	25.46 (6,825)
Too Expensive or No Computer	39.66 (8,184)	53.74 (2,359)	38.40 (331)	60.01 (3,244)	42.37 (11,361)
Not Available in Area	6.17 (1,273)	2.07 (91)	1.16 (10)	1.18 (64)	5.27 (1,413)
Lack of Confidence or Skill	2.64 (544)	2.19 (96)	7.77 (67)	2.05 (111)	2.72 (730)
Central City:					
Don't Need It, Not Interested	40.01 (1,031)	29.66 (559)	42.81 (143)	26.41 (533)	36.05 (1,785)

	Race			Ethnicity	
Too Expensive	23.90 (616)	34.43 (649)	17.37 (58)	36.12 (729)	27.75 (1,374)
Too Expensive or No Computer	41.33 (1,065)	55.65 (1,049)	33.83 (113)	60.70 (1,225)	46.60 (2,307)
Not Available in Area	1.59 (41)	0.64 (12)	0.60 (2)	0.69 (14)	1.17 (58)
Lack of Confidence or Skill	2.83 (73)	2.81 (53)	11.98 (40)	2.18 (44)	3.43 (170)
Suburbs:					
Don't Need It, Not Interested	40.11 (4,403)	32.89 (571)	38.86 (178)	25.38 (726)	38.84 (5,253)
Too Expensive	24.64 (2,704)	32.26 (560)	24.67 (113)	38.87 (1,112)	25.93 (3,507)
Too Expensive or No Computer	40.25 (4,418)	51.38 (892)	42.58 (195)	60.92 (1,743)	41.99 (5,679)
Not Available in Area	5.09 (559)	3.00 (52)	1.31 (6)	1.43 (41)	4.68 (633)
Lack of Confidence or Skill	2.74 (301)	1.44 (25)	5.02 (23)	2.03 (58)	2.65 (358)
Rural:					
Don't Need It, Not Interested	39.52 (2,799)	32.77 (252)	41.43 (29)	33.97 (179)	38.17 (3,182)
Too Expensive	21.93 (1,553)	31.21 (240)	18.57 (13)	29.41 (155)	23.32 (1,944)
Too Expensive or No Computer	38.13 (2,701)	54.36 (418)	32.86 (23)	52.37 (276)	40.49 (3,375)
Not Available in Area	9.50 (673)	3.51 (27)	2.86 (2)	1.71 (9)	8.66 (722)
Lack of Confidence or Skill	2.40 (170)	2.34 (18)	5.71 (4)	1.71 (9)	2.42 (202)

Note: Entries are weighted percentages with sample sizes in parentheses.

African Americans are 14% more likely to give this reason than whites, while Latinos are 20% more likely to face this barrier than white non-Hispanics. The no computer or inadequate computer category is most important for Latinos, although it affects African Americans as well. Just as we saw distinct patterns of technology use in minority populations in the previous chapters, race/ethnicity is an important factor in understanding barriers to high-speed Internet at home.

Table 7.2 also indicates that nationally, whites are much more likely to say they are not interested in technology than minority groups, and whites are more likely to live in an area where broadband is not available than racial and ethnic minorities. Thus, federal government policy focusing on rural broadband disproportionately benefits white non-Hispanic Americans.

In central cities, 56% of African Americans without broadband at home say the reason is expense or lack of a computer, compared with 54% for blacks nationally. Cost is a slightly more important barrier for urban minorities. Suburban African American and Latino residents are less likely to cite affordability or a lack of computer than their central city counterparts. Only 51% of suburban African Americans cite cost or lack of a computer, compared with 56% of urban African Americans. Rural whites are more likely than minorities living in rural areas to say they don't have home broadband because they are not interested or high-speed Internet is not available.

BARRIERS TO INTERNET USE: INCOME AND GEOGRAPHIC REGIONS

Beyond race, a long-standing influence on home adoption is personal income. Table 7.3 shows the percentage of Americans who experience the five barriers to high-speed Internet at home by annual income. Nationally, the poor (or those earning less than $20,000 a year) are 12% more likely to say they don't have access because it is too expensive and 25% more likely to say the reason is cost or the lack of a computer than the wealthiest Americans, or those earning $100,000 per year or more. The poor and those earning between $20,000 and $39,000 are much less likely to say broadband is not available in their area (2 and 4%, respectively). On the other hand, this response is given by 15% of those with incomes in the six digits. Affluent rural residents cite availability, but poor rural residents experience other barriers as most important. Across geographic regions and income groups, roughly the same percent say they are not interested in broadband. A lack of skill or confidence is slightly more commonly cited among the poor than the affluent, but the differences are minimal.

Table 7.3 indicates that cost is a more common problem among the urban poor. Fifty-nine percent of those with annual incomes less than $20,000 who live in urban areas mention cost or lack of a home computer, compared with 54% nationally, a 5-point difference. And 55% of urban residents with incomes between $20,000–40,000 cite expense or lack of a home computer, compared with over 47% nationally, a 7% increase for central city residents. Even urban residents with incomes between $40,000–59,000 are 7% more likely to give this reason compared with the national averages or their suburban counterparts. Reasons for not having high-speed Internet at home nationally mirror those in the suburbs. Notably, as income increases for rural residents, the percentage of the population saying "not available in area" jumps dramatically, suggesting

Table 7.3   **Reason for No High-Speed Home Access by Income (2009 CPS)**

	Income				
	Less than 20,000	*20,000 to 39,999*	*40,000 to 59,999*	*60,000 to 99,999*	*100,000 or more*
National (All):					
Don't Need It, Not Interested	32.25 (2,748)	35.56 (3,023)	32.67 (1,228)	33.37 (889)	28.64 (242)
Too Expensive	32.13 (2,738)	29.08 (2,472)	27.51 (1,034)	23.65 (630)	21.42 (181)
Too Expensive or No Computer	54.40 (4,635)	47.45 (4,034)	42.86 (1,611)	35.81 (954)	28.64 (242)
Not Available in Area	1.75 (149)	3.71 (315)	8.38 (315)	11.19 (298)	14.79 (125)
Lack of Confidence or Skill	3.40 (290)	2.42 (206)	1.94 (73)	1.58 (42)	1.78 (15)
Central City:					
Don't Need It, Not Interested	28.40 (603)	30.61 (532)	31.40 (216)	38.48 (172)	25.30 (42)
Too Expensive	35.28 (749)	31.65 (550)	30.81 (212)	25.28 (113)	30.12 (50)
Too Expensive or No Computer	58.78 (1,248)	55.12 (958)	49.71 (342)	37.14 (166)	39.76 (66)
Not Available in Area	0.38 (8)	1.21 (21)	1.16 (8)	0.67 (3)	1.20 (2)
Lack of Confidence or Skill	3.72 (79)	2.01 (35)	2.18 (15)	2.46 (11)	0.00 (0)
Suburbs:					
Don't Need It, Not Interested	30.47 (1,169)	36.15 (1,571)	33.91 (688)	32.66 (515)	31.33 (146)
Too Expensive	33.67 (1,292)	29.80 (1,295)	29.23 (593)	25.75 (406)	21.24 (99)
Too Expensive or No Computer	55.85 (2,143)	46.92 (2,039)	43.72 (887)	38.11 (601)	29.18 (136)

(*continued*)

Table 7.3   **(continued)**

	Income				
	Less than 20,000	20,000 to 39,999	40,000 to 59,999	60,000 to 99,999	100,000 or more
Not Available in Area	1.59 (61)	2.88 (125)	7.20 (146)	10.53 (166)	10.94 (51)
Lack of Confidence or Skill	3.23 (124)	2.76 (120)	1.63 (33)	1.78 (28)	3.22 (15)
Rural:					
Don't Need It, Not Interested	38.11 (976)	38.05 (920)	31.09 (324)	31.56 (202)	25.35 (54)
Too Expensive	27.22 (697)	25.93 (627)	21.98 (229)	17.34 (111)	15.02 (32)
Too Expensive or No Computer	48.57 (1,244)	42.89 (1,037)	36.66 (382)	29.22 (187)	18.78 (40)
Not Available in Area	3.12 (80)	6.99 (169)	15.45 (161)	20.16 (129)	33.80 (72)
Lack of Confidence or Skill	3.40 (87)	2.11 (51)	2.40 (25)	0.47 (3)	0.00 (0)

Note: Entries are weighted percentages with sample sizes in parentheses.

either greater awareness of availability problems or a lack of other barriers. Among rural residents who are very poor, only 3% mention lack of availability as the main reason for not having home broadband. But this increases to 20% of those with incomes between $70,000–100,000 per year, and 34% among those earning more than $100,000. This strongly suggests higher income rural residents are the most likely beneficiaries of a program that addresses only availability, and that awareness or affordability or other barriers will be issues for less affluent rural residents. Among those who do not now have broadband at home, the highest percentage of Americans saying they don't need it are among the wealthiest citizens (earning $100,000 or more) residing in urban or in rural areas, with both high-income cohorts citing this 25% of the time. Wealthy suburban residents without broadband are less likely say they don't need it.

Appendix Tables A7.1 and A7.2 list these five reasons for lacking home broadband by education and age, respectively. Nationally, the young (ages 18–29) are 30% more likely than respondents 65 years or older to say they lack home access because it is too expensive or they lack a computer. This gap is even slightly wider among central city residents. The young are almost 32% more likely to cite expense or a lack of a computer than older respondents if they live in an urban area, and the gap is 30% among suburban residents.

Predicting Barriers to Internet Use by Geography

Next, we explore how overlapping individual-level demographic, economic, and occupational influences shape the probability of facing these barriers across geographic areas. Following the previous chapters of this volume, we use multivariate regression to isolate the independent effects of multiple factors on barriers to technology use. Our multivariate analyses model the five main barriers to home broadband as dependent or outcome variables. We use the same detailed set of explanatory or predictor variables from the 2009 CPS as in chapter 3, including race; ethnicity; language; income; education; age; marital status; parental status; an interaction term to measure a single parent with children; business ownership; and occupation. Appendix B lists these variables and how they are coded.

Multivariate Results

RACE/ETHNICITY AND BARRIERS TO INTERNET USE BY GEOGRAPHIC REGION

Appendix Table A7.3 presents a multivariate logistic regression model predicting the probability of citing a lack of interest as the main reason for no home broadband (coded 1 with other reasons coded 0). The sample is restricted to those individuals without high-speed Internet at home. In column 1 the sample is the entire nation (all respondents), column 2 includes only respondents residing in central cities, column 3 shows respondents residing in suburbs, and column 4 gives results for rural residents. Appendix Tables A7.4–A7.7 model the other four primary reasons for lacking Internet access, including cost, cost plus no home computer, availability, or lack of skill. Because the dependent variables for each reason are binary, logistic regression coefficients are reported. The model standard errors are clustered by household using VCE (variance-covariance estimator). As it is difficult to understand the substantive meaning of the variables from the logistic regression coefficients, we present the results graphically as predicted probabilities, holding all other variables in the model constant at mean/modal values.

Appendix Table A7.3 indicates that Latinos and African Americans are statistically less likely than white non-Hispanics to say the reason they lack home broadband is that they don't need it, and this pattern holds nationally and among residents of central cities. Substantively, however, the differences are rather small. Holding other demographic and economic factors constant, Figure 7.1 suggests that urban whites have a .30 probability of saying not interested, compared with .27 if the respondent is a Latino or African American. But there are no statistically significant differences based on race/ ethnicity for rural residents. Although the graph appears to show differences by race/ ethnicity for rural residents, these differences are not statistically significant. The bars for varying racial and ethnic groups in suburban areas are roughly the same, showing little difference among whites, Latinos, and African Americans in citing a lack of interest as the reason for not adopting broadband.

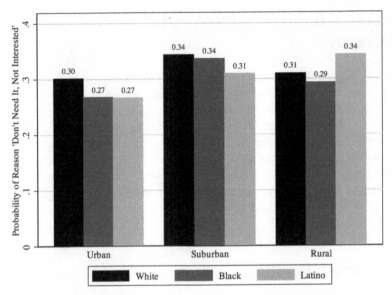

Figure 7.1 Reason No High-Speed: Predicted Probability of Responding Don't Need It, Not Interested by Race/Ethnicity (from Appendix Table A7.3). Note: All other explanatory variables held constant at mean values.

Appendix Table A7.4 shows that African Americans are statistically more likely to say they lack home broadband because it is too expensive, nationally and among urban African Americans. But we do not see this pattern for suburban or rural African Americans. In contrast, Latinos are not more likely than white non-Hispanics to mention cost as a reason for lacking access regardless of geography, while Asian Americans are actually less likely than whites to cite affordability as the main reason for no Internet access. Figure 7.2 shows these results graphically; the probability of saying "too expensive" for urban African Americans is .33, compared with .29 for urban whites, a .04 difference. Since this gap only matters in urban areas, it suggests cost barriers to Internet use are more important in central cities, especially for some minorities.

The most frequently mentioned reason for lacking home broadband is the combined category of cost or the lack of a home computer. The logistic regressions modeling this outcome variable are reported in Appendix Table A7.5. In this case, Latinos and African Americans are statistically more likely to give this reason than white non-Hispanics nationally and among subsamples of urban respondents and suburban respondents (using a 90% confidence interval). Rural Latinos are more likely to give this reason than rural whites, but there is no statistically significant difference between rural whites and African Americans. Figure 7.3 graphs these results, showing a varied pattern among racial and ethnic groups for all geographic areas. Among urban residents, whites have a .48 probability of citing cost or lack of a computer as the main barrier, compared with .54 for Latinos and African Americans, a 6-point difference. Only 42% of suburban whites give this as the primary reason, compared with 46% of suburban African Americans and 50% of suburban Latinos, an 8-point difference between non-Hispanic whites and Latinos. Minorities across geographic areas are more likely to face affordability concerns or lack a computer than white non-Hispanics.

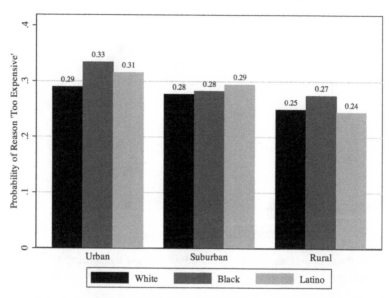

Figure 7.2 Reason No High-Speed: Predicted Probability of Responding Too Expensive by Race/Ethnicity (from Appendix Table A7.4). Note: All other explanatory variables held constant at mean values.

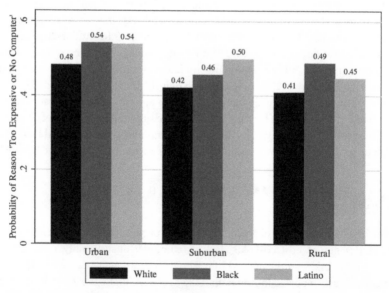

Figure 7.3 Reason No High-Speed: Predicted Probability of Responding Too Expensive or No Home Computer by Race/Ethnicity (from Appendix Table A7.5). Note: All other explanatory variables held constant at mean values.

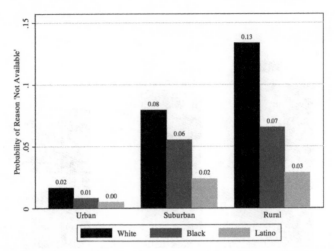

Figure 7.4 Reason No High-Speed: Predicted Probability of Responding Not Available by Race/Ethnicity (from Appendix Table A7.6). Note: All other explanatory variables held constant at mean values.

Geography matters the most when modeling responses to "not available in area" as shown in Appendix Table A7.6 and graphed in Figure 7.4. Across racial and ethnic groups there is an extremely low probability of giving this reason among urban residents, as expected, since most urban areas have some type of broadband available. Among suburban residents, white non-Hispanics are significantly more likely to cite this barrier than racial or ethnic minorities; 8% of suburban whites indicate broadband is not available, compared with 6% of African Americans and 2% of Latinos, controlling for other demographic factors. This may reflect some spotty availability at the fringes of metropolitan areas, which also tend to be predominantly white (Brookings Institution 2010).

But the largest disparities by race/ethnicity are found among rural residents. Figure 7.4 indicates the probability of citing "not available" as the primary barrier among rural whites is relatively high at .13, compared with only .07 for rural blacks and .03 for rural Latinos. Again, a lack of broadband infrastructure appears to be a primary factor for white rural residents but not for rural minorities. Because the probability of citing a lack of confidence or skill is so low (1–2%) and the sample sizes are small and less reliable, we do not present a graph, but the statistical results are found in Appendix Table A7.7.

INCOME/EDUCATION AND BARRIERS TO INTERNET USE BY GEOGRAPHIC REGION

Figures 7.5–7.8 graph the probability of saying the primary reason for not having home broadband is interest, cost, cost plus a lack of a computer, or availability, varying respondents' income. Like the previous graphs, the figures are generated from the logistic regression models reported in Appendix Tables A7.3–A7.6. Figure 7.5 indicates that as annual income increases, the probability of citing lack of interest in the Internet rises steadily across geographic areas. But, suburban residents are about 5 percentage points more likely to give this reason than urban residents. The effect of increased income on lack of interest or perceived lack of need is the smallest for those living in rural areas. Figure 7.6 shows the opposite pattern. As income increases, the probability of citing cost as a barrier falls steadily, from a .40 probability for poor suburban residents to .25 for wealthy suburbanites. Overall, there is less variation in the probability of citing cost as income decreases among urban residents compared with those living in suburban or rural areas. Further evidence that the lack of an adequate computer is a proxy for cost is found in Figure 7.7. As income increases, the probability of mentioning expense and

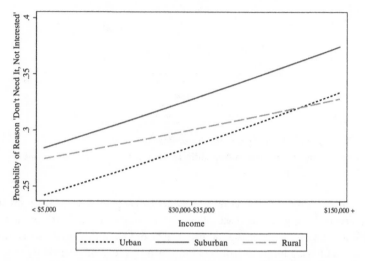

Figure 7.5   Reason No High-Speed: Predicted Probability of Responding Don't Need It, Not Interested by Income (from Appendix Table A7.3). Note: All other explanatory variables held constant at mean values.

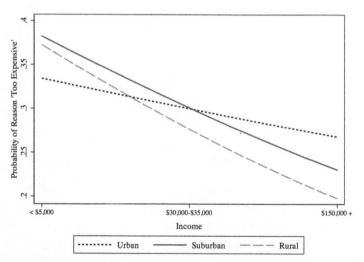

Figure 7.6   Reason No High-Speed: Predicted Probability of Responding Too Expensive by Income (from Appendix Table A7.4). Note: All other explanatory variables held constant at mean values.

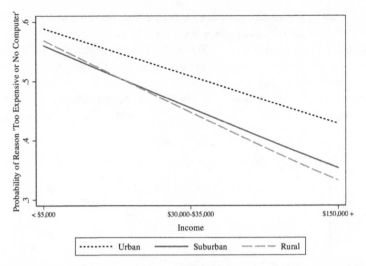

Figure 7.7 Reason No High-Speed: Predicted Probability of Responding Too Expensive or No Computer by Income (from Appendix Table A7.5). Note: All other explanatory variables held constant at mean values.

lack of a home computer falls rather steeply across geographic areas, with urban residents more likely to give this reason than those living in the suburbs or rural areas. Among the urban poor there is a .60 probability of giving this response as the main reason for not having home broadband, but this drops to a .45 probability among the wealthy urbanites.

As expected, Figure 7.8 shows that the probability for availability as the barrier to Internet use is much higher among rural residents than those living in the suburbs or

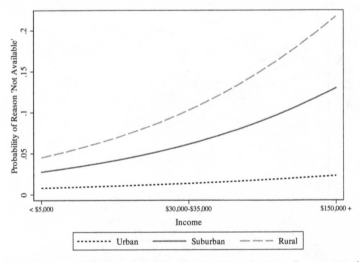

Figure 7.8 Reason No High-Speed: Predicted Probability of Responding Not Available by Income (from Appendix Table A7.6). Note: All other explanatory variables held constant at mean values.

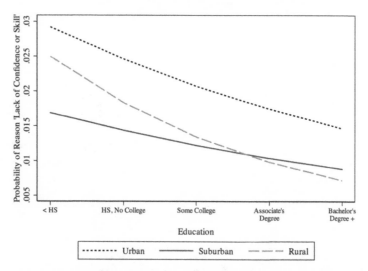

Figure 7.9 Reason No High-Speed: Predicted Probability of Responding Lack of Confidence or Skill by Education (from Appendix Table A7.7). Note: All other explanatory variables held constant at mean values.

urban areas, but an unexpected finding is that this barrier is much higher for the rural wealthy than the rural poor. While not shown graphically, the probability of citing a lack of confidence or skill remains steady as incomes rise for urban or suburban residents. Rural residents, however, are less likely to say they lack technology skills as income rises. A similar pattern is evident in Figure 7.9, which plots the probability of citing "lack of confidence or skill" as education level increases. Across geographic areas, as formal education increases the probability of lacking technology skills falls, with the largest gaps in urban areas. As education rises, there is little substantive difference in the probability of naming the other barriers as reasons for not having the Internet at home.

AGE AND BARRIERS TO INTERNET USE BY GEOGRAPHIC REGION

The patterns evident so far suggest that there is significant overlap for some barriers across geographic regions, but for other barriers, place of residence shapes broadband use. The last set of predicted probability graphs, which we briefly summarize, are again based on logistic regression models presented in Appendix Tables A7.3–A7.7 and show the probability of naming each of the five barriers as age increases. Figure 7.10 shows that regardless of residence in urban, suburban, or rural areas, as age increases from 20 years to over 70, the probability of lack of interest/lack of need rises from a .20 probability to .60. Age remains a factor in broadband disparities. And the young also tend to be poorer, so even controlling for individual income and education, as age increases the probability of citing cost as the reason drops from nearly 50% for 20-year-olds to 20% for those over 70, again with little variation by geographic region (see Figure 7.11). A very similar pattern is shown in Figure 7.12 graphing the probability of citing cost or no

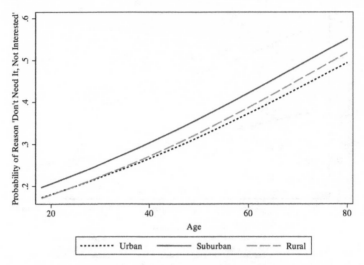

Figure 7.10 Reason No High-Speed: Predicted Probability of Responding Don't Need It, Not Interested by Age (from Appendix Table A7.3). Note: All other explanatory variables held constant at mean values.

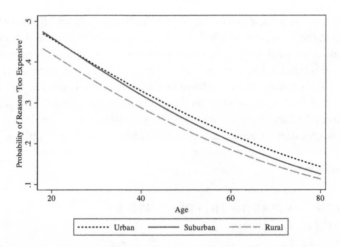

Figure 7.11 Reason No High-Speed: Predicted Probability of Responding Too Expensive by Age (from Appendix Table A7.4). Note: All other explanatory variables held constant at mean values.

home computer, with urban residents more likely to mention this barrier across age cohorts. Divergences by geographic area come into play in Figure 7.13, which graphs the probability of citing lack of availability by age. Young rural residents are much more likely than older rural residents to give availability as the primary reason for lacking broadband, and the same is true (to a lesser extent) for the suburban young and old. This suggests the young would otherwise be broadband adopters, but that older residents don't view this as the main barrier. For urban residents, who live in wired areas,

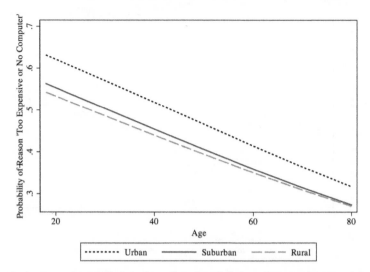

Figure 7.12 Reason No High-Speed: Predicted Probability of Responding Too Expensive or No Computer by Age (from Appendix Table A7.5). Note: All other explanatory variables held constant at mean values.

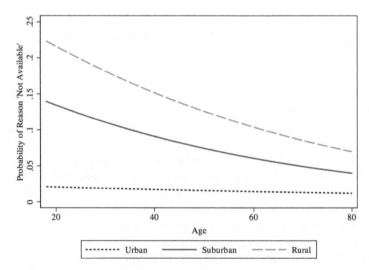

Figure 7.13 Reason No High-Speed: Predicted Probability of Responding Not Available by Age (from Appendix Table A7.6). Note: All other explanatory variables held constant at mean values.

there are no differences based on age. Finally, Figure 7.14 shows that age increases the probability of saying lack of confidence or skill is the main barrier; it rises about 2% from the young (age 20) to those over 70 for residents of urban areas. The differences across age cohorts in all geographic areas are relatively small with older individuals only slightly more likely to name skill as a barrier.

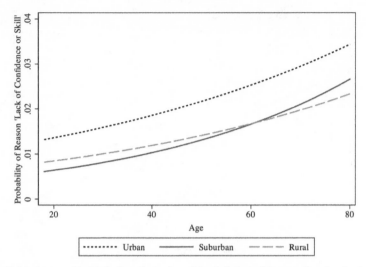

Figure 7.14 Reason No High-Speed: Predicted Probability of Responding Lack of Confidence or Skill by Age (from Appendix Table A7.7). Note: All other explanatory variables held constant at mean values.

Conclusion: Tracking National Barriers Across Place

The contribution of this chapter has been to model the main reasons that people do not have broadband at home, controlling for overlapping factors and disaggregating results by geography. There are some differences by geography that have policy implications. Urban African Americans are more likely to view cost as a barrier, although Latinos everywhere are among those most likely to report cost as a reason for not having broadband. The category of cost plus computer constraints is an important one for African Americans and Latinos, especially Latinos. Self-reported difficulty using the Internet, while modest, trends higher in central cities.

The largest geographic differences, of course, are for availability. While this was expected, our analysis reveals an important finding. Among rural residents, availability is the main barrier for those who are in more technologically advantaged groups—for more affluent, white, and younger respondents. Improving infrastructure in rural areas will create new opportunities for some, but will not address the major barriers for others—rural minorities and the poor.

General patterns emerge based on social and demographic factors across place. While the results are quite similar to the descriptive statistics described in other reports, the multivariate models clarify these relationships. African Americans, Latinos, the poor, and the young are most likely to report that cost is the primary reason for not having high-speed connections at home. Combining the categories of cost and no computer/inadequate computer strengthens these results, and more accurately reflects the prevalence of affordability as a barrier to home adoption. Similarly, while the percentage of those who mention lack of confidence or skill as the major reason for not having broadband is small, these individuals tend to be older and less educated. Those who experience barriers of cost or difficulty cite needs rather than lack of interest and may be a ready audience for public policy solutions that address those problems.

Nationally, affordability is the single largest barrier for broadband adoption, when we consider that lack of an adequate computer is most often related to cost. Descriptive statistics show that this is the main reason for not adopting broadband in the home, given by nearly half (45%) of respondents.

Lack of interest is most frequently mentioned by older, more affluent, and white respondents. For high-income nonadopters in particular, this may simply be a lifestyle choice, as Selwyn suggests. Some older individuals, however, may be coaxed online if they can be introduced to applications that matter to them. Motivations to use the Internet may include keeping in touch with family members, especially grandchildren, or accessing health information. Both social ties and better information may lead to healthier aging, and Internet use may assist in this regard.

The urban differences, while modest in the aggregate, suggest that affordability and lack of skill may be crucial issues in some urban neighborhoods. The literature review at the beginning of this chapter raises social networks as a possible influence on attitudes and resources for technology use. Social networks often have a strong place-based element (Wellman 1996). These and other environmental factors will be considered in more depth in the next chapter, which examines barriers to adoption at the neighborhood level in Chicago.

8

Barriers to Adoption in Chicago Neighborhoods

WITH DANIEL BOWEN AND BENEDICT JIMENEZ

A large body of urban policy research suggests that place-effects such as segregation and concentrated poverty within inner-city neighborhoods affect experiences and opportunities for the poor, especially African Americans and Latinos (e.g., Wilson 1987; Jargowsky 1997; Massey and Denton 1993; Wilson 1996). Chapter 6 demonstrated that neighborhood factors exercise an independent effect on Internet use and home access in Chicago; residents of community areas with high percentages of African Americans and Latinos are particularly disadvantaged, and these results are significant holding constant influences like race or income at the individual level. Outside of these high-minority neighborhoods, African Americans are just as likely as whites to use the Internet in some place, but disparities for Latinos are wider and seem less place-specific.

Other studies indicate that the neighborhood context is significant for shaping opportunity and communication using information technology. The Chicago study is consistent with national research showing that neighborhood income affects the prospects for Internet use across races, and that controls for neighborhood characteristics explain disparities between African Americans and whites (Mossberger, Tolbert, and Gilbert 2006). Fong and Cao (2008) find that in metropolitan areas with higher levels of Latino segregation and poverty, Latino households are less likely to use the Internet at home.[1] This suggests place effects for Latinos, but the Fong and Cao study measures segregation and concentrated poverty within the metropolitan context rather than the actual neighborhood of respondents. Some other research has found various neighborhood influences on Internet use: outside the home, on the job, and in various ways across racially and ethnically different communities (Kim, Jung, and Ball-Rokeach 2007; Mossberger, Kaplan, and Gilbert 2008; Kaplan and Mossberger 2012). These studies will be explored further in this chapter. But, the evidence raises questions about why place effects are significant. Do poor neighborhoods present particular barriers for adoption or magnify disparities in some way?

The previous chapter showed that African Americans in central cities are more sensitive to cost as a barrier, and that while skill barriers are infrequently cited, there is a greater tendency for urban residents to report this as the main reason for not having broadband at home. Urban poverty may influence technology use in ways that are different from rural poverty. While public access technology may be more available in urban areas, disparities in education and in the labor market may still present hurdles for gaining skill or for affording high-speed access at home.

The Chicago study offers an unusual opportunity to explore differences in urban neighborhoods. We estimate barriers to home adoption[2] across Chicago's census tracts and the 77 official community areas of the city using survey questions that parallel the previous chapter exploring national barriers. We find significant diversity in why some residents are offline or less-connected. Barriers to technology use vary by neighborhood as well as by individual demographic characteristics, such as race, ethnicity, and age. Modeling interactions between variables demonstrates the differential effects of age across racial and ethnic groups, and the amplification of individual disparities in segregated neighborhoods, especially for Latinos.

Chicago has large populations of both African Americans and Latinos and offers a good view of similarities and contrasts between these groups. With comparisons to previous research on technology use and place, we use the Chicago study to suggest more general patterns of need in poor urban neighborhoods.

Urban Place Effects and Technology Use

Research on spatially concentrated poverty indicates that the neighborhood environment may structure opportunities and constraints for technology use.[3] Concentrated poverty represents a "double burden" for the poor who live in very poor areas (Federal Reserve and Brookings Institution 2008, 5). How might community characteristics affect attitudes and resources for home Internet use, applying the theory of planned behavior from chapter 7 to the environment of high-poverty neighborhoods?

Attitudes and Subjective Norms—Interest. Do poor and segregated neighborhoods have values or attitudes that downplay the utility of the Internet because of social isolation or opposition to mainstream culture? The theory of planned behavior, argues that technology adoption is influenced by peer pressure and social norms. The literature on concentrated poverty in American cities suggests that segregation and the prevalence of poverty can breed different attitudes and values within social networks in such communities (Wilson 1987). Likewise, the networks within poor neighborhoods may lack information about the Internet and its potential benefits, and do little to encourage interest in going online. Ono and Zavodny (2007) hypothesized that segregation for poor Latino immigrants may produce social networks that are isolated from the Web, although they did not test these spatial effects in their work.

Some research indicates, however, that poor neighborhoods may not have very different values, despite whatever experience and information is available within local networks. Neighborhood-level factors predicted using the Internet without easy access in one study: living in a predominantly African American neighborhood was associated with a higher probability of Internet use without home access (including public access), controlling for other factors (Mossberger, Kaplan, and Gilbert 2008).[4] These neighborhood patterns of use may reflect interest in digital society despite economic constraints and are consistent with other research on attitudes toward technology (Dailey 2010; Mossberger, Tolbert, and Stansbury 2003).

Resources—Cost. How might neighborhoods affect cost barriers? While urban areas generally have some availability of broadband, costs may be higher in poor communities due to a lack of competition or the options available for service. There is little systematic evidence to test this explanation, however. The FCC published data at the time of this study on the number of broadband providers per census tract, but this is not useful for identifying the alternatives available for residential services.[5] Anecdotally, some low-income areas in Chicago have only one residential provider, which is higher cost cable modem rather than lower cost DSL. Still, until better data becomes available through federal broadband mapping initiatives, it is difficult to tell the extent of competition in poor areas.

There are other ways in which high costs within poor neighborhoods may influence perceived adequacy of resources for technology. The availability and prices of goods and services tend to be worse in poor neighborhoods, and financing or credit are less available in low-income areas (Caplovitz 1967; Federal Reserve and Brookings Institution 2008). Higher prices or lack of credit may impose extra burdens for acquiring the hardware and software needed for home broadband access. Additionally, higher prices for food and other necessities in poor neighborhoods may limit investments in competing goods such as Internet access.

Pricing practices may cause individuals to drop Internet service, such as high installation costs or pressure to bundle services beyond ability to pay (Dailey et al. 2010). While these constraints are related to an individual's income and consumer knowledge, there may be some place effects that exacerbate these problems in poor neighborhoods. It is unclear from the cited study whether companies operating in poor areas are more likely to charge extra fees or to push aggressive pricing, or whether there is just a lack of experience or good consumer information in neighborhood social networks. Any of these, however, could contribute to community influences beyond an individual's income or knowledge.

Resources—Skill. There may be a spatial dimension to skill in areas where there is little exposure to technology at work and other places, and where members of resident social networks have little familiarity with computers or the Internet. Residents of poor urban neighborhoods may be disadvantaged for employment that includes opportunities for learning about technology. Individuals living in neighborhoods with high unemployment were less likely to use the Internet for their jobs in one metropolitan area (Kaplan and Mossberger 2012). Residents of poor neighborhoods may have fewer educational skills to navigate the information on the Web and to learn about technology. Both neighborhood influences and school quality affect student achievement in high-poverty communities (Jargowsky and El Komi 2011), and disadvantages for those who lived in high-poverty communities during adolescence often persist for years (Holloway and Mulherin 2004).

Neighborhood effects may also be visible in gateway communities where recent immigrants who are less educated and poor cluster together in high-poverty neighborhoods. There may be some differences between Latino and African American neighborhoods in terms of perceived skill as a barrier, because of more exposure to technology outside the home in African American communities and better resources for informal learning and support within social networks.[6]

There are myriad reasons to expect that place matters for urban residents who are offline or less-connected. It is difficult, however, to tease out causal mechanisms underlying potential place effects. Indeed, causes for neighborhood effects are complex and not easily addressed in the research (Federal Reserve and Brookings 2008; Sampson, Morenoff, and Gannon-Rowley 2002; Birch, Newburger, and Wachter 2011).

Barriers for the Less-Connected in Chicago

We are interested in understanding barriers to home Internet use at both the individual level and by place or neighborhood. The Chicago survey included a number of questions about why individuals lacked Internet access at home.[7] Common responses in both the Chicago survey and the national CPS were lack of interest, cost, and difficulty using the technology. Our analyses therefore concentrate on these three reasons for lacking home Internet access. From the previous chapter, we would expect that at the individual level, those who are less interested in technology will be older, less educated, and white. African Americans and Latinos will be less likely than non-Hispanic whites without home Internet access to say they are uninterested. Based on the national results, those who cite costs are more likely to be African American, Latino, and low income, but this may be especially true for Latinos. Those who cite difficulty with technology are more likely to be older and less educated, according to the analysis in the last chapter. Latinos may also be in this group, given lower levels of education.

Residents of poor minority neighborhoods, we hypothesize, are more likely to cite cost or difficulty with technology (but not lack of interest). Most of the potential neighborhood effects indicate reasons why costs may be higher in poor neighborhoods, or why residents of such areas may experience more skill deficits. Based on high rates of public access use in poor communities, we believe that lack of interest is not likely to be grounded in the neighborhood context.

Finally, we explore interactive effects. Age is an important factor in digital inequality, and the national data shows strong relationships between age and some barriers, such as lack of interest and skill. We expect that age has differential effects on home adoption for African Americans, Latinos, and non-Hispanic whites, just as we expect differences in general between these groups. Older minorities are among those who are most isolated from technology. Understanding whether barriers are similar for all older individuals can yield better information for addressing disparities among older African Americans and Latinos, in Chicago and other cities.

The final set of interactions we investigate is related to segregation, which chapter 6 showed was a significant influence on Internet use anywhere and home access. Residents of both predominantly African American and Latino neighborhoods were disadvantaged, controlling for individual-level factors. Here, we take a further step in examining the reasons for not using the Internet at home for African Americans and Latinos living in a neighborhood with a high percentage of minorities. If neighborhood matters for digital inclusion, these individuals may be, to use Wilson's (1987) term, truly disadvantaged.

To explore these questions, we draw on the Chicago survey of 3,453 residents conducted in summer 2008. The survey was merged with census tract-level data measuring neighborhood racial and ethnic context, educational attainment, and relative affluence or poverty. The results are presented first using only the individual-level survey data, and then using a series of multilevel statistical models controlling for neighborhood-level factors, used in the previous chapters. We conclude by examining interactions between race/ethnicity and age, and cross-level interactions of the race/ethnicity of the respondent by the minority population of the neighborhood.

Barriers to Home Access in Chicago

Home access is an important resource for regular and effective technology use. The telephone survey used in this analysis included a question asking why respondents did not use the Internet at home, which serves as our primary outcome variable. We asked those who do not use the Internet at all and those who do not use it at home to choose any and all reasons for not using the Internet at home.[8] In this way, we could better understand whether respondents who said that they cannot afford the Internet might be uninterested as well, and therefore not motivated to spend money on a computer or a monthly Internet bill.

Table 8.1 shows that lack of interest, affordability, and skill stand out as the most important main reasons for not having a home connection in Chicago.[9] When respondents are allowed to give multiple answers, issues such as privacy and danger online emerge as secondary reasons for many, even though few residents cite them as the main reason for not having the Internet at home. Difficulty is also more important as a secondary reason—people who do not have the Internet at home may not choose this as the primary reason for not investing in an Internet connection, but they are less confident of their skills nonetheless.[10]

Table 8.1   **Reasons for No Internet at Home, Chicago Sample**

	Main reason	*One reason*
Don't need it/not interested	30%	48%
Cost is too high	27%	52%
Too difficult to use	9%	43%
Can use it elsewhere	5%	52%
Don't have time	5%	24%
I am worried about privacy	2%	57%
The Internet is dangerous	2%	46%
Hard to use information in English	1%	19%
Physical impairment	3%	13%
Other	16%	—

Note: N = 1,011

Table 8.2   **Main Reason for No Internet at Home by Race and Ethnicity, Chicago Sample**

	White Non-Hispanic	Black	Asian	Latino	Total
Don't need it/not interested	42%	29%	42%	19%	31%
Cost is too high	14%	30%	12%	37%	27%
Too difficult to use	9%	8%	9%	13%	9%

As in the national data, there is considerable variation by race and ethnicity in the main reason for not having the Internet at home as seen in Table 8.2. More white and Asian American residents who do not currently use the Internet at home are not interested, and African Americans and Latinos are more concerned about cost than white non-Hispanics. Thirty percent of African Americans and almost 40% of Latinos offline cite affordability as the primary barrier to home access.[11] Cost and lack of interest are nearly tied for African Americans in the Chicago sample, but in comparison with whites, a much lower percentage of African Americans say they are not interested. A lack of interest is the number one reason cited by white non-Hispanics for not having the Internet at home, with more than 40% giving this reason. In contrast with the CPS, Latinos are the group most likely to say that difficulty using the Internet is the main reason for not having it at home. Additionally, there are more respondents in the Chicago sample who cite difficulty, even for the main reason for being less-connected. Overall, however, results are comparable to the CPS.

Predicting Barriers to Home Access at the Individual Level

To sort out differences among Chicago residents in reasons for not having home access, we conducted multivariate logistic regression. This first layer of the analysis focuses exclusively on individual-level predictors as explanatory factors. We examine only the most frequently cited answers for the main reason, which were "I don't need it/not interested," "the cost is too high," and "it's too difficult to use." We allow respondents to include multiple barriers to technology access to measure the full scope of the problem. Appendix Table A8.1 models who reports they are not interested as a reason for being offline, who reports cost as a barrier, and who reports a lack of skills. Primary explanatory variables measure demographic factors paralleling previous research on digital inequality (Mossberger, Tolbert, and Stansbury 2003; Fairlie 2004).[12]

Because logistic regression coefficients are difficult to interpret in terms of substantive magnitude, we convert the coefficients in Appendix Table A8.1 into predicted probabilities shown in Table 8.3. We hold constant all other explanatory variables in the model at their mean/modal values, and then vary each explanatory variable from minimum to maximum values to understand the independent effect of age, for example, on barriers to home Internet access.

Table 8.3 shows diversity in the barriers individuals face in lacking technology access at home. Older individuals and those with more income are more likely to say they are not interested as reasons for not using the Internet at home, controlling for other factors. These individuals make conscious choices to stay offline, and some may be resistant to new technology or see it as irrelevant (Selwyn 2003). However, the poor, Latinos, females, and those with less education are significantly more likely to cite affordability as the main reason for not having the Internet at home. A lack of skill is a barrier for older respondents and Latinos. Notably, African Americans and those with higher education are significantly less likely than other groups to mention a lack of skill as a reason for not having home access. Higher rates of public access use by African Americans may have some positive effects on confidence in skills.

Table 8.3 shows older individuals are 24% more likely to cite a lack of interest as the reason they are offline compared to young respondents; a 31-year-old (one standard deviation below the mean) has only a 32% probability of saying he or she is not interested, compared to an older individual (67 years, one standard deviation above the mean), who has a 56% probability of citing this reason. Higher income residents are also more likely to say that they are uninterested. Nonadopters with annual family incomes between $75,000 and $100,000 are 15% more likely to cite lack of interest than respondents with incomes between $10,000 and $20,000. In comparison, education makes a smaller difference than age and income. Residents with a high school diploma are 9% more likely than college graduates to say they are not interested in the Internet. African Americans are 7% *less* likely than whites to cite a lack of interest in home access.

Not surprisingly, residents citing cost are, in fact, low income. However, Latinos (not African Americans) emerge as the ethnic group most likely to view cost as a barrier to technology access, once we control for factors such as income. The poor (with incomes between $10,000 and $20,000) are 30% more likely to perceive cost as a barrier to home access than the affluent (incomes between $75,000 and $100,000), all else equal. Poor Chicago residents have a 60% probability of citing cost barriers, compared to higher income residents, who have less than a 30% chance of saying this. Holding other factors constant, Latinos were 15% more likely to say cost is a problem in acquiring Internet access than white non-Hispanics. African Americans, in contrast, were only 3% more likely than whites to say cost is the main issue for home access, controlling for other factors. This difference was not statistically significant. The differences between African Americans and whites in sensitivity to cost (apparent in the descriptive statistics) may therefore be due to higher levels of poverty rather than race per se. We explore this in more detail later. Interestingly, women were 15% more likely than men to mention cost as a reason for not having home access, all else equal.

The last column of Table 8.3 demonstrates that less educated, older, and Latino respondents are more likely to say that they have difficulty using the Internet. Older respondents (one standard deviation above the mean) were 30% more likely to cite skill barriers compared to the young (one standard deviation below the mean). This is a very large difference based on age alone and is not surprising given the national data and prior research. A lack of formal education also corresponds with a lack of skills. Respondents with only a high school degree were 15% more likely to say the Internet

Table 8.3 **Predicted Probabilities: Reasons Chicago Residents Do Not Have Home Internet (from models reported in Appendix Table A8.1)**

	Not Interested	Cost is Too High	Too Difficult to Use
White non-Hispanic (baseline)	.50 (.04)	.54 (.04)	.43 (.04)
Latino	.48 (.04)	.69 (.05)	.57 (.04)
Difference Latino vs. White	−.02	+.15	+.14
Black	.43 (.04)	.57 (.03)	.36 (.03)
Difference Black vs. White	−.07	+.03	−.07
Male	.55 (.04)	.39 (.04)	.37 (.04)
Difference Female vs. Male	−.05	+.15	+.06
Annual Income			
Very low ($0, −2 SD)	.40 (.05)	.72 (.04)	.50 (.05)
Low ($10,000–$20,000, −1 SD)	.47 (.04)	.59 (.03)	.45 (.04)
Mean/Average ($40,000–$50,000)	.50 (.04)	.54 (.04)	.43 (.04)
High ($75–$100,000, + 1 SD)	.62 (.05)	.29 (.04)	.35 (.05)
Very high (more than $150,000, + 2 SD)	.66 (.05)	.21 (.04)	.31 (.05)
Difference Low to High	+.15	−.30	−.10
Education level			
Less than HS	.54 (.04)	.58 (.04)	.52 (.04)
High school graduate	.52 (.04)	.56 (.04)	.47 (.04)
Some college	.46 (.04)	.52 (.04)	.37 (.04)
College Graduate	.43 (.04)	.50 (.04)	.32 (.04)
Graduate degree	.40 (.05)	.47 (.05)	.28 (.04)
Difference HS to College	−.09	−.06	−.15
Age of respondent			
Very young (18 yrs., −2 SD)	.24 (.05)	.50 (.06)	.15 (.04)
Young (31 yrs., −1 SD)	.32 (.05)	.51 (.05)	.22 (.04)
Mean/Average (49 yrs)	.50 (.04)	.54 (.04)	.43 (.04)
Old (67 yrs., + 1 SD)	.56 (.03)	.55 (.03)	.52 (.03)
Very old (85 yrs., + 2 SD)	.68 (.03)	.57 (.03)	.67 (.03)
Difference young to old (27–67 yrs.)	+.24	+.04	+.30

Note: All other explanatory variables held constant at mean/modal values. Standard errors of the probability estimate in parentheses. Modal/mean values are a female, white non-Hispanic Chicago resident with no children and average age, income, and education.

was "too difficult to use" compared with those who have a college degree. Latinos were 14% more likely to cite a lack of skills or difficulty going online than white non-Hispanics, again indicating greater disparities for Latinos. In contrast, African Americans were 7% *less* likely to cite skills as a barrier to use compared with whites who did not have home access. This may reflect Internet use outside the home among African Americans.

Predicting Barriers to Home Access for Individuals Controlling for Neighborhood Context

As a second layer to our analysis, we merge our survey data with geographic information from the respondent's community area or census tract, as we did in previous chapters. Scholars have found measurement error may occur unless researchers account for the geography in which individuals reside (Primo, Jacobsmeier, and Milyo 2007). Chicago's community areas and census tracts vary dramatically in terms of affluence, education, and racial/ethnic composition. Geographic variables included in the models are the percentage of African Americans, Latinos, Asian Americans, high school graduates, and population living below poverty levels from the U.S. Census.[13] These variables correspond to the urban literature on segregation and concentrated poverty.

Because of the multilevel data, we clustered the respondents by either census tract (column 1) or community area (column 2) reported in Appendix Tables A8.2–A8.4.[14] This analysis allows us to understand how context interacts with individual-level factors to predict technology access. We report traditional predicted probabilities of the substantive effects of our explanatory variables. Probabilities from the multilevel models are also used to create geographic estimates of the reasons for no home access for each of Chicago's 77 community areas. The maps are produced using the multilevel models that combine neighborhood and individual characteristics.

LACK OF INTEREST

Appendix Table A8.2 shows that when we add in contextual predictors, income matters at the tract and community level as well as at the individual level. Residents of more affluent neighborhoods without home Internet access are more likely to say that they are not interested in going online. Those who are offline by choice tend to be more affluent and live in higher income areas. The darkest shading on the map in Figure 8.1 indicates where lack of interest as the reason for not having home Internet access is highest in Chicago, and this follows community areas where Internet use is highest (see chapter 6), including the affluent north lakefront, Beverly, and the far North Side.

COST TOO HIGH

While at the individual level African Americans were not more likely than whites to report cost as a reason for not having technology access at home (a 3% difference), the

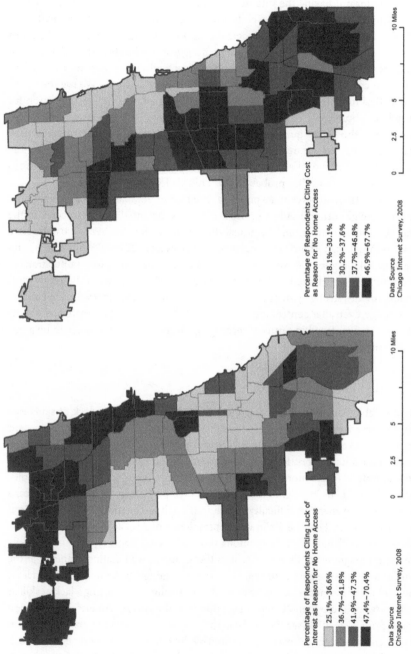

Percentage of Respondents Citing Lack of
Interest as Reason for No Home Access

25.1%–36.6%
36.7%–41.8%
41.9%–47.3%
47.4%–70.4%

Data Source
Chicago Internet Survey, 2008

Percentage of Respondents Citing Cost
as Reason for No Home Access

18.1%–30.1%
30.2%–37.6%
37.7%–46.8%
46.9%–67.7%

Data Source
Chicago Internet Survey, 2008

Figures 8.1–8.2 Predicted Probability of Citing Lack of Interest (left) or Cost (right) as Reason for No Home Internet by Chicago Community Area (from Appendix Table A8.2 and A8.3) models reported in Appendix Table 8A.3 show that residents of communities with higher African American populations are significantly more likely to state that cost is a main reason for not having the Internet at home (see Figure 8.4). This is an example where using only the individual-level data may mask important variation in what we seek to explain. Similarly, residents in neighborhoods with high proportions of Latinos are also more likely to cite cost. These patterns suggest neighborhoods with high concentrations of African Americans and Latinos are particularly sensitive to cost burdens or perceived costs. These are areas of concentrated poverty as well. We use the multilevel statistical models to map the probability of citing affordability as the reason for being offline at home.

Figure 8.2 shows by quartile darker shaded community areas, where a high percentage of the less-connected cite costs. Such neighborhoods are largely on the South and West Sides of the city, where there are greater concentrations of African Americans and Latinos. The probability of citing affordability as a barrier doubles, rising by more than 40 percentage points, as the Latino population increases from 20 to 80% in a neighborhood. A less pronounced but substantial increase occurs in the African American population. The probability of citing affordability as a barrier rises by 20%, as the African American population increases from 20 to 80% in a community (see Figure 8.4). Figure 8.4 even suggests that higher Asian American populations in a community area are linked with barriers to home technology access based on cost. The map provides strong evidence that place and context matter in predicting barriers to technology, even after controlling for individual-level factors. Segregated neighborhoods are disadvantaged in terms of technology access and cost appears to be a primary explanation.

DIFFICULTY/LACK OF SKILL

Appendix Table A8.4 introduces neighborhood effects to predict a lack of skills as a barrier to home access. The results show individuals residing in higher poverty census tracts are less likely to cite a lack of skills as a reason for not having home access, controlling for other factors. Residents in poor neighborhoods, whether white, Latino, or African American, are more likely to cite cost as a barrier rather than a lack of skills. Additionally, residents in neighborhoods with a high percentage of African Americans are more likely to mention difficulty in use (although at the individual level African Americans are not). Figure 8.3 shows the prevalence of African American neighborhoods on the South and West Sides among those where residents report a lack of skill. Some Latino neighborhoods are evident in this group as well. Latino ethnicity at the individual level is associated with skill as a barrier, although at the neighborhood level the percentage of Latinos is not significant. The probability of reporting a lack of skill as a barrier rises by more than 20 percentage points as the African American population increases from 20 to 80% (see Figure 8.4). This may suggest some skill deficits or problems concentrated in these areas not captured by the other factors examined here, such as unequal educational opportunities not measured by formal educational attainment. Again, relying on individual-level survey data alone would hide this variation based on neighborhood racial characteristics.

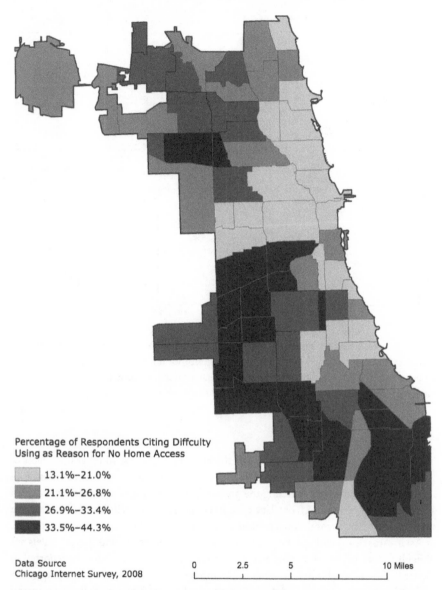

Percentage of Respondents Citing Diffculty
Using as Reason for No Home Access

- 13.1%–21.0%
- 21.1%–26.8%
- 26.9%–33.4%
- 33.5%–44.3%

Data Source
Chicago Internet Survey, 2008

0   2.5   5   10 Miles

Figure 8.3 Predicted Probability of Citing Difficulty as Reason for No Home Internet by
Chicago Community Area (from Appendix Table A8.4)

INTERACTION EFFECTS: AGE AND RACE/ETHNICITY

But how might these individual-level and neighborhood-level patterns interact in mag-
nifying or diminishing the barriers we have shown so far? One plausible avenue is to
explore how race/ethnicity and age interact in shaping barriers to technology. Age
accounts for some of the largest gaps in access and use and is implicated in many of the

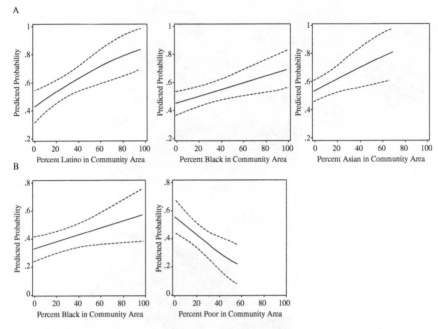

Figure 8.4 Predicted Probability of Citing Cost (top panel) and Too Difficult (bottom panel) as Reasons for No Home Internet by Neighborhood Demographics (from Appendix Tables A8.3 and A8.4). Note: Dashed lines represent 95% confidence interval around the predicted values. All other explanatory variables held constant at mean values.

barriers in prior research, and so it is worthwhile to understand whether the effects of age differ across racial and ethnic groups. Appendix Table A8.5 replicates the multilevel models reported earlier, predicting the probability of citing a lack of interest (column 1), affordability (column 2), or a lack of skill (column 3), but includes three interaction terms measuring the conditional relationship between race (African American, Latino, or Asian-American) and age. Because the substantive effects of conditional models are difficult to interpret from the logit coefficients, predicted probabilities are reported in Figure 8.5, holding all other variables in the model constant. The top panel graphs the probability of citing interest, cost, or difficulty for Latinos (solid black line) compared to non-Latinos (light gray line). The dashed lines represent the 95% confidence interval around the predicted values. The bottom three graphs report the same data for African Americans (black line) compared to white non-Hispanics (light gray line).

A striking pattern emerges for both Latinos and African Americans, compared with white non-Hispanics. As whites become older, they are significantly *less* likely to cite affordability as the reason for not having the Internet at home, as noted by the falling light gray lines. In contrast, as African Americans and Latinos get older, they are significantly *more* likely to cite cost constraints as the reason for lacking technology access (rising black lines). Thus older racial and ethnic minorities may face the greatest technology barriers in terms of affordability, while white non-Hispanics may be offline by

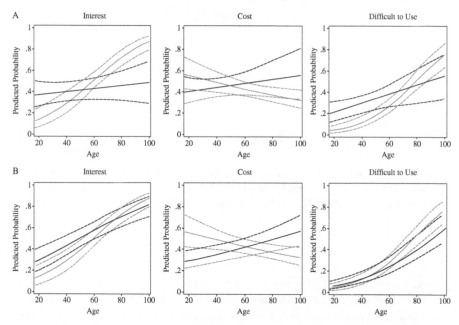

Figure 8.5 Probability of Citing a Lack or Interest, Cost, or Skill as a Reason for No Home Internet, for Latinos and Non-Latinos (top panel) and Blacks and Whites (bottom panel) by Varying Age (from Appendix Table A8.5). Note: Dashed lines represent 95% confidence interval around the predicted values. All other explanatory variables held constant at mean values.

choice. The graphs also show a consistent pattern where older non-Hispanic whites are considerably more likely to cite a lack of interest, compared with similarly aged African Americans and Latinos. For older whites in Chicago, a lack of interest is the barrier, but for minorities it is cost.

Finally, Figure 8.5 shows that Latinos are considerably more likely to cite a lack of skill than non-Hispanics across age cohorts. But, the most dramatic gaps are for the young; young Latinos are much more likely than young white non-Hispanics to mention difficulty as a barrier. This may indicate a lack of educational opportunities, language barriers, or limited experience with technology in neighborhoods with concentrated Latino populations. These graphs are some of the first we are aware of to illustrate these intriguing interactive effects of race and age in shaping the contours of digital inequality.

INTERACTION EFFECTS: RACE/ETHNICITY AND NEIGHBORHOOD MINORITY POPULATIONS

We conclude by empirically testing a major theme of this research. Do individual and place effects interact to shape urban disparities, especially self-reported barriers to home Internet access? Table A8.6 reports three final multilevel models identical to those already discussed, but the table includes cross-level interactions of a Latino

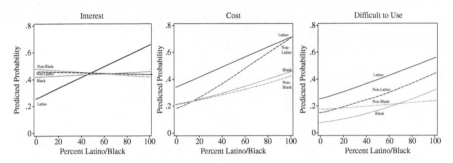

Figure 8.6 Probability of Citing a Lack of Interest, Cost, or Skill as a Reason for No Home Internet, Latinos and the Percent Latino in their Neighborhood, and for Blacks and the Percent Black in their Neighborhood (from Appendix Table A8.6). Note: All other explanatory variables held constant at mean values.

respondent multiplied by the percent Latino in his or her neighborhood, as well as cross-level interactions for an African American respondent multiplied by the percent of African Americans in his or her community area. That is, are Latinos and African Americans relatively better off for information technology access when residing in more ethnically diverse neighborhoods or when residing in heavily minority areas of Chicago that also are known for concentrated poverty?

Again we turn to graphs of the predicted probabilities (see Figure 8.6) with all other variables in the model held constant to understand the substantive results. Following the previous presentation, Figure 8.6 presents the probabilities of reporting the reasons for no home access: lack of interest (far left), affordability (center), and difficulty or a lack of skill (far right), as the percent African American or Latino population in the neighborhood increases. Probabilities for African Americans and Latinos are shown in the same graph. For African Americans (solid gray line), non-Blacks (dotted gray line), and non-Hispanics (dotted black line), as the percent minority population in a neighborhood increases, there is no measurable change in the probability of citing a lack of interest as a barrier. But for Latinos (solid black line), as the percent Latino increases in the neighborhood, so does the probability of not being interested in technology. The effects are dramatic, increasing nearly 40 percentage points over the range of the variable measuring percent Latino in Chicago neighborhoods. Latinos residing in heavily Latino neighborhoods are not only offline, but they have less interest in the information online. The results suggest that there are additional barriers for Latinos living in segregated Latino communities, including perhaps a lack of knowledge about technology.

The middle graph in Figure 8.6 plots parallel information, but this time for the probability of citing affordability as a barrier. Again, the most dramatic effects are for Latinos. A Latino living in a neighborhood that is only 20% Latino has approximately a 40% probability of citing cost as a barrier. For the same Latino living in a neighborhood that is 80% Latino, the probability of citing cost rises to 70%; a .30 probability difference based on place alone. Neighborhood ethnicity has an independent effect in driving concerns about affordability of home Internet access. This pattern is significantly different than for non-Hispanics living in the same neighborhoods, who are much less likely to cite affordability concerns. Thus, Latino ethnicity and concentrated Latino populations combine to increase barriers to technology access.

While increased proportions of African Americans in a neighborhood are associated with a higher probability of citing affordability as a barrier, the same pattern is found for African Americans and whites living in predominantly black neighborhoods (the lines for both races are nearly identical). Thus concentrated poverty and higher African American population are driving this effect, and it is similar for whites or African Americans living in the area. This explains why the coefficient for African Americans at the individual level was not statistically significant in the previous models.

Finally, the far right graph in Figure 8.6 shows that Latinos living in neighborhoods that are primarily Latino are significantly more likely to cite a lack of skills as a barrier, compared with Latinos living in more ethnically mixed neighborhoods or non-Hispanics living in the same areas. Interestingly, as the percentage of African Americans increases in a neighborhood, there is no change in the probability of whites citing skill as a barrier, but African Americans living in homogeneous African American neighborhoods do face a higher probability of reported skill deficits.

Overall, the analysis provides strong evidence that place matters in Chicago's map of digital inequality. There are independent effects for neighborhoods (percent minority) as well as individual demographic factors (race/ethnicity, age) at work.

Conclusion: The Role of Place in Technology Barriers

Theoretically, this chapter lends credence to the need for considering how digital inequalities vary by place, not only between cities and rural areas, but across neighborhoods as well. By drawing on large-sample survey data and measures of neighborhood context, our research provides a more nuanced analysis of barriers to technology access than is possible in national studies. The analysis demonstrates that barriers to technology access vary across neighborhood contexts and vary across different demographic groups, and that race and place interact to shape barriers to access.

Costs are an important dimension of urban digital inequalities. While individual-level models show that cost barriers are not significantly different for African Americans compared with whites, costs barriers are more pronounced in neighborhoods with high proportions of either African Americans or Latinos. These effects are the most dramatic for Latinos living in more homogenous neighborhoods, although they are significant for Latinos overall. Additionally, at the individual level, low-income respondents are those most concerned with cost. To date, federal policies have supported public access and training in urban areas, but there has been little policy addressing affordability.

Two issues that stand out in this analysis would not be visible analyzing data on a national scale: the amplification of cost and skill barriers in poor neighborhoods, and the extent of barriers faced by Latinos in predominantly Latino communities. For African Americans in particular, individual-level models do not reveal the disadvantage experienced by those who live in areas of concentrated poverty. Latinos face substantial and multiple barriers in terms of technology access. Wide gaps for Latinos were apparent in earlier chapters, especially for the Spanish dominant. The constraint is not just Spanish language but also living in a segregated environment. While we often think of concentrated poverty and segregation in terms of African American populations, urban Latino communities may face the greatest technology challenges in the 21st century.

As expected, residents of more affluent neighborhoods are most likely to say they are simply not interested in going online, and at the individual level, it is older and higher income nonadopters who also mention lack of interest. Interaction models show that as whites age, they are much more likely to report a lack of interest as the reason for not going online, but the same is not true for older African Americans and Latinos. Rather, it is older racial and ethnic minorities who are much more likely to cite cost as a barrier than white non-Hispanics. This suggests that older African Americans and Latinos may be enticed online with affordable broadband and other support.

Self-reported difficulty or skill barriers are less frequently mentioned as the main reason for not having home access but are given as a contributing factor by 43%. Moreover, residence in a high-poverty neighborhood is correlated with such skill barriers. While African Americans are not more likely to cite skill deficits at the individual level, Chicagoans in neighborhoods with high proportions of African Americans are, indicating some additional disadvantage in these areas. In general, it is African Americans in poor communities who lag behind technologically, and so without controlling for the neighborhood context, disparities for African Americans are less visible. At the individual level, older, less educated, and Latino respondents were those most concerned with difficulties using technology. Most important, Latinos residing in heavily Latino neighborhoods are the most likely to cite skill as a barrier to access.

These findings raise issues for research as well as for public policy. Why exactly does neighborhood matter? Costs may be affected by perceptions in the community or by how the Internet is valued compared with competing needs. It is also possible that higher prices of other goods and services crowd out technology purchases, or the lack of competition among service providers may make monthly prices higher. Neighborhood effects for skill deficits may reflect long-standing educational disparities in poor communities, limited access to jobs that can encourage skill development, or lack of exposure to technology within social networks (especially in areas with many new immigrants). Future research might address some of these possible causes of community disadvantage. Broadband mapping is being supported by stimulus funding, and better data on competition among Internet providers could inform further study on costs in poor neighborhoods. Systematic evaluation of federally supported inclusion programs may also provide some answers about the causes for these barriers and effective strategies to overcome them.

Public policies that target poor urban neighborhoods are justified by these findings, for both African American and Latino communities. But, the strategies for encouraging digital citizenship will differ, given higher rates of existing experience within African American neighborhoods. Affordability may be the policy key in those areas, along with continued support of public access. In Latino communities, the need to combine outreach, training, and affordable solutions is apparent.

Urban neighborhoods have strengths as well as challenges. Chicago, in particular, has a long history of neighborhood organizing, dating back to Saul Alinsky in the 1930s and the civil rights movement of the 1960s. The diversity of organizations and efforts in Chicago is a resource for implementing programs that are responsive to the varied needs across neighborhoods. The final chapter on policy solutions discusses such an effort, the Smart Communities program, which is part of the city's digital excellence agenda.

9

From Neighborhoods to Washington: Conclusions and Policy Solutions

Drawing together theory, evidence, and policy experience, in this chapter we revisit two important questions. How does broadband matter for public policy? And how and why does place matter for broadband? First, we consider these questions from a theoretical and conceptual perspective, and then we summarize the empirical contributions made throughout these chapters and the policy implications of these findings. We conclude with a discussion of various policy solutions to address barriers and disparities, from the neighborhood to the national level, including both public and private sectors. Chicago's Smart Communities program is described as an example of a community-based initiative. We also consider the Comcast Internet Essentials programs and the reforms of the federal Universal Service Fund in light of the findings in this study.

Broadband as Access to Information

We have argued that broadband is a critical issue for public policy rather than simply another consumer good best left to the market and private consumption. One reason is that broadband use has spillover benefits for society, affecting communities as well as the nation. Another basis for public policy attention is the need for digital citizenship for individuals, for an equal opportunity to participate in society online. While federal policy has placed broadband on the national agenda, there is a need to redefine the issue.

As the opening quote to chapter 2 illustrates, the Internet and broadband have been compared by federal policymakers to railroads, electricity, and other transformative infrastructures, past and present. These analogies matter because they frame policy problems, debates, and solutions (Stone 2001). Yet, such comparisons are limited as metaphors, missing the fundamental nature of the Internet.

Others have equated the Internet with the printing press for its role in spreading a revolution of information worldwide (West 2011; Glaeser 2011). While each of these metaphors is true in part, even the printing press comparison fails to capture the essential power of the Internet. The foundation of the Internet is access to information and knowledge, as well as a means to communicate information to others. The printing press was a technical achievement, but it was the much later development of public education and widespread literacy that truly democratized access to information.

More than an infrastructure, the Internet has become a social institution that fosters the use of information, much like public education. For this reason, the United Nations has defined access to the Internet as a human right (Kravets 2011). Like education, broadband facilitates equality of opportunity for individuals and creates spillover benefits for the rest of society. These were the primary arguments for public education in the 19th century, and they apply to the Internet today.

Finally, the infrastructure metaphor suggests that the root of the policy problem is availability. As the previous chapters demonstrated, the broadband policy problem is a matter of adoption and use, not just availability. Without policies that address barriers to adoption, many in urban and rural areas will continue to be marginalized in what Susan Crawford has called an "information-driven society" (Crawford 2011, 1).

Why Place Matters

We explore the significance of cities for both opportunity and equity in broadband use and then analyze evidence across multiple layers of geography. Discussing how places matter for broadband policy seems ironic at best. Hasn't technology rendered the world placeless? Phrases like the "death of distance" are commonly used to describe the effects of the Internet to extend information and communication networks beyond the limits of geography (Kolko 2000). Bandwidth-driven advances in applications such as video conferencing and cloud computing facilitate collaboration without respect to location (West 2011, 46).

Yet, technology is shaped by the existing institutional context (Fountain 2001). Within a decentralized federal system, public policy is inescapably influenced by geography. Authority and resources for policies are often situated at the state and local level. Dependence on local revenues for municipal governments means that the distribution of resources does not often meet the policy need. Spatial inequalities like the concentration of poverty and segregation affect access to labor markets and services such as education. Federal policy is currently place-based and targeted but uses the policy lens of infrastructure availability.

We argue, in contrast, that broadband investment and technology policy should be focused on cities and urban areas. Containing 85% of the nation's population, metropolitan areas offer the greatest spillover benefits for broadband policies. Yet, over 90% of federal broadband funding has been invested in rural areas where 15% of the population resides.

Technology has increased the significance of cities, particularly major cities that serve as hubs in global communication networks (Castells 1991; Sassen 2001; Glaeser 2011). The density of ideas and information has always fostered urban growth. Indeed, Americans who live in metropolitan areas with over a million residents are, on average, more than 50% more productive than Americans who lives in small metropolitan areas. Productivity is higher for firms that locate near the geographic center of inventive activity (Glaeser 2011, ch. 2). These advantages are enhanced by technology, as businesses in urban areas use the Internet in more sophisticated ways and produce higher wage growth from the use of the Internet in firms (Forman, Goldfarb, and Greenstein 2005, 2008, 2009). Technology has the potential to enrich the face-to-face interactions that proximity creates, so that face-to-face and online interactions support, rather than undermine, one another. Better connections from information technology make cities more relevant, not less.

Cities are also important sites in the geography of opportunity. Poverty in cities is not necessarily a harbinger of their decline; it is precisely the economic advantages of cities that attract the poor and immigrants in search of employment and prosperity. Glaeser (2011, ch. 2) argues that cities should be judged not by their poverty, but by their track record in helping poorer people gain upward mobility. Cities must adapt themselves to an age of information in order to survive, and addressing inequalities in access and use are critical for continued innovation and economic growth.

The Geography of Digital Citizenship

The evidence indicates that there is indeed variation in technology use by place, although the story is more complex than rural disadvantage. Chapters 3 and 4 offered a broad view of Internet use, broadband access, and mobile access in urban, suburban, and rural areas. The chapters utilized two national surveys with comparable findings and different strengths: the CPS with its large sample, and the FCC study with its more detailed questions. Together chapters 3 and 4 described the geography of digital citizenship, with different forms of access: individuals with full access through broadband, and less-connected individuals who depend on mobile access, dial-up, or public sites.

Overall, the percentage of the population with broadband at home was 59% in cities and 52% in rural areas, compared with 65.5% in suburban communities in 2010. Internet use anywhere followed similar patterns, suggesting that the problem is not just the availability of broadband infrastructure. While rural rates were lowest, we need to probe further and investigate the factors that account for these gaps. Using multivariate analysis, we can see that socioeconomic inequalities trumped place on this broader plane, comparing urban and rural.

Regardless of region, home broadband was largely driven by income. There were also important differences by race and ethnicity. Both African Americans and Latinos were more likely than similarly situated whites to depend on Internet use outside the home or to be "less-connected" Internet users. This was especially true for African Americans. Latinos, however, were the demographic group most likely to have no experience online, and Spanish-dominant urban residents had the lowest probability of having broadband access—only 20%.

Chapter 4 presented a comparison of mobile-phone-only Internet users and home broadband adopters. Little research has focused on the less-connected, defined in this study as those without high-speed access at home. Fewer yet have systematically measured the impact of reliance on smartphones as a primary means of going online, a trend that some have argued has now leveled the playing field because of high rates of smartphone use by minorities and low-income youth. Consistent with the idea of digital citizenship, we examined the relationship of mobile access to activities online, for banking, employment, government services, news, and more. While mobile-only Internet users performed a few more activities online than other less-connected individuals, such as reading online news and using e-government, they were substantially disadvantaged compared with individuals who had broadband at home. Patterns in urban, suburban, and rural areas were similar in this case. Mobile phones did not perform any better for promoting online activities among African Americans and Latinos, although they are more likely to depend on cell phones for Internet use. These results call into question the popular argument that smartphones and mobile access alone will erase disparities. As Crawford (2011) noted, the less-connected, including mobile-only users, have second-class access. Our data demonstrates that this leads to second-class citizenship online.

Comparing Cities and Neighborhoods

Depicting the urban geography of broadband access and Internet use, chapters 5 and 6 break new ground as well. Moving beyond the broad geographic categories of urban, rural, and suburban, chapter 5 ranked the nation's 50 largest central cities and suburban areas by the percent of the city population with broadband Internet at home or Internet use at any location. We estimated access and use in major cities and their suburban areas, as this data has not been systematically available below the state level. Using multilevel statistical models, this chapter compared digital cities on measures that count, including disparities by race and ethnicity. By identifying more technologically inclusive places, as well as those lagging behind, public policy can better address digital inequalities.

There is a surprising amount of variation across cities and across suburban regions. As chapter 5 showed, some American cities are truly digital cities, where most residents are online. But others are falling behind and have failed to accumulate the human and information capital provided by widespread technology use. While city and suburban rankings tended to track each other, there were some instances in which low-ranking cities had high-ranking suburban areas, posing interesting questions about metropolitan inequalities. The rankings were fairly stable over a two-year period, although a handful of cities moved up 20–30% in broadband access during this period. Southern and Midwestern areas tended to fare worse, and cities with high proportions of minorities were low on the rankings as well. Subsamples for African Americans and Latinos demonstrated that while these groups lagged behind in all cities, they did measurably better in cities or suburbs where there was widespread technology use. This suggests that context matters for opportunity.

Following this theme, the neighborhood-level data in chapter 6 allowed us to observe the implications of concentrated poverty for Internet access and use. Geographic variation exists within cities, as well as between cities and suburbs. Chapter 6 mapped Internet access and online activities across neighborhoods in one U.S. city, Chicago. Neighborhood factors exercised a significant influence on technology use, over and above individual characteristics. African Americans were no less likely to use the Internet than similarly situated whites (when we controlled for neighborhood characteristics), but they were still disadvantaged regarding home access. The Chicago results mirrored the patterns in national data, also indicating that Latinos were least likely to use the Internet anywhere.

Despite the availability of infrastructure, we found that large areas of Chicago met federal definitions for underserved areas, where less than 40% of the population had broadband at home. Thousands of residents live in these underserved neighborhoods, and the policy impact of efforts in cities like Chicago could well outweigh the benefits of rural investments. Patterns of online activity across neighborhoods demonstrated the potential consequences of being a less-connected community—for employment, economic development, civic engagement, and health care opportunities. A lack of connectivity in poor neighborhoods has the possibility of amplifying existing disadvantage across policy areas. Moving down another level of geography from cities to neighborhoods more precisely illustrates patterns of opportunity and inequality online.

Barriers to Broadband Adoption

Chapters 7 and 8 described barriers to broadband and Internet access at home; how these varied nationally by place, and in Chicago by neighborhood. Cost was a prevalent barrier overall, but especially for low-income residents and minorities. Even in rural areas, availability as a barrier mainly affected those who are more advantaged—wealthier, more educated, and younger rural residents. Our analysis of national data suggests that infrastructure initiatives are most likely to benefit those who are already better off or more Internet savvy in rural communities. This echoed the finding in chapter 3 on socioeconomic inequality as a cause of rural disparities (as well as urban).

The Chicago-neighborhood data offered a unique view of the role of concentrated poverty within urban neighborhoods. Neighborhood environments magnified the difficulties that individuals face. Barriers such as cost and skill became more important for African Americans, for example, within the context of segregated and high-poverty communities. Interaction terms showed that cost rose with age as a barrier for African Americans and Latinos, while for non-Hispanic whites it declined with age as a reason for not having home access. Living in high-minority neighborhoods dramatically raised the probability that African Americans and Latinos cited difficulties such as cost and skill as barriers. These effects were most pronounced for Latinos in homogenous neighborhoods, who were more likely to mention a lack of interest as well. As chapter 3 showed, urban Latinos who were Spanish dominant had the lowest rates of broadband access and Internet use. Residents of poor and segregated neighborhoods experienced the most difficulty in achieving full access to the Internet, and Latinos in particular faced multiple barriers.

Several key policy implications emerge from these findings. Affordability is an important requirement for achieving universal access and digital citizenship. Nationally, addressing cost is important across places, but it is especially a hurdle in poor urban communities. This suggests solutions such as targeting low-income individuals for assistance and low-income communities for interventions. Programs in poor neighborhoods need to address both the cost of broadband and the skills that residents require to participate online. But, strategies for fostering digital citizenship will vary somewhat even in these communities, and so public policies must be responsive to different needs and neighborhood contexts. Low-income African American neighborhoods are likely to have residents who have some experience online because of high use of public access. Predominantly Latino neighborhoods may be more isolated from Internet use and face multiple barriers as a result. Community-based programs have the potential to offer assistance through strategies that are sensitive to the particular needs and aspirations in those communities.

The remainder of this chapter focuses on policy solutions to address both innovation and inequalities in effective technology use. Actions can be taken by different levels of government and by both public- and private-sector actors. We turn first to the City of Chicago's Smart Communities program as an example of grassroots organizing and local initiative. Building on this foundation, we discuss a range of policies, some under way and some only proposed. We conclude with what we see as a need for continued local initiatives and more equitable federal policy to address the need for digital citizenship in America's cities and rural communities.

Local Initiative: Chicago's Smart Communities Program

Policy experimentation, learning, and diffusion are advantages in decentralized federal systems (Mooney and Lee 1995; Mintrom 1999; Shipan and Volden 2006; Volden 2006; Mossberger 1999). Often states have been described as laboratories of democracy, but the more numerous local governments (and the varied neighborhoods within them) offer nearly unlimited possibilities for such experimentation. Neighborhoods have been portrayed as sites for fostering social capital (Putnam 2000; Hero 2007), civic engagement, and collective problem-solving (Fung and Wright 2003; Briggs 2008; Berry, Portney, and Thomson 1993), and grassroots efforts to bring people online can be responsive to different needs across neighborhoods.

The Smart Communities program illustrates the potential strengths of community-based initiatives as well as the limitations for what they can accomplish without assistance for affordable broadband. The Smart Communities neighborhoods in Chicago received a grant for $7 million to do outreach and training, and to integrate technology into the context of neighborhood-revitalization efforts. The goal is to create a "culture" of technology use in the five pilot neighborhoods, with community-based organizations and strategies drawn from their toolkits of community organizing (Smart Communities 2009, 1). For example, tech organizers do outreach in the neighborhoods and bring together a variety of groups for technology training and activities. Technology use is embedded in assistance for employment, small business development, school reform, health education, youth programs, and more. While there are different lead agencies and other partners in each neighborhood, the Chicago Local Initiative Support Corporation (LISC) coordinates the effort. The City of Chicago is the grant recipient, and support has been provided by funders such as the Chicago Community Trust, the MacArthur Foundation, Microsoft, and the Illinois Department of Commerce and Economic Opportunity.[1]

Originally, the city envisioned the Smart Communities program as nested within a triad of efforts to improve technology use throughout the city. In addition to the Smart Communities grant, the City of Chicago received a $9 million Public Computer Centers grant for upgrading public access in 150 locations across the city. Not funded, however, was a proposal for a fiber-optic network serving community institutions, with pilot projects for residential service in two of the Smart Community neighborhoods. This meant that plans drawn up through community participation prioritizing the use of wireless networks and affordable fiber to the home had to be changed, according to our interviews with neighborhood organizations. The next section demonstrates the needs within these neighborhoods and the strategies that have been devised.

ACCESS AND NEED IN THE SMART COMMUNITIES NEIGHBORHOODS

While there are five neighborhoods and lead agencies involved in the Smart Communities program, there are three project areas: Pilsen, Humboldt Park, and the Southwest Smart Communities (a collaboration between Englewood, Auburn Gresham, and Chicago Lawn). Table 9.1 describes the populations of the community areas in Chicago's Smart Communities program (compared to city averages) and also shows home broadband adoption and barriers to home access by community area. Collectively, there were nearly 133,000 residents without broadband at home in these neighborhoods. The communities are diverse in their composition and histories, but they well illustrate the different barriers and patterns of technology use that were evident in the previous chapters.

Pilsen lies just southwest of Chicago's downtown Loop and is formally known as the Lower West Side community area. Pilsen has been "a center for Mexican-American culture in Chicago for more than 50 years" (Pilsen Smart Communities Plan 2010, 4) and is 82% Latino, with many recent immigrants and predominantly Spanish-speaking residents (American Community Survey 2005–09; see Table 9.1). The lead agency is the Resurrection Project, which was formed by six parishes in 1990 to organize the community and to provide affordable housing.

Humboldt Park, on the West Side of Chicago, is 43% African American and 53% Latino. The eastern section of the neighborhood is a center for Chicago's Puerto Rican community, although the Mexican American population has increased in the area in recent years. To the west, the community is predominantly African American. The lead agency for Humboldt Park is Bickerdike Redevelopment Corporation, which was formed in 1967 and has become a major developer of affordable housing in an area that has experienced gentrification during the past decade.

The Southwest collaboration includes the lead agencies for three different neighborhoods: Englewood, Auburn Gresham, and Chicago Lawn. In the planning phase, neighborhood organizations discussed the ways in which technology could be used for "DSL" or digitally and socially linking the Southwest communities. Englewood's population is 99% African American, and it has the highest poverty rate of any of the five Smart Communities neighborhoods, at 43%. Teamwork Englewood is the lead agency and was established in 2003 by several community institutions, including St. Bernard Hospital, the Pullman Bank, and Greater Englewood Parish United Methodist Church. Auburn Gresham is also 99% African

American, but the 27% poverty rate is much lower than in Englewood. The neighborhood is populated by single-family homes with long-time residents and homeowners, including many seniors. Yet, it has struggled with decline and disinvestment in recent decades. The Greater Auburn Gresham Development Corporation (GAGDC) is the lead agency. Like Auburn Gresham, Chicago Lawn has a lower poverty rate. It has experienced rapid growth in the Latino population in recent years and has a number of Arab residents as well. In 1966, the Reverend Martin Luther King marched through Chicago Lawn in the battle for open housing. Today, the neighborhood is 56% African American and 37% Latino. The lead agency, Greater Southwest Development Corporation, was founded in 1974 and is involved in economic development, housing, senior living, and financial counseling.

All five Smart Communities areas have estimated broadband adoption rates that are lower than the city average (Mossberger and Tolbert 2009), as shown in Table 9.1. Two of the community areas (Pilsen and Auburn Gresham) fall below the 40% threshold that defines "underserved" populations for the federal government, and another neighborhood, Humboldt Park, hovers just above that boundary. Englewood and Chicago Lawn have slightly lower rates of broadband access than the citywide average. While Englewood is clearly a poor neighborhood, estimates for use of the Internet anywhere demonstrate the tendency to use the Internet outside the home in some African American neighborhoods.

Tracking the analysis in chapter 8, the barriers to adoption differ across the Smart Communities in some respects. Among Smart Communities residents who do not have the Internet at home, concerns about cost generally outrank the other two major barriers (see Table 9.1). All three of the main reasons for not having access at home, however, affect the disconnected and less-connected in these neighborhoods. Cost issues stand out especially in Pilsen, which has the highest concentration of Latinos, and where 62% of those without home access cite costs. Skill barriers are mentioned by only 18% in Englewood (which has high rates of public use), but are more substantial in other neighborhoods, especially Pilsen, where they are cited by 41% of respondents as a reason for not having the Internet at home. Pilsen most clearly demonstrates the multiplicity of barriers in neighborhoods with high proportions of Latino residents, illustrating the trends in the multilevel analysis.

BUILDING A CULTURE OF TECHNOLOGY USE

Within the Smart Communities initiatives, there is a common core of programs and activities intended to foster a culture of technology use. This core includes FamilyNet Centers, which offer training and drop-in assistance; Business Resource Networks; Digital Youth Network afterschool programs; Digital Youth summer job programs; and YouMedia library programs for middle school students. Youth programs emphasize new ways of learning through digital media. EveryDay Digital classes offer basic skills, and

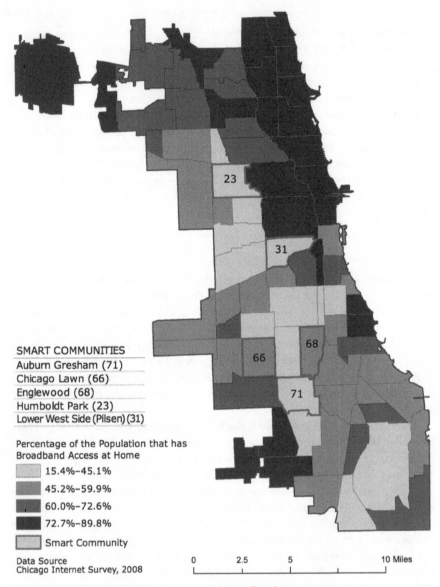

SMART COMMUNITIES
Auburn Gresham (71)
Chicago Lawn (66)
Englewood (68)
Humboldt Park (23)
Lower West Side (Pilsen) (31)

Percentage of the Population that has
Broadband Access at Home

15.4%–45.1%
45.2%–59.9%
60.0%–72.6%
72.7%–89.8%

Smart Community

Data Source
Chicago Internet Survey, 2008

0   2.5   5   10 Miles

Figure 9.1 Chicago Smart Communities and Broadband Access at Home

Civic 2.0 training for block clubs, schools, and other neighborhood groups introduces information about government services and online research for neighborhood and policy issues. Connecting these programs is an awareness campaign featuring ads on bus shelters and "tech organizers" who conduct community outreach. Neighborhood portals feature information about Smart Communities programs alongside community news, directories of businesses and services, technology tips, and opportunities for residents to comment or contribute items.

Table 9.1 **Broadband Adoption and Barriers in Smart Communities (numbers are percentages unless otherwise noted)**

CCA	Demographic Characteristics (%)						Internet Use (%), 2008				
	Total Population (in thousands)	Black	Latino	Asian	Poor	High School Grad	Home Broadband	Residents without Broadband (in thousands)	Reason: Cost	Reason: No Interest	Reason: Difficult to Use
Auburn Gresham	55,258	99	1	0	27	78	38	34,260	49	41	35
Pilsen	37,477	3	82	1	30	56	39	22,861	62	39	41
Humboldt Park	57,763	43	53	0	34	63	43	32,925	53	33	29
Chicago Lawn	56,019	56	37	1	27	68	51	27,449	50	39	32
Englewood	35,186	99	0	0	43	73	56	15,482	35	39	18
City Avg.	2,868,060	34	27	5	20	79	61	1,118,543	52	48	43

Sources: U.S. Bureau of the Census, American Community Survey 5 Year Estimates, 2005-09 for Demographic Characteristics; 2008 Chicago Internet Survey for Internet Use.

Neighborhood residents and organizations participated in planning processes for each neighborhood and have employed different strategies for outreach and training, according to interviews. For example, in Pilsen, word about the Smart Communities program is spread at Sunday Mass. In Auburn Gresham, organizers there have emphasized intergenerational programs to connect seniors and youth through technology. Chicago Lawn has strengthened networks of parents active in the schools through Civic 2.0 training, while in Englewood block clubs work on projects together. Different approaches have been required to address barriers. In some neighborhoods, more basic content was added when it soon became apparent that many participants had no experience with the Internet at all. While costs are frequently cited in Latino neighborhoods, organizers have pointed to potential savings by using Skype for contacting distant relatives and friends abroad. Neighborhood organizations also have knowledge and relationships that allow them to leverage additional resources. Humboldt Park is able to channel trainees into local vocational classes for technology certification after their initial EveryDay Digital coursework.

As the program began to roll out across the five participating neighborhoods, hundreds of Chicago residents attended the launches and each community accumulated a waiting list for the free classes, taught in English and Spanish. It is anticipated that over 5,000 residents will attend training or workshops during the two-year grant period.[2] Yet, there is clearly additional demand. For many, this is driven by the need for jobs, according to interviews.

Neighborhood-level approaches allow for responsiveness and creativity, but the Smart Communities, like other programs, face some limitations as well. One issue is a matter of scale. The FamilyNet Centers have one instructor and a dozen computers each, and even with six locations and multiple classes they cannot reach everyone who might benefit from the classes. The program has also provided some hardware, software, and short-term broadband access for residents, but demand has outstripped the supply for these as well. A total of 1,500 netbook computers have been distributed among participants, but there are not enough to accommodate everyone who has earned them. Organizers acknowledge that this is a chance to test new approaches and curricula, and to pilot strategies that could be replicated later (Mossberger 2012).

Additionally, while community groups have worked to identify resources for those who cannot afford broadband, there is limited assistance available. Chicago was the first city to participate in Comcast's Internet Essentials program, which offers discounted broadband at $9.95 per month for households with children in the school free-lunch program. The Smart Communities have helped spread the word about the program, and Cook County has more participants than any other county in the United States, according to an early Comcast report (Comcast 2012). But, many residents in need are not eligible for Internet Essentials. Classes and counseling in the FamilyNet Centers help individuals budget for broadband and compare prices and features in different plans. But, the Smart Communities program itself is unable to offer low-cost broadband, and cost will continue to be a barrier for many participants.

Despite the focus of the Smart Communities federal funding on skills and digital literacy, federal grants use home broadband adoption as the measure of program success and will hold grantees accountable for achieving these results. On the programmatic level, the expected results do not match the resources available. But, it also brings into question the effectiveness of the federal investments. Digital literacy is essential, but home access and high-speed access are also critical for gaining skills and experience, and for exercising digital citizenship. Without a way to reduce the cost of broadband at home, the outcome may be to encourage Internet use without increasing home adoption, perpetuating the problems of the less-connected in low-income neighborhoods.

Affordability has been an issue for urban SBA programs in other cities. Other SBA (outreach and training) programs have made efforts to secure low-cost broadband for program participants, despite a lack of infrastructure grants. Some grantees have developed wireless networks that serve a housing development (One Economy) or a particular neighborhood within their service area in (Detroit).[3] In these cases, however, networks generally serve a relatively small area. They provide needed support for particular programs but have limited scale. Others cities, such as New York and Boston, have obtained introductory discounts from existing Internet service providers for program participants. The uncertainty is whether participants will be able to sustain broadband subscriptions after the program lapses. The experience so far raises questions about whether the federal goal of greater home broadband adoption can be achieved on a large scale in urban communities without programs that offer more affordable broadband on a widespread and sustainable basis. While the stimulus program missed an opportunity to connect urban residents with both broadband and digital literacy, there are some private and federal efforts that bear watching for future policy solutions.

National Programs: Affordable Broadband Policy

PRIVATE INITIATIVE: COMCAST'S INTERNET ESSENTIALS PROGRAM

Comcast announced in summer 2008 that it would offer discounted broadband access nationwide as part of its bid to secure federal permission for a merger with NBC. The Internet Essentials program provides basic broadband at $9.95 per month for households with children enrolled in the school free-lunch program; Comcast plans to expand this for children qualifying for reduced-price lunches (Comcast 2012). Discounts will be honored as long as there is an eligible child in the household, so it could potentially assist families for a number of years. Participation in the Internet Essentials program also requires training and the purchase of a refurbished computer for $150. Interviews with city respondents indicated some barriers for participation. Participants must not currently be Comcast customers and may not have a history of arrears with the company. Installation kits are provided for participants, who must connect to the Internet themselves.[4]

Home broadband access for children is an important educational resource and can provide other benefits for families. Program implementation, however, will be important. Will discounts be marketed widely by the company, and will it be easy for recipients to sign up? To what extent will requirements like self-installation or $150 for a discounted computer be a barrier?

Like other existing solutions for addressing affordability, the Internet Essentials program is a potentially important but partial one. Many low-income households (including seniors and adults with disabilities) will not be eligible. Others will not qualify because Comcast does not serve their area, and still others will be excluded because of a history of delinquent bills. We can learn from Internet Essentials, from the variety of temporary discounts, and programs that offer financial counseling. Yet, there is a need for a more holistic approach to affordability in order to achieve the goal of universal access, as well as a comprehensive urban broadband policy. Some of these changes are currently being debated and tested in Washington.

CHANGES TO THE FEDERAL UNIVERSAL SERVICE FUND

At the federal level, recent changes to the Universal Service Fund under the FCC have included a pilot program for subsidizing broadband access under the Lifeline program, which affects urban as well as rural residents. The Universal Service Fund is supported by fees collected on telecommunications services, and the fund subsidizes monthly telephone service through the Lifeline program. Individuals who qualify for federal assistance programs such as food stamps or public housing are eligible for the program, as well as those with incomes below 135% of the Federal Poverty Guidelines (Rosen 2011). Use of the program's subsidy for Internet access is advocated in the National Broadband Plan (FCC 2010a) and has long been debated, with substantial resistance in Congress (Rosen 2011).

Through some changes to address inefficiencies in the current program, a total of $25 million was designated by the FCC in early 2012 for a pilot project to subsidize broadband home access. Experiments are intended to provide better information on levels of subsidy to support broadband adoption. The $25 million also includes funding for digital-literacy training at libraries and schools (FCC 2012).

The experimental program is a critical step forward for providing affordable broadband. As a national effort, it has the potential to reach a broad range of low-income individuals. However, experience with the current telephone subsidy program indicates that a number of changes may be needed to promote widespread impact. In 2008, only about 7 million households were enrolled in Lifeline—approximately 29% of those eligible. In some states, adoption rates are as low as 10% (Rosen 2011). The program is administered by participating telecommunication firms, and one problem may be limited outreach by providers. Surveys indicate that low-participation rates may be due to a lack of public awareness (Holt and Jamison 2006). The National Broadband Plan recommends that state social service agencies become responsible for outreach and administration in the future (Rosen 2011; FCC 2010a). This has the potential to streamline applications and certification as well as to improve outreach.

Yet, the future inclusion of broadband in the Lifeline program is not assured. Congressional resistance has stymied past efforts to include broadband in the Lifeline and other Universal Service Fund programs. One issue has been worries about increased costs for the program, which is funded through fees on telephone service. The FCC discussion of the Lifeline experiment reveals such concerns.[5] But according to Rosston and Wallsten (2011), wiring the last 5% of U.S. housing units for broadband implies a subsidy that could range between $3,400 to $4,800 per subscribing household. Many low-income metropolitan and rural residents, currently offline, could gain access for considerably less than that through Lifeline subsidies.

Another factor, however, is that interest groups which currently benefit from policy can be expected to stand in the way of reform. Even in regard to telephone service, policies "heavily emphasize rural build-out and subsidy, at the expense of low-income adoption," with only 14% of subsidy funds currently supporting low-income adoption of telephones (Rosston and Wallsten 2011, 3). The lion's share of funding has gone to rural telecommunications providers to support infrastructure and for subsidies in the High Cost program (Rosen 2011; Rosston and Wallsten 2011). The argument has been made that the greatest problem is the inefficiency of the High Cost program (see Rosen 2011; FCC 2012).

As our analysis in chapter 3 shows, income is an important determinant of broadband adoption in both urban and rural communities. A shift toward a Universal Service Fund that subsidizes broadband access based on income rather than telephone service and rural infrastructure would be more equitable and more effective in many respects. It would clearly benefit urban residents and bring national policy into the information age.

UBIQUITOUS BROADBAND IN DIGITAL CITIES

Federal programs have also bypassed opportunities to explore the social benefits of high-speed ubiquitous broadband in cities. Google's gigabyte experiments in the neighboring Kansas Citys will prove interesting, but applications in a variety of cities would surely yield more information for the future. Much more could likely be accomplished through creative uses of somewhat lower bandwidths (West 2011), using a number of cities as living laboratories. Any further federal infrastructure investments must recognize this and support urban innovation.

In a recent *Scientific American* article, researchers from MIT Labs argued that "our cities are quickly becoming like 'computers in open air'" with high-speed fiber-optic networks that support wireless and mobile technologies, public kiosks, and open data that enable new applications (Ratti and Townsend 2011, 43). Ubiquitous broadband has possibilities for solving a number of policy problems—for providing commuting information to improve traffic flow and air quality, for monitoring energy and water use, for tracking the flow of waste streams and encouraging recycling, and more. Clearly, ubiquitous broadband has applications for public safety and emergency services, as well as more efficient communications for a variety of city services. Cities with ubiquitous broadband should be attractive for economic investment and for the development of start-up businesses. New York respondents spoke about the desire to create "a blanket of access" in parks, libraries, mobile vans, and hot spots; training in community centers and libraries; increased bandwidth and longer hours for public access; laptop checkout programs; and other supports for greater connectivity throughout neighborhoods.

Experimentation in cities can foster decentralized, democratic, and bottom-up approaches to technology use, just as the Internet is itself a decentralized network (Ratti and Townsend 2011). Concepts like crowdsourcing of policy ideas, and collaborative platforms like cloud computing, increase in value with the extension of the network.

Future innovation for policy solutions can be enhanced with greater inclusion and online participation in cities (extending the network for more of the population), and in employing flexible and bottom-up approaches to policy, like the Smart Communities initiative.

A number of city officials who were interviewed referred to ubiquitous broadband in their municipalities as the platform for further technology innovation. Local governments can play an important role in this evolving scenario, utilizing public services and resources to foster ubiquitous technology use. Seattle is studying a business plan for a municipal fiber-optic network, but costs are an issue for local governments.

Federal stimulus programs did not support infrastructure investments that may have competed with current providers in cities. But limited competition has already created the lack of affordability and innovation that characterizes broadband in the United States. According to the Berkman Center at Harvard University, open access and greater competition have provided faster and cheaper broadband in other nations (Berkman Center 2010). Local governments that offer open access networks may enhance competition and improve the broadband markets in their cities.

The Future of Digital Cities and a Digital Society

American cities have been innovative, but they cannot do it alone. Our respondents described cities as "the innovators in this space" or the "cauldrons of creativity" for both economic development and digital citizenship. Cities know their neighborhoods and local needs. Yet, cities have fewer resources and less authority than other levels of government, and need support from the federal system. State governments are potential partners for digital cities. They regulate utilities and provide the rules of the game for broadband in many ways. Under the current Lifeline program, states have the option of increasing the subsidy for low-income households. In the future, they may provide an important source for funding, outreach, and administration of a low-income broadband program (Rosen 2011). States are also strategically positioned to promote technology use through programs in K–12 schools, universities, job training programs, libraries, and in other areas. Illinois, for example, has long provided funding for community technology centers, and there is a statewide broadband council, with planning and collaboration on the state level. States have at times constrained cities, however, restricting municipal wireless programs. Since local governments are legally of the state, support for local efforts is needed at this level as well (Rusk 1995).

Universal access is necessary for continued economic growth and prosperity, as well as social and democratic outcomes. What is needed is a federal policy going forward that addresses the potential for urban innovation and the problem of urban inequalities in Internet access and use—a federal policy that goes beyond a rural infrastructure program. The National Broadband Plan calls for continued investment to encourage universal access, but to date there are few programs that will truly achieve that goal. The current federal policy avoids conflict with incumbent telecommunications providers by intervening in areas that are not profitable. But it fails to take on the issues of a lack of competition among service providers and high costs in urban areas. And unless it can address issues such as affordability, federal policy will not narrow the persistent gaps in technology use in both urban and rural areas, which are rooted in social inequalities, not infrastructure. Federal, state, and local investment and cooperation are necessary to turn the present geography of inequality into the geography of opportunity and to create the digital cities of the 21st century.

Chapter 2

Table A2.1 **Municipal Officials Interview Questions**

Q1.	What policies or programs does your city have to promote broadband deployment and use—by residents, businesses, and public institutions? [We will have looked at website—is there anything new, something that you want to emphasize or add that we wouldn't find on the website?]
Q2.	Why is this an issue that city government is concerned with? Why is the city involved in promoting broadband use?
Q3.	What needs do you see for addressing the digital divide in your programs?
Q4.	More generally, what are challenges that the city faces in promoting broadband deployment and use?
Q5.	What do you see as the role of cities in this policy area in the future? What do cities need to do, and why?
Q6.	What do you see as the role of the state and federal governments as it relates to city policies on broadband?
Q7.	What should be the relationship between cities and the private sector regarding broadband policy at the local level?
Q8.	Is there anything else that I should have asked, or that you would like to add?

Chapter 3

Table A3.1.1 **Uses High–Speed Internet at Home (2009 CPS)**

	National		Urban		Suburban		Rural	
	b/(s.e.)	p	b/(s.e.)	p	b/(s.e.)	p	b/(s.e.)	p
Hispanic	-0.849 (0.035)	0.000	-0.967 (0.065)	0.000	-0.810 (0.045)	0.000	-0.708 (0.107)	0.000
Black	-0.655 (0.035)	0.000	-0.692 (0.059)	0.000	-0.563 (0.050)	0.000	-1.057 (0.102)	0.000
Asian	-0.394 (0.052)	0.000	-0.387 (0.084)	0.000	-0.438 (0.071)	0.000	-0.212 (0.176)	0.228
Spanish Only Language	-0.664 (0.091)	0.000	-0.794 (0.148)	0.000	-0.594 (0.122)	0.000	-0.428 (0.350)	0.221
Income	0.116 (0.003)	0.000	0.103 (0.006)	0.000	0.121 (0.004)	0.000	0.114 (0.006)	0.000
Education	0.414 (0.007)	0.000	0.415 (0.016)	0.000	0.420 (0.010)	0.000	0.391 (0.016)	0.000
Age	-0.035 (0.001)	0.000	-0.036 (0.001)	0.000	-0.036 (0.001)	0.000	-0.031 (0.001)	0.000

	National		Urban		Suburban		Rural	
	b/(s.e.)	p	b/(s.e.)	p	b/(s.e.)	p	b/(s.e.)	p
Male	-0.032 (0.014)	0.025	0.063 (0.033)	0.057	-0.040 (0.019)	0.032	-0.103 (0.028)	0.000
Not Married	-0.354 (0.041)	0.000	-0.282 (0.089)	0.002	-0.408 (0.055)	0.000	-0.284 (0.087)	0.001
Parent of Child	-0.053 (0.030)	0.078	-0.052 (0.071)	0.465	-0.109 (0.040)	0.007	0.041 (0.061)	0.506
Not Married X Parent	0.026 (0.045)	0.565	0.090 (0.099)	0.363	0.055 (0.060)	0.360	-0.101 (0.095)	0.286
Business Owner	0.227 (0.033)	0.000	0.441 (0.085)	0.000	0.219 (0.046)	0.000	0.148 (0.058)	0.010
Occupation:								
Other	-0.089 (0.040)	0.025	-0.033 (0.097)	0.733	-0.110 (0.054)	0.041	-0.108 (0.076)	0.156
Business	0.502 (0.047)	0.000	0.670 (0.116)	0.000	0.495 (0.063)	0.000	0.364 (0.091)	0.000

(continued)

Table A3.1.1 (continued)

	National		Urban		Suburban		Rural	
	b/(s.e.)	p	b/(s.e.)	p	b/(s.e.)	p	b/(s.e.)	p
Professional	0.518 (0.046)	0.000	0.754 (0.110)	0.000	0.459 (0.062)	0.000	0.399 (0.092)	0.000
Service	0.034 (0.043)	0.430	0.114 (0.103)	0.265	−0.041 (0.058)	0.477	0.121 (0.084)	0.147
Sales	0.340 (0.047)	0.000	0.381 (0.113)	0.001	0.288 (0.063)	0.000	0.407 (0.095)	0.000
Office Support	0.422 (0.046)	0.000	0.502 (0.109)	0.000	0.402 (0.062)	0.000	0.370 (0.092)	0.000
Construction	−0.194 (0.052)	0.000	−0.206 (0.129)	0.109	−0.213 (0.069)	0.002	−0.152 (0.098)	0.121
Installation & Repair	0.076 (0.061)	0.213	−0.014 (0.160)	0.932	0.037 (0.080)	0.640	0.198 (0.116)	0.089
Transportation	−0.053 (0.051)	0.295	−0.060 (0.126)	0.632	−0.084 (0.068)	0.218	−0.004 (0.095)	0.968

	National		Urban		Suburban		Rural	
	b/(s.e.)	p	b/(s.e.)	p	b/(s.e.)	p	b/(s.e.)	p
Production (reference)								
Urban	-0.048 (0.027)	0.078						
Rural	-0.476 (0.026)	0.000						
Constant	0.056 (0.062)	0.369	0.004 (0.141)	0.980	0.103 (0.083)	0.211	-0.503 (0.121)	0.000
N	101249		20887		59117		21245	
Pseudo R^2	0.238		0.266		0.233		0.195	

Note: Unstandardized logistic regression coefficients with robust standard errors in parentheses. Probabilities based on two–tailed significance tests. Standard errors clustered by household using VCE (variance–covariance estimator).

Table A3.1.2 **Uses High–Speed Internet at Home (2009 FCC)**

	National		Urban		Suburban		Rural	
	b/(s.e.)	p	b/(s.e.)	p	b/(s.e.)	p	b/(s.e.)	p
Hispanic	-0.663 (0.137)	0.000	-1.017 (0.229)	0.000	-0.777 (0.192)	0.000	0.331 (0.400)	0.407
Black	-0.330 (0.129)	0.010	-0.759 (0.220)	0.001	0.216 (0.195)	0.269	-0.794 (0.366)	0.030
Asian	-0.152 (0.307)	0.621	-0.033 (0.438)	0.939	-0.386 (0.491)	0.432	-1.041 (1.227)	0.396
Income	0.277 (0.020)	0.000	0.279 (0.038)	0.000	0.288 (0.029)	0.000	0.267 (0.041)	0.000
Education	0.663 (0.042)	0.000	0.729 (0.083)	0.000	0.643 (0.060)	0.000	0.619 (0.084)	0.000
Age	-0.041 (0.003)	0.000	-0.044 (0.005)	0.000	-0.047 (0.004)	0.000	-0.027 (0.005)	0.000
Male	0.123 (0.075)	0.101	0.047 (0.149)	0.753	0.235 (0.109)	0.032	-0.012 (0.152)	0.939
Not Married	-0.541 (0.094)	0.000	-0.295 (0.187)	0.115	-0.807 (0.132)	0.000	-0.269 (0.188)	0.153
Parent of Child	0.174 (0.116)	0.132	0.223 (0.235)	0.342	0.260 (0.173)	0.134	0.084 (0.225)	0.709

	National		Urban		Suburban		Rural	
	b/(s.e.)	p	b/(s.e.)	p	b/(s.e.)	p	b/(s.e.)	p
Not Married X Parent	0.445	0.008	0.463	0.146	0.535	0.035	0.310	0.366
	(0.167)		(0.319)		(0.253)		(0.343)	
Employed	0.018	0.828	0.297	0.060	-0.070	0.569	-0.111	0.519
	(0.083)		(0.157)		(0.123)		(0.171)	
Urban	0.005	0.955						
	(0.087)							
Rural	-0.633	0.000						
	(0.098)							
Constant	-0.499	0.027	-0.682	0.111	-0.100	0.752	-1.652	0.000
	(0.225)		(0.428)		(0.318)		(0.459)	
N	4550		1285		2250		1015	
Pseudo R^2	0.285		0.325		0.299		0.188	

Note: Unstandardized logistic regression coefficients with robust standard errors in parentheses. Probabilities based on two-tailed significance tests.

Table A3.2.1   Uses Internet Anywhere (2009 CPS)

	National		Urban		Suburban		Rural	
	b/(s.e.)	p	b/(s.e.)	p	b/(s.e.)	p	b/(s.e.)	p
Hispanic	-1.025 (0.036)	0.000	-1.085 (0.069)	0.000	-1.007 (0.046)	0.000	-0.944 (0.109)	0.000
Black	-0.599 (0.036)	0.000	-0.598 (0.059)	0.000	-0.539 (0.052)	0.000	-0.939 (0.094)	0.000
Asian	-0.706 (0.055)	0.000	-0.720 (0.090)	0.000	-0.696 (0.075)	0.000	-0.614 (0.195)	0.002
Spanish Only Language	-0.739 (0.086)	0.000	-0.925 (0.137)	0.000	-0.618 (0.114)	0.000	-0.867 (0.366)	0.018
Income	0.097 (0.003)	0.000	0.082 (0.006)	0.000	0.101 (0.004)	0.000	0.104 (0.006)	0.000
Education	0.523 (0.008)	0.000	0.508 (0.018)	0.000	0.520 (0.011)	0.000	0.542 (0.018)	0.000
Age	-0.044 (0.001)	0.000	-0.044 (0.001)	0.000	-0.044 (0.001)	0.000	-0.042 (0.001)	0.000
Male	-0.133 (0.017)	0.000	-0.017 (0.038)	0.660	-0.118 (0.022)	0.000	-0.268 (0.034)	0.000

	National		Urban		Suburban		Rural	
	b/(s.e.)	p	b/(s.e.)	p	b/(s.e.)	p	b/(s.e.)	p
Not Married	-0.215 (0.046)	0.000	-0.002 (0.096)	0.983	-0.274 (0.062)	0.000	-0.273 (0.096)	0.004
Parent of Child	-0.013 (0.033)	0.680	-0.023 (0.075)	0.760	-0.026 (0.044)	0.545	-0.007 (0.066)	0.911
Not Married X Parent	-0.031 (0.049)	0.534	-0.044 (0.105)	0.677	-0.026 (0.067)	0.700	-0.005 (0.103)	0.959
Business Owner	0.225 (0.035)	0.000	0.459 (0.090)	0.000	0.229 (0.049)	0.000	0.114 (0.060)	0.058
Occupation:								
Other	-0.209 (0.042)	0.000	-0.166 (0.100)	0.096	-0.237 (0.057)	0.000	-0.208 (0.082)	0.011
Business	0.761 (0.054)	0.000	0.963 (0.132)	0.000	0.749 (0.073)	0.000	0.649 (0.103)	0.000
Professional	0.867 (0.055)	0.000	1.004 (0.123)	0.000	0.799 (0.073)	0.000	0.849 (0.114)	0.000
Service	0.039 (0.046)	0.391	0.054 (0.106)	0.608	-0.004 (0.062)	0.954	0.089 (0.090)	0.326

(continued)

Table A3.2.1 (continued)

	National		Urban		Suburban		Rural	
	b/(s.e.)	p	b/(s.e.)	p	b/(s.e.)	p	b/(s.e.)	p
Sales	0.483 (0.053)	0.000	0.521 (0.120)	0.000	0.427 (0.071)	0.000	0.543 (0.109)	0.000
Office Support	0.821 (0.053)	0.000	0.842 (0.121)	0.000	0.798 (0.070)	0.000	0.820 (0.109)	0.000
Construction	-0.217 (0.054)	0.000	-0.241 (0.131)	0.065	-0.200 (0.074)	0.007	-0.249 (0.104)	0.016
Installation & Repair	0.149 (0.066)	0.025	0.008 (0.166)	0.960	0.095 (0.088)	0.283	0.334 (0.129)	0.010
Transportation	-0.065 (0.053)	0.224	-0.069 (0.130)	0.595	-0.079 (0.072)	0.276	-0.055 (0.100)	0.579
Production (reference)								
Urban	-0.074 (0.029)	0.009						

	National		Urban		Suburban		Rural	
	b/(s.e.)	p	b/(s.e.)	p	b/(s.e.)	p	b/(s.e.)	p
Rural	-0.354 (0.026)	0.000						
Constant	0.948 (0.065)	0.000	0.871 (0.147)	0.000	0.983 (0.087)	0.000	0.515 (0.127)	0.000
N	101249		20887		59117		21245	
Pseudo R²	0.294		0.314		0.289		0.274	

Note: Unstandardized logistic regression coefficients with robust standard errors in parentheses. Probabilities based on two−tailed significance tests. Standard errors clustered by household using VCE (variance−covariance estimator).

Table A3.2.2 Uses Internet Anywhere (2009 FCC)

	National		Urban		Suburban		Rural	
	b/(s.e.)	p	b/(s.e.)	p	b/(s.e.)	p	b/(s.e.)	p
Hispanic	-0.966 (0.148)	0.000	-1.328 (0.254)	0.000	-1.058 (0.218)	0.000	-0.359 (0.428)	0.401
Black	-0.367 (0.144)	0.011	-0.750 (0.242)	0.002	0.054 (0.232)	0.816	-0.527 (0.316)	0.096
Asian	-0.560 (0.398)	0.159	-0.726 (0.535)	0.175	-0.745 (0.730)	0.308	0.113 (0.780)	0.885
Income	0.187 (0.024)	0.000	0.179 (0.047)	0.000	0.201 (0.035)	0.000	0.192 (0.048)	0.000
Education	0.979 (0.050)	0.000	0.902 (0.096)	0.000	0.996 (0.074)	0.000	1.040 (0.105)	0.000
Age	-0.058 (0.003)	0.000	-0.061 (0.006)	0.000	-0.064 (0.005)	0.000	-0.045 (0.006)	0.000
Male	-0.118 (0.087)	0.175	-0.039 (0.169)	0.819	-0.089 (0.130)	0.493	-0.241 (0.171)	0.157
Not Married	-0.516 (0.104)	0.000	-0.533 (0.211)	0.012	-0.712 (0.150)	0.000	-0.124 (0.200)	0.535
Parent of Child	-0.011 (0.144)	0.941	-0.162 (0.286)	0.571	-0.159 (0.217)	0.466	0.451 (0.276)	0.102

	National		Urban		Suburban		Rural	
	b/(s.e.)	p	b/(s.e.)	p	b/(s.e.)	p	b/(s.e.)	p
Not Married X Parent	0.457	0.024	0.749	0.047	0.621	0.047	−0.087	0.830
	(0.203)		(0.378)		(0.313)		(0.406)	
Employed	0.364	0.000	0.776	0.000	0.208	0.153	0.270	0.143
	(0.096)		(0.184)		(0.146)		(0.184)	
Urban	−0.152	0.135						
	(0.102)							
Rural	−0.221	0.040						
	(0.107)							
Constant	1.123	0.000	1.308	0.007	1.506	0.000	−0.162	0.744
	(0.259)		(0.488)		(0.382)		(0.495)	
N	4550		1285		2250		1015	
Pseudo R^2	0.350		0.389		0.358		0.293	

Note: Unstandardized logistic regression coefficients with robust standard errors in parentheses. Probabilities based on two–tailed significance tests.

Chapter 4

Table A4.1 **Connects to Internet on Mobile Phone, but No High–Speed Connection at Home (2009 FCC)**

	National		Urban		Suburban		Rural	
	b/(s.e.)	p	b/(s.e.)	p	b/(s.e.)	p	b/(s.e.)	p
Hispanic	0.687 (0.223)	0.002	0.552 (0.388)	0.155	0.947 (0.312)	0.002	0.921 (0.618)	0.136
Black	0.906 (0.208)	0.000	1.276 (0.342)	0.000	0.253 (0.431)	0.556	1.115 (0.428)	0.009
Asian	-0.965 (0.996)	0.333					2.141 (0.855)	0.012
Income	-0.116 (0.039)	0.003	-0.240 (0.076)	0.002	-0.074 (0.064)	0.248	-0.031 (0.071)	0.663
Education	-0.330 (0.086)	0.000	-0.129 (0.169)	0.446	-0.424 (0.128)	0.001	-0.500 (0.177)	0.005
Age	-0.038 (0.006)	0.000	-0.037 (0.010)	0.000	-0.036 (0.008)	0.000	-0.042 (0.014)	0.002
Male	0.155 (0.164)	0.344	0.305 (0.281)	0.277	-0.262 (0.263)	0.319	0.535 (0.341)	0.117
Not Married	-0.077 (0.227)	0.734	0.468 (0.446)	0.295	-0.275 (0.335)	0.411	-0.476 (0.513)	0.353
Parent of Child	-0.097 (0.255)	0.703	0.395 (0.527)	0.454	-0.968 (0.414)	0.020	0.593 (0.487)	0.224

	National		Urban		Suburban		Rural	
	b/(s.e.)	p	b/(s.e.)	p	b/(s.e.)	p	b/(s.e.)	p
Not Married X Parent	0.113	0.725	−1.237	0.053	1.120	0.030	0.342	0.583
	(0.321)		(0.640)		(0.518)		(0.623)	
Employed	0.273	0.115	0.297	0.362	0.196	0.455	0.534	0.165
	(0.173)		(0.326)		(0.263)		(0.385)	
Urban	0.086	0.639						
	(0.183)							
Rural	0.377	0.058						
	(0.199)							
Constant	−0.546	0.301	−0.993	0.289	−0.055	0.944	−0.589	0.570
	(0.528)		(0.936)		(0.781)		(1.035)	
N	4549		1254		2213		1015	
Pseudo R^2	0.120		0.150		0.119		0.181	

Note: Unstandardized logistic regression coefficients with robust standard errors in parentheses. Probabilities based on two-tailed significance tests.

Table A4.2 Internet Use by Disadvantaged Groups, Black and Latino Subsamples (2009 CPS)

| | Uses High-Speed Internet at Home | | | | Uses Internet Anywhere | | | |
| | Black | | Latino | | Black | | Latino | |
	b/(s.e.)	p	b/(s.e.)	p	b/(s.e.)	p	b/(s.e.)	p
Spanish Only Language			-0.608 (0.102)	0.000			-0.728 (0.093)	0.000
Income	0.106 (0.008)	0.000	0.124 (0.008)	0.000	0.084 (0.008)	0.000	0.094 (0.008)	0.000
Education	0.364 (0.023)	0.000	0.523 (0.023)	0.000	0.460 (0.026)	0.000	0.587 (0.025)	0.000
Age	-0.030 (0.002)	0.000	-0.027 (0.002)	0.000	-0.040 (0.002)	0.000	-0.035 (0.002)	0.000
Male	0.036 (0.048)	0.446	0.098 (0.046)	0.032	-0.138 (0.053)	0.009	0.025 (0.047)	0.593
Not Married	-0.450 (0.111)	0.000	-0.060 (0.098)	0.541	-0.352 (0.119)	0.003	0.129 (0.097)	0.182
Parent of Child	-0.222 (0.106)	0.037	-0.093 (0.082)	0.258	-0.263 (0.113)	0.020	-0.014 (0.082)	0.861
Not Married X Parent	0.205 (0.130)	0.114	-0.005 (0.121)	0.965	0.193 (0.137)	0.160	-0.105 (0.119)	0.377
Business Owner	0.707 (0.153)	0.000	0.458 (0.110)	0.000	0.755 (0.166)	0.000	0.502 (0.113)	0.000

| | Uses High-Speed Internet at Home | | | | Uses Internet Anywhere | | | |
| | Black | | Latino | | Black | | Latino | |
	b/(s.e.)	p	b/(s.e.)	p	b/(s.e.)	p	b/(s.e.)	p
Occupation:								
Other	-0.020 (0.132)	0.877	-0.129 (0.104)	0.212	-0.289 (0.129)	0.025	-0.150 (0.102)	0.143
Business	0.530 (0.161)	0.001	0.608 (0.139)	0.000	0.913 (0.189)	0.000	0.966 (0.151)	0.000
Professional	0.590 (0.147)	0.000	0.685 (0.137)	0.000	0.750 (0.157)	0.000	0.852 (0.148)	0.000
Service	0.185 (0.137)	0.176	-0.029 (0.108)	0.784	0.077 (0.135)	0.570	0.051 (0.106)	0.628
Sales	0.365 (0.152)	0.016	0.323 (0.128)	0.012	0.283 (0.156)	0.070	0.515 (0.132)	0.000
Office Support	0.484 (0.146)	0.001	0.609 (0.125)	0.000	0.837 (0.154)	0.000	0.890 (0.129)	0.000
Construction	-0.283 (0.201)	0.159	-0.099 (0.130)	0.444	-0.368 (0.193)	0.056	-0.153 (0.125)	0.222
Installation & Repair	0.474 (0.225)	0.035	0.001 (0.175)	0.998	0.310 (0.221)	0.161	-0.013 (0.175)	0.940

(continued)

Table A4.2 (continued)

| | Uses High–Speed Internet at Home | | | | Uses Internet Anywhere | | | |
| | Black | | Latino | | Black | | Latino | |
	b/(s.e.)	p	b/(s.e.)	p	b/(s.e.)	p	b/(s.e.)	p
Transportation	0.021 (0.157)	0.894	-0.151 (0.130)	0.245	0.016 (0.155)	0.917	-0.189 (0.129)	0.144
Production (reference)								
Urban	-0.102 (0.066)	0.124	-0.202 (0.067)	0.003	-0.051 (0.066)	0.442	-0.179 (0.065)	0.006
Rural	-0.966 (0.111)	0.000	-0.375 (0.116)	0.001	-0.742 (0.101)	0.000	-0.340 (0.110)	0.002
Constant	-0.558 (0.194)	0.004	-1.601 (0.158)	0.000	0.684 (0.191)	0.000	-0.757 (0.153)	0.000
N	9295		11286		9295		11286	
Pseudo R^2	0.196		0.222		0.251		0.244	

Note: Unstandardized logistic regression coefficients with robust standard errors in parentheses. Probabilities based on two–tailed significance tests. Standard errors clustered by household using VCE (variance–covariance estimator).

Table A4.3 Uses the Internet for Various Activities, Mobile Phone Internet vs. High–Speed Home Access (2009 FCC)

	(local news)	(govt website)	(natl news)	(apply job)	(govt info.)	(online banking)	(take a class)
	b/(p)	b/(p)	b/(p)	b/(p)	b/(p)	b/(p)	b/(p)
High–Speed at Home	1.117 (0.000)	0.919 (0.000)	1.077 (0.000)	0.538 (0.000)	0.414 (0.002)	1.090 (0.000)	0.772 (0.000)
Mobile Phone Internet, No High Speed Access	0.680 (0.024)	1.023 (0.002)	0.819 (0.017)	0.609 (0.085)	0.229 (0.441)	0.054 (0.860)	-0.128 (0.786)
Hispanic	0.006 (0.980)	-0.562 (0.015)	0.097 (0.696)	-0.047 (0.849)	0.020 (0.928)	-0.130 (0.580)	0.038 (0.893)
Black	0.275 (0.238)	-0.268 (0.236)	0.006 (0.979)	0.951 (0.000)	0.165 (0.407)	-0.497 (0.016)	0.370 (0.103)
Asian	-0.904 (0.025)	-0.751 (0.102)	-0.109 (0.805)	0.267 (0.448)	0.118 (0.766)	0.179 (0.667)	-0.831 (0.155)
Income (<$30k)	-0.054 (0.729)	-0.192 (0.215)	-0.198 (0.215)	0.162 (0.307)	-0.346 (0.014)	-0.579 (0.000)	0.189 (0.305)
Education	0.354 (0.000)	0.563 (0.000)	0.403 (0.000)	0.087 (0.198)	0.327 (0.000)	0.342 (0.000)	0.341 (0.000)
Age	-0.024 (0.000)	-0.011 (0.026)	-0.022 (0.000)	-0.063 (0.000)	-0.004 (0.284)	-0.019 (0.000)	-0.039 (0.000)

(continued)

Table A4.3   (continued)

	(local news) b/(p)	(govt website) b/(p)	(natl news) b/(p)	(apply job) b/(p)	(govt info.) b/(p)	(online banking) b/(p)	(take a class) b/(p)
Male	-0.126 (0.301)	0.026 (0.836)	0.270 (0.026)	0.045 (0.695)	-0.077 (0.464)	-0.102 (0.370)	-0.244 (0.082)
Not Married	-0.007 (0.964)	0.176 (0.289)	-0.233 (0.148)	-0.035 (0.822)	-0.201 (0.152)	-0.048 (0.747)	-0.107 (0.593)
Parent of Child	0.290 (0.105)	0.142 (0.448)	-0.134 (0.433)	-0.063 (0.699)	0.226 (0.129)	0.323 (0.049)	0.080 (0.677)
Not Married X Parent	-0.055 (0.841)	-0.239 (0.380)	0.013 (0.960)	0.157 (0.541)	-0.147 (0.520)	-0.387 (0.114)	0.307 (0.286)
Employed	0.213 (0.117)	0.060 (0.672)	-0.015 (0.910)	0.073 (0.555)	-0.022 (0.848)	0.212 (0.086)	0.133 (0.393)
Urban	0.283 (0.060)	-0.026 (0.863)	0.280 (0.049)	0.222 (0.099)	0.223 (0.068)	0.291 (0.030)	0.240 (0.124)
Rural	0.158 (0.311)	0.087 (0.602)	0.195 (0.214)	-0.412 (0.010)	-0.001 (0.994)	-0.022 (0.882)	0.344 (0.068)

	(local news)	(govt website)	(natl news)	(apply job)	(govt info.)	(online banking)	(take a class)
	b/(p)	b/(p)	b/(p)	b/(p)	b/(p)	b/(p)	b/(p)
Constant	0.040	-0.664	-0.060	2.115	-1.064	-0.500	-1.609
	(0.922)	(0.137)	(0.877)	(0.000)	(0.002)	(0.181)	(0.000)
N	1627	1619	1586	1588	1586	1586	1588
Pseudo R²	0.106	0.093	0.098	0.174	0.044	0.122	0.093

Note: Models estimate whether the respondent ever uses the Internet: (1) to get local or community news online; (2) to visit local, state or federal government website; (3) to get national or international news; (4) to get information or apply for a job; (5) to get information from a government agency; (6) for online banking; (7) to take a class for credit toward a degree. Unstandardized logistic regression coefficients with probabilities based on two–tailed significance tests in parentheses. Standard errors omitted from table to provide space for all seven models. Split sample design used for activities questions, reducing sample size to half of the 3,500 Internet users.

Chapter 5

Table A5.1 **Internet Use in Central Cities, Random Intercept Models (2009 CPS)**

	Internet Anywhere		Connects at Home		High–Speed at Home	
	b/(s.e.)	p	b/(s.e.)	p	b/(s.e.)	p
Individual–Level						
Hispanic	-1.099	0.000	-1.016	0.000	-0.989	0.000
	(0.069)		(0.065)		(0.064)	
Black	-0.582	0.000	-0.670	0.000	-0.696	0.000
	(0.064)		(0.059)		(0.058)	
Asian	-0.743	0.000	-0.670	0.000	-0.494	0.000
	(0.094)		(0.087)		(0.085)	
Spanish Only Language	-0.887	0.000	-0.741	0.000	-0.777	0.000
	(0.112)		(0.113)		(0.117)	
Income	0.079	0.000	0.105	0.000	0.103	0.000
	(0.006)		(0.006)		(0.006)	
Education	0.493	0.000	0.429	0.000	0.406	0.000
	(0.019)		(0.018)		(0.017)	
Age	-0.045	0.000	-0.037	0.000	-0.037	0.000
	(0.001)		(0.001)		(0.001)	
Male	-0.009	0.853	0.025	0.582	0.091	0.043
	(0.049)		(0.046)		(0.045)	

	Internet Anywhere		Connects at Home		High–Speed at Home	
	b/(s.e.)	p	b/(s.e.)	p	b/(s.e.)	p
Not Married	-0.004 (0.103)	0.972	-0.325 (0.097)	0.001	-0.296 (0.095)	0.002
Parent of Child	-0.030 (0.075)	0.693	-0.050 (0.071)	0.483	-0.032 (0.069)	0.645
Not Married X Parent	-0.037 (0.115)	0.750	0.104 (0.108)	0.334	0.059 (0.107)	0.582
Business Owner	0.477 (0.095)	0.000	0.520 (0.085)	0.000	0.436 (0.080)	0.000
Occupation:						
Other	-0.216 (0.118)	0.068	-0.104 (0.116)	0.369	-0.113 (0.116)	0.328
Business	0.987 (0.157)	0.000	0.714 (0.142)	0.000	0.655 (0.138)	0.000
Professional	0.976 (0.145)	0.000	0.714 (0.133)	0.000	0.692 (0.130)	0.000
Service	0.051 (0.124)	0.681	0.044 (0.121)	0.714	0.041 (0.121)	0.734
Sales	0.556 (0.143)	0.000	0.382 (0.136)	0.005	0.316 (0.134)	0.018

(continued)

Table AS.1 **(continued)**

	Internet Anywhere		Connects at Home		High–Speed at Home	
	b/(s.e.)	p	b/(s.e.)	p	b/(s.e.)	p
Office Support	0.858 (0.141)	0.000	0.507 (0.132)	0.000	0.430 (0.130)	0.001
Construction	−0.299 (0.151)	0.048	−0.208 (0.149)	0.162	−0.249 (0.149)	0.095
Installation & Repair	0.061 (0.208)	0.769	0.062 (0.200)	0.759	−0.115 (0.196)	0.557
Transportation	−0.009 (0.151)	0.950	−0.074 (0.148)	0.616	−0.124 (0.148)	0.402
Production (reference)						
MSA–Level						
% Black	−0.003 (0.004)	0.493	0.001 (0.004)	0.798	−0.001 (0.004)	0.800
% Hispanic	−0.002 (0.006)	0.753	0.006 (0.006)	0.314	0.004 (0.006)	0.492
Per Capita Income	0.000 (0.000)	0.433	0.000 (0.000)	0.215	0.000 (0.000)	0.266
% High School Grad.	0.015 (0.022)	0.493	0.020 (0.022)	0.363	0.011 (0.020)	0.588

	Internet Anywhere			Connects at Home			High–Speed at Home		
	b/(s.e.)		p	b/(s.e.)		p	b/(s.e.)		p
% Age 65 +	0.006		0.846	-0.003		0.920	-0.015		0.593
	(0.029)			(0.029)			(0.027)		
% Employed in Information	-0.102		0.053	-0.083		0.115	-0.075		0.131
	(0.053)			(0.053)			(0.050)		
Constant	0.280		0.793	-1.130		0.290	-0.515		0.609
	(1.064)			(1.068)			(1.006)		
σ^2_{L2}	-1.349		0.000	-1.312		0.000	-1.385		0.000
	(0.163)			(0.152)			(0.152)		
N	14699			14699			14699		
LL	-6163.870			-6890.318			-7142.694		

Note: Random intercept multilevel logistic regressions models with standard errors in parentheses. Probabilities based on two–tailed significance tests.

Table A5.2 **Internet Use in Suburbs, Random Intercept Models (2009 CPS)**

	Internet Anywhere		Connects at Home		High–Speed at Home	
	b/(s.e.)	p	b/(s.e.)	p	b/(s.e.)	p
Individual–Level						
Hispanic	−1.070 (0.051)	0.000	−0.988 (0.049)	0.000	−0.905 (0.047)	0.000
Black	−0.507 (0.057)	0.000	−0.615 (0.053)	0.000	−0.565 (0.051)	0.000
Asian	−0.817 (0.074)	0.000	−0.638 (0.070)	0.000	−0.537 (0.067)	0.000
Spanish Only Language	−0.469 (0.089)	0.000	−0.464 (0.089)	0.000	−0.511 (0.091)	0.000
Income	0.098 (0.005)	0.000	0.119 (0.004)	0.000	0.120 (0.004)	0.000
Education	0.490 (0.014)	0.000	0.437 (0.013)	0.000	0.408 (0.012)	0.000
Age	−0.044 (0.001)	0.000	−0.037 (0.001)	0.000	−0.037 (0.001)	0.000
Male	−0.089 (0.035)	0.010	−0.055 (0.032)	0.092	−0.031 (0.031)	0.320
Not Married	−0.198 (0.081)	0.015	−0.452 (0.073)	0.000	−0.414 (0.071)	0.000

	Internet Anywhere		Connects at Home		High–Speed at Home	
	b/(s.e.)	p	b/(s.e.)	p	b/(s.e.)	p
Parent of Child	-0.022 (0.050)	0.661	-0.105 (0.047)	0.025	-0.094 (0.044)	0.034
Not Married X Parent	-0.066 (0.088)	0.457	0.098 (0.080)	0.222	0.051 (0.078)	0.510
Business Owner	0.298 (0.055)	0.000	0.344 (0.051)	0.000	0.278 (0.047)	0.000
Occupation:						
Other	-0.281 (0.080)	0.000	-0.199 (0.077)	0.010	-0.191 (0.076)	0.011
Business	0.841 (0.104)	0.000	0.582 (0.094)	0.000	0.564 (0.090)	0.000
Professional	0.637 (0.099)	0.000	0.422 (0.091)	0.000	0.388 (0.086)	0.000
Service	-0.074 (0.086)	0.389	-0.100 (0.083)	0.229	-0.095 (0.081)	0.240
Sales	0.446 (0.099)	0.000	0.313 (0.092)	0.001	0.261 (0.088)	0.003
Office Support	0.707 (0.097)	0.000	0.438 (0.090)	0.000	0.352 (0.086)	0.000

(continued)

Table A5.2 (continued)

	Internet Anywhere		Connects at Home		High–Speed at Home	
	b/(s.e.)	p	b/(s.e.)	p	b/(s.e.)	p
Construction	-0.253 (0.102)	0.013	-0.288 (0.098)	0.003	-0.280 (0.096)	0.004
Installation & Repair	0.154 (0.127)	0.225	0.058 (0.120)	0.629	0.058 (0.116)	0.620
Transportation	-0.146 (0.102)	0.151	-0.143 (0.098)	0.144	-0.174 (0.096)	0.070
Production (reference)						
MSA–Level						
% Black	-0.004 (0.004)	0.351	-0.003 (0.004)	0.517	-0.003 (0.006)	0.601
% Hispanic	0.012 (0.004)	0.008	0.011 (0.004)	0.010	0.012 (0.006)	0.035
Per Capita Income	0.000 (0.000)	0.099	0.000 (0.000)	0.101	0.000 (0.000)	0.439
% High School Grad.	0.046 (0.016)	0.004	0.036 (0.016)	0.024	0.034 (0.020)	0.096
% Age 65 +	0.005 (0.015)	0.758	0.013 (0.015)	0.369	0.024 (0.019)	0.219

	Internet Anywhere		Connects at Home		High–Speed at Home	
	b/(s.e.)	p	b/(s.e.)	p	b/(s.e.)	p
% Employed in Information	−0.023	0.553	−0.013	0.726	−0.047	0.323
	(0.039)		(0.038)		(0.047)	
Constant	−3.246	0.023	−3.142	0.026	−3.090	0.092
	(1.428)		(1.408)		(1.831)	
σ^2_{L2}	−1.719	0.000	−1.716	0.000	−1.380	0.000
	(0.167)		(0.165)		(0.133)	
N	31951		31951		31951	
LL	−12652.528		−14166.411		−15118.737	

Note: Random intercept multilevel logistic regressions models with standard errors in parentheses. Probabilities based on two–tailed significance tests.

Table A5.3 Internet Use in Central Cities, Random Intercept Models (2007 CPS)

	Internet Anywhere		Connects at Home		High–Speed at Home	
	b/(s.e.)	p	b/(s.e.)	p	b/(s.e.)	p
Individual–Level						
Hispanic	-1.001 (0.068)	0.000	-0.922 (0.066)	0.000	-0.893 (0.065)	0.000
Black	-0.674 (0.060)	0.000	-0.798 (0.057)	0.000	-0.775 (0.057)	0.000
Asian	-0.487 (0.090)	0.000	-0.375 (0.084)	0.000	-0.300 (0.081)	0.000
Spanish Only Language	-0.929 (0.120)	0.000	-0.971 (0.127)	0.000	-1.032 (0.136)	0.000
Income	0.083 (0.006)	0.000	0.108 (0.006)	0.000	0.105 (0.006)	0.000
Education	0.480 (0.018)	0.000	0.415 (0.017)	0.000	0.394 (0.017)	0.000
Age	-0.039 (0.001)	0.000	-0.031 (0.001)	0.000	-0.035 (0.001)	0.000
Male	-0.047 (0.048)	0.329	0.052 (0.045)	0.249	0.086 (0.044)	0.052
Not Married	-0.139 (0.099)	0.159	-0.367 (0.096)	0.000	-0.332 (0.095)	0.000

	Internet Anywhere		Connects at Home		High–Speed at Home	
	b/(s.e.)	p	b/(s.e.)	p	b/(s.e.)	p
Parent of Child	-0.149 (0.072)	0.040	-0.232 (0.069)	0.001	-0.143 (0.066)	0.031
Not Married X Parent	0.123 (0.110)	0.264	0.220 (0.107)	0.040	0.108 (0.106)	0.307
Business Owner	0.481 (0.085)	0.000	0.584 (0.078)	0.000	0.608 (0.072)	0.000
Occupation:						
Other	-0.250 (0.110)	0.023	-0.026 (0.111)	0.812	0.043 (0.113)	0.706
Business	0.993 (0.142)	0.000	0.811 (0.131)	0.000	0.645 (0.128)	0.000
Professional	0.961 (0.131)	0.000	0.778 (0.124)	0.000	0.681 (0.122)	0.000
Service	0.003 (0.116)	0.982	0.071 (0.117)	0.542	0.116 (0.120)	0.331
Sales	0.389 (0.130)	0.003	0.415 (0.128)	0.001	0.291 (0.128)	0.023
Office Support	0.766 (0.126)	0.000	0.625 (0.123)	0.000	0.589 (0.124)	0.000

(*continued*)

Table A5.3 (continued)

	Internet Anywhere		Connects at Home		High-Speed at Home	
	b/(s.e.)	p	b/(s.e.)	p	b/(s.e.)	p
Construction	-0.428 (0.142)	0.003	-0.335 (0.144)	0.020	-0.277 (0.148)	0.061
Installation & Repair	0.442 (0.179)	0.014	0.439 (0.175)	0.012	0.422 (0.174)	0.015
Transportation	0.195 (0.144)	0.175	0.262 (0.145)	0.071	0.271 (0.148)	0.067
Production (reference)						
MSA-Level						
% Black	-0.009 (0.003)	0.005	-0.005 (0.004)	0.134	-0.005 (0.004)	0.222
% Hispanic	-0.008 (0.005)	0.097	-0.001 (0.005)	0.874	0.000 (0.006)	0.964
Per Capita Income	0.000 (0.000)	0.833	-0.000 (0.000)	0.551	0.000 (0.000)	0.944
% High School Grad.	0.003 (0.017)	0.869	0.014 (0.018)	0.427	0.001 (0.019)	0.954
% Age 65 +	-0.009 (0.022)	0.693	-0.002 (0.024)	0.923	-0.001 (0.025)	0.956

	Internet Anywhere		Connects at Home		High–Speed at Home	
	b/(s.e.)	p	b/(s.e.)	p	b/(s.e.)	p
% Employed in Information	−0.046	0.171	−0.033	0.362	−0.014	0.721
	(0.034)		(0.036)		(0.038)	
Constant	0.826	0.304	−0.733	0.396	−0.474	0.599
	(0.804)		(0.864)		(0.902)	
σ^2_{L2}	−1.822	0.000	−1.651	0.000	−1.554	0.000
	(0.190)		(0.185)		(0.162)	
N	14404		14404		14404	
LL	−6471.969		−7020.969		−7241.855	

Note: Random intercept multilevel logistic regressions models with standard errors in parentheses. Probabilities based on two–tailed significance tests.

Chapter 6

Table A6.1   **Uses Internet Anywhere, Chicago Sample**

	Coef.	*Robust Std. Err.*	*z*	*P>|z|*
Age	−.077	.004	−19.40	.000
Latino	−1.263	.177	−7.15	.000
Black	−.525	.134	−3.93	.000
Asian	.296	.464	0.64	.524
Income	.363	.031	11.74	.000
Education	.472	.037	12.65	.000
Parent	.073	.140	0.52	.603
Female	−.144	.112	−1.27	.205
Constant	2.077	.302	6.89	.000
Number of obs = 3259				
Wald chi2(8) = 738.45				
Prob > chi2 = 0.0000				
Pseudo R2 = 0.4042				
Log pseudo likelihood = −1097.8317				

Note: Unstandardized logistic regressions coefficients. Probabilities based on two–tailed significance tests.

Table A6.2   **Uses Internet at Home, Chicago Sample**

	Coef.	*Robust Std. Err.*	*z*	*P>|z|*
Age	−.051	.003	−16.56	.000
Latino	−.546	.154	−3.56	.000
Black	−.559	.117	−4.77	.000
Asian	.447	.375	1.19	.233
Income	.379	.027	13.96	.000
Education	.371	.034	10.79	.000
Parent	.228	.119	1.92	.055

	Coef.	*Robust Std. Err.*	*z*	*P>|z|*
Female	−.043	.100	−0.42	.672
Constant	.348	.248	1.40	.161

Number of obs = 3259

Wald chi2(8) = 778.28

Prob > chi2 = 0.0000

Pseudo R2 = 0.3283

Log pseudo likelihood = −1355.5936

Note: Unstandardized logistic regressions coefficients. Probabilities based on two–tailed significance tests.

Table A6.3   **Uses High Speed Internet at Home, Chicago Sample**

	Coef.	*Robust Std. Err.*	*z*	*P>|z|*
Age	−.033	.004	−7.58	.000
Latino	−.553	.192	−2.87	.004
Black	.004	.179	0.02	.984
Asian	1.337	.766	1.75	.081
Income	.247	.037	6.63	.000
Educate	.212	.051	4.13	.000
Parent	−.201	.155	−1.30	.193
Female	−.130	.146	−0.88	.376
Constant	1.522	.365	4.17	.000

Number of obs = 2226

Wald chi2(8) = 186.15

Prob > chi2 = 0.0000

Pseudo R2 = 0.1242

Log pseudo likelihood = −693.87635

Note: Unstandardized logistic regressions coefficients. Probabilities based on two–tailed significance tests.

Table A6.4 **Uses Internet at the Public Library, Chicago Sample**

	Coef.	Robust Std. Err.	z	P>|z|
Uses Internet at home	1.143	.125	9.14	.000
Awareness of public Internet facility in neighborhood	.187	.055	3.37	.001
Ease of access to public Internet facility in neighborhood	.608	.141	4.31	.000
Age	-.037	.003	-13.15	.000
Latino	.318	.138	2.30	.021
Black	.563	.111	5.06	.000
Asian	.077	.281	0.28	.783
Income	-.108	.025	-4.39	.000
Education	.176	.034	5.17	.000
Parent	.104	.096	1.08	.281
Female	-.021	.090	-0.23	.818
Constant	-1.48	.302	-4.91	.000

Number of obs = 2815

Wald chi2(11) = 440.46

Prob > chi2 = 0.0000

Pseudo R2 = 0.1424

Log pseudo likelihood = -1582.1751

Note: Unstandardized logistic regressions coefficients. Probabilities based on two-tailed significance tests.

Table A6.5 **Uses Internet in Anyplace by Chicago Neighborhoods**

	Model 1: Census Tract		Model 2: Community Area	
	Coef. (S.E.)	*p>|z|*	*Coef. (S.E.)*	*p>|z|*
Individual Level Variables				
Age	-0.078 (0.004)	0.000	-0.077 (0.004)	0.000
Latino	-0.964 (0.201)	0.000	-1.041 (0.211)	0.000
Black	-0.099 (0.205)	0.630	-0.281 (0.177)	0.112
Asian	0.374 (0.470)	0.426	0.335 (0.431)	0.438
Income	0.359 (0.032)	0.000	0.366 (0.034)	0.000
Education	0.470 (0.038)	0.000	0.464 (0.042)	0.000
Parent	0.118 (0.147)	0.425	0.112 (0.143)	0.435
Female	-0.117 (0.111)	0.294	-0.115 (0.113)	0.309

(continued)

Table A6.5 (continued)

Geographic Level Variables	Model 1: Census Tract		Model 2: Community Area	
% Latino	-0.010	0.039	-0.006	0.348
	(0.005)		(0.006)	
% Black	-0.009	0.007	-0.009	0.013
	(0.003)		(0.004)	
% Asian	-0.001	0.911	-0.011	0.267
	(0.010)		(0.010)	
% Below Poverty Line	0.006	0.367	0.023	0.004
	(0.007)		(0.008)	
% High School Graduate	0.002	0.762	0.014	0.158
	(0.007)		(0.010)	
Constant	2.208	0.002	1.024	0.285
	(0.718)		(0.959)	
Observations	3117		3117	
Pseudo R–squared	0.4107		0.4102	
Log–likelihood	-1045.5454		-1046.4632	
Wald Chi2	776.7520		821.2099	
Prob. > chi2	0.0000		0.0000	

Unstandardized logistic regression coefficients with robust standard errors in parentheses. Standard errors adjusted by clustering cases by geographic area (census tract or Chicago community area). Probabilities based on two–tailed significance tests.

Table A6.6 **Uses High Speed Internet at Home by Chicago Neighborhoods**

	Model 1: Census Tract		Model 2: Community Area	
	Coef. (S.E.)	p>|z|	Coef. (S.E.)	p>|z|
Individual Level Variables				
Age	-0.051 (0.003)	0.000	-0.051 (0.003)	0.000
Latino	-0.276 (0.176)	0.117	-0.327 (0.178)	0.067
Black	-0.333 (0.192)	0.082	-0.482 (0.151)	0.001
Asian	0.410 (0.419)	0.327	0.417 (0.293)	0.155
Income	0.373 (0.028)	0.000	0.378 (0.026)	0.000
Education	0.364 (0.036)	0.000	0.365 (0.033)	0.000
Parent	0.284 (0.126)	0.025	0.273 (0.140)	0.052
Female	-0.011 (0.099)	0.915	-0.011 (0.096)	0.907

(continued)

Table A6.6 **(continued)**

	Model 1: Census Tract		Model 2: Community Area	
	Coef. (S.E.)	p>|z|	Coef. (S.E.)	p>|z|
Geographic Level Variables				
% Latino	-0.007	0.031	-0.009	0.003
	(0.003)		(0.003)	
% Black	-0.003	0.221	-0.005	0.083
	(0.003)		(0.003)	
% Asian	0.015	0.099	0.003	0.657
	(0.009)		(0.007)	
% Below Poverty Line	-0.002	0.708	0.009	0.132
	(0.005)		(0.006)	
Constant	0.474	0.112	0.445	0.180
	(0.298)		(0.332)	
Observations	3117		3117	
Pseudo R–squared	0.3318		0.3308	
Log–likelihood	-1298.6818		-1300.7910	
Wald Chi2	780.9496		827.6910	
Prob. > chi2	0.0000		0.0000	

Unstandardized logistic regression coefficients with robust standard errors in parentheses. Standard errors adjusted by clustering cases by geographic area (census tract or Chicago community area). Probabilities based on two–tailed significance tests.

Table A6.7 **Uses Internet at Work by Chicago Neighborhoods**

	Model 1: Census Tract		Model 2: Community Area	
	Coef. (S.E.)	p>|z|	Coef. (S.E.)	p>|z|
Individual Level Variables				
Age	-0.013 (0.005)	0.008	-0.013 (0.004)	0.002
Latino	-0.833 (0.190)	0.000	-0.754 (0.192)	0.000
Black	-0.495 (0.243)	0.042	-0.521 (0.245)	0.033
Asian	-0.443 (0.327)	0.176	-0.413 (0.392)	0.292
Income	0.226 (0.036)	0.000	0.225 (0.032)	0.000
Education	0.499 (0.050)	0.000	0.494 (0.052)	0.000
Parent	-0.070 (0.139)	0.615	-0.047 (0.124)	0.703
Female	-0.035 (0.124)	0.775	-0.049 (0.101)	0.626

(continued)

Table A6.7 (continued)

	Model 1: Census Tract		Model 2: Community Area	
	Coef. (S.E.)	p>|z|	Coef. (S.E.)	p>|z|
Geographic Level Variables				
% Latino	0.025 (0.006)	0.000	0.030 (0.007)	0.000
% Black	0.009 (0.004)	0.014	0.010 (0.004)	0.022
% Asian	0.001 (0.008)	0.924	-0.003 (0.013)	0.829
% Below Poverty Line	0.006 (0.007)	0.435	0.013 (0.010)	0.187
% High School Graduate	0.030 (0.009)	0.001	0.041 (0.011)	0.000
Constant	-5.513 (0.905)	0.000	-6.596 (1.115)	0.000
Observations	1546		1546	
Pseudo R–squared	0.2332		0.2323	
Log–likelihood	-784.3304		-785.3172	
Wald Chi2	328.0555		293.6138	
Prob. > chi2	0.0000		0.0000	

Unstandardized logistic regression coefficients with robust standard errors in parentheses. Standard errors adjusted by clustering cases by geographic area (census tract or Chicago community area). Probabilities based on two–tailed significance tests. Subsample of employed respondents (full or part–time) only.

Table A6.8   Uses Online Job Search by Chicago Neighborhoods

	Model 1: Census Tract		Model 2: Community Area	
	Coef. (S.E.)	p>|z|	Coef. (S.E.)	p>|z|
Individual Level Variables				
Age	-0.078 (0.003)	0.000	-0.078 (0.003)	0.000
Latino	-0.286 (0.162)	0.078	-0.329 (0.164)	0.045
Black	0.473 (0.161)	0.003	0.381 (0.174)	0.029
Asian	0.329 (0.258)	0.203	0.335 (0.217)	0.123
Income	0.054 (0.023)	0.020	0.057 (0.028)	0.040
Education	0.314 (0.032)	0.000	0.319 (0.032)	0.000
Parent	0.015 (0.109)	0.891	0.011 (0.134)	0.937
Female	0.011 (0.095)	0.905	0.008 (0.096)	0.936

(continued)

Table A6.8 (continued)

Geographic Level Variables	Model 1: Census Tract		Model 2: Community Area	
	Coef. (S.E.)	p>|z|	Coef. (S.E.)	p>|z|
% Latino	-0.006	0.173	-0.008	0.191
	(0.004)		(0.006)	
% Black	-0.002	0.338	-0.003	0.358
	(0.003)		(0.003)	
% Asian	0.001	0.907	-0.004	0.699
	(0.009)		(0.011)	
% Below Poverty Line	0.001	0.906	0.001	0.939
	(0.005)		(0.007)	
% High School Graduate	-0.004	0.587	-0.010	0.336
	(0.007)		(0.010)	
Constant	2.313	0.001	2.844	0.005
	(0.675)		(1.019)	
Observations	3115		3115	
Pseudo R–squared	0.2715		0.2715	
Log–likelihood	-1572.6548		-1572.6726	
Wald Chi2	889.7194		738.0208	
Prob. > chi2	0.0000		0.0000	

Unstandardized logistic regression coefficients with robust standard errors in parentheses. Standard errors adjusted by clustering cases by geographic area (census tract or Chicago community area). Probabilities based on two–tailed significance tests.

Table A6.9 **Uses the City of Chicago's Website by Chicago Neighborhoods**

	Model 1: Census Tract		Model 2: Community Area	
	Coef. (S.E.)	*p>|z|*	*Coef. (S.E.)*	*p>|z|*
Individual Level Variables				
Age	-0.027 (0.002)	0.000	-0.027 (0.003)	0.000
Latino	-0.167 (0.138)	0.226	-0.196 (0.132)	0.138
Black	-0.080 (0.166)	0.628	-0.059 (0.138)	0.670
Asian	-0.202 (0.254)	0.426	-0.169 (0.250)	0.500
Income	0.208 (0.024)	0.000	0.209 (0.025)	0.000
Education	0.314 (0.030)	0.000	0.321 (0.031)	0.000
Parent	0.311 (0.102)	0.002	0.305 (0.092)	0.001
Female	0.184 (0.085)	0.031	0.176 (0.084)	0.035

(continued)

Table A6.9 **(continued)**

Geographic Level Variables	Model 1: Census Tract		Model 2: Community Area	
	Coef. (S.E.)	p>|z|	Coef. (S.E.)	p>|z|
% Latino	−0.002 (0.003)	0.649	−0.004 (0.005)	0.351
% Black	0.002 (0.002)	0.513	−0.000 (0.002)	0.968
% Asian	0.008 (0.006)	0.230	0.003 (0.005)	0.559
% Below Poverty Line	−0.002 (0.004)	0.595	−0.003 (0.006)	0.648
% High School Graduate	−0.008 (0.005)	0.119	−0.016 (0.008)	0.049
Constant	−0.827 (0.536)	0.123	−0.203 (0.788)	0.797
Observations	3112		3112	
Pseudo R−squared	0.1573		0.1578	
Log−likelihood	−1816.7383		−1815.7021	
Wald Chi2	541.2771		634.1826	
Prob. > chi2	0.0000		0.0000	

Unstandardized logistic regression coefficients with robust standard errors in parentheses. Standard errors adjusted by clustering cases by geographic area (census tract or Chicago community area). Probabilities based on two−tailed significance tests.

Table A6.10 **Uses Online Political Information by Chicago Neighborhoods**

	Model 1: Census Tract		Model 2: Community Area	
	Coef. (S.E.)	*p>|z|*	*Coef. (S.E.)*	*p>|z|*
Individual Level Variables				
Age	−0.043 (0.003)	0.000	−0.042 (0.003)	0.000
Latino	−0.585 (0.151)	0.000	−0.538 (0.142)	0.000
Black	−0.411 (0.163)	0.011	−0.388 (0.164)	0.018
Asian	0.067 (0.263)	0.798	0.020 (0.240)	0.934
Income	0.238 (0.025)	0.000	0.240 (0.029)	0.000
Education	0.394 (0.033)	0.000	0.381 (0.032)	0.000
Parent	−0.298 (0.110)	0.007	−0.282 (0.098)	0.004
Female	−0.166 (0.088)	0.059	−0.157 (0.085)	0.066

(continued)

Table A6.10 (continued)

	Model 1: Census Tract		Model 2: Community Area	
	Coef. (S.E.)	p>|z|	Coef. (S.E.)	p>|z|
Geographic Level Variables				
% Latino	0.007 (0.004)	0.059	0.013 (0.006)	0.021
% Black	0.003 (0.002)	0.238	0.003 (0.003)	0.397
% Asian	0.004 (0.007)	0.615	0.007 (0.008)	0.341
% Below Poverty Line	0.006 (0.006)	0.252	0.024 (0.009)	0.007
% High School Graduate	0.018 (0.006)	0.004	0.036 (0.010)	0.000
Constant	-2.155 (0.618)	0.000	-3.879 (0.892)	0.000
Observations	3115		3115	
Pseudo R–squared	0.2609		0.2640	
Log–likelihood	-1592.5272		-1585.8280	
Wald Chi2	832.9049		783.1396	
Prob. > chi2	0.0000		0.0000	

Unstandardized logistic regression coefficients with robust standard errors in parentheses. Standard errors adjusted by clustering cases by geographic area (census tract or Chicago community area). Probabilities based on two–tailed significance tests.

Table A6.11 **Uses Online Health Information by Chicago Neighborhoods**

	Model 1: Census Tract		Model 2: Community Area	
	Coef. (S.E.)	*p>|z|*	*Coef. (S.E.)*	*p>|z|*
Individual Level Variables				
Age	-0.048	0.000	-0.048	0.000
	(0.003)		(0.003)	
Latino	-0.529	0.001	-0.566	0.000
	(0.159)		(0.155)	
Black	-0.038	0.828	-0.121	0.471
	(0.174)		(0.168)	
Asian	0.203	0.509	0.200	0.444
	(0.308)		(0.261)	
Income	0.304	0.000	0.308	0.000
	(0.026)		(0.031)	
Education	0.366	0.000	0.362	0.000
	(0.032)		(0.030)	
Parent	0.250	0.033	0.244	0.028
	(0.117)		(0.111)	
Female	0.283	0.002	0.283	0.004
	(0.091)		(0.098)	

(continued)

Table A6.11 (continued)

	Model 1: Census Tract		Model 2: Community Area	
	Coef. (S.E.)	p>|z|	Coef. (S.E.)	p>|z|
Geographic Level Variables				
% Latino	-0.007 (0.004)	0.095	-0.006 (0.004)	0.170
% Black	-0.005 (0.003)	0.059	-0.007 (0.003)	0.011
% Asian	0.014 (0.008)	0.083	0.006 (0.006)	0.277
% Below Poverty Line	0.005 (0.006)	0.398	0.018 (0.006)	0.003
% High School Graduate	0.002 (0.006)	0.719	0.008 (0.008)	0.285
Constant	-0.139 (0.649)	0.830	-0.761 (0.772)	0.324
Observations	3116		3116	
Pseudo R-squared	0.2923		0.2922	
Log-likelihood	-1438.2169		-1438.3387	
Wald Chi2	742.3475		935.8000	
Prob. > chi2	0.0000		0.0000	

Unstandardized logistic regression coefficients with robust standard errors in parentheses. Standard errors adjusted by clustering cases by geographic area (census tract or Chicago community area). Probabilities based on two–tailed significance tests.

Chapter 7

Table A7.1 **Reason No High-Speed Home Access by Education (weighted percent, sample sizes in parentheses) 2009 CPS**

| | Education | | | |
	Less than High School	High School Graduate	Some College, Associate's	Bachelor's or Higher
National (All)				
Don't Need It, Not Interested	36.70 (2,932)	37.48 (5,016)	32.71 (2,310)	36.99 (1,400)
Too Expensive	28.10 (2,245)	27.19 (3,639)	29.30 (2,069)	22.93 (868)
Too Expensive or No Computer	49.84 (3,982)	45.64 (6,108)	45.14 (3,188)	35.06 (1,327)
Not Available in Area	1.90 (152)	4.69 (627)	5.89 (416)	7.45 (282)
Lack of Confidence or Skill	3.86 (308)	2.52 (337)	1.88 (133)	1.66 (63)
Central City				
Don't Need It, Not Interested	32.65 (669)	33.57 (852)	32.04 (479)	35.85 (318)
Too Expensive	32.26 (661)	28.72 (729)	32.98 (493)	24.80 (220)

(continued)

Table A7.1 (continued)

	Education			
	Less than High School	High School Graduate	Some College, Associate's	Bachelor's or Higher
Too Expensive or No Computer	55.64 (1,140)	51.30 (1,302)	49.90 (746)	38.78 (344)
Not Available in Area	0.54 (11)	1.30 (33)	0.74 (11)	1.92 (17)
Lack of Confidence or Skill	3.76 (77)	3.15 (80)	2.88 (43)	1.58 (14)
Suburbs:				
Don't Need It, Not Interested	35.14 (1,341)	38.03 (2,608)	33.51 (1,235)	39.24 (795)
Too Expensive	29.82 (1,138)	28.30 (1,941)	28.81 (1,062)	23.59 (478)
Too Expensive or No Computer	51.23 (1,955)	45.64 (3,130)	43.95 (1,620)	35.39 (717)
Not Available in Area	1.76 (67)	3.94 (270)	5.64 (208)	6.37 (129)
Lack of Confidence or Skill	3.56 (136)	2.58 (177)	1.76 (65)	1.88 (38)

	Education			
	Less than High School	High School Graduate	Some College, Associate's	Bachelor's or Higher
Rural:				
Don't Need It, Not Interested	43.41 (922)	39.04 (1,556)	31.69 (596)	32.91 (287)
Too Expensive	21.00 (446)	24.31 (969)	27.33 (514)	19.50 (170)
Too Expensive or No Computer	41.76 (887)	42.05 (1,676)	43.70 (822)	30.50 (266)
Not Available in Area	3.48 (74)	8.13 (324)	10.47 (197)	15.60 (136)
Lack of Confidence or Skill	4.47 (95)	2.01 (80)	1.33 (25)	1.26 (11)

Table A7.2 **Reason No High–Speed Home Access by Age (weighted percent, sample sizes in parentheses) 2009 CPS**

	Age			
	18–29	30–49	50–64	65 +
National (All):				
Don't Need It, Not Interested	20.74 (1,127)	24.94 (2,255)	37.47 (2,930)	53.87 (5,346)
Too Expensive	41.38 (2,248)	38.75 (3,504)	24.34 (1,903)	11.75 (1,166)
Too Expensive or No Computer	59.75 (3,246)	55.59 (5,027)	41.82 (3,270)	30.86 (3,062)
Not Available in Area	4.75 (258)	5.55 (502)	6.29 (492)	2.27 (225)
Lack of Confidence or Skill	0.88 (48)	1.54 (139)	2.93 (229)	4.28 (425)
Central City:				
Don't Need It, Not Interested	19.80 (276)	25.05 (544)	36.25 (580)	50.92 (918)
Too Expensive	41.97 (585)	40.33 (876)	26.06 (417)	12.48 (225)
Too Expensive or No Computer	64.35 (897)	59.71 (1,297)	46.69 (747)	32.78 (591)

		Age		
	18–29	30–49	50–64	65 +
Not Available in Area	0.72 (10)	1.24 (27)	1.44 (23)	0.67 (12)
Lack of Confidence or Skill	1.22 (17)	2.03 (44)	3.44 (55)	5.44 (98)
Suburbs:				
Don't Need It, Not Interested	20.24 (547)	24.18 (1,096)	38.87 (1,557)	54.00 (2,779)
Too Expensive	43.15 (1,166)	40.78 (1,848)	24.84 (995)	11.85 (610)
Too Expensive or No Computer	60.36 (1,631)	56.75 (2,572)	41.06 (1,645)	30.59 (1,574)
Not Available in Area	4.63 (125)	4.83 (219)	5.52 (221)	2.12 (109)
Lack of Confidence or Skill	0.74 (20)	1.46 (66)	2.85 (114)	4.20 (216)
Rural:				
Don't Need It, Not Interested	22.74 (304)	26.29 (615)	35.83 (793)	55.45 (1,649)

(continued)

Table A7.2   (**continued**)

	Age			
	18–29	*30–49*	*50–64*	*65 +*
Too Expensive	37.17 (497)	33.35 (780)	22.19 (491)	11.13 (331)
Too Expensive or No Computer	53.70 (718)	49.51 (1,158)	39.67 (878)	30.16 (897)
Not Available in Area	9.20 (123)	10.94 (256)	11.21 (248)	3.50 (104)
Lack of Confidence or Skill	0.82 (11)	1.24 (29)	2.71 (60)	3.73 (111)

Table A7.3 Reason No High–Speed: Probability of Responding Don't Need It, Not Interested (2009 CPS)

	National		Urban		Suburban		Rural	
	b/(s.e.)	p	b/(s.e.)	p	b/(s.e.)	p	b/(s.e.)	p
Hispanic	-0.117 (0.062)	0.060	-0.175 (0.113)	0.119	-0.153 (0.085)	0.070	0.153 (0.154)	0.319
Black	-0.098 (0.053)	0.065	-0.182 (0.092)	0.048	-0.026 (0.079)	0.738	-0.080 (0.117)	0.493
Asian	0.199 (0.113)	0.080	0.208 (0.180)	0.247	0.115 (0.158)	0.467	0.182 (0.340)	0.594
Spanish Only Language	0.027 (0.117)	0.820	0.086 (0.192)	0.656	-0.009 (0.158)	0.952	0.348 (0.424)	0.411
Income	0.024 (0.005)	0.000	0.020 (0.010)	0.043	0.030 (0.006)	0.000	0.016 (0.009)	0.063
Education	-0.035 (0.012)	0.005	-0.014 (0.027)	0.598	-0.017 (0.017)	0.322	-0.096 (0.024)	0.000
Age	0.026 (0.001)	0.000	0.025 (0.002)	0.000	0.026 (0.001)	0.000	0.027 (0.002)	0.000
Male	0.105 (0.020)	0.000	0.097 (0.049)	0.045	0.127 (0.028)	0.000	0.054 (0.037)	0.147

(continued)

Table A7.3 (continued)

	National		Urban		Suburban		Rural	
	b/(s.e.)	p	b/(s.e.)	p	b/(s.e.)	p	b/(s.e.)	p
Not Married	-0.215 (0.082)	0.009	-0.601 (0.167)	0.000	-0.139 (0.119)	0.244	-0.031 (0.155)	0.842
Parent of Child	0.289 (0.063)	0.000	-0.060 (0.136)	0.656	0.420 (0.090)	0.000	0.310 (0.118)	0.009
Not Married X Parent	0.279 (0.087)	0.001	0.769 (0.181)	0.000	0.135 (0.126)	0.287	0.152 (0.164)	0.353
Business Owner	-0.049 (0.067)	0.465	0.420 (0.180)	0.020	-0.118 (0.100)	0.235	-0.084 (0.106)	0.428
Occupation:								
Other	0.201 (0.067)	0.003	0.272 (0.160)	0.088	0.160 (0.094)	0.090	0.214 (0.120)	0.074
Business	-0.059 (0.089)	0.503	0.120 (0.220)	0.586	-0.019 (0.123)	0.877	-0.193 (0.158)	0.224
Professional	-0.156 (0.087)	0.074	-0.266 (0.207)	0.198	-0.078 (0.119)	0.514	-0.262 (0.170)	0.123

	National		Urban		Suburban		Rural	
	b/(s.e.)	p	b/(s.e.)	p	b/(s.e.)	p	b/(s.e.)	p
Service	0.057 (0.073)	0.439	0.147 (0.171)	0.388	0.049 (0.103)	0.635	-0.001 (0.135)	0.991
Sales	0.032 (0.086)	0.712	0.166 (0.197)	0.400	-0.022 (0.119)	0.853	0.001 (0.163)	0.997
Office Support	-0.002 (0.081)	0.976	-0.012 (0.191)	0.952	-0.012 (0.113)	0.917	0.021 (0.152)	0.892
Construction	0.063 (0.087)	0.466	0.121 (0.198)	0.542	-0.024 (0.125)	0.847	0.188 (0.157)	0.231
Installation & Repair	0.079 (0.107)	0.462	-0.047 (0.275)	0.864	0.092 (0.148)	0.536	0.130 (0.191)	0.494
Transportation	0.134 (0.084)	0.110	0.091 (0.196)	0.644	0.019 (0.122)	0.874	0.356 (0.146)	0.015
Production (reference)								
Urban	-0.029 (0.046)	0.528						

(continued)

Table A7.3 **(continued)**

	National		Urban		Suburban		Rural	
	b/(s.e.)	p	b/(s.e.)	p	b/(s.e.)	p	b/(s.e.)	p
Rural	0.037 (0.040)	0.357						
Constant	-2.463 (0.109)	0.000	-2.251 (0.243)	0.000	-2.629 (0.150)	0.000	-2.314 (0.197)	0.000
N	32111		6957		16310		8844	
Pseudo R^2	0.067		0.065		0.070		0.068	

Note: Unstandardized logistic regression coefficients with robust standard errors in parentheses. Probabilities based on two–tailed significance tests. Standard errors clustered by household using VCE (variance–covariance estimator).

Table A7.4 Reason No High–Speed: Probability of Responding Too Expensive (2009 CPS)

	National		Urban		Suburban		Rural	
	b/(s.e.)	p	b/(s.e.)	p	b/(s.e.)	p	b/(s.e.)	p
Hispanic	0.085 (0.061)	0.161	0.120 (0.113)	0.289	0.086 (0.083)	0.297	−0.034 (0.162)	0.836
Black	0.115 (0.057)	0.043	0.208 (0.099)	0.035	0.026 (0.085)	0.764	0.130 (0.127)	0.307
Asian	−0.331 (0.135)	0.014	−0.535 (0.232)	0.021	−0.168 (0.179)	0.347	−0.367 (0.489)	0.454
Spanish Only Language	0.249 (0.112)	0.026	0.322 (0.177)	0.069	0.179 (0.152)	0.237	0.819 (0.588)	0.163
Income	−0.044 (0.005)	0.000	−0.022 (0.011)	0.041	−0.047 (0.008)	0.000	−0.060 (0.010)	0.000
Education	0.005 (0.014)	0.718	−0.007 (0.028)	0.818	−0.009 (0.020)	0.667	0.052 (0.029)	0.067
Age	−0.029 (0.001)	0.000	−0.027 (0.002)	0.000	−0.030 (0.001)	0.000	−0.029 (0.002)	0.000
Male	−0.077 (0.023)	0.001	−0.042 (0.051)	0.410	−0.109 (0.031)	0.000	−0.030 (0.044)	0.490
Not Married	0.064 (0.066)	0.331	0.164 (0.135)	0.225	0.004 (0.094)	0.964	0.098 (0.131)	0.455

(continued)

Table A7.4 (continued)

	National		Urban		Suburban		Rural	
	b/(s.e.)	p	b/(s.e.)	p	b/(s.e.)	p	b/(s.e.)	p
Parent of Child	−0.305 (0.061)	0.000	−0.209 (0.133)	0.115	−0.445 (0.084)	0.000	−0.104 (0.118)	0.381
Not Married X Parent	−0.202 (0.076)	0.008	−0.305 (0.160)	0.057	−0.112 (0.108)	0.300	−0.311 (0.150)	0.038
Business Owner	−0.280 (0.081)	0.001	−0.603 (0.230)	0.009	−0.225 (0.118)	0.056	−0.230 (0.127)	0.069
Occupation:								
Other	−0.304 (0.067)	0.000	−0.362 (0.147)	0.014	−0.303 (0.095)	0.001	−0.273 (0.122)	0.025
Business	−0.226 (0.090)	0.013	−0.335 (0.210)	0.110	−0.202 (0.125)	0.104	−0.255 (0.171)	0.136
Professional	−0.067 (0.085)	0.433	−0.032 (0.187)	0.865	−0.039 (0.118)	0.739	−0.201 (0.166)	0.227
Service	−0.072 (0.071)	0.312	−0.202 (0.156)	0.194	−0.058 (0.100)	0.560	−0.017 (0.133)	0.899

	National		Urban		Suburban		Rural	
	b/(s.e.)	p	b/(s.e.)	p	b/(s.e.)	p	b/(s.e.)	p
Sales	-0.108 (0.084)	0.199	-0.176 (0.180)	0.328	-0.124 (0.118)	0.293	-0.032 (0.163)	0.843
Office Support	0.017 (0.080)	0.831	0.030 (0.173)	0.861	-0.066 (0.113)	0.560	0.144 (0.149)	0.334
Construction	-0.199 (0.085)	0.019	-0.207 (0.184)	0.262	-0.138 (0.120)	0.247	-0.358 (0.162)	0.026
Installation & Repair	-0.153 (0.109)	0.158	-0.041 (0.256)	0.872	-0.233 (0.152)	0.125	-0.077 (0.198)	0.698
Transportation	-0.118 (0.083)	0.158	-0.247 (0.185)	0.181	-0.064 (0.118)	0.584	-0.163 (0.156)	0.297
Production (reference)								
Urban	-0.048 (0.051)	0.348						

(continued)

Table A7.4   (continued)

	National		Urban		Suburban		Rural	
	b/(s.e.)	p	b/(s.e.)	p	b/(s.e.)	p	b/(s.e.)	p
Rural	−0.229	0.000						
	(0.047)							
Constant	1.393	0.000	1.068	0.000	1.602	0.000	1.042	0.000
	(0.109)		(0.234)		(0.150)		(0.196)	
N	32111		6957		16310		8844	
Pseudo R^2	0.081		0.074		0.088		0.073	

Note: Unstandardized logistic regression coefficients with robust standard errors in parentheses. Probabilities based on two−tailed significance tests. Standard errors clustered by household using VCE (variance−covariance estimator).

Table A7.5 Reason No High–Speed: Probability of Responding Too Expensive or No Computer (2009 CPS)

	National		Urban		Suburban		Rural	
	b/(s.e.)	p	b/(s.e.)	p	b/(s.e.)	p	b/(s.e.)	p
Hispanic	0.276 (0.056)	0.000	0.221 (0.103)	0.032	0.306 (0.077)	0.000	0.151 (0.142)	0.289
Black	0.224 (0.050)	0.000	0.250 (0.088)	0.004	0.134 (0.076)	0.076	0.317 (0.109)	0.004
Asian	-0.169 (0.112)	0.131	-0.418 (0.184)	0.023	0.050 (0.154)	0.745	-0.370 (0.393)	0.347
Spanish Only Language	0.087 (0.107)	0.416	0.115 (0.176)	0.514	0.047 (0.145)	0.746	-0.000 (0.398)	1.000
Income	-0.055 (0.005)	0.000	-0.033 (0.009)	0.001	-0.059 (0.007)	0.000	-0.067 (0.009)	0.000
Education	-0.051 (0.012)	0.000	-0.068 (0.025)	0.007	-0.059 (0.018)	0.001	-0.015 (0.024)	0.529
Age	-0.020 (0.001)	0.000	-0.021 (0.002)	0.000	-0.020 (0.001)	0.000	-0.019 (0.002)	0.000
Male	-0.116 (0.020)	0.000	-0.039 (0.047)	0.402	-0.154 (0.028)	0.000	-0.097 (0.037)	0.008

(continued)

Table A7.5 (continued)

	National		Urban		Suburban		Rural	
	b/(s.e.)	p	b/(s.e.)	p	b/(s.e.)	p	b/(s.e.)	p
Not Married	0.265 (0.067)	0.000	0.473 (0.142)	0.001	0.121 (0.097)	0.214	0.335 (0.126)	0.008
Parent of Child	-0.176 (0.056)	0.002	-0.012 (0.126)	0.927	-0.391 (0.079)	0.000	0.078 (0.105)	0.459
Not Married X Parent	-0.324 (0.074)	0.000	-0.661 (0.160)	0.000	-0.121 (0.107)	0.259	-0.409 (0.139)	0.003
Business Owner	-0.385 (0.069)	0.000	-0.905 (0.196)	0.000	-0.334 (0.101)	0.001	-0.280 (0.106)	0.008
Occupation:								
Other	-0.254 (0.062)	0.000	-0.126 (0.143)	0.376	-0.282 (0.088)	0.001	-0.306 (0.112)	0.006
Business	-0.178 (0.083)	0.033	-0.198 (0.198)	0.315	-0.222 (0.116)	0.056	-0.175 (0.149)	0.238
Professional	-0.174 (0.080)	0.029	0.108 (0.183)	0.556	-0.231 (0.111)	0.037	-0.306 (0.149)	0.040
Service	-0.042 (0.067)	0.533	0.071 (0.151)	0.640	-0.090 (0.095)	0.344	-0.055 (0.124)	0.659

	National		Urban		Suburban		Rural	
	b/(s.e.)	p	b/(s.e.)	p	b/(s.e.)	p	b/(s.e.)	p
Sales	-0.113 (0.079)	0.150	0.035 (0.175)	0.840	-0.168 (0.110)	0.125	-0.131 (0.149)	0.379
Office Support	-0.055 (0.075)	0.462	0.147 (0.170)	0.389	-0.122 (0.105)	0.243	-0.109 (0.139)	0.431
Construction	-0.090 (0.080)	0.262	0.085 (0.180)	0.638	-0.063 (0.113)	0.579	-0.281 (0.146)	0.054
Installation & Repair	-0.170 (0.100)	0.091	0.224 (0.243)	0.358	-0.253 (0.141)	0.073	-0.259 (0.181)	0.151
Transportation	-0.054 (0.078)	0.492	0.142 (0.178)	0.425	-0.061 (0.112)	0.586	-0.216 (0.141)	0.126
Production (reference)								
Urban	0.032 (0.045)	0.481						
Rural	-0.129 (0.040)	0.001						

(continued)

Table A7.5 **(continued)**

	National		Urban		Suburban		Rural	
	b/(s.e.)	p	b/(s.e.)	p	b/(s.e.)	p	b/(s.e.)	p
Constant	1.770	0.000	1.522	0.000	2.040	0.000	1.447	0.000
	(0.101)		(0.223)		(0.141)		(0.178)	
N	32111		6957		16310		8844	
Pseudo R^2	0.064		0.072		0.069		0.048	

Note: Unstandardized logistic regression coefficients with robust standard errors in parentheses. Probabilities based on two–tailed significance tests. Standard errors clustered by household using VCE (variance–covariance estimator).

Table A7.6 **Reason No High–Speed: Probability of Responding Not Available (2009 CPS)**

	National		Urban		Suburban		Rural	
	b/(s.e.)	p	b/(s.e.)	p	b/(s.e.)	p	b/(s.e.)	p
Hispanic	-1.318 (0.210)	0.000	-1.233 (0.494)	0.013	-1.258 (0.269)	0.000	-1.630 (0.503)	0.001
Black	-0.568 (0.168)	0.001	-0.745 (0.480)	0.121	-0.386 (0.226)	0.088	-0.773 (0.290)	0.008
Asian	-1.576 (0.456)	0.001	-1.180 (1.069)	0.270	-1.751 (0.635)	0.006	-1.128 (0.705)	0.110
Spanish Only Language	-0.057 (0.513)	0.911	1.123 (0.704)	0.111	-0.469 (0.795)	0.555	— —	—
Income	0.108 (0.012)	0.000	0.075 (0.035)	0.031	0.098 (0.019)	0.000	0.122 (0.018)	0.000
Education	0.119 (0.027)	0.000	0.065 (0.123)	0.595	0.090 (0.039)	0.021	0.158 (0.040)	0.000
Age	-0.021 (0.002)	0.000	-0.009 (0.008)	0.244	-0.022 (0.003)	0.000	-0.021 (0.003)	0.000
Male	0.028 (0.039)	0.484	0.239 (0.174)	0.169	-0.040 (0.056)	0.473	0.090 (0.059)	0.131

(continued)

Table A7.6 (continued)

	National		Urban		Suburban		Rural	
	b/(s.e.)	p	b/(s.e.)	p	b/(s.e.)	p	b/(s.e.)	p
Not Married	-0.543 (0.154)	0.000	-0.218 (0.612)	0.722	-0.647 (0.227)	0.004	-0.484 (0.225)	0.031
Parent of Child	-0.106 (0.113)	0.348	-0.459 (0.463)	0.322	0.017 (0.166)	0.919	-0.173 (0.165)	0.295
Not Married X Parent	-0.070 (0.172)	0.685	-0.202 (0.695)	0.771	-0.001 (0.252)	0.997	-0.128 (0.250)	0.608
Business Owner	0.571 (0.113)	0.000	0.780 (0.597)	0.191	0.538 (0.168)	0.001	0.583 (0.161)	0.000
Occupation:								
Other	0.012 (0.140)	0.930	0.227 (0.618)	0.714	-0.111 (0.218)	0.610	0.109 (0.191)	0.567
Business	0.097 (0.169)	0.565	-1.623 (1.150)	0.158	0.155 (0.255)	0.543	0.119 (0.238)	0.616
Professional	0.265 (0.160)	0.097	0.430 (0.654)	0.511	0.271 (0.245)	0.270	0.230 (0.224)	0.305
Service	-0.148 (0.157)	0.346	-0.369 (0.621)	0.553	-0.256 (0.247)	0.301	-0.018 (0.215)	0.933

	National		Urban		Suburban		Rural	
	b/(s.e.)	p	b/(s.e.)	p	b/(s.e.)	p	b/(s.e.)	p
Sales	0.122 (0.172)	0.478	0.738 (0.627)	0.239	0.048 (0.253)	0.851	0.081 (0.260)	0.755
Office Support	0.059 (0.162)	0.714	−1.021 (0.907)	0.261	0.133 (0.244)	0.586	0.023 (0.230)	0.922
Construction	0.114 (0.172)	0.508	−0.486 (0.682)	0.476	0.033 (0.272)	0.903	0.211 (0.234)	0.367
Installation & Repair	0.096 (0.208)	0.645	— —	—	0.314 (0.302)	0.298	−0.043 (0.301)	0.886
Transportation	0.027 (0.181)	0.880	−0.643 (0.909)	0.479	0.109 (0.274)	0.692	−0.003 (0.252)	0.990
Production (reference)								
Urban	−1.076 (0.192)	0.000						
Rural	0.644 (0.087)	0.000						

(continued)

Table A7.6 (continued)

	National		Urban		Suburban		Rural	
	b/(s.e.)	p	b/(s.e.)	p	b/(s.e.)	p	b/(s.e.)	p
Constant	-3.014	0.000	-4.151	0.000	-2.769	0.000	-2.612	0.000
	(0.234)		(0.822)		(0.344)		(0.315)	
N	32111		6849		16310		8773	
Pseudo R^2	0.135		0.072		0.092		0.112	

Note: Unstandardized logistic regression coefficients with robust standard errors in parentheses. Probabilities based on two–tailed significance tests. Standard errors clustered by household using VCE (variance–covariance estimator).

Table A7.7 **Reason No High–Speed: Probability of Responding Lack of Confidence or Skill (2009 CPS)**

	National		Urban		Suburban		Rural	
	b/(s.e.)	*p*	*b/(s.e.)*	*p*	*b/(s.e.)*	*p*	*b/(s.e.)*	*p*
Hispanic	-0.220 (0.177)	0.214	-0.158 (0.328)	0.630	-0.223 (0.233)	0.338	0.049 (0.464)	0.915
Black	-0.160 (0.148)	0.280	0.101 (0.254)	0.690	-0.501 (0.242)	0.039	-0.022 (0.290)	0.940
Asian	1.254 (0.190)	0.000	1.648 (0.282)	0.000	0.916 (0.314)	0.004	0.954 (0.787)	0.225
Spanish Only Language	0.634 (0.308)	0.039	0.499 (0.554)	0.368	0.902 (0.371)	0.015	— —	—
Income	-0.012 (0.013)	0.372	-0.022 (0.025)	0.380	0.020 (0.019)	0.280	-0.064 (0.028)	0.020
Education	-0.201 (0.038)	0.000	-0.164 (0.066)	0.012	-0.174 (0.053)	0.001	-0.318 (0.096)	0.001
Age	0.020 (0.003)	0.000	0.016 (0.005)	0.002	0.024 (0.004)	0.000	0.017 (0.006)	0.002
Male	0.007 (0.061)	0.909	-0.071 (0.124)	0.568	0.033 (0.087)	0.702	0.020 (0.119)	0.868

(continued)

Table A7.7 (continued)

	National		Urban		Suburban		Rural	
	b/(s.e.)	p	b/(s.e.)	p	b/(s.e.)	p	b/(s.e.)	p
Not Married	-0.369 (0.372)	0.320	-1.153 (0.688)	0.094	-0.541 (0.599)	0.366	0.973 (0.839)	0.246
Parent of Child	0.647 (0.239)	0.007	0.380 (0.363)	0.296	0.497 (0.365)	0.172	1.693 (0.724)	0.019
Not Married X Parent	0.556 (0.376)	0.139	1.106 (0.683)	0.105	1.013 (0.615)	0.099	-1.149 (0.854)	0.178
Business Owner	0.005 (0.207)	0.982	-1.094 (0.599)	0.068	0.189 (0.303)	0.533	0.016 (0.312)	0.958
Occupation:								
Other	0.349 (0.247)	0.158	0.684 (0.620)	0.270	0.227 (0.318)	0.474	0.233 (0.518)	0.654
Business	-0.218 (0.340)	0.521	0.483 (0.740)	0.514	-0.817 (0.513)	0.111	0.058 (0.630)	0.926
Professional	-0.120 (0.345)	0.727	0.160 (0.739)	0.829	-0.419 (0.481)	0.384	0.385 (0.714)	0.590
Service	0.260 (0.270)	0.335	0.341 (0.659)	0.605	0.216 (0.355)	0.543	0.280 (0.542)	0.606

	National		Urban		Suburban		Rural	
	b/(s.e.)	p	b/(s.e.)	p	b/(s.e.)	p	b/(s.e.)	p
Sales	-0.053 (0.320)	0.869	0.490 (0.721)	0.497	-0.172 (0.431)	0.690	-0.524 (0.742)	0.480
Office Support	-0.703 (0.336)	0.037	-0.444 (0.795)	0.577	-1.119 (0.489)	0.022	-0.153 (0.600)	0.799
Construction	0.521 (0.290)	0.072	0.425 (0.757)	0.574	0.496 (0.374)	0.184	0.692 (0.565)	0.221
Installation & Repair	-0.317 (0.437)	0.469	-0.217 (1.200)	0.856	-0.244 (0.544)	0.654	-0.918 (0.964)	0.341
Transportation	0.385 (0.295)	0.192	0.757 (0.674)	0.261	0.318 (0.394)	0.419	0.199 (0.593)	0.737
Production (reference)								
Urban	0.202 (0.117)	0.085						
Rural	-0.108 (0.114)	0.343						

(continued)

Table A7.7 (continued)

	National		Urban		Suburban		Rural	
	b/(s.e.)	p	b/(s.e.)	p	b/(s.e.)	p	b/(s.e.)	p
Constant	−5.182	0.000	−4.688	0.000	−5.662	0.000	−5.280	0.000
	(0.392)		(0.925)		(0.515)		(0.894)	
N	32111		6957		16310		8773	
Pseudo R²	0.061		0.081		0.066		0.061	

Note: Unstandardized logistic regression coefficients with robust standard errors in parentheses. Probabilities based on two−tailed significance tests. Standard errors clustered by household using VCE (variance–covariance estimator).

Chapter 8

Table A8.1 **Reason No Internet at Home, Chicago Sample**

Independent Variables	I Am Not Interested			The Cost Is Too High		
	Coef.	Robust Std. Err.	P>|z|	Coef.	Robust Std. Err.	P>|z|
Age	.029	.004	.000	.005	.004	.263
Latino	−.079	.225	.725	.647	.225	.004
Black	−.280	.161	.082	.104	.166	.529
Asian	.784	.746	.293	−.879	.815	.281
Income	.120	.041	.004	−.256	.043	.000
Female	−.158	.145	.275	.607	.146	.000
Education	−.115	.045	.012	−.084	.047	.073
Parent	−.168	.196	.392	−.176	.197	.370
Constant	−1.45	.391	.000	.405	.371	.275

Number of obs = 1011   Number of obs = 1011

Wald chi2(8) = 90.17   Wald chi2(8) = 103.14

Prob > chi2 = 0.0000   Prob > chi2 = 0.0000

Pseudo R2 = 0.0763   Pseudo R2 = 0.0876

Log pseudo likelihood = −645.9321   Log pseudo likelihood = −637.9946

Independent Variables	It's Too Difficult to Use		
	Coef.	Robust Std. Err.	P>|z|
Age	.037	.005	.000
Latino	.573	.228	.012
Black	−.273	.169	.107
Asian	−.412	.648	.525
Income	−.087	.041	.033
Female	.250	.147	.089
Education	−.201	.047	.000
Parent	.260	.191	.173
Constant	−1.62	.382	.000

Number of obs = 1011

Wald chi2(8) = 103.36

Prob > chi2 = 0.0000

Pseudo R2 = 0.0930

Log pseudo likelihood = −627.89249

Note: Unstandardized logistic regression coefficients. Probabilities based on two–tailed significance tests.

Table A8.2 **Reason No Home Internet: Probability of Responding Don't Need It, Not Interested by Chicago Neighborhood**

	Model 1: Census Tract		Model 2: Community Area	
	Coef. (S.E.)	*p>|z|*	*Coef. (S.E.)*	*p>|z|*
Individual Level Variables				
Age	0.028 (0.005)	0.000	0.029 (0.005)	0.000
Latino	−0.084 (0.240)	0.727	−0.127 (0.243)	0.603
Black	0.176 (0.269)	0.512	−0.021 (0.229)	0.926
Asian	0.828 (0.780)	0.288	0.824 (0.791)	0.298
Income	0.110 (0.045)	0.015	0.119 (0.045)	0.008
Education	−0.123 (0.048)	0.010	−0.130 (0.050)	0.010
Parent	−0.190 (0.193)	0.326	−0.216 (0.191)	0.257
Female	−0.154 (0.152)	0.311	−0.138 (0.150)	0.358

	Model 1: Census Tract		Model 2: Community Area	
	Coef. (S.E.)	p>|z|	Coef. (S.E.)	p>|z|
Geographic Level Variables				
% Latino	0.003 (0.004)	0.538	0.009 (0.007)	0.189
% Black	−0.003 (0.004)	0.500	0.004 (0.005)	0.453
% Asian	0.010 (0.014)	0.465	0.020 (0.014)	0.166
Median Income	0.000 (0.000)	0.099	0.000 (0.000)	0.033
Constant	−1.962 (0.540)	0.000	−2.728 (0.749)	0.000
Observations	984		984	
Pseudo R−squared	0.0812		0.0816	
Log−likelihood	−625.1008		−624.8473	
Wald Chi2	90.5790		86.2566	
Prob. > chi2	0.0000		0.0000	

Note: Unstandardized logistic regression coefficients with robust standard errors in parentheses. Probabilities based on two–tailed tests. Standard errors adjusted by clustering cases by geographic area (census tract or Chicago community area).

Table A8.3 **Reason No Home Internet: Probability of Responding Cost Too High by Chicago Neighborhood**

	Model 1: Census Tract		Model 2: Community Area	
	Coef. (S.E.)	*p>|z|*	*Coef. (S.E.)*	*p>|z|*
Individual Level Variables				
Age	0.006	0.143	0.005	0.313
	(0.004)		(0.005)	
Latino	0.310	0.212	0.509	0.009
	(0.248)		(0.196)	
Black	-0.020	0.946	0.052	0.804
	(0.299)		(0.210)	
Asian	-0.951	0.215	-0.906	0.228
	(0.767)		(0.752)	
Income	-0.253	0.000	-0.253	0.000
	(0.047)		(0.046)	
Education	-0.091	0.065	-0.099	0.029
	(0.049)		(0.046)	
Parent	-0.181	0.387	-0.199	0.309
	(0.209)		(0.196)	
Female	0.585	0.000	0.587	0.000
	(0.147)		(0.126)	

	Model 1: Census Tract		Model 2: Community Area	
	Coef. (S.E.)	p>|z|	Coef. (S.E.)	p>|z|
Geographic Level Variables				
% Latino	0.020 (0.006)	0.002	0.020 (0.007)	0.007
% Black	0.008 (0.004)	0.084	0.010 (0.004)	0.013
% Asian	0.011 (0.013)	0.371	0.018 (0.009)	0.038
% Below Poverty Line	0.006 (0.007)	0.382	-0.008 (0.011)	0.473
% High School Graduate	0.019 (0.010)	0.047	0.020 (0.013)	0.114
Constant	-1.807 (1.018)	0.076	-1.737 (1.273)	0.172
Observations	984		984	
Pseudo R–squared	0.0959		0.0924	
Log–likelihood	-615.4857		-617.8867	
Wald Chi2	100.6470		101.4212	
Prob. > chi2	0.0000		0.0000	

Note: Unstandardized logistic regression coefficients with robust standard errors in parentheses. Probabilities based on two–tailed tests. Standard errors adjusted by clustering cases by geographic area (census tract or Chicago community area).

Table A8.4 **Reason No Home Internet: Probability of Responding Too Difficult/Lack Skills by Chicago Neighborhood**

	Model 1: Census Tract		Model 2: Community Area	
	Coef. (S.E.)	p>|z|	Coef. (S.E.)	p>|z|
Individual Level Variables				
Age	0.038 (0.005)	0.000	0.038 (0.005)	0.000
Latino	0.603 (0.264)	0.022	0.586 (0.300)	0.051
Black	−0.231 (0.296)	0.435	−0.303 (0.262)	0.248
Asian	−0.352 (0.598)	0.557	−0.326 (0.638)	0.610
Income	−0.094 (0.043)	0.027	−0.096 (0.042)	0.021
Education	−0.203 (0.049)	0.000	−0.210 (0.049)	0.000
Parent	0.256 (0.198)	0.197	0.259 (0.207)	0.210
Female	0.229 (0.157)	0.144	0.218 (0.165)	0.185

	Model 1: Census Tract		Model 2: Community Area	
	Coef. (S.E.)	p>|z|	Coef. (S.E.)	p>|z|
Geographic Level Variables				
% Latino	0.003 (0.006)	0.659	0.012 (0.007)	0.107
% Black	0.005 (0.004)	0.189	0.010 (0.005)	0.036
% Asian	0.007 (0.013)	0.569	0.010 (0.011)	0.388
% Below Poverty Line	−0.025 (0.008)	0.001	−0.027 (0.010)	0.009
% High School Graduate	−0.007 (0.009)	0.477	0.008 (0.013)	0.538
Constant	−1.034 (0.943)	0.273	−2.408 (1.198)	0.045
Observations	984		984	
Pseudo R−squared	0.1043		0.1039	
Log−likelihood	−602.4645		−602.7304	
Wald Chi2	120.5170		125.6407	
Prob. > chi2	0.0000		0.0000	

Note: Unstandardized logistic regression coefficients with robust standard errors in parentheses. Standard errors adjusted by clustering cases by geographic area (census tract or Chicago community area). Probabilities based on two−tailed significance tests.

Table A8.5 **Reasons for No Home Internet, Age and Race/Ethnicity Interactions (Chicago Sample)**

	Not Interested		Cost to High		Too Difficult	
	Coef. (S.E.)	p>|z|	Coef. (S.E.)	p>|z|	Coef. (S.E.)	p>|z|
Age	0.046 (0.009)	0.000	-0.013 (0.007)	0.057	0.053 (0.009)	0.000
Latino	2.118 (0.738)	0.004	-1.111 (0.670)	0.097	2.434 (0.742)	0.001
Latino * Age	-0.041 (0.012)	0.001	0.022 (0.013)	0.079	-0.033 (0.013)	0.009
Black	1.306 (0.744)	0.079	-1.841 (0.617)	0.003	0.766 (0.752)	0.309
Black * Age	-0.017 (0.011)	0.125	0.030 (0.009)	0.001	-0.015 (0.011)	0.171
Asian	12.570 (8.203)	0.125	1.738 (3.920)	0.657	-3.993 (5.468)	0.465
Asian * Age	-0.163 (0.108)	0.133	-0.038 (0.062)	0.534	0.050 (0.075)	0.507
Income	0.123 (0.046)	0.007	-0.257 (0.047)	0.000	-0.088 (0.044)	0.042
Education	-0.128 (0.049)	0.009	-0.094 (0.050)	0.059	-0.210 (0.051)	0.000

	Not Interested		Cost to High		Too Difficult	
	Coef. (S.E.)	p>|z|	Coef. (S.E.)	p>|z|	Coef. (S.E.)	p>|z|
Parent	-0.301 (0.193)	0.120	-0.132 (0.211)	0.531	0.175 (0.198)	0.376
Female	-0.154 (0.153)	0.314	0.604 (0.149)	0.000	0.236 (0.157)	0.134
% Latino	0.003 (0.005)	0.626	0.019 (0.006)	0.003	0.002 (0.006)	0.714
% Black	-0.003 (0.004)	0.452	0.005 (0.004)	0.208	0.006 (0.004)	0.174
% Asian	0.004 (0.014)	0.765	0.011 (0.013)	0.395	0.006 (0.013)	0.647
% Below Poverty Line	-0.006 (0.008)	0.437	0.008 (0.007)	0.284	-0.025 (0.008)	0.001
% High School Graduate	0.001 (0.009)	0.918	0.019 (0.009)	0.043	-0.007 (0.010)	0.438
Intercept	-2.663 (1.023)	0.009	-0.433 (1.042)	0.678	-1.990 (1.047)	0.057

(continued)

Table A8.5 (continued)

	Not Interested		Cost to High		Too Difficult	
	Coef. (S.E.)	p>|z|	Coef. (S.E.)	p>|z|	Coef. (S.E.)	p>|z|
Observations	984		984		984	
Pseudo R–squared	0.091		0.104		0.110	
Log–likelihood	–618.361		–609.905		–598.520	
Wald Chi2	101.369		107.547		129.573	
Prob. > chi2	0.000		0.000		0.000	

Note: Unstandardized logistic regression coefficients with robust standard errors in parentheses. Standard errors adjusted by clustering cases by census tract. Probabilities based on two–tailed significance tests.

Table A8.6 **Reasons for No Home Internet, Race/Ethnicity and Percent Minority in Chicago Neighborhood Interactions**

	Not Interested		Cost to High		Too Difficult	
	Coef. (S.E.)	p>|z|	Coef. (S.E.)	p>|z|	Coef. (S.E.)	p>|z|
Latino	-.881 (.422)	.037	.841 (.278)	.002	.660 (.359)	.066
Latino * % Latino	.017 (.009)	.042	-.008 (.006)	.209	-.002 (.008)	.801
% Latino	-.001 (.009)	.909	.023 (.009)	.006	.015 (.008)	.073
Black	-.241 (.345)	.485	.037 (.296)	.900	-.919 (.405)	.023
Black * % Black	.004 (.005)	.472	.001 (.005)	.879	.013 (.005)	.014
% Black	-.002 (.006)	.685	.010 (.005)	.049	.004 (.005)	.425
Individual Level Variables						
Age	.028 (.005)	.000	.005 (.005)	.299	.038 (.005)	.000
Income	.116 (.045)	.010	-.250 (.046)	.000	-.098 (.042)	.019

(continued)

Table A8.6 (continued)

	Not Interested		Cost to High		Too Difficult	
	Coef. (S.E.)	p>|z|	Coef. (S.E.)	p>|z|	Coef. (S.E.)	p>|z|
Education	-.130 (.052)	.013	-.099 (.046)	.030	-.212 (.049)	.000
Parent	-.204 (.189)	.279	-.198 (.196)	.314	.290 (.209)	.165
Female	-.164 (.153)	.283	.593 (.126)	.000	.215 (.163)	.186
Asian	.815 (.761)	.284	-.919 (.743)	.216	-.319 (.621)	.608
Geographic Level Variables						
% Asian	.015 (.013)	.245	.018 (.009)	.038	.011 (.011)	.330
% Below Poverty Line	-.009 (.013)	.499	-.007 (.011)	.506	-.023 (.011)	.031
% High School Graduate	.004 (.015)	.779	.021 (.014)	.128	.014 (.013)	.301

	Not Interested		Cost to High		Too Difficult	
	Coef. (S.E.)	p>|z|	Coef. (S.E.)	p>|z|	Coef. (S.E.)	p>|z|
Constant	-1.594	.271	-1.879	.156	-2.877	.020
	(1.447)		(1.326)		(1.234)	
Observations	984.000		984.000		984.000	
Pseudo R–squared	.085		.093		.108	
Log–likelihood	-622.549		-617.264		-600.299	
Wald Chi2	94.740		112.126		126.355	
Prob. > chi2	.000		.000		.000	

Note: Unstandardized logistic regression coefficients with robust standard errors in parentheses. Standard errors adjusted by clustering cases by census tract. Probabilities based on two–tailed significance tests.

Survey Questions and Variable Coding

Source: 2009 CPS

Variable Name	Description	Coding	Source Variable/Question Wording
No High-Speed Reason: Don't Need It, Not Interested	The main reason for not having high-speed Internet access at home = "Don't need it, not interested"	1 = true, 0 = other	HENET5: What is the main reason that you do not have high-speed (that is, faster than dial-up) Internet access at home?
			[1 = Don't need it, not interested; 2 = Too expensive; 3 = Can use it somewhere else; 4 = Not available in area; 5 = No computer or computer inadequate; 6 = Privacy and security; 7 = Concern for children's access; 8 = Lack of confidence or skill; 9 = Other reasons]
No High-Speed Reason: Too Expensive	The main reason for not having high-speed Internet access at home = "Too expensive"	1 = true, 0 = other	HENET5
No High-Speed Reason: Too Expensive or No Computer	The main reason for not having high-speed Internet access at home = "Too expensive" or "No computer or computer inadequate"	1 = true, 0 = other	HENET5
No High-Speed Reason: Not Available	The main reason for not having high-speed Internet access at home = "Not available in area"	1 = true, 0 = other	HENET5
No High-Speed Reason: Lack of Confidence or Skill	The main reason for not having high-speed Internet access at home = "Lack of confidence or skill"	1 = true, 0 = other	HENET5

Source: 2007 & 2009 CPS

Variable Name	Description	Coding	Source Variable/Question Wording
Uses High-Speed at Home	Connects to the Internet from home using DSL, cable modem, fiber optics, satellite,	1 = true, 0 = other	*HENET4:* Do you currently access the Internet at home using— [1 = A regular "dial-up" telephone; 2 = DSL, cable modem, fiber optics, satellite, wireless (such as Wi-Fi), mobile phone or PDA, or some other broadband Internet connection;
	wireless (such as Wi-Fi), mobile phone or PDA, or some other broadband Internet connection		3 = Something else]
Uses Internet at Home	Connects to the Internet from home	1 = true, 0 = other	*HENET3:* (Do you/Does anyone in this household) connect to the Internet from home? [1 = Yes; 2 = No]
Uses Internet Anywhere	Uses the Internet at any location	1 = true, 0 = other	*PENET2:* Who is that? (Does this person use the Internet at any location?) [1 = Yes; 2 = No]
Hispanic	Hispanic ethnicity	1 = true, 0 = other	*PEHSPNON:* Hispanic or non-Hispanic. [1 = Hispanic; 2 = non-Hispanic]

(*continued*)

Variable Name	Description	Coding	Source Variable/Question Wording
Black	African-American race	1 = true, 0 = other	*PTDTRACE*: Race. [1 = White Only; 2 = Black Only; 3 = American Indian, Alaskan Native Only; 4 = Asian Only; 5 = Hawaiian/Pacific Islander Only; 6 = White-Black; 7 = White-AI; 8 = White-Asian; 9 = White-Hawaiian; 10 = Black-AI; 11 = Black-Asian; 12 = Black-HP; 13 = AI-Asian; 14 = Asian-HP; 15 = W-B-AI; 16 = W-B-A; 17 = W-AI-A; 18 = W-A-HP; 19 = W-B-AI-A; 20 = 2 or 3 Races; 21 = 4 or 5 Races]
Asian	Asian race	1 = true, 0 = other	*PTDTRACE*
Spanish Only Language	Spanish is only language spoken	1 = true, 0 = other	*HUSPNISH*: Is Spanish the only language spoken by all members of this household who are 15 years of age or older? [1 = Spanish only language spoken]
Income	Household family income	1–16 (1 = lowest, 16 = highest)	*HUFAMINC*: Combined income of all family members during the last 12 months. Includes money from jobs, net income from business, farm or rent, pensions, dividends, interest, social security payments and any other money income received by family members who are 15 years of age or older. [1 = less than $5,000; 2 = 5,000 to 7,499; 3 = 7,500 to 9,999; 4 = 10,000 to 12,499; 5 = 12,500 to 14,999; 6 = 15,000 to 19,999; 7 = 20,000 to 24,999; 8 = 25,000 to 29,999; 9 = 30,000 to 34,999; 10 = 35,000 to 39,999; 11 = 40,000 to 49,999; 12 = 50,000 to 59,999; 13 = 60,000 to 74,999; 14 = 75,000 to 99,999; 15 = 100,000 to 149,999; 16 = 150,000 or more]

Variable Name	Description	Coding	Source Variable/Question Wording
Education	Highest level of school completed	1–5 (1 = lowest, 5 = highest)	PEEDUCA: Highest level of school completed or degree received.
			[31 = less than 1st grade; 32 = 1st, 2nd, 3rd or 4th grade; 33 = 5th or 6th grade; 34 = 7th or 8th grade; 35 = 9th grade; 36 = 10th grade; 37 = 11th grade; 38 = 12th grade no diploma; 39 = high school grad-diploma or equiv. (GED); 40 = some college but no degree; 41 = associate degree-occupational/vocational; 42 = associate degree-academic program; 43 = bachelor's degree (ex: BA, AB, BS); 44 = master's degree (ex: MA, MS, MEng, MEd, MSW); 45 = professional school deg. (ex: MD, DDS, DVM); 46 = doctorate degree (ex: PhD, EdD)]
Age	Age in years	0–79 = age in years, 80 = 80–84 years old, 85 = 85 + years old	PEAGE: Persons age as of the end of survey week.
Male	Male gender	1 = true, 0 = other	PESEX: Sex.
			[1 = Male; 2 = Female]
Not Married	Not currently married	1 = true, 0 = other	PEMARITL: Marital status.
			[1 = married—spouse present; 2 = married—spouse absent; 3 = widowed; 4 = divorced; 5 = separated; 6 = never married]

(continued)

Variable Name	Description	Coding	Source Variable/Question Wording
Parent of Child	Has a child under the age of 18	1 = true, 0 = other	PRNMCHLD: Number of own children <18 years of age.
Business Owner	Owns a business or farm	1 = true, 0 = other	HUBUS: Does anyone in this household have a business or a farm? [1 = Yes; 2 = No]
Other	Farming, fishing, and forestry, armed forces, or unidentified occupation	1 = true, 0 = other	PRMJOCC1: Major occupation recode—Job 1. [1 = Management, business, and financial occupations; 2 = Professional and related occupations; 3 = Service occupations; 4 = Sales and related occupations; 5 = Office and administrative support occupations; 6 = Farming, fishing, and forestry occupations; 7 = Construction and extraction occupations; 8 = Installation, maintenance, and repair occupations; 9 = Production occupations; 10 = Transportation and material moving occupations; 11 = Armed Forces]
Business	Management, business, or financial occupation	1 = true, 0 = other	PRMJOCC1
Professional	Professional or related occupation	1 = true, 0 = other	PRMJOCC1
Service	Service occupation	1 = true, 0 = other	PRMJOCC1
Sales	Sales or related occupation	1 = true, 0 = other	PRMJOCC1
Office Support	Office or administrative support occupation	1 = true, 0 = other	PRMJOCC1

Variable Name	Description	Coding	Source Variable/Question Wording
Construction	Construction or extraction occupation	1 = true, 0 = other	PRMJOCC1
Installation & Repair	Installation, maintenance, or repair occupation	1 = true, 0 = other	PRMJOCC1
Transportation	Transportation or material moving occupation	1 = true, 0 = other	PRMJOCC1
Production (reference)	Production occupation	1 = true, 0 = other	PRMJOCC1
Urban	Principal city status	1 = true, 0 = other	GTCBSAST: Principal city/balance status. [1 = principal city; 2 = balance; 3 = nonmetropolitan; 4 = not identified]
Suburban (reference)	Balance city status or not identified	1 = true, 0 = other	GTCBSAST
Rural	Nonmetropolitan status	1 = true, 0 = other	GTCBSAST
% Employed in Information	Percent of population employed in the information sector (weighted estimates based on Census industry classification)	0–100%	PEIO1ICD: Industry code for primary job.

Source: 2009 FCC

Variable Name	Description	Coding	Source Variable/Question Wording
Uses High-Speed at Home	Connects to the Internet from home using a high-speed, broadband connection	1 = true, 0 = other	q11.1: At home, do you now connect to the internet through a slow-speed connection such as dial-up or do you have a high-speed, broadband connection?
			[1 = Slow-speed connection; 2 = High-speed broadband connection; 3 = (DO NOT READ) Both/Neither; 4 = (DO NOT READ) Don't have internet at home]
Uses Internet at Home	Connects to the Internet from home	1 = true, 0 = other	q9a: Now please tell me if you access the internet at any of the following places? (First/Next) Do you ever access the Internet….At home?
			[1 = Yes; 2 = No]
Uses Internet Anywhere	Uses the Internet at any location	1 = true, 0 = other	q8: Do you ever access the internet… or send and receive e-mail?
			[1 = Yes; 2 = No]

Variable Name	Description	Coding	Source Variable/Question Wording
Mobile Internet User Without High-Speed	Uses the Internet on mobile phone, but does not have high-speed Internet at home	1 = true, 0 = other	q30a: Please tell me if you ever use your cell phone to do any of the following things. Do you ever use it to—Send or receive email or not?
			[1 = Yes; 2 = No]
			q30a: Please tell me if you ever use your cell phone to do any of the following things. Do you ever use it to—Access webpages on the internet or not?
Local News	Ever uses the Internet: to get local or community news online	1 = true, 0 = other	q14a: Please tell me if you EVER use the internet to do any of the following things. Do you ever use the internet to...Get local or community news online?
			[1 = Yes; 2 = No]
Govt Website	Ever uses the Internet: to visit a local, state or federal government website	1 = true, 0 = other	q14c: Please tell me if you EVER use the internet to do any of the following things. Do you ever use the internet to...Visit a local, state or federal government website?
			[1 = Yes; 2 = No]

(continued)

Variable Name	Description	Coding	Source Variable/Question Wording
Natl News	Ever uses the Internet: to get national or international news	1 = true, 0 = other	q14i: Please tell me if you EVER use the internet to do any of the following things. Do you ever use the internet to . . . Get international or national news online? [1 = Yes; 2 = No]
Apply Job	Ever uses the Internet:) to get information or apply for a job	1 = true, 0 = other	q14j: Please tell me if you EVER use the internet to do any of the following things. Do you ever use the internet to . . . Get information about or apply for a job? [1 = Yes; 2 = No]
Govt Info	Ever uses the Internet: to get information from a government agency	1 = true, 0 = other	q14l: Please tell me if you EVER use the internet to do any of the following things. Do you ever use the internet to . . . Get advice or information from a government agency about a health or safety issue? [1 = Yes; 2 = No]
Online Banking	Ever uses the Internet: for online banking	1 = true, 0 = other	q14n: Please tell me if you EVER use the internet to do any of the following things. Do you ever use the internet to . . . Do any banking online? [1 = Yes; 2 = No]

Variable Name	Description	Coding	Source Variable/Question Wording
Take a Class	Ever uses the Internet: to take a class for credit toward a degree	1 = true, 0 = other	q14o: Please tell me if you EVER use the internet to do any of the following things. Do you ever use the internet to . . . Take a class online for credit towards a degree of some kind, like a high school or college diploma or an advanced degree? [1 = Yes; 2 = No]
Hispanic	Hispanic ethnicity	1 = true, 0 = other	raceethn: Combining race and ethnicity variables. [1 = White, non Hispanic; 2 = Black, non-Hispanic; 3 = Hispanic; 4 = Asian non-Hispanic; 5 = American Indian/Alaska Native; 6 = Native Hawaiian/Pacific Islander; 7 = Other/Mixed Race]
Black	African-American race	1 = true, 0 = other	raceethn

(continued)

Variable Name	Description	Coding	Source Variable/Question Wording
Asian	Asian race	1 = true, 0 = other	*raceethn*
Income	Household family income	1–9 (1 = lowest, 9 = highest)	*inc*: Last year, that is in 2008, what was your total family income from all sources, before taxes? Just stop me when I get to the right category (READ 1–9).
			[1 = Less than $10,000; 2 = $10,000 to under $20,000; 3 = $20,000 to under $30,000; 4 = $30,000 to under $40,000; 5 = $40,000 to under $50,000; 6 = $50,000 to under $75,000; 7 = $75,000 to under $100,000; 8 = $100,000 to under $150,000; 9 = $150,000 or more]
Education	Highest level of school completed	1–4 (1 = lowest, 4 = highest)	*receduc*: Recoded education. [1 = Lower than HS; 2 = HS grad; 3 = Some college; 4 = College +]
Age	Age in years	0–96 = age in years, 97 = 97 + years old	*age*: What is your age?
Male	Male gender	1 = true, 0 = other	*sex*: Record respondent's sex.

Variable Name	Description	Coding	Source Variable/Question Wording
Not Married	Not currently married	1 = true, 0 = other	*mar*: Are you currently married, living with a partner, divorced, separated, widowed, or have you never been married?
			[1 = Married; 2 = Living with a partner; 3 = Divorced; 4 = Separated; 5 = Widowed; 6 = Never been married; 7 = Single (VOL.)]
Parent of Child	Has a child under the age of 18 living in household	1 = true, 0 = other	*hh3*: How many children, under age 18, currently live in your household?
Employed	Employed full-time, part-time, or is self-employed	1 = true, 0 = other	*empl*: Are you now employed full-time, part-time, retired, or are you not employed for pay?
			[1 = Employed full-time; 2 = Employed part-time; 3 = Retired; 4 = Not employed for pay; 5 = (VOL.) Have own business/self-employed; 6 = (VOL.) Disabled; 7 = (VOL.) Student; 8 = (VOL.) Other]
Urban	Community type = urban	1 = true, 0 = other	*usr*: Community type from zip merge—alpha.
			[R = Rural; S = Suburban; U = Urban]
Suburban (reference)	Community type = suburban	1 = true, 0 = other	*usr*
Rural	Community type = rural	1 = true, 0 = other	*usr*

Source: American Community Survey and State and Metropolitan Area Data Book*

Variable Name	Description	Coding
% Black	Percent of the population that is African-American	0–100%
% Hispanic	Percent of the population that is Hispanic	0–100%
Per Capita Income	State income per resident	Continuous
% High School Grad.	Percent of the population with a high school degree	0–100%
% Age 65 +	Percent of the population 65 years of age or older	0–100%

*Note: The American Community Survey (three-year estimates 2007–2009) was used for urban area model estimates, and the State and Metropolitan Area Data Book was used for suburban area model estimates.

University of Iowa Hawkeye Poll
Department of Political Science
Chicago Internet Survey Conducted June
23–August 7, 2008 Questionnaire

Introduction

Hello, I am ———, calling from the University of Iowa. We are studying the role of the internet in Chicago. Your phone number was selected at random to represent your neighborhood in this study. I am not selling anything and just need a few minutes.

Attempt to Improve Young Male Response Rates

YNGMALE:

I'd like to ask some questions of the youngest male who is 18 years or older and now at home. [IF R IS MALE] Would that be you?
IF RESP: YES → CONTINUE WITH [**AGESCREEN**]
IF RESP: LET ME GET HIM →WAIT FOR NEW PERSON, GO TO [**REINTRO**]
IF RESP: NO MALE, ASK:
    Is there another person over 18 I can speak with? Could I speak with you?
IF CURRENT R. → GO TO [**AGESCREEN**]
IF WILL GET SOMEONE, → WAIT FOR NEW PERSON, GO TO [**REINTRO**]
IF NO, GO TO [**SCHEDULE**].

REINTRO:

Hello, I am _____, calling from the University of Iowa. We are studying the role of the internet in Chicago. Your phone number was selected at random to represent your neighborhood in this study. I am not selling anything and just need a few minutes.

AGESCREEN:

Screen age for 18 and over

Q1A
AGE   First, I need to make sure we are reaching people of all ages 18 or over. Would you tell me your age?

_____ years
97   97 or older
99   Don't know/Refused [**VOL.**]

If Not 18 Or Over→ Go to End [Ineligible]
Consent:

We invite you to participate in a study about technology access in Chicago being conducted by researchers from the University of Iowa. Your phone number was chosen at random to represent your neighborhood. If you agree, we would like to ask you a series of questions. You may skip any questions that you prefer not to answer. This will take about 12 minutes.

Your responses are confidential and it will not be possible to link you to them. This survey is voluntary. Your willingness to answer my questions will indicate your consent to use your answers in our research project.

Q1B
Are you willing to participate in this survey?

0   NO → **GO TO END** [**ATTEMPT CONVERT**]
1   YES

Q2
INTUSE   OK, thanks! First, do you ever use the Internet in any place (home, work, school, anywhere else)?
0   No
1   Yes
8   Don't Know
9   Refused

Q3
INFO   We are interested in the information people feel they need in their daily lives whether or not it comes from the internet. Would you say that it is very important, important, not very important, or not important at all for you to get information on: [PROMPT WITH RESPONSE OPTIONS AS NEEDED]
Q3A   Jobs or better job opportunities
Q3B   Education or training for myself

Q3   CMy child's school
Q3   DHealth care or health issues
Q3   EMy neighborhood
Q3   FGovernment or services provided by government
Q3   GPlaces to live

RESPONSE OPTIONS
    1   Very important
    2   Important
    3   Not very important
    4   Not at all important
    8   Don't Know
    9   Refused

If Q2 Is Not Yes (1) Go To Q6

Q4
FREQUSE   About how often do you use the Internet? [Read options]
    1   Several times a day
    2   About once a day
    3   3–5 days a week
    4   1–2 days a week
    5   Every few weeks
    6   Less often
    9   Refused

Q5
HOWLONG   About how many years have you been an Internet user? [ENTER YEARS]
    _____ years

    8   Don't Know
    9   Refused

Q6
HCOMP   Do you have a computer at home?
    0   NO → **GO TO Q8**
    1   YES
    8   Don't Know→ **GO TO Q8**
    9   Refused → **GO TO Q8**

Q7
INETHOM   Do you ever use the Internet at home?

    0   NO
    1   YES→ **GO TO Q10**
    8   Don't Know
    9   Refused

Q8

NOACCESS   I am going to read a list of reasons why some people don't use the Internet at home. For each, just tell me whether it applies to you by saying yes if it does, or no if it does not.

    Q8A I don't need it, I'm not interested
    Q8B The cost is too high for me
    Q8C I can use it somewhere else
    Q8D I don't have time to use the Internet
    Q8E It's too difficult to use
    Q8F I am worried about privacy and personal information online
    Q8G The Internet is dangerous
    Q8H It's hard for me to use the information in English
    Q8I I have a physical impairment that makes it difficult to use the Internet

    RESPONSE OPTIONS
       0   NO
       1   YES
       8   Don't Know
       9   Refused

Q9

MAIN   Now, please tell me in a couple words the MAIN reason you don't use the Internet at home? [DON'T READ, CODE ANSWER TO BEST FIT]

    1   I don't need it, I'm not interested
    2   The cost is too high for me
    3   I can use it somewhere else
    4   I don't have time to use the Internet
    5   It's too difficult to use
    6   I am worried about privacy and personal information online
    7   Te Internet is dangerous
    8   It's hard for me to use the information in English
    9   I have a physical impairment that makes it difficult to use the Internet
   10   Other
   11   Don't Know
   12   Refused

Q9A

INTFUT   Is there anything that might make you interested in using the internet in the future? If so, just tell me in a couple words what it is. If not, just tell me no. [OPEN ENDED, RECORD VERBATIM]

IF Q7 IS NOT 1 GO TO Q14

Q10
HCONTYP   Does the computer you use at HOME connect to the Internet through a
          dial-up telephone line, or do you have some type of high speed connec-
          tion,?
    1   Dial-up telephone
    2   High Speed Connection → **GO TO Q12**
    8   Don't Know → **GO TO Q12**
    9   Refused→ **GO TO Q12**

Q11
NOBBND   What is the MAIN reason you do not have high-speed (that is, faster than
         dial-up) Internet access at home? [DON'T READ, CODE ANSWER TO
         BEST FIT]
    1   Don't need it or not interested
    2   Costs are too high for me
    3   Can use it somewhere else
    4   I don't have time to use the Internet
    5   Too difficult to use or don't now how to use
    6   No computer or computer inadequate
    7   Privacy and security
    8   Not available in area
    9   Other
    10 Don't Know
    11 Refused

Q12
WHEREINT   Where would you say that you use the Internet **most often?** [DON'T
           READ, CODE ANSWER TO BEST FIT]
    1   Home
    2   Work
    3   School
    4   A library or public place
    5   Friend or relative's house
    6   Coffee Shop or Internet Cafe
    7   Other
    8   Don't Know (Vol.)
    9   Refused (Vol.)

Q13
WHERESEC   Where would you say that you use the Internet **most often after that?**
           [DON'T READ, CODE ANSWER TO BEST FIT]
    1   Home
    2   Work

3   School
4   A library or public place
5   Friend or relative's house
6   Coffee Shop or Internet Cafe
7   Other
8   Don't Know (Vol.)
9   Refused (Vol.)

Q14

CTCAWAR   As far as you know, is there a place you can go in your neighbor-hood where the Internet is publicly available to anyone who wants to use it? Such places are often called Community Technology Centers.

0   NO
1   YES
8   Don't Know (Vol.)
9   Refused (Vol.)

IF Q2 IS NOT YES (1) SKIP TO Q16

Q15

CTCHELP   Have you ever used the Internet or gotten help using the Internet at a Community Technology Center?

0   NO
1   YES
8   Don't Know (Vol.)
9   Refused (Vol.)

Q16

PUBLICACC   Would you say that it is easy or difficult to get to places in your community with public access to the Internet, like a library or a community technology center? Would you say that it is very easy, somewhat easy, somewhat difficult or very difficult?

1   Very easy
2   Somewhat easy
3   Somewhat difficult
4   Very difficult
8   Don't know (Vol)
9   Refused (Vol)

IF Q2 IS NOT YES (1) SKIP TO Q24

Q17
LIBRARY   Have you used the Internet at the Chicago Public Library?
    0   NO
    1   YES
    8   Don't Know (Vol.)
    9   Refused (Vol.)

IF Q15 IS NOT YES (1) AND Q17 IS NOT YES (1) GO TO Q19

Q18
WHYLIB   I am going to read a number of statements about why you use the Internet at the library or at a community technology center. Please respond yes or no to each statement.
  Q18 A   I don't have a computer at home or my computer it slow
  Q18 B   I don't have an Internet connection at home
  Q18 C   I needed help to find information
  Q18D   I needed help to use the computer
  Q18 E   My computer or Internet connections at home aren't working
  Q18 F   It is convenient
  Q18G   To take a class
  Q18 H   To take my children to do their homework

RESPONSE OPTIONS
    0   NO
    1   YES
    8   Don't Know (Vol.)
    9   Refused (Vol.)

Q19
ACTIVITIES   I am going to read a list of things you might do on the internet. Please tell me how frequently you do each by saying if you do these things daily, a few times per week, a few times per month, rarely, or never. [PROMPT WITH OPTIONS AS NEEDED]
  Q19 A   Get news online
  Q19B   Do work for your job
  Q19C   Use a social networking site like Facebook
  Q19D   Send or receive email

Q19E   Use a cell phone to connect to the Internet
Q19F   Read a blog
Q19G   Use wireless access to connect to the Internet in a public place

RESPONSE OPTIONS
1   Daily
2   A few times per week
3   A few times per month
4   Rarely
5   Never
8   Don't Know (Vol.)
9   Refused (Vol.)

Q20
ONLINE   I'm going to read another list. For each item please tell me if you ever use the Internet to do any of the following things by just saying yes or no. Do you ever use the Internet to; [PROMPT AS NECESSARY—JUST TELL ME YES OR NO]
Q20A   Find health information
Q20B   Look for a job or information on jobs
Q20C   Take a class or training online
Q20D   Get information about politics
Q20E   Get information about trains or buses using the CTA or RTA website
Q20F   Find information on government
Q20G   Use the City of Chicago website

RESPONSE OPTIONS
0   NO
1   YES
8   Don't Know (Vol.)
9   Refused (Vol.)

IF Q20G IS YES(1) ASK Q21 OTHERWISE SKIP TO Q23

Q21
CHICAGO   Please tell me if you have ever used the City of Chicago website to do any of the following. Just tell me yes or no. [PROMPT AS NECESSARY—JUST TELL ME YES OR NO]
Q21A   Get an address or phone number
Q21B   Contact officials
Q21C   Get tourist or recreation information

Q21D   Get information about services (other than recreation or tourism)

Q21E   Complete a transaction online, such as paying a bill or fine, or filing a form online

Q21F   Look for government policies or documents

RESPONSE OPTIONS
- 0   NO
- 1   YES
- 8   Don't Know (Vol.)
- 9   Refused (Vol.)

Q22

EVALCHI   I am going to read you some statements about the City of Chicago website. Please tell me whether you strongly agree, agree, disagree or strongly disagree with each statement. [PROMPT AS NECESSARY WITH RESPONSE OPTIONS]

Q22A   The website had the information I needed.

Q22B   The website was easy to use and find information.

Q22C   The website was difficult to use and complex.

RESPONSE OPTIONS
- 1   Strongly Agree
- 2   Agree
- 3   Disagree
- 4   Strongly Disagree
- 8   Don't Know (Vol.)
- 9   Refused (Vol.)

Q23

SKILLS   I am going to read some things people sometimes do online. Please tell me if you already know how to do each one, or if you would need someone else to help you.

Q23A   Use a search engine to find information online

Q23B   Send and receive email

Q23C   Download and fill out a form

Q23D   Upload images or files to a website or email

Q23E   Create a website

RESPONSE OPTIONS
- 1   Know how
- 2   Need help
- 8   Don't Know (Vol.)
- 9   Refused (Vol.)

Q24

POLICY1   There's been talk about building a wireless network in neighborhoods in Chicago. Which of the following should be the focus in doing this project? Should it be on making wireless available: [RANDOMIZE ORDER OF FIRST THREE OPTIONS; READ IN ORDER]

1   all over the city
2   in low-income neighborhoods
3   in public schools, libraries and other public places
4   or do you think they should not work on this project?
8   Don't Know (Vol.)
9   Refused (Vol.)

Q25

POLICY2   Would you support a project to provide free wireless internet access if it caused a small increase in fees or taxes?

0   NO
1   YES
8   Don't Know (Vol.)
9   Refused (Vol.)

Demographic Information—ALL RESPONDENTS

Now, just a few last questions for statistical purposes only. We're almost done. I appreciate the time you've given me.

Q26

EDUC   What is the last grade or class that you completed in school?
[DO NOT READ; MARK CLOSEST]

1   None, or grade 1–8
2   High school incomplete (Grades 9–11)
3   High school graduate (Grade 12 or GED certificate)
4   Technical, trade, or vocational school AFTER high school
5   Some college, no 4-year degree (including associate degree)
6   College graduate (B.S., B.A., or other 4-year degree)
7   Post-graduate training or professional schooling after college (e.g., toward a master's Degree or Ph.D.; law or medical school)
8   Don't know (**Vol.**)
9   Refused (**Vol.**)

Q27

RACE   What is your race? Are you white, black, Asian, or some other?

1   White
2   Black
3   Asian
4   Other or mixed race

8   Don't know (**Vol.**)
9   Refused (**Vol.**)

Q28
HISP   Are you, yourself, of Hispanic origin or descent, such as Mexican, Puerto Rican, Cuban, or some other Spanish background?

0   NO
1   YES
8   Don't know (Vol)
9   Refused (Vol)

Q29
MARITAL   What is your marital status? Are you ... [**READ**]
1   Married, or with a committed partner
2   Divorced
3   Separated
4   Widowed
5   Never been married
8   Don't know (**Vol.**)
9   Refused (**Vol.**)

Q31
INCOME   Last year, that is in 2007, what was your total family income from all sources, before taxes? Just stop me when I get to the right category. [**READ**]
1   Less than $5,000
1   5 to under $10,000
2   10 to under $20,000
3   20 to under $30,000
4   30 to under $40,000
5   40 to under $50,000
6   50 to under $75,000
7   75 to under $100,000
8   100 to under $150,000
9   $150,000 or more
10   Don't know (**Vol.**)
11   Refused (**Vol.**)

IF Q31 IS REFUSED(11) ASK:

Q31A
INCOME2   Just for statistical purposes it would be really helpful if you would tell me if your family income is above $20,000. Is it: [read options]
1   Above $20,000
2   At or Below $20,000

8   Don't Know
9   Refused

Q32

CHILD   Are you the parent or guardian of any children under 18 now living in your household?

0   NO
1   YES
8   Don't know
9   Refused

Q33

JOB   What is your employment status? Are you: [**READ**]

1   Employed full time
2   Employed part time
3   A homemaker or stay at home parent
4   Retired
5   A student
6   Unemployed
7   Laid off
8   Disabled
9   Don't know
10 Refused

Q34

ZIPCODE   What is your zipcode?

_____Enter Zipcode

8   Don't know (**Vol.**)
9   Refused (**Vol.**)

Q35

OCCUP   What is your occupation? [OPEN ENDED, RECORD VERBATIM]

Q36

CHA   Are you currently a CHA [Chicago Housing Authority] resident or are you a former resident who will be returning to CHA housing in the future?

0   NO
1   YES
8   Don't know (**Vol.**)
9   Refused (**Vol.**)

Q37

STREETS   What are the cross-streets nearest your residence? [OPEN ENDED, RECORD VERBATIM]

Q38
SEX   [**DO NOT ASK; ENTER RESPONDENT'S APPARENT SEX**]
   1   Male
   2   Female

End of interview. Thank respondent → GO TO [COMPLETE]

[COMPLETE]

OK, that's all I have for your today. Thank you again for your time. Have a nice day/evening. [END; complete]

[ATTEMPT CONVERT]

I understand why you might not want to take the time right now to talk with us. But what we are doing is important to Chicago and your answers will help the city better understand what kind of technology people need. It will only take about 12 minutes. Could you help us out?

   1. YES → RETURN TO Q2
   2. NO → GO TO [SCHEDULE]

[SCHEDULE]

Would it be possible to schedule another time to talk with you or someone else in your household? I'd be happy to set up a specific day and time to call.

   1. YES
   2. NO → OK, thanks for your time. [END; Refusal]

Great, thanks. I am calling you at [read phone number]. When would you like me to call back? [ENTER DAY AND TIME FOR CALLBACK] Could you give me your first name so I know who to ask for when I call? [RECORD FIRST NAME].

   Thanks, we'll talk to you soon. [END, Callback scheduled]

[PARTIAL]

   I'm sorry this is taking so long right now, and I know you are busy. Could I schedule a time to call you back to finish the survey? We only have a few more minutes to go and your answers are very important to the study since you've been randomly selected to represent your neighborhood. Would it be possible for us to call you back at another time or day to finish this survey?

   1. YES
   2. NO → OK, thanks for your time. [END; Partial Refusal]

Great, thanks. I am calling you at [read phone number]. When would you like me to call back? [ENTER DAY AND TIME FOR CALLBACK] Could you give me your first name so I know who to ask for when I call? [RECORD FIRST NAME].

Thanks, talk to you soon. [END, Partial Callback]

[INELIGIBLE]

OK, we're only talking to people 18 or over today. Thanks for your time.
[END, ineligible]
OTHER CODES TO RECORD AS NEEDED
OUT OF SAMPLE—Business Line
DISCONNECT—Number not in service
LANGUAGE—Respondent does not speak English or Spanish

Notes

Chapter 1

1. See OECD 2011.
2. See the Google Fiber website at http://www.google.com/appserve/fiberrfi/.
3. For a description of broadband recovery grants (American Recovery and Reinvestment Act), see U.S. Dept. of Commerce, NTIA, "About" page, BroadbandUSA website, http://www2.ntia.doc.gov/about. (Hereafter BroadbandUSA.)
4. FCC 2010a. *Connecting America: The National Broadband Plan*. Washington, D.C.: The Federal Communications Commission. http://www.broadband.gov.
5. In 2009, IBM announced a partnership with Dubuque, Iowa, to create the first "Smart City" in the United States, utilizing information technology to make water, electricity, and transportation systems more efficient (Hamm 2009). The MIT Media Lab has a smart cities research program on information technology use for mobility and sustainability. Cisco has also been piloting a smart city project in Holyoke, Massachusetts, especially focused on the smart grid. In 2011, there were 102 smart city projects worldwide, with 35 in North America, according to ABI Research (Schelmetic 2011).
6. http://change.gov/agenda/technology_agenda/. Barack Obama presidential announcement speech in Springfield, IL, February 10, 2007. Quote is from p. 1, website for Office of the President-Elect. Accessed July 22, 2012.
7. The Broadband Technology Opportunities Program (BTOP) is part of the American Recovery and Reinvestment Act (ARRA), which is more popularly known as the economic stimulus program.
8. The full list of grantees is available at "Grants Awarded" page, Broadband USA, http://www2.ntia.doc.gov/awards.
9. See a sample reporting form for the Sustainable Broadband Adoption training and outreach program, "Sustainable Broadband Adoption Annual Performance Progress Report Introduction," BroadbandUSA, http://www2.ntia.doc.gov/files/sbaannualfinal.pdf.
10. For example, the problem of addressing cost as a barrier for broadband subscribership was discussed by Public Computer Center and Sustainable Broadband Adoption grantees at the national Community Broadband Adoption, Impact, and Sustainability conference held in Cleveland in June 2011 (see http://www.connectcommunity.org/2011/05/09/community-broadband-adoption-impact-sustainability-conference/).
11. Alternatives such as DSL are slower than cable, and even AT&T's U-verse, which has about 4% of the market, has slower speeds because its fiber-optic broadband signal switches to copper lines before reaching the home. Fiber-optic networks (such as Verizon's FiOS) are faster than cable but are available to only about 10% of the nation's households (Crawford 2011).

Chapter 2

1. Based on author calculations, reviewing grant awards available online at http://www2.ntia. doc.gov/awards. Authors estimated grants made for urban or metropolitan areas (including nonprofits, cities, or other governments, and for both individual or multiple-site grants) for BTOP, including Sustainable Broadband Adoption, Public Computer Centers, and Comprehensive Community Infrastructure grants. Totaling these grants, we then estimated the total of urban/metropolitan awards as a proportion of the grant awards. See note 10 for a discussion of how we defined awards in urban and metropolitan areas.

2. Federal programs to assist community technology centers and to spur adoption by local governments and nonprofits established during the Clinton administration were eliminated by the George W. Bush administration. The National Technology and Information Administration (NTIA), which played a leading role in federal technology policy, issued a 2001 report entitled *A Nation Online*, which summed up the attitude of the Bush administration—problem solved. Michael Powell, chairman of the Federal Communications Commission (FCC) appointed by President Bush famously remarked that the digital divide was not a public policy issue that government should address, because there was a Mercedes divide as well (Mossberger, Tolbert, and Stansbury 2003, chapter 1).

3. FCC, National Broadband Plan, xi, emphasis added.

4. See a description of the American Recovery and Reinvestment Act passed on February 17, 2009, including a description of broadband programs at http://www.ntia.doc.gov/ page/2011/american-recovery-and-reinvestment-act-2009. The FCC broadband.gov website contains a number of hearings, workshops, and panels held during 2009 on issues related to the National Broadband Plan. See http://www.broadband.gov/news.html.

5. For more information, see http://www.gig-u.org/.

6. See http://www2.ntia.doc.gov/awards.

7. For information-sharing in Homeland Security see http://www.dhs.gov/files/programs/ sharing-information.shtm.

8. Philadelphia, Kansas City, MO, and Kansas City, KS, were contacted, but did not respond to the invitation for an interview.

9. See Appendix Table A2.1 for the questions, which were used for semistructured interviewing. Respondents were promised confidentiality, unless they were contacted for attribution. The interviews were conducted by the authors with the assistance of Adrian Brown, PhD student in Public Administration at the University of Illinois at Chicago.

10. This includes cities of at least 50,000, which are large enough to meet the definition of a core city for a metropolitan area, and suburbs such as Cambridge, MA, which are within metropolitan areas. There are also statewide grants or others that serve multiple locations around the country, both urban and rural. Estimating the exact spending on urban or metropolitan areas is difficult given the complexity of these grants. Here, we assumed that about one-third of the spending on statewide and multilocational grants went toward metropolitan areas.

11. Some, like the One Economy and One Community projects, have substantial investments in central cities and metropolitan areas as well as rural programs. Many statewide projects are less focused on urban areas.

12. A total of $2.5 billion was designated for infrastructure in rural areas through the Broadband Initiatives Program (BIP) administered by the Rural Utilities Service (RUS).

13. BTOP has several types of grants, including Comprehensive Community Infrastructure (CCI), Public Computer Centers (PCC), training and outreach through Sustainable Broadband Adoption (SBA), and another program for mapping broadband availability through grants in each of the states.

14. Unserved areas eligible for infrastructure grants were required to have broadband available in less than 10% of the area and were overwhelmingly rural.

15. The Notice of Funding Availability was released on July 9, 2009, and Round 1 proposals were due on August 14 (Federal Register 2009, p. 33104). Available online at http://www.ntia. doc.gov/files/ntia/publications/fr_bbnofa_090709.pdf.

16. Notice of Funding Availability, Federal Register, January 22, 2010, Broadband Technology Opportunities Program, p. 3794, available online at http://www.ntia.doc.gov/files/ntia/publications/fr_btopnofa_100115_0.pdf.

17. These institutional networks can provide infrastructure that could later be built out for affordable home access in adjacent neighborhoods, if government or private providers fund such improvements (providing last-mile coverage from middle-mile infrastructure). These are not part of the plans submitted by the cities in the second round, because of the require-ments that networks are intended for community anchor institutions, especially public safety. Whether such investments will occur in the future is an open question.

Chapter 3

1. Urban clusters include smaller towns outside of metropolitan areas, so this suggests that the lack of availability affects mostly sparsely populated regions. For example, a census block in urbanized areas on average has a population of 2,900 persons, whereas those outside urban-ized areas average 13.8 people (FCC 2010b).

2. U.S. Bureau of the Census, *Current Population Survey, October 2009: School Enrollment and Internet Use Supplement Technical Documentation.* Documentation of the abstract, ques-tionnaire, and record layouts of the file are available on the Census Bureau's website at http://www.census.gov/.

3. Each household is interviewed once a month for four consecutive months one year and again for the corresponding time period a year later. Because of this feature, we cluster respondents in our statistical analysis by household to control for any shared characteristics. The CPS samples from 2,025 geographic areas called primary sampling units (PSUs) in the entire United States providing broad coverage of the country.

4. The CPS is the only source of monthly estimates of total employment (both farm and non-farm); nonfarm self- employed persons, domestics, and unpaid helpers in nonfarm family enterprises; wage and salaried employees; and, finally, estimates of total unemployment.

5. For an MSA with multiple principal cities, we only consider the largest principal city as an urban area. This is mainly a concern for the largest MSAs, such as Chicago, Los Angeles, and New York, where cities outside of these main urban areas are designated as principal cities simply because they meet the Census Bureau's population threshold.

Chapter 4

1. Pew Internet and American Life. 2012. "What Internet Users Do Online," February 2012 Survey, http://pewinternet.org/Trend-Data-(Adults)/Online-Activites-Total.aspx (accessed June 25, 2012).

2. Hargittai and Hsieh (2011) have pointed out that the selected FCC measures differ some-what from the validated skill measures, for example, using double-barreled questions and introducing less variation than combinations tested by the authors. For our purposes, how-ever, there is enough variation to demonstrate differences between the less-connected and those with full access.

3. We omit e-commerce from this analysis, as it represents a gray area between entertainment and economic participation.

Chapter 5

1. Among the cities we interviewed that have conducted surveys or done other studies to understand levels of Internet use or broadband adoption in the past several years are Los Angeles, San Francisco, New York, and Seattle, in addition to Chicago.

2. Some metropolitan authorities coordinate policy in a few functional areas (such as Minne-apolis and Portland), or some counties have formed consolidated governments, covering a

larger part of the region than previously (as in Louisville/Jefferson County, Miami/Dade County). Yet even these examples are exceptional, and none constitute truly metropolitan government (Lefevre and Weir 2012).

3. The data can be found in the State and Metropolitan Area Data Book online at http://www. census.gov/compendia/smadb/SMADBmetro.html.

4. Rather than reduce the set of contextual variables to reduce concerns about multicollinearity, we use the full set of aggregate variables to create the best possible rankings of cities and suburbs possible. Our focus is not on statistical significance of the place variables per se but on portraying the variation in city rankings as much as possible with the best and most complete set of predictor variables.

5. See 2010 census data for Los Angeles at http://quickfacts.census.gov/qfd/states/06/0644000. html. The population of LA is around 3.8 million; nearly half the residents are Hispanic and almost 10% are black.

Chapter 6

1. SOCDS Census Data: Output for Chicago City, IL, http://socds.huduser.org/census/industry.odb. State of the Cities Data Systems (SOCDS), HUD User, U.S. Department of Housing and Urban Development.

2. Available online at http://quickfacts.census.gov/qfd/states/00000.html.

3. Source: American Factfinder, Chicago City, Illinois, Census 2010 Median Household Income (White Non-Hispanic B19013H, Black Alone B19013B, and Hispanic All Races Alone B19013I at http://factfinder2.census.gov).

4. Traditionally, concentrated poverty has been defined as occurring in census tracts with poverty rates of 40% or more, although those with poverty rates of over 20% have also been depicted as disadvantaged (Jargowsky 1997). There has been debate in recent years about whether this definition is overly restrictive (Swanstrom, Ryan, and Stigers, 2007; Federal Reserve and Brookings Institution 2008), in part because the federal poverty line refers primarily to costs for a minimally nutritional diet rather than a broader range of needs (Swanstrom, Ryan, and Stigers 2007).

5. "City of Chicago," webpage, BroadbandUSA website, http://www2.ntia.doc.gov/grantees/CityofChicago2.

6. This rate is comparable to recent surveys for the Pew Internet and American Life Project, for example (see pewinternet.org). The margin of error is 1.7% and the cooperation rate was 26.7%.

7. Cell phones were not sampled in this study. While this has now become more common (with the growth of cell phone ownership and the decrease in land lines), there are still some debates over the most effective way in which to draw such samples, and evidence that higher nonresponse rates are biased toward more technologically sophisticated cell phone users (American Association of Public Opinion Research 2010). This will remain a challenge for telephone survey research for the future.

8. Because Latinos may be any race, the totals exceed 100%.

9. For example, the community areas in Chicago's Smart Communities project range between 35,000 and 58,000 residents, as described in chapter 9 (Table 9.1).

10. All are estimated to have less than 40% home broadband adoption. New City is listed in the table at 40% because of rounding up.

11. Pew Internet and American Life Project, May 2008, Internet trends over time at pewinternet.org; Mossberger, Tolbert, and Stansbury 2003.

12. In comparison with Chicago 2008 survey findings for general e-government use as well, use of the city's website is more diverse, as women and minorities are otherwise less likely to use government websites. This is consistent with some national studies, which have indicated that women and African Americans are more likely to use local government websites. See Mossberger and Tolbert 2009.

13. Krueger 2002; Mossberger, Tolbert, and Stansbury 2003 among others.
14. Fox 2005.

Chapter 7

1. In his more general work on the diffusion of innovations, Rogers (1995) argues that an innovation must have some relative advantage over the current way of doing things.
2. See links to the portals on the Smart Communities website at http://www.smartcommunitieschicago.org/index.html. See the Beehive at http://www.thebeehive.org/.
3. See for example, the "Usage Over Time" spreadsheet that aggregates historical results from Pew surveys, at http://www.pewinternet.org.

Chapter 8

1. Fong and Cao (2008) also find that African American households are more likely to use the Internet at home in metropolitan areas with higher levels of racial segregation and concentrated poverty, but, this effect is stronger for households with a head who is college educated. This may say something about the metropolitan context, but not necessarily the neighborhood where better-educated African Americans live. This may simply underscore that middle-class and better-educated African Americans are likely to be online (Gant et al. 2010; Mossberger, Tolbert, and Gilbert 2006).
2. Although we ask about barriers to home Internet adoption rather than broadband only, most Chicagoans with Internet access at home have broadband; only 8% had dial-up in 2008.
3. The term "concentrated poverty" has generally been applied to census tracts with a poverty rate of 40% or more (Jargowsky 1997), although recent work has argued that all high-poverty neighborhoods have place effects (Federal Reserve and Brookings Institution 2008) or that the traditional definition is too restrictive (Swanstrom et al. 2007).
4. This study used "buffers" that constructed a unique geography for each respondent within a half-mile radius, using data from the 2000 Census. See Mossberger, Kaplan, and Gilbert 2008 for a fuller explanation of the methodology.
5. The FCC codes from one to three providers as a single provider, and more detailed information is guarded as proprietary data. Federal broadband mapping promises better data on providers, but the initial results have been criticized for relying on incomplete data from providers (Lennett and Meinrath 2011).
6. A number of studies, including the Chicago survey analyzed here, have shown high rates of public access and other technology use outside the home among African Americans in poor communities. See also Mossberger, Kaplan, and Gilbert 2008 and Mossberger, Tolbert, and McNeal 2008, ch. 5.
7. The Chicago study asked respondents about barriers to home adoption rather than broadband home access. Given that most Chicago residents with Internet access at home had broadband connections, there are still close parallels. In the Chicago survey, only eight respondents cited a lack of broadband availability in their area as one reason for not having broadband at home.
8. See appendix C for question wording. The data analyzed in models here is from the multiple reasons respondents don't use the Internet at home.
9. The frequencies are weighted to correct for differences between the sample and the population, but weights are not used in multivariate models.
10. Only 5% say that use outside the home is their main reason for not having home access, but over half the respondents can use the Internet somewhere else.
11. The survey did not have separate questions regarding the cost of Internet services versus the cost of hardware. But, only 20% of respondents who cited cost as a barrier to home use had computers at home. For most respondents, then, cost barriers likely included both computers and Internet services.

12. Age is measured in years, while binary variables for African Americans, Latinos, and Asian Americans are included with white non-Hispanics as the reference group. Binary variables are included for females (coded 1, males coded 0) and parents with children. Educational attainment and family income are measured on seven-point indices.

13. Median household income is used instead of percent below the poverty line in modeling a lack of interest as a barrier because of improved fit of the model based on the neighborhood factors. From the 2000 U.S. Census.

14. Models were estimated using both this method and hierarchical linear modeling with HLM 6.0. There were no differences in results, and we report this simpler model specification.

Chapter 9

1. The Smart Communities program is the result of a series of digital inclusion initiatives in Chicago dating back to 2006, when the Mayor's Advisory Council on Closing the Digital Divide was formed during the Richard M. Daley administration to study the feasibility of a municipal wireless network and programs in low-income communities. The wireless proposal failed due to a lack of private-sector bidders, but the city launched some initial outreach and planning in several neighborhoods with support from the MacArthur Foundation, the Illinois Department of Commerce and Economic Opportunity, and Microsoft (see Mayor's Advisory Council to Close the Digital Divide 2007; Smart Communities 2009). These early projects led to the Smart Communities and to the establishment of a Smart Chicago Collaborative housed at the Chicago Community Trust. Smart Chicago will continue to support technology use in the city's low-income neighborhoods.

2. See grant application available online at http://www2.ntia.doc.gov/files/grantees/City_of_Chicago_Application.pdf.

3. For information on One Economy programs in affordable housing, see http://www.one-economy.com/how-were-able-to-reduce-the-cost-of-internet-access-in-affordable-housing/#.UBRBGrR2SSo. The Detroit wireless initiative is part of Connect Your Community's SBA grant in multiple cities. For a description of the wireless project in Detroit see http://www.focushope.edu/page.aspx?content_id=209&content_type=news.

4. Interviews with city officials in multiple cities.

5. See http://www.fcc.gov/document/fcc-reforms-modernizes-lifeline-program-low-income-americans.

References

AAPOR Cell Phone Task Force. 2010. *New Considerations for Survey Researchers When Planning and Conducting RDD Telephone Surveys in the U.S. With Respondents Reached Via Cell Phone Numbers.* American Association for Public Opinion Research. http://www.aapor.org/ Reports1.htm.

Aaron, Craig. 2008. "The Promise of Municipal Broadband." *The Progressive.* http://www. progressive.org/mag/aaron0808.html.

Ajzen, Icek. 1991. "The Theory of Planned Behavior." *Organizational Behavior and Human Decision Processes* 50 (2): 179–211.

ALA. 2010. *Job-Seeking in U.S. Public Libraries.* Chicago: Office for Research & Statistics, American Library Association. http://www.ala.org/ala/research/initiatives/plftas/ issuesbriefs/jobseeking.cfm.

———. 2011. *ALA Library Fact Sheet 6.* American Library Association. http://www.ala.org/ala/ professionalresources/libfactsheets/alalibraryfactsheet06.cfm.

Alex-Assensoh, Yvette. 1997. "Race, Concentrated Poverty, Social Isolation, and Political Behavior." *Urban Affairs Review* 33 (2): 209–227.

Allard, Scott, and Benjamin Roth. 2010. *Strained Suburbs: The Social Service Challenges of Rising Suburban Poverty.* Washington, D.C.: Brookings Institution. http://www.brookings.edu/ reports/2010/1007_suburban_poverty_allard_roth.aspx.

Barreto, Matt A. 2010. *Ethnic Cues: The Role of Shared Ethnicity in Latino Political Participation.* Ann Arbor, MI: University of Michigan Press.

Barseghian, Tina. 2011. "For At-Risk Youth, Is Learning Digital Media a Luxury?" KQED, National Public Radio.

Bartik, Timothy J. 2003. *Local Economic Development Policies.* Upjohn Institute Working Papers. http://research.upjohn.org/up_workingpapers/91/.

Bayer, Patrick, Stephen L. Ross, and Giorgio Topa. 2008. "Place of Work and Place of Residence: Informal Hiring Networks and Labor Market Outcomes." *Journal of Political Economy* 116 (6): 1150–1196.

Becker, Samantha, Michael D. Crandall, Karen E. Fisher, Bo Kinney, Carol Landry, and Anita Bocha. 2010. *Opportunity for All: How the American Public Benefits from Internet Access at U.S. Libraries.* Washington, D.C.: Institute of Museum and Library Services.

Benkler, Yochai. 2010. "Ending the Internet's Trench Warfare." *New York Times.* http:// www.nytimes.com/2010/03/21/opinion/21Benkler.html.

Bennett, Larry. 2010. *The Third City: Chicago and American Urbanism.* Chicago, IL: University of Chicago Press.

Berkman Center. 2010. *Next Generation Connectivity: A Review of Broadband Internet Transitions and Policy from Around the World.* The Berkman Center for the Internet and Society at Harvard University. http://cyber.law.harvard.edu/sites/cyber.law.harvard.edu/files/Berkman_ Center_Broadband_Final_Report_15Feb2010.pdf.

Berry, Jeffrey M., Kent E. Portney, and Ken Thomson. 1993. *The Rebirth of Urban Democracy*. Washington, DC: The Brookings Institution.

Bertot, John Carlo, Paul T. Jaeger, Lesley A. Langa, and Charles R. McClure. 2006. "Public Access Computing and Internet Access in Public Libraries: The Role of Public Libraries in E-Government and Emergency Situations." *First Monday* 11 (9). http://www.firstmonday.org/issues/issue11_9/bertot/index.html.

Berube, Alan, and Elizabeth Kneebone. 2006. *Two Steps Back: City and Suburban Poverty Trends 1999–2005*. Washington, D.C.: The Brookings Institution. http://dspace.cigilibrary.org/jspui/handle/123456789/5867.

Bettencourt, Luis M. A., and Geoffrey B. West. 2011. "Bigger Cities Do More with Less: New Science Reveals Why Cities Become More Productive and Efficient as They Grow." *Scientific American Magazine*. Sept., 52–53.

Bimber, Bruce A. 2003. *Information and American Democracy: Technology in the Evolution of Political Power*. Cambridge: Cambridge University Press.

Blackburn, Bradley. 2011. "Japan Earthquake and Tsunami: Social Media Spreads News, Raises Relief Funds." *ABC News*. http://abcnews.go.com/Technology/japan-earthquake-tsunami-drive-social-media-dialogue/story?id=13117677#.T0J6Tcyjrgw.

Boulianne, Shelley. 2009. "Does Internet Use Affect Engagement? A Meta-Analysis of Research." *Political Communication* 26 (2): 193–211.

Boyce, Angie. 2002. "Online Job Hunting: A Pew Internet Project Data Memo." Pew Internet and American Life Project. http://www.pewinternet.org/Press-Releases/2002/Online-Job-Hunting-A-Pew-Internet-Project-Data-Memo.aspx.

Briggs, Xavier de Souza. 2005. *The Geography of Opportunity: Race and Housing Choice in Metropolitan America*. Washington, D.C.: The Brookings Institution.

———. 2008. *Democracy as Problem-Solving*. Cambridge, MA: MIT Press.

Brookings Institution. 2007. *MetroNation: How U.S. Metropolitan Areas Fuel American Prosperity*. Washington, D.C.: The Brookings Institution. http://www.brookings.edu/reports/2007/1106_metronation_berube.aspx.

———. 2010. *State of Metropolitan America*. Washington, D.C.: The Brookings Institution. http://www.brookings.edu/metro/StateOfMetroAmerica.aspx.

Brown, Katie, Scott W. Campbell, and Rich Ling. 2011. "Mobile Phones Bridging the Digital Divide for Teens in the US?" *Future Internet* 3 (2): 144–158.

Brynjolfsson, Erik, and Adam Saunders. 2010. *Wired for Innovation. How Information Technology Is Reshaping the Economy*. Cambridge, MA: MIT Press.

Bushwick, Sophie. 2011. "The Top Ten Cities for Technology." *Scientific American*. http://www.scientificamerican.com/article.cfm?id=the-top-10-cities-for-techology.

Campbell, Angus, Philip E Converse, Warren E Miller, and Donald E Stokes. 1960. *The American Voter*. New York: Wiley.

Campbell, Heather, and Susan Fainstein. 2012. "The Just City." In *The Oxford Handbook of Urban Politics*, ed. Karen Mossberger, Susan E. Clarke, and Peter John. New York, NY: Oxford University Press.

Caplovitz, David. 1967. *The Poor Pay More: Consumer Practices of Low-Income Families*. New York: Free Press.

Castells, Manuel. 1991. *The Informational City: Information Technology, Economic Restructuring, and the Urban-Regional Process*. Oxford: Blackwell.

Chapple, Karen, Ann Markusen, Greg Schrock, Daisaku Yamamoto, and Pingkang Yu. 2004. "Gauging Metropolitan 'High-Tech' and 'I-Tech' Activity." *Economic Development Quarterly* 18 (1): 10–29.

City of New York. 2011. *Road Map for the Digital City: Achieving New York City's Digital Future*. New York: The City of New York. www.nyc.gov/html/media/media/PDF/90dayreport.pdf.

Clotfelter, Charles T. 1999. "Public School Segregation in Metropolitan Areas." *Land Economics* 75 (4): 487–504.

Clucas, Richard A. 2001. "Principal-Agent Theory and the Power of State House Speakers." *Legislative Studies Quarterly* 26 (2): 319–338.

Comcast. 2012. *Conquering the Digital Divide: Closing the Broadband Opportunity Gap*. Launch Report. http://blog.comcast.com/assets/InternetEssentialsfromComcast.pdf.

Crandall, Robert W., William Lehr, and Robert E. Litan. 2007. *The Effects of Broadband Deployment on Output and Employment: A Cross-sectional Analysis of U.S. Data.* Washington, D.C.: The Brookings Institution. http://www.brookings.edu/papers/2007/06labor_crandall.aspx.

Crawford, Susan P. 2007. *The Internet and the Project of Communications Law.* SSRN eLibrary. http://papers.ssrn.com/sol3/papers.cfm?abstract_id=962594.

———.2011. "Internet Access and the New Divide." *New York Times.* http://www.nytimes.com/2011/12/04/opinion/sunday/internet-access-and-the-new-divide.html.

Currie, Janet. 2011. "Health and Residential Location." In *Neighborhood and Life Chances: How Place Matters in Modern America,* ed. Harriet B. Newburger, Eugenie L. Birch, and Susan M. Wachter, 3–17. Philadelphia: University of Pennsylvania Press.

Dailey, Dharma, Amelia Bryne, Alison Powell, Joe Karaganis, and Jaewon Chung. 2010. *Broadband Adoption in Low-Income Communities.* Washington, D.C.: The Federal Communications Commission and the Social Science Research Council. http://www.ssrc.org/publications/view/1EB76F62-C720-DF11-9D32-001CC477EC70/.

Davis, Fred D. 1989. "Perceived Usefulness, Perceived Ease of Use, and User Acceptance of Information Technology." *MIS Quarterly* 13 (3): 319–340.

Diaz, Sam. 2010. *Study: Minorities Leading in Mobile Web Usage; Helping Close Digital Divide.* ZDNet. http://www.zdnet.com/blog/btl/study-minorities-leading-in-mobile-web-usage-helping-close-digital-divide/36523.

DiMaggio, Paul, and Bart Bonikowski. 2008. "Make Money Surfing the Web? The Impact of Internet Use on the Earnings of U.S. Workers." *American Sociological Review* 73 (2): 227–250.

DiMaggio, Paul J., and Coral E. Celeste. 2004. "Technological Careers: Adoption, Deepening, and Dropping Out in a Panel of Internet Users." Eastern Sociological Society Annual Meetings. New York, NY.

DiMaggio, Paul, Eszter Hargittai, Coral Celeste, and Steven Shafer. 2004. "Digital Inequality: From Unequal Access to Differentiated Use." In *Social Inequality,* ed. Kathryn M. Neckerman, 355–400. New York: Russell Sage Foundation.

DiMaggio, Paul, Eszter Hargittai, W. Russell Neuman, and John P. Robinson. 2001. "Social Implications of the Internet." *Annual Review of Sociology* 27 (1): 307–336.

Dobransky, Kerry, and Eszter Hargittai. 2006. "The Disability Divide in Internet Access and Use." *Information, Communication and Society* 9 (3): 313–314.

Dreier, Peter, John Mollenkopf, and Todd Swanstrom. 2004. *Place Matters: Metropolitics for the Twenty-first Century.* 2nd ed. Lawrence: University Press of Kansas.

Dunbar, John. 2011. *Wealthy Suburbs Get Best Broadband Deals; D.C., Rural Areas Lag Behind.* Washington, D.C.: Investigative Reporting Workshop.

Economist. 2007. "City-wide Wireless Internet. WiFi for the Masses: America's Cities Are Learning to Love the Idea of Universal Internet Access." *The Economist.* http://www.economist.com/node/8780650.

Ellen, Ingrid Gould, and Katherine O'Regan. 2011. "Exploring Changes in Low-Income Neighborhoods in the 1990s." In *Neighborhood and Life Chances: How Place Matters in Modern America,* ed. Harriet Newburger, Eugenie L. Birch, and Susan M. Wachter, 103–121. Philadelphia: University of Pennsylvania Press.

Ellen, Pam Scholder, William O. Bearden, and Subhash Sharma. 1991. "Resistance to Technological Innovations: An Examination of the Role of Self-Efficacy and Performance Satisfaction." *Journal of the Academy of Marketing Science* 19 (4): 297–307.

Elliott, James R. 1999. "Social Isolation and Labor Market Insulation: Network and Neighborhood Effects on Less-Educated Urban Workers." *The Sociological Quarterly* 40 (2): 199–216.

Ezell, Stephen. 2010. *Explaining International IT Application Leadership: Intelligent Transportation Systems.* The Information Technology and Innovation Foundation. http://archive.itif.org/index.php?id=332.

Fairlie, Robert. 2007. "Explaining Differences in Access to Home Computers and the Internet: A Comparison of Latino Groups to Other Ethnic and Racial Groups." *Electronic Commerce Research* 7 (3): 265–291.

Fairlie, Robert W. 2004. "Race and the Digital Divide." *The BE Journal of Economic Analysis & Policy* 3 (1). http://www.bepress.com/bejeap/contributions/vol3/iss1/art15/.

FCC. 2010a. *Connecting America: The National Broadband Plan*. Washington, D.C.: The Federal Communications Commission. http://www.broadband.gov.

———.2010b. *The Broadband Availability Gap*. Washington, D.C.: The Federal Communications Commission. http://www.broadband.gov/plan/broadband-working-reports-technical-papers .html.

———.2012. *FCC Reforms, Modernizes Lifeline Program for Low-Income Americans*. Washington, D.C.: Federal Communications Commission. http://www.fcc.gov/document/fcc-reforms-modernizes-lifeline-program-low-income-americans.

Federal Register. 2009. "Broadband Initiatives Program; Broadband Technology Opportunities Program; Notice". Vol. 74, No. 130.

Federal Register. 2010. "Broadband Technology Opportunities Program; Notices". Vol. 75, No. 14.

Federal Reserve and Brookings Institution. 2008. *The Enduring Challenge of Concentrated Poverty in America: Case Studies from Across the U.S.* Washington, D.C.: The Brookings Institution.

Feld, Harold, Gregory Rose, Mark Cooper, and Ben Scott. 2005. *Connecting the Public: The Truth About Municipal Broadband*. Consumer Federation of America, Consumers Union, Media Access Project, Free Press. http://www.ci.longmont.co.us/lpc/tc/documents/mb_white_paper.pdf.

Fong, Eric, and Xingshan Cao. 2008. "Bridges Across the Racial Digital Divide: Residential Ecology of Internet Use." *Canadian Studies in Population* 35: 243–268.

Foreign Policy. 2008. "The 2008 Global Cities Index." *Foreign Policy*, October 15. http://www.foreignpolicy.com/articles/2008/10/15/the_2008_global_cities_index.

Foreign Policy. 2010. "The Global Cities Index 2010." *Foreign Policy*, August 11. http://www.foreignpolicy.com/articles/2010/08/11/the_global_cities_index_2010.

Forlano, Laura, Alison Powell, Gwen Shaffer, and Benjamin Lennett. 2010. *From the Digital Divide to Digital Excellence: Global Best Practices for Municipal and Community Wireless Networks*. Washington, D.C.: New America Foundation. http://www.newamerica.net/publications/policy/from_the_digital_divide_to_digital_excellence.

Forman, Chris, Avi Goldfarb, and Shane Greenstein. 2005. *Technology Adoption In and Out of Major Urban Areas: When Do Internal Firm Resources Matter Most?* NBER Working Paper No. 11642. http://www.nber.org/papers/w11642.

———.2008. "Understanding the Inputs into Innovation: Do Cities Substitute for Internal Firm Resources?" *Journal of Economics & Management Strategy* 17 (2): 295–316.

———.2009. *The Internet and Local Wages: Convergence or Divergence?* NBER Working Paper No. 14750. http://www.nber.org/papers/w14750.

———.2011. *Local Capabilities and Broadband Bandwidth at Community Anchor Institutions*. Atlanta, GA: Georgia Institute of Technology. http://mgt.gatech.edu/directory/faculty/forman/pubs/BroadbandBandwidth--FormanGoldfarbGreenstein.pdf.

Fountain, Jane E. 2001. *Building the Virtual State: Information Technology and Institutional Change*. Washington, D.C.: Brookings Institution Press.

Fox, Susannah. 2005. *Health Information Online*. Washington, D.C.: Pew Internet and American Life Project. http://www.pewinternet.org/Reports/2005/Health-Information-Online.aspx.

———.2009. *Latinos Online, 2006–2008*. Washington, D.C.: Pew Internet and American Life Project. http://www.pewinternet.org/Commentary/2009/December/Latinos-Online-20062008.aspx.

Frey, William H. 2010. *Analysis of 2010 Census Data*. Brookings Institution and University of Michigan Social Science Data Analysis Network. http://www.censusscope.org/.

———.2011. *The New Metro Minority Map: Regional Shifts in Hispanics, Asians, and Blacks from Census 2010*. Washington, D.C.: The Brookings Institution. http://www.brookings.edu/papers/2011/0831_census_race_frey.aspx.

Fung, Archon, and Erik Olin Wright. 2003. *Deepening Democracy: Institutional Innovations in Empowered Participatory Governance*. London: Verso.

Gallaga, Omar L. 2010. "Can Mobile Phones Narrow the Digital Divide? Increasingly, Latino and African-American Teens Are Using Cell Phones as Their Main Device to Get Online." *American-Statesman*. www.statesman.com/business/technology/can-mobile-phones-narrow-the-digital-divide-784691.html.

Gant, Jon P., Nicol E. Turner-Lee, Ying Li, and Joseph S. Miller. 2010. *National Minority Broadband Adoption: Comparative Trends in Adoption, Acceptance, and Use*. Washington, D.C.: Joint Center for Political and Economic Studies. http://www.jointcenter.org/research/national-minority-broadband-adoption-comparative-trends-in-adoption-acceptance-and-use.

Gerken, Heather. 2009. *The Democracy Index: Why Our Election System Is Failing and How to Fix It*. Princeton, NJ: Princeton University Press.

Gilder, George. 1995. "Gilder Meets His Critics." *Forbes ASAP*.

Gillett, Sharon E. 2005. "Municipal Wireless Broadband: Hype or Harbinger?" *Southern California Law Review* 79:561–593.

Gillett, Sharon E., William H. Lehr, Carlos A. Osorio, and Marvin A. Sirbu. 2006. *Measuring Broadband's Economic Impact*. National Technical Assistance, Training, Research, and Evaluation Project #99-07-13829. http://cfp.mit.edu/publications/CFP_Papers/Measuring_bb_econ_impact-final.pdf.

Glaeser, Edward. 2011. *Triumph of the City: How Our Greatest Invention Makes Us Richer, Smarter, Greener, Healthier, and Happier*. New York: Penguin Press.

Goolsbee, Austan, and Peter J. Klenow. 2002. "Evidence on Learning and Network Externalities in the Diffusion of Home Computers." *Journal of Law and Economics* 45 (2): 317–343.

Granovetter, Mark S. 1973. "The Strength of Weak Ties." *American Journal of Sociology* 78 (6): 1360–1380.

Greenstein, Shane, and Ryan C. McDevitt. 2010. *Evidence of a Modest Price Decline in US Broadband Services*. NBER Working Paper No. 16166. http://www.nber.org/papers/w16166.

Grogan, Paul S., and Tony Proscio. 2000. *Comeback Cities: A Blueprint for Urban Neighborhood Revival*. New York: Westview Press.

Gross, Grant. 2011. "Universities Launch Ultra-High-Speed Broadband Initiative." *CIO*, July 27. http://www.cio.com/article/print/686793.

Guest, Avery M., and Barrett A. Lee. 1983. "The Social Organization of Local Areas." *Urban Affairs Review* 19 (2): 217–240.

Hackler, Darrene. 2003. "Invisible Infrastructure and the City: The Role of Telecommunications in Economic Development." *American Behavioral Scientist* 46 (8): 1034–1055.

———. 2006. *Cities in the Technology Economy*. Armonk, NY: M.E. Sharpe.

Haddon, Leslie. 2000. "Social Exclusion and Information and Communication Technologies: Lessons from Studies of Single Parents and the Young Elderly." *New Media & Society* 2 (4): 387–406.

Hamilton, Amanda, and Caroline Tolbert. "Political Engagement and the Internet in the 2008 U.S. Presidential Election: A Panel Survey." In *Digital Media and Political Engagement Worldwide: A Comparative Study*, ed. Eva Anduiza, Mike Jensen, and Laia Jorba, 56–79. New York: Cambridge University Press.

Hamm, Steve. 2009. "Dubuque, Iowa: The First American 'Smart City'?" *Businessweek*. http://www.businessweek.com/innovate/content/sep2009/id20090918_187656.htm.

Hampton, Keith N. 2010. "Internet Use and the Concentration of Disadvantage: Globalization and the Urban Underclass." *American Behavioral Scientist* 53 (8): 1111–1132.

Hampton, Keith N., Lauren F. Sessions, and Eun Ja Her. 2010. "Core Networks, Social Isolation, and New Media: How Internet and Mobile Phone Use Is Related to Network Size and Diversity." *Information, Communication & Society* 14 (1): 130–155.

Hargittai, Eszter. 2002. "Second-Level Digital Divide: Differences in People's Online Skills." *First Monday* 7 (4): 1–20.

———. 2003. "The Digital Divide and What to Do About It." In *New Economy Handbook*, ed. Derek C. Jones, 821–839. San Diego, CA: Academic Press.

Hargittai, Eszter, and Amanda Hinnant. 2008. "Digital Inequality: Differences in Young Adults' Use of the Internet." *Communication Research* 35 (5): 602–621.

Hargittai, Eszter, and Yuli Patrick Hsieh. 2012. "Succinct Survey Measures of Web-Use Skills." *Social Science Computer Review* 30 (1): 95–107.

Hargittai, Eszter, and Steven Shafer. 2006. "Differences in Actual and Perceived Online Skills: The Role of Gender." *Social Science Quarterly* 87 (2): 432–448.

Hassani, Sara Nephew. 2006. "Locating Digital Divides at Home, Work, and Everywhere Else." *Poetics* 34: 250–72.

Helft, M. 2010. "Hoping for a Gift from Google? Go Jump in the Lake." *New York Times.* http://www.nytimes.com/2010/03/22/technology/22stunts.html.

Hendrick, Rebecca. 2012. *Managing the Fiscal Metropolis: Financial Policies, Practices and Health of Chicago Suburban Municipalities.* Washington, D.C.: Georgetown University Press.

Hero, Rodney E. 1992. *Latinos and the U.S. Political System: Two-Tiered Pluralism.* Philadelphia, PA: Temple University Press.

———. 1998. *Faces of Inequality: Social Diversity in American Politics.* New York: Oxford University Press.

———. 2003. "Multiple Traditions in American Politics and Racial Policy Inequality." *Political Research Quarterly* 56 (4): 401–08.

———. 2007. *Racial Diversity and Social Capital: Equality and Community in America.* New York: Cambridge University Press.

Hero, Rodney E., and Caroline J. Tolbert. 1996. "A Racial/Ethnic Diversity Interpretation of Politics and Policy in the States of the U.S." *American Journal of Political Science* 40 (3): 851–871.

High, Kristal. 2011. *Joint Center Explores Impact of Broadband Plan on Underserved.* Politic 365. http://politic365.com/2011/03/03/joint-center-explores-impact-of-broadband-plan-on-underserved/.

Ho, Alfred Tat-Kei. 2002. "Reinventing Local Governments and the E-Government Initiative." *Public Administration Review* 62 (4): 434–444.

Hoffman, Judy, John Carlo Bertot, Denise M. Davis, and Larra Clark. 2011. *Libraries Connect Communities: Public Library Funding and Public Access Study, 2010–11.* Chicago, IL: American Library Association. http://www.ors.ala.org/libconnect/2010/09/07/2010_2011_npls/.

Holloway, Steven R., and Stephen Mulherin. 2004. "The Effect of Adolescent Neighborhood Poverty on Adult Employment." *Journal of Urban Affairs* 26 (4): 427–454.

Holt, Lynne, and Mark A. Jamison. 2006. *Making Telephone Service Affordable for Low-Income Households: An Analysis of Lifeline and Link-Up Programs in Florida.* PURC, University of Florida. http://warrington.ufl.edu/purc/purcdocs/papers/0605_Holt_Make_Telephone_Service.pdf.

Holzer, Harry J. 1999. *What Employers Want: Job Prospects for Less-Educated Workers.* New York: Russell Sage Foundation.

Horak, Martin, and Talja Blokland. 2012. "Neighborhoods and Civic Practice." In *The Oxford Handbook of Urban Politics*, ed. Karen Mossberger, Susan E. Clarke, and Peter John. New York: Oxford University Press.

Horrigan, John. 2004. *Broadband Penetration on the Upswing.* Washington, D.C.: Pew Internet & American Life Project. http://www.pewinternet.org/Reports/2004/Broadband-Penetration-on-the-Upswing.aspx.

———. 2009. *Home Broadband Adoption 2009.* Pew Internet and American Life Project. http://www.pewinternet.org/Reports/2009/10-Home-Broadband-Adoption-2009.aspx.

———. 2010. *Broadband Adoption and Use in America.* Washington, D.C.: The Federal Communications Commission. http://online.wsj.com/public/resources/documents/FCCSurvey.pdf.

———. 2012. *Broadband Adoption in 2012: Little Movement Since '09 & Stakeholders Can Do More to Spur Adoption.* TechNet. http://www.technet.org/wp-content/uploads/2012/03/TechNet-NBP-Broadband-Report-3-20-2012-FINAL1.pdf.

Horrigan, John, and Lee Rainie. 2002. *The Broadband Difference: How Online Behavior Changes with High-Speed Internet Connections*. Washington, D.C.: Pew Internet and American Life Project. http://www.pewinternet.org/Reports/2002/The-Broadband-Difference-How-online-behavior-changes-with-highspeed-Internet-connections.aspx.

Howard, Philip E. N., Lee Rainie, and Steve Jones. 2001. "Days and Nights on the Internet: The Impact of Diffusing Technology." *American Behavioral Scientist* 45: 383–404.

Ihlanfeldt, Keith R., and David L. Sjoquist. 1998. "The Spatial Mismatch Hypothesis: A Review of Recent Studies and Their Implications for Welfare Reform." *Housing Policy Debate* 9 (4): 849–892.

Ioannides, Yannis M., and Giorgio Topa. 2010. "Neighborhood Effects: Accomplishments and Looking Beyond Them." *Journal of Regional Science* 50 (1): 343–362.

Jacob, Brian A., and Jens Ludwig. 2011. "Educational Interventions: Their Effects on the Achievement of Poor Children." In *Neighborhood and Life Chances: How Place Matters in Modern America*, ed. Harriet B. Newburger, Eugenie L. Birch, and Susan M. Wachter, 37–49. Philadelphia: University of Pennsylvania Press.

Jain, Abhijit, Munir Mandviwalla, and Rajiv Banker. 2007. *Can Governments Create Universal Internet Access? The Philadelphia Municipal Wireless Network Story*. IBM Business of Government.

Jargowsky, Paul A. 1997. *Poverty and Place: Ghettos, Barrios, and the American City*. New York: Russell Sage Foundation.

———. 2003. *Stunning Progress, Hidden Problems: The Dramatic Decline of Concentrated Poverty in the 1990s*. Washington, D.C.: The Brookings Institution. http://www.brookings.edu/reports/2003/05demographics_jargowsky.aspx.

Jargowsky, Paul A., and Mohamed El Komi. 2011. "Before or After the Bell? School Context and Neighborhood Effects on Student Achievement." In *Neighborhood and Life Chances: How Place Matters in Modern America*, ed. Harriet B. Newburger, Eugenie L. Birch, and Susan M. Wachter, 37-49, 50–72. Philadelphia: University of Pennsylvania Press.

Joassart-Marcelli, Pascale M., Juliet A. Musso, and Jennifer R. Wolch. 2005. "Fiscal Consequences of Concentrated Poverty in a Metropolitan Region." *Annals of the Association of American Geographers* 95 (2): 336–356.

Kain, John F. 1968. "Housing Segregation, Negro Employment, and Metropolitan Decentralization." *Quarterly Journal of Economics* 82 (2): 175–197.

Kang, Cecilia. 2010. "Going Wireless All the Way to the Web." *Washington Post*, July 10. www.washingtonpost.com.

———. 2011. "Obama Touts Plan to Get Wireless Internet to 98 Percent of U.S." *Washington Post*. www.washingtonpost.com.

Kang, Cecilia, and Krissah Thompson. 2011. "Hispanics Trail Other Groups in Web Usage, Confidence." *Washington Post*. http://www.washingtonpost.com/.

Kantor, Paul, and Ivan Turok. 2012. "The Politics of Growth and Decline." In *The Oxford Handbook of Urban Politics*, ed. Karen Mossberger, Susan E. Clarke, and Peter John. New York: Oxford University Press.

Kaplan, David, and Karen Mossberger. 2012. "Prospects for Poor Neighborhoods in the Broadband Era: Neighborhood-Level Influences on Technology Use at Work." *Economic Development Quarterly* 26 (1): 95–105.

Kasarda, John D. 1990. "City Jobs and Residents on a Collision Course: The Urban Underclass Dilemma." *Economic Development Quarterly* 4 (4): 313–319.

Katz, James E., and Ronald E. Rice. 2002. *Social Consequences of Internet Use: Access, Involvement, and Interaction*. Cambridge, MA: MIT Press.

Katz, Yaacov J. 1994. "Self-Image, Locus Control and Computer Related Attitudes." In *Lessons from Learning*, ed. Robert Lewis and Patrick Mendelsohn, 105–109. Amsterdam: Elsevier Science.

Kim, Yong-Chan, Joo-Young Jung, and Sandra J. Ball-Rokeach. 2007. "Ethnicity, Place, and Communication Technology: Effects of Ethnicity on Multi-Dimensional Internet Connectedness." *Information Technology & People* 20 (3): 282–303.

King, Gary, Michael Tomz, and Jason Wittenberg. 2000. "Making the Most of Statistical Analyses: Improving Interpretation and Presentation." *American Journal of Political Science* 44 (2): 347–361.

Kleit, Rachel Garshick. 2001. "The Role of Neighborhood Social Networks in Scattered-Site Public Housing Residents' Search for Jobs." *Housing Policy Debate* 12 (3): 541–573.

Kneebone, Elizabeth. 2011. *The Great Recession and Poverty in Metropolitan America*. Washington, D.C.: The Brookings Institution. http://www.brookings.edu/papers/2010/1007_suburban_poverty_acs_kneebone.aspx.

Kolko, Jed. 2000. "The Death of Cities? The Death of Distance? Evidence from the Geography of Commercial Internet Usage." In *The Internet Upheaval: Raising Questions, Seeking Answers in Communications Policy*, ed. Ingo Vogelsang and Benjamin M. Compaine, 73–98. Cambridge, MA: MIT Press.

———. 2010. *Does Broadband Boost Local Economic Development?* San Francisco: Public Policy Institute of California. http://www.ppic.org/main/publication.asp?i=866.

Koval, John P. 2006. "An Overview and Point of View." In *The New Chicago: A Social and Cultural Analysis*, ed. John P. Koval, Larry Bennett, Michael I. J. Bennett, Fassil Demissie, Roberta Garner, and Kiljoong Kim, 3–15; 1. Philadelphia, PA: Temple University Press.

Kravets, David. 2011. "U.N. Report Declares Internet Access a Human Right." *Wired*, June 3. http://www.wired.com/threatlevel/2011/06/internet-a-human-right/.

Krueger, Brian S. 2002. "Assessing the Potential of Internet Political Participation in the United States: A Resource Approach." *American Politics Research* 30 (5): 476–98.

———. 2006. "A Comparison of Conventional and Internet Political Mobilization." *American Politics Research* 34 (6): 759–776.

LaRue, Frank. 2011. *Report of the Special Rapporteur on the Promotion and Protection of the Right to Freedom of Opinion and Expression*. United Nations General Assembly.

Lax, Jeffrey R., and Justin H. Phillips. 2009a. "Gay Rights in the States: Public Opinion and Policy Responsiveness." *American Political Science Review* 103 (03): 367–386.

———. 2009b. "How Should We Estimate Public Opinion in The States?" *American Journal of Political Science* 53 (1): 107–121.

Ledebur, Larry, and William Barnes. 1998. *The New Regional Economies: The U.S. Common Market and the Global Economy*. London: Sage.

Lee, Barrett A., and Karen E. Campbell. 1999. "Neighbor Networks of Black and White Americans." In *Networks In The Global Village: Life In Contemporary Communities*, ed. Barry Wellman, 119–146. Boulder, CO: Westview Press.

Lefevre, Christian, and Margaret Weir. 2012. "Regional Institution-Building." In *The Oxford Handbook of Urban Politics*, ed. Karen Mossberger, Susan E. Clarke, and Peter John. New York: Oxford University Press.

Lenhart, Amanda. 2003. *The Ever-Shifting Internet Population: A New Look at Internet Access and the Digital Divide*. Washington, D.C.: Pew Internet & American Life Project. http://www.pewinternet.org/Reports/2003/The-EverShifting-Internet-Population-A-new-look-at-Internet-access-and-the-digital-divide.aspx.

———. 2010. *Cell Phones and American Adults*. Washington, D.C.: Pew Internet & American Life Project. http://pewinternet.org/Reports/2010/Cell-Phones-and-American-Adults.aspx.

Lennett, Benjamin, and Sascha Meinrath. 2011. *Map to Nowhere*. New America Foundation. http://newamerica.net/node/51483.

Lewis, James H., and David K. Hamilton. 2011. "Race and Regionalism: The Structure of Local Government and Racial Disparity." *Urban Affairs Review* 47 (3): 349–384.

Litan, Robert E., and Alice M. Rivlin, eds. 2001. *The Economic Payoff from the Internet Revolution*. Washington, D.C.: Brookings Institution.

Livingston, Gretchen. 2010. *The Latino Digital Divide: The Native Born Versus The Foreign Born*. Washington, D.C.: Pew Hispanic Center. http://www.pewhispanic.org/2010/07/28/the-latino-digital-divide-the-native-born-versus-the-foreign-born/.

Livingston, Gretchen, Kim Parker, and Susannah Fox. 2009. *Latinos Online, 2006–2008: Narrowing the Gap*. Washington, D.C.: Pew Hispanic Center. http://www.pewhispanic.org/2009/12/22/latinos-online-2006-2008-narrowing-the-gap/.

Logan, John R., and Brian J. Stults. 2011. *The Persistence of Segregation in the Metropolis: New Findings from the 2010 Census*. Brown University. http://www.s4.brown.edu/us2010.

Long, J. Scott. 1997. *Regression Models for Categorical and Limited Dependent Variables*. Thousand Oaks, CA: Sage.

Massey, Douglas S., and Nancy A. Denton. 1993. *American Apartheid: Segregation and the Making of the Underclass*. Cambridge, MA: Harvard University Press.

Mata, Arnoldo. 2011. *Connected Hispanics & Civic Engagement*. Washington, D.C.: The Hispanic Institute. http://thehispanicinstitute.net/files/u2/Connected_Hispanics_and_Civic_Engagement__3_.pdf.

Mayor's Advisory Council for Closing the Digital Divide. 2007. *The City That NetWorks: Transforming Society and Economy Through Digital Excellence*. Chicago, IL: The City of Chicago.

McCann, Bailey. 2012. "Georgia Considers Bill to Curb Municipal Broadband." *CivSource*, January 27. http://civsourceonline.com/2012/01/27/georgia-considers-bill-to-curb-municipal-broadband/.

Mintrom, Michael. 2000. *Policy Entrepreneurs and School Choice*. Washington, D.C.: Georgetown University Press.

Misur, Susan. 2012. "East Haven Schools Invest in Reading Technology." *New Haven Register*, February 12. http://nhregister.com/articles/2012/02/12/news/metro/doc4f385e050a0c2202663898.txt.

Moon, M. Jae. 2002. "The Evolution of E-Government Among Municipalities: Rhetoric or Reality?" *Public Administration Review* 62 (4): 424–33.

Mooney, Christopher Z. 1997. *Monte Carlo Simulation*. Thousand Oaks, CA: Sage.

Mooney, Christopher Z., and Mei-Hsien Lee. 1995. "Legislative Morality in the American States: The Case of Pre-Roe Abortion Regulation Reform." *American Journal of Political Science* 39 (3): 599–627.

Morris, Michael G., and Viswanath Venkatesh. 2000. "Age Differences in Technology Adoption Decisions: Implications for a Changing Work Force." *Personnel Psychology* 53 (2): 375–403.

Moskow, Michael H., Perritt Henry H., and Adele Simmons. 2007. *The Global Edge: An Agenda for Chicago's Future*. Chicago: The Chicago Council on Global Affairs.

Moss, Mitchell L., and Anthony M. Townsend. 2000. "The Internet Backbone and the American Metropolis." *Information Society* 16 (1): 35–47.

Mossberger, Karen. 1999. "State-Federal Diffusion and Policy Learning in a Federal System: From Enterprise Zones to Empowerment Zones." *Publius: The Journal of Federalism* 29 (3): 31–50.

———. 2012. *Smart Communities—Formative Evaluation*. Department of Public Administration, University of Illinois at Chicago.

Mossberger, Karen, David Kaplan, and Michele A. Gilbert. 2008. "Going Online Without Easy Access: A Tale of Three Cities." *Journal of Urban Affairs* 30 (5): 469–488.

Mossberger, Karen, and Caroline J. Tolbert. 2009. "Digital Excellence in Chicago: A Citywide View of Technology Use." http://www.cityofchicago.org/city/en/depts/doit/supp_info/digital_excellenceinchicagoacitywideviewoftechnologyuse.html.

Mossberger, Karen, Caroline J. Tolbert, and Michele Gilbert. 2006. "Race, Place, and Information Technology." *Urban Affairs Review* 41 (5): 583–620.

Mossberger, Karen, Caroline J. Tolbert, and Ramona S. McNeal. 2008. *Digital Citizenship: The Internet, Society, and Participation*. Cambridge, MA: MIT Press.

Mossberger, Karen, Caroline J. Tolbert, and Mary Stansbury. 2003. *Virtual Inequality: Beyond the Digital Divide*. Washington, D.C.: Georgetown University Press.

Mossberger, Karen, and Yonghong Wu. 2012. *Civic Engagement and Local E-Government: Social Networking Comes of Age*. Institute for Policy and Civic Engagement, University of Illinois at Chicago. http://www.uic.edu/cuppa/ipce/research.shtml.

Mossberger, Karen, Yonghong Wu, and Benedict Jimenez. 2010. "Can E-Government Promote Informed Citizenship and Civic Engagement? A Study of Local Government Websites in the U.S." Paper presented at the Annual Meeting of the Midwest Political Science Association, Chicago, IL.

Munger, Michael C. 2000. *Analyzing Policy: Choices, Conflicts, and Practices.* New York: W.W. Norton.

Nagel, David. 2011. *Will Smart Phones Eliminate the Digital Divide?* The Journal. http://thejournal.com/articles/2011/02/01/will-smart-phones-eliminate-the-digital-divide.aspx.

National Center for Education Statistics. 2011. *Fast Facts.* U.S. Department of Education. http://nces.ed.gov/fastfacts/display.asp?id=46.

Negroponte, Nicholas. 1995. *Being Digital.* New York: Vintage Books.

Newburger, Harriet, Eugenie L. Birch, and Susan M. Wachter, eds. 2011. *Neighborhood and Life Chances: How Place Matters in Modern America.* Philadelphia: University of Pennsylvania Press.

Nicolai, Megan. 2012. "Fox Valley Schools Face Challenge of Prepping for the E-Future." *Appleton (WI) Post-Crescent.* http://www.postcrescent.com/article/20120213/APC0101/202130395/Valley-schools-face-challenge-prepping-e-future?odyssey=mod%7Ctopnews%7Ctext%7CFRONTPAGE.

Nolan, Sarah. 2011. *How Technology Fuels Learning.* KQED, National Public Radio. http://mindshift.kqed.org/2011/09/how-technology-fuels-learning/.

Norris, Pippa. 2001. *Digital Divide: Civic Engagement, Information Poverty, and the Internet Worldwide.* Cambridge: Cambridge University Press.

NTIA. 1995. *Falling Through the Net: A Survey of the "Have Nots" in Rural and Urban America.* Washington, D.C.: U.S. Department of Commerce. http://www.ntia.doc.gov/ntiahome/fallingthru.html.

———. 2004. *A Nation Online: Entering the Broadband Age.* Washington, D.C.: U.S. Department of Commerce. http://www.ntia.doc.gov/report/2004/nation-online-entering-broadband-age.

———. 2010a. *Digital Nation: 21st Century America's Progress Toward Universal Broadband Access.* Washington, D.C.: U.S. Department of Commerce. http://www.ntia.doc.gov/reports/2010/NTIA_internet_use_report_Feb2010.pdf.

———. 2010b. *Expanding Broadband Access and Adoption in Communities Across America, Overview of Grant Awards.* Washington, D.C.: U.S. Department of Commerce: National Telecommunications and Information Administration. internal-pdf://NTIA_Report_on_BTOP_12142010-2692435712/NTIA_Report_on_BTOP_12142010.pdf.

———. 2011. *Digital Nation: Expanding Internet Usage.* Washington, D.C.: U.S. Department of Commerce: National Telecommunications and Information Administration. http://www.ntia.doc.gov/files/ntia/publications/ntia_internet_use_report_february_2011.pdf.

Obama, Barack. 2007. "Connecting and Empowering All Americans Through Technology and Innovation." Cairns Blog. http://cairns.typepad.com/blog/files/fact_sheet_innovation_and_technology_plan_final.pd.

OECD. 2011. *OECD Broadband Portal.* Organization for Economic Cooperation and Development. http://www.oecd.org/document/54/0,3746,en_2649_34225_38690102_1_1_1_1,00.html.

Ono, Hiroshi, and Madeline Zavodny. 2007. "Digital Inequality: A Five Country Comparison Using Microdata." *Social Science Research* 36 (3): 1135–1155.

———. 2008. "Immigrants, English Ability and the Digital Divide." *Social Forces* 86 (4): 1455–1479; 1455.

Orfield, Gary, and Chungmei Lee. 2005. *Why Segregation Matters: Poverty and Educational Inequality.* Cambridge, MA: Civil Rights Project, Harvard University.

Orfield, Gary, Daniel Losen, Johanna Wald, and Christopher B. Swanson. 2004. *Losing Our Future: How Minority Youth Are Being Left Behind by the Graduation Rate Crisis.* Washington, D.C.: The Urban Institute. http://www.urban.org/publications/410936.html.

Orfield, Myron. 1997. *Metropolitics: A Regional Agenda for Community and Stability.* Rev. ed. Washington, D.C.: Brookings Institution Press.

Pacione, Michael. 2001. "Geography and Public Finance: Planning for Fiscal Equity in a Metropolitan Region." *Progress in Planning* 56: 1–59.

Pallares, Amalia, and Nilda Flores-Gonzalez. 2011. "Regarding Family: New Actors in the Chicago Protests." In *Rallying for Immigrant Rights: The Fight for Inclusion in 21st Century America*, ed. Kim Voss and Irene Bloemraad, 161–179. Berkeley: University of California Press.

Park, Robert E., Ernest W. Burgess, and Roderick D. McKenzie. 1984. *The City*. Chicago: University of Chicago Press.

Pastor, Manuel, Peter Dreier, J. Eugene III Grigsby, and Marta Lopez-Garza. 2000. *Regions That Work: How Cities and Suburbs Can Grow Together*. Minneapolis, MN: University of Minnesota Press.

Pastor, Manuel, T. William Lester, and Justin Scoggins. 2009. "Why Regions? Why Now? Who Cares?" *Journal of Urban Affairs* 31 (3): 269–296.

Pattillo, Mary. 2007. *Black on the Block: The Politics of Race and Class in the City*. Chicago: University of Chicago Press.

Peterson, Latoya. 2010. *A Digital Revolution In The Palm Of Your Hand*. National Public Radio. http://www.npr.org/blogs/tellmemore/2010/07/21/128674384/a-digital-revolution-in-the-palm-of-your-hand.

Peterson, Paul E. 1981. *City Limits*. Chicago: University of Chicago Press.

Pilsen Smart Communities Plan. 2010. *Connecting Our Communities*. Smart Communities, Chicago Digital Excellence Initiative. http://www.smartcommunitieschicago.org/uploads/smartchicago/documents/pilsen_smart_communities.pdf.

Prieger, James E., and Wei-Min Hu. 2008. "The Broadband Digital Divide and the Nexus of Race, Competition, and Quality." *Information Economics and Policy* 20 (2): 150–167.

Primo, David M, Matthew L Jacobsmeier, and Jeffrey Milyo. 2007. "Estimating the Impact of State Policies and Institutions with Mixed-Level Data." *State Politics and Policy Quarterly* 7 (4): 446–459.

Putnam, Robert. 2000. *Bowling Alone: The Collapse and Revival of American Community*. New York: Simon and Schuster.

Quillien, Ian. 2011. "Duncan Unveils Digital Promise." Education Week. http://blogs.edweek.org/edweek/DigitalEducation/2011/09/duncan_announces_digital_promi.html.

Radcliff, Benjamin, and Martin Saiz. 1995. "Race, Turnout, and Public Policy In the American States." *Political Research Quarterly* 48 (4) (Dec. 1): 775–794.

Ratti, Carlo, and Anthony M. Townsend. 2011. "The Social Nexus: The Best Way to Harness a City's Potential for Creativity and Innovation Is to Jack People Into the Network and Get Out of the Way." *Scientific American*. Sept., 42–48.

Raudenbush, Stephen W., and Anthony S. Bryk. 2002. *Hierarchical Linear Models: Applications and Data Analysis Methods*. Thousand Oaks, CA: Sage.

Reardon, Sean F. 2011. "The Widening Academic Achievement Gap Between the Rich and the Poor: New Evidence and Possible Explanations." In *Whither Opportunity? Rising Inequality, Schools, and Children's Life Chances*, ed. Greg J. Duncan and Richard J. Murnane, 91–116. New York: Russell Sage Foundation.

Reardon, Sean F., and Kendra Bischoff. 2011. "Income Inequality and Income Segregation." *American Journal of Sociology* 116 (4): 1092–1153.

Reuters. 2010. "$800 Million in Stimulus Will Expand Broadband." *New York Times*, July 3, B2.

Rogers, Everett M. 1995. *Diffusion of Innovations*. New York: Simon and Schuster.

Rosen, Jeffrey. 2011. *Universal Service Fund Reform: Expanding Broadband Internet Access in the United States*. Washington, D.C.: The Brookings Institution. http://www.brookings.edu/papers/2011/04_universal_service_fund_rosen.aspx.

Rosston, Gregory L., and Scott J. Wallsten. 2011. "The Path to Universal Broadband: Why We Should Grant Low-Income Subsidies, and Use Auctions and Experiments to Determine the Specifics." Berkeley Electronic Press.

Rue, Frank La. 2011. *Report of the Special Rapporteur on the Promotion and Protection of the Right to Freedom of Opinion and Expression*. UN Human Rights Council. http://www.unhcr.org/.

Rusk, David. 1995. *Cities Without Suburbs*. 2nd ed. Washington, D.C.: Woodrow Wilson Center Press.

Sampson, Robert J., Jeffrey D. Morenoff, and Thomas Gannon-Rowley. 2002. "Assessing 'Neighborhood Effects': Social Processes and New Directions in Research." *Annual Review of Sociology* 28 (1): 443–478.

Sampson, Robert J., Stephen W. Raudenbush, and Felton Earls. 1997. "Neighborhoods and Violent Crime: A Multilevel Study of Collective Efficacy." *Science* 277 (5328): 918–924.

Sassen, Saskia. 2001. *The Global City: New York, London, Tokyo*. 2nd ed. Princeton, NJ: Princeton University Press.

Saxenian, Anna Lee. 1996. *Regional Advantage: Culture and Competition in Silicon Valley and Route 128*. Cambridge, MA: Harvard University Press.

Schelmetic, Tracey E. 2011. *The Rise of the First Smart Cities*. ThomasNet News. http://smart-grid.tmcnet.com/topics/smart-grid/articles/216406-rise-the-first-smart-cities.htm.

Schement, Jorge Reina, and Scott C. Forbes. 2000. "Identifying Temporary and Permanent Gaps in Universal Service." *The Information Society* 16 (2): 117–126.

Schlozman, Kay Lehman, Sidney Verba, and Henry E. Brady. 2010. "Weapon of the Strong? Participatory Inequality and the Internet." *Perspectives on Politics* 8 (2): 487–509.

Schmeida, Mary, and Ramona S. McNeal. 2007. "The Telehealth Divide: Disparities in Searching Public Health Information Online." *Journal of Health Care for the Poor and Underserved* 18 (3): 637–647.

Schwarz, Alan. 2011. "Out With Textbooks, In With Laptops for an Indiana School District." *New York Times*, Oct. 18, A17.

Selwyn, Neil. 2003. "Apart from Technology: Understanding People's Non-Use of Information and Communication Technologies in Everyday Life." *Technology in Society* 25 (1): 99–116.

Selwyn, Neil, Stephen Gorard, and John Furlong. 2005. "Whose Internet Is It Anyway?" *European Journal of Communication* 20 (1): 5–26.

Sen, Amartya. 1993. "Capability and Well-Being." In *The Quality of Life*, ed. Martha Nussbaum and Amartya Sen, 30–53. Oxford: Clarendon Press.

Servon, Lisa J., and Marla K. Nelson. 2001. "Community Technology Centers: Narrowing the Digital Divide in Low-Income, Urban Communities." *Journal of Urban Affairs* 23 (3–4): 279–90.

Settles, Craig. 2011. "A Tale of Two Kansas Cities and Google." *GigaOM*, July 4. http://gigaom.com/broadband/a-tale-of-two-kansas-cities-and-google/.

Shah, Dhavan V., Jaeho Cho, William P. Eveland, and Nojin Kwak. 2005. "Information and Expression in a Digital Age." *Communication Research* 32 (5): 531–565.

Shipan, Charles R., and Craig Volden. 2006. "Bottom-Up Federalism: The Diffusion of Antismoking Policies from U.S. Cities to States." *American Journal of Political Science* 50 (4): 825–843.

Smart Communities. 2009. *A Platform for Participation and Innovation*. Chicago, IL: LISC/Chicago. www.lisc-chicago.org/uploads/lisc-chicago/documents/scpmasterplan.pdf.

Smith, Aaron. 2010. *Mobile Access 2010*. Washington, D.C.: Pew Internet and American Life Project. http://www.pewinternet.org/Reports/2010/Mobile-Access-2010.aspx.

———. 2011. *Smartphone Adoption and Usage*. Washington, D.C.: Pew Internet and American Life Project. http://pewinternet.org/Reports/2011/Smartphones.aspx.

Stansbury, Meris. 2012. "Six Ed-Tech Resources for ELL/ESL Instruction." *eSchool News*, February 10. http://www.eschoolnews.com/2012/02/10/six-ed-tech-resources-for-ellesl-instruction/.

Steenbergen, Marco R, and Bradford S Jones. 2002. "Modeling Multilevel Data Structures." *American Journal of Political Science* 46 (1): 218–237.

Steketee Greiner and Co. 2010. "Google Fiber: Share of Voice Report (Update 3.24.2010)." http://blog.agent-x.com/wp-content/uploads/2010/03/Google_Fiber_Share_of_Voice_ReportUpdate3-24-10.pdf.

Stimson, James A., Michael B. Mackuen, and Robert S. Erikson. 1995. "Dynamic Representation." *The American Political Science Review* 89 (3): 543–565.

Stiroh, Kevin J. 2004. *Reassessing the Impact of IT on the Production Function: A Meta-Analysis and Sensitivity Tests.* Federal Reserve Bank of New York.

Stone, Clarence N., Jeffrey R. Henig, Bryan D. Jones, and Carol Pierannunzi. 2001. *Building Civic Capacity: The Politics of Reforming Urban Schools.* Lawrence: University Press of Kansas.

Stone, Deborah. 2001. *Policy Paradox: The Art of Political Decision Making.* 3rd ed. New York: W.W. Norton.

Swabey, Pete. 2012. "IBM, Cisco and the Business of Smart Cities." *Information Age.* February 23. http://www.information-age.com/channels/comms-and-networking/company-analysis/2087993/ibm-cisco-and-the-business-of-smart-cities.thtml.

Swanstrom, Todd, Colleen Casey, Robert Flack, and Peter Dreier. 2004. *Pulling Apart: Economic Segregation Among Suburbs and Central Cities in Major Metropolitan Areas.* Washington, D.C.: The Brookings Institution. http://www.brookings.edu/reports/2004/10metropolitanpolicy_swanstrom.aspx.

Swanstrom, Todd, Rob Ryan, and Katherine M. Stigers. 2007. *Measuring Concentrated Poverty: Did It Really Decline in the 1990s?* Berkeley, CA: IURD Working Paper Series, Institute of Urban and Regional Development, UC Berkeley.

Tapia, A. H., and J. A. Ortiz. 2008. "Keeping Promises: Municipal Communities Struggle to Fulfill Promises to Narrow the Digital Divide with Municipal Community Wireless Networks." *The Journal of Community Informatics* 4 (1). http://ci-journal.net/index.php/ciej/article/view/436/400.

Tapia, Andrea, Matt Stone, and Carleen Maitland. 2005. "Public-Private Partnerships and the Role of State and Federal Legislation in Wireless Municipal Networks." Telecommunications Policy Research Conference. Arlington, VA.

Timberlake, Jeffrey M., Aaron J. Howell, and Amanda J. Staight. 2011. "Trends in the Suburbanization of Racial/Ethnic Groups in U.S. Metropolitan Areas, 1970 to 2000." *Urban Affairs Review* 47 (2): 218–255.

Todman, John, and Elizabeth Monaghan. 1994. "Qualitative Differences in Computer Experience, Computer Anxiety, and Students' Use of Computers: A Path Model." *Computers in Human Behavior* 10 (4): 529–539.

Tolbert, Caroline. 2010. "Editor's Introduction: Race and the 2008 Presidential Election." *Political Research Quarterly* 63 (3): 860–862.

Tolbert, Caroline J., and Ramona S. McNeal. 2003. "Unraveling the Effects of the Internet on Political Participation?" *Political Research Quarterly* 56 (2): 175–185.

Tolbert, Caroline, and Karen Mossberger. 2006. "The Effects of E-Government on Trust and Confidence in Government." *Public Administration Review* 66 (3): 354–69.

Tolbert, Caroline, Karen Mossberger, Bridgett King, and Gena Miller. 2007. "Are All American Women Making Progress Online? African-Americans and Latinas." *Information Technologies and International Development* 4 (2): 61–88.

Tolva, John. 2012. "Data-Driven Chicago." February 24, Speech of Chief Technology Officer of City of Chicago at University of Illinois at Chicago, Department of Urban Planning and Policy. http://www.ustream.tv/recorded/20666748.

U.S. Census Bureau. 2010. *Current Population Survey, October 2009: School Enrollment and Internet Use Supplement Technical Documentation.* Washington, D.C. http://www.census.gov/apsd/techdoc/cps/cpsoct09.pdf.

U.S. Department of Homeland Security. 2007. *Tactical Interoperability Communication Scorecards: Summary Report and Findings.* Washington, D.C. http://www.dhs.gov/files/gc_1167770109789.shtm.

Van Deursen, Alexander J.A.M., and Jan A.G.M. Van Dijk. 2009a. "Improving Digital Skills for the Use of Online Public Information and Services." *Government Information Quarterly* 26 (2): 333–340.

———. 2009b. "Using the Internet: Skill Related Problems in Users' Online Behavior." *Interacting with Computers* 21 (5–6): 393–402.

———. 2009c. "Improving Digital Skills for the Use of Online Public Information and Services." *Government Information Quarterly* 26 (2): 333–340.

Van Dijk, Jan A.G.M. 2005. *The Deepening Divide: Inequality in the Information Society.* Thousand Oaks, CA: Sage.

———. 2008. "One Europe, Digitally Divided." In *Routledge Handbook of Internet Politics,* ed. Andrew Chadwick and Philip N. Howard, 288–305. London: Routledge.

Volden, Craig. 2006. "States as Policy Laboratories: Emulating Success in the Children's Health Insurance Program." *American Journal of Political Science* 50 (2): 294–312.

Vos, Esme. 2010. "Updated List of U.S. Cities and Counties with Large Scale WiFi Networks." MuniWireless. http://www.muniwireless.com/2010/06/07/updated-list-of-cities-and-counties-with-wifi/.

Warschauer, Mark. 2003. *Technology and Social Inclusion: Rethinking the Digital Divide.* Cambridge, MA: MIT Press.

———. 2010. "New Reports on Technology in US Schools: The Changing Divide." http://papyrusnews.com/2010/10/26/new-reports-on-technology-in-us-schools-the-changing-divide.

Washington, Jesse. 2011. "For Minorities, New 'Digital Divide' Seen." *USA Today,* Jan. 10. http://www.usatoday.com/tech/news/2011-01-10-minorities-online_N.htm.

Wellman, Barry. 1996. "Are Personal Communities Local? A Dumptarian Reconsideration." *Social Networks* 18 (4): 347–354.

West, Darrell M. 2000. *Assessing E-Government: The Internet, Democracy, and Service Delivery by State and Federal Governments.* Inside Politics. http://www.insidepolitics.org/egovtreport00.html.

———. 2011. *The Next Wave: Using Digital Technology to Further Social and Political Innovation.* Washington, D.C.: Brookings Institution Press.

Wilson, W. J. 1996. *When Work Disappears.* New York: Alfred A. Knopf.

Wilson, William Julius. 1987. *The Truly Disadvantaged: The Inner City, the Underclass, and Public Policy.* Chicago: University of Chicago Press.

Wolman, Hal, and Martin Horak. 2010. "Contexts for Neighborhood Regeneration: A Comparative Overview." Paper presented at the Annual Meeting of the Midwest Political Science Association, Chicago, IL.

Wolman, Harold. 2012. "What Cities Do: How Much Does Urban Policy Matter?" In *The Oxford Handbook of Urban Politics,* ed. Karen Mossberger, Susan E. Clarke, and Peter John. New York: Oxford University Press.

Worden, Nat. 2011. "Motorola CEO: It's Not a Wireless World Just Yet." *Digits—WSJ Blogs.* http://blogs.wsj.com/digits/2011/06/16/motorola-ceo-its-not-a-wireless-world-just-yet/.

Wortham, Jenna. 2009. "Mobile Internet Use Shrinks Digital Divide." *New York Times.* http://bits.blogs.nytimes.com/2009/07/22/mobile-internet-use-shrinks-digital-divide/.

Zickuhr, Kathryn, and Aaron Smith. *Digital Differences.* Washington, D.C.: Pew Internet and American Life Project. http://pewinternet.org/Reports/2012/Digital-differences.aspx.

Index